2001 Race Odyssey

2001
RACE ODYSSEY

African Americans and Sociology

Edited by

Bruce R. Hare

Syracuse University Press

Library of Congress Cataloging-in-Publication Data

2001 race odyssey : African Americans and sociology / edited by Bruce R. Hare.— 1st ed.
    p. cm.
Includes bibliographical references and index.
ISBN 0–8156–2938–9 (alk. paper)
1. African Americans—Social conditions—1975– 2. United States—Race relations. 3. United
States—Social conditions—1980– 4. Sociology—United States. I. Hare, Bruce R.
E185.86 .A195 2002
305.896'073—dc21   2002009678

Contents

Illustrations

Tables

Foreword

Charles Vert Willie

Bruce Hare has performed a wonderful and useful service to society and to the social sciences by assembling seventeen essays that are representative of contributions to accumulated knowledge by African American sociologists. He has placed in one volume the scientific work of some of the finest scholars in the United States. They use their analytical studies of the way of life of people of color in this and other nations to provide new insights that remain unresolved. Their conclusions are decisive when warranted but cautious if necessary because of insufficient information.

Bruce Hare sets the stage in his introductory essay entitled "Toward Cultural Pluralism and Economic Justice." His use of the concept "culture" rather than "race" is deliberate. While he acknowledges that racism is alive and well in contemporary society, he casts doubt on the way race is used as a classification concept of people and the groups with which they are affiliated. Hare believes, based on his studies, that "cultural diversity [is] the true fabric of an emerging pluralistic America." A major goal of this book is to provide evidence on and an understanding of the cultural dynamics of community life among African Americans and of the dynamics between them and other groups regarding differentiation and similarity, inclusion and rejection.

These and other concepts having to do with change, stability, and simultaneous happenings are, for Bruce Hare, intriguing ways of analyzing data about "race" and race-related events. Bruce Hare's interest in simultaneity and my interest in complementarities move us away from the static structural concepts used in the past to describe and analyze dominant and subdominant people of power. In a multicultural society, Hare sees unity and separation, differentiation and inclusion, as continuous happenings. Since cultural groups, even those sometimes identified as "racial" cultural groups, may differentiate, separate, and reconnect again and again, it is inappropriate to label the current status of any group "permanent," as Gunnar Myrdal did for "Negroes" and other "colored people" in his book *An American Dilemma,* published in 1944, more than a half-century ago.

In his study, Myrdal used "caste," a static concept, to help us understand the way of life of African Americans. He assumed that "The American caste system . . . stays rigid and unblurred" and concluded that the "American definition of Negro . . . has its significance in making the caste line absolutely rigid [for any person who has the slightest amount of Negro ancestry]" (668). The conception of a rigid, unchanging caste system for people of color in the United States is incompatible with Bruce Hare's notion of cultural pluralism and the continuing process of both inclusion and rejection. From Hare's perspective, the "racial" odyssey in America is not fixed and unchangeable.

Sarah Susannah Willie comments on this theme in her chapter "Performing Blackness." She writes that "[the] tendency to see race as a variable with fixed meaning runs the risk of obscuring how individuals and groups are also proactive agents and how race can play a positive role in group and individual identity." Her ideas are in opposition to Myrdal's notion that blackness in America is a permanent disability.

Donald Cunnigen has examined the classification of African American sociologists by generational groups and tells us that the second generation (those who began their careers between the First and the Second World War) tended to focus their research on conditions that immediately affected the African American community.

The work of earlier sociologists focused on conditions within the black community as well as on investigations about relationships in important social institutions in the micro-community of African Americans and at large in the macro-society. For example, Patricia Hill-Collins and Walter R. Allen discuss relationships in the black family.

Hill-Collins also studies the workplace and the roles of black women there. Elijah Anderson studies the workplace of corporations and the various adaptations of participating black executives. Edgar G. Epps analyzes schools as learning communities for African Americans and is particularly concerned about the test score gap between white students and black students. In this connection, Howard F. Taylor's chapter, "Deconstructing the Bell Curve," asserts that "one of the biggest . . . problems facing African Americans . . . [today] involves the structure of the educational institution in America."

The research of Patricia Hill-Collins, Elijah Anderson, and several other scholars in this book reveals great diversity among African Americans in their adaptations to various institutional systems in the community. Regarding the caste and class controversy, Edgar Epps, based on his extensive review of the literature, tells us that the "race versus class question is too simplistic . . . [that] both factors are at work and they interact in different ways depending upon the person's or family's position in the race/class structure." Several of the studies in this book reveal a new status—that of marginality, attained by some African Americans because of their new identity triggered by changing social circumstances and participation in new and different groups.

In my own investigations, I have discovered that the search for identity seems to be a search for security and acceptance, a need to be needed by others. However, identity is complicated because it is a twofold function of self-affirmation and community confirmation, not one or the other but both. My identity as well as the identity of others emerges from a process of negotiation regarding who I say I am and who others say I am. This negotiation process is continuous throughout the life cycle. Because of our new multicultural society and an increasing process of inclusion in the nation at large, some individuals—particularly African Americans—find themselves occupying new space in groups with which they were not affiliated in the past. Some resolve the stress of change by attempting to identify exclusively with the new groups; others attempt to hold tenaciously to their old groups and fully identify with them. Still others function between multiple cultural groups, helping them to discover ways of achieving mutual enhancement.

Individuals betwixt and between different cultural groups occupy a challenging new marginal space with few guidelines for how to persevere and survive. While adaptation to this new space and its required roles is not easy, marginality because of membership in multiple groups that are not always compatible (as opposed to marginality on the edge of one group) may not be a pleasant experience but is not necessarily harmful. Sociologist Robert Park (one of the teachers of many second-generation African American professional sociologists) wrote this in the introduction to Everett Stonequist's book *The Marginal Man* (1937): The marginal person who is positioned between two or more cultural groups is "the individual with wider horizon, the keener intelligence, the more detached and rational viewpoint."

In summary, "The marginal [person] is always relatively the more civilized human being." Stonequist goes further and states that, "The Marginal [person] is the key-personality in the contacts of cultures. It is in his [or her] mind that the cultures come together, conflict, and eventually work out some kind of mutual adjustment" (222).

Marginal people can have tragic or transcendent relationships with others. They may fall between the cracks, pulled apart by incompatible goals of the groups in which they hold membership; they also may mobilize sufficient energy to rise above the differences of their multiple groups. Without denying the negative consequences of marginality, I emphasize its positive consequences such as rising above, conciliating, and reconciling differences. These possible adaptations of marginal people have been neglected as legitimate problems for sociological analysis.

Attention should be called to this research oversight because of Bruce Hare's conception of multicultural pluralism and his belief about cultural diversity as the "true fabric" of an emerging pluralistic America. An important feature of this book is the variety of perspectives used to interpret the findings reported and the use of both quantitative and qualitative methods for collecting and analyzing data. This book also offers a global perspective on immigration, "primitive" societies, and African experience in three fine chapters authored by Roy Simon Bryce-Laport, S. N. Sangmpam, and Pade Badru. Also included are fine chapters on racial classification in criminology by Jeanette Covington, a study on linguistics and multicultural turns by Paget Henry and an excellent essay on political-class racism by Joseph W. Scott.

Truly, this is a comprehensive and exciting book about the African American way of life, African American scholarship, and African American sociologists. This book is interesting because of the diversity of scholars invited to write about their research. By age they vary from "thirty-something" to "seventy-something." By gender and location they are males and females who live in northern and southern regions of the nation. And they work in private and public colleges and universities in the eastern and western United States. All are accomplished authors who write with skill and grace.

Preface

Edgar G. Epps

The essays in this volume bring into sharp focus the continuing significance of racism in America as it impacts the life chances of African Americans and other people of color in the new century. Whether, as Bruce Hare argues, the concept of race has outlived its usefulness or, as others contend, changing to ethnic labels will have little effect on politically constructed social barriers that have been erected to privilege some groups while disadvantaging others, there is little disagreement concerning the pervasiveness of racism in America. I welcome Hare's focus on cultural pluralism, however, because of my interest in the educational implications of this approach, as described in my book *Cultural Pluralism* (1974). Cultural pluralism acknowledges the value of diversity; it encourages inclusion without submersion of one's ethnic heritage, and it recognizes the contributions of Native Americans, Africans, Asians, and Europeans to the rich cultural, economic, and political mosaic that we celebrate in America.

Professor Hare should be commended for bringing this project to fruition. As a contributor to the special issue of *Sociological Forum* in which some of these essays first appeared, I am very pleased that the work was significantly expanded and will reach a wider audience. The mix of scholarship is quite impressive both for its quality and for its diversity. The authors have all been deeply involved in one way or another in the struggles to gain acceptance in society and in the profession of sociology. No one can come away from this volume without being impressed by the wide range of conceptual and methodological approaches embodied within the ranks of African American sociologists. Our ideological positions and our policy recommendations often take us in different directions. And that is as it should be. Each of us brings to this research the weight of our experiences, having grown up in different eras and in different social, economic, and geographic contexts. This difference enables us to examine issues of race/ethnic relations from multiple perspectives, which, in turn, lead to alternative explanations and policy recommendations. While multiple perspectives subvert the possibility of a single "African American position" on any issue, they help to validate our searches for sociological "truths."

A theme that emerges in several of the essays is the importance of agency, both individual agency and collective agency, in the struggle for racial/ethnic equality in America. This is an emphasis that has rarely surfaced in "mainstream" scholarship in this area. The authors remind us of the debt that is owed to African Americans and the Civil Rights movement by women, Latinos, Native Americans, Asian Americans, and other groups that have used collective action to promote change in their social and economic circumstances and to overcome legal and semi-legal obstacles to progress. I thank the authors for reminding us that only through our own efforts, especially through organized social movements, will we be able to attain the equality that we have been seeking for hundreds of years.

The authors of these essays located the origins and the persistence of racial, ethnic, class, and gender inequality in the historical and contemporary legal structures and institutional practices that can be traced to the founding fathers' assumptions about superiority and inferiority. In their view, the task facing us in this new century is the dismantling of all vestiges of the historical legacy of white male domination and the establishment of a social democracy based on equality, inclusion, and social justice.

Finally, several contributors to this volume address the increasing diversity both within the African American community and the nation. Social class distinctions within the African American community are becoming more prevalent as the middle class expands while a substantial proportion of the population remains mired in poverty. Does this development weaken the ability of the African American community to define political goals that are common to all segments of the race/ethnic group? In addition, the increasing presence of immigrants from Africa and the African diaspora adds to the diversity of this population. When the recent wave of immigration from Asia, Latin America, and Eastern Europe is taken into consideration, it becomes clear that it may be necessary to rethink the way we view American race and ethnic relations in the twenty-first century.

Introduction

Bruce R. Hare

As a child born in Harlem Hospital in New York City in 1946, raised in Harlem as a young child, and then subsequently in a multiethnic, brand new public housing project in the Bronx called Edenwald, I am the product of multiethnic and multiculture exposure, having been raised by Harlem-grown parents on the heels of the famous Harlem Renaissance, and subsequently in a pluralistic community full of recent immigrants from Italy, Ireland, Poland, Cuba, Jamaica, and the Dominican Republic, and migrants from Puerto Rico and elsewhere. Consequently, I never quite bought the deprived ghetto stereotype of "black" Harlem nor the idea that all "white" groups or people were the same. I was thus disturbed to learn as an undergraduate sociology major at CCNY (City College of the City University of New York) that my world was being woefully presented as either poor and "black" or rich and "white." Despite what mainstream America and sociology told me, I knew, experientially, neither stereotype to be true. I was proud of both my Harlem and Bronx home communities. I had known ethnic diversity and unity both within and between communities and wondered how my lived experience was so out of touch with what I was being taught. I thus worried that my complex lenses were delusional and wondered whether there was a respectable place for me and my multiethnic experiences in sociology.

Then, in the early 1970s while I was a graduate student in sociology and education at the University of Chicago, I was privileged to attend a most amazing conference. Professor James E. Blackwell, then chair of the sociology department at the University of Massachusetts at Boston, and Professor Morris Janowitz, then chair of the sociology department at the University of Chicago, co-hosted a conference attended by a group of distinguished African American sociologists. It was at that conference that my eyes were opened to the works of such founding fathers of African American/Black Sociology as W. E. B. DuBois, E. Franklin Frazier, and Charles S. Johnson, who were discussed by such scholars as G. Franklin Edwards, Jacquelyn Johnson Jackson, James E. Blackwell, Walter L. Wallace, William Julius Wilson, and Edgar G. Epps.

Among issues discussed were the history of African American sociologists in "black" and "white" universities, race relations, the usefulness of sociological theory in studying black Americans, the intersections of sociology and black studies and black female sociologists.

I was impressed and inspired by the clarity, complexity, cultural integrity, and relevancy of their critiques of the African American experience. Their ability to combine sociological expertise and their lived African American/black experience in constructing theory, analyzing data, and drawing conclusions with policy implications convinced me that the use of sociological tools could indeed provide useful information concerning the plight of African Americans and the American society. The subsequent publication of *Black Sociologists—Contemporary and Historical Perspectives* (University of Chicago Press, 1974), which contained many of the conference presentations, has proven to be an historic sociological contribution to understanding "race" relations in America.

It was with this model in mind that I began the process, almost five years ago, of seeking to recruit a new generation of distinguished African American, African Caribbean, and African sociologists to publish together in a single volume. This book is the result of that effort.

As were the authors in the 1974 publication, these authors are all highly accomplished, having published extensively and acquired standing. All are currently senior tenured scholars with national reputations. Some hold named endowed chairs and others are current or former sociology and/or African American Studies unit chairs. By design, these are among the best Pan African sociologists and social scientists of our generation, complemented by a sprinkling of distinguished elders.

The issues these authors raise are urgent. The analyses they provide, both quantitative and qualitative, are cogent, and their recommendations are compelling, timely, and useful. I thank each of them for lending their prestige and wisdom to this collective enterprise.

This volume looks at the problem of the "color line," which W. E. B. DuBois defined as the problem of the twentieth century, and offers an analysis of the strengths and weaknesses of the traditional sociological "race relations" approach in search of twenty-first-century solutions to the problem of American and "Third World" racism. The authors also address issues of social and economic oppression in complex ways that have implications far beyond the black/white dichotomy. The problematic intersections of racism, sexism, and classism are frequently raised by these authors, suggesting the need for a paradigm shift that would address these core social problems simultaneously rather than separately, and cooperatively rather than competitively.

It is expected that the volume will prove useful in sociology, psychology, social work, education, and other social science-related courses. It should also prove useful to practitioners in such varied fields as psychiatry, psychology, medicine, and nursing, where knowledge of the culture, class, and social context in which the patients live could significantly increase the effectiveness of treatment. Additionally, the volume could prove valuable to other policymakers and practitioners interested in fresh ways of thinking about social problems and possible solutions as seen through the informed perspectives of African American sociologists.

I hope that my own two contributions to this volume, "Toward Cultural Pluralism and Economic Justice" (chapter 1) and "Black Youth at Risk" (chapter 6), might also contribute to a paradigm shift in thinking about these problems and to an ongoing discourse about possible solutions.

I again thank my distinguished colleagues for their contributions to this volume; I also thank my children, family, and friends for their support. I thank Spring Genovese for her secretarial help and Deborah Y. Banks for preparing the manuscript with editorial expertise and cultural knowledge.

I would like to thank Norman Goodman for his support during my tenure in the department of sociology at Stony Brook and Stephen Cole for the opportunity to edit a special issue of *Sociological Forum* in 1995. I also thank the editorial staff of Syracuse University Press for patience and support during this elongated project.

I especially thank my wife, Diane Ackerman Hare, for her moral and spiritual support. Her confidence in me and in the value of this book project has been a constant source of inspiration.

Finally, as the fortunate son of proud and conscious African American parents, I dedicate this book to the memory of my late father, Stephen Henry Hare Jr., and to my mother, Ann Johnson Hare. She continues to encourage her children and grandchildren to be knowledgeable of the past, look beyond the present, actively engage the world and be optimistic about the future.

Contributors

Walter R. Allen is currently professor of sociology at the University of California, Los Angeles. His research and teaching focuses on family patterns, socialization and personality development, race and ethnic relations, African American males, health inequalities, and higher education. He has coauthored (with R. Farley) *The Color Line and the Quality of Life in America* and has to his credit more than eighty publications appearing in the *Harvard Educational Review, Journal of Marriage and Family Therapy, Phylon, Sociological Quarterly, Journal of Negro Education,* and many other journals and publications.

Elijah Anderson is the Charles and William L. Day Distinguished Professor of the Social Sciences and professor of sociology at the University of Pennsylvania, Philadelphia. He is the author of the widely regarded sociological work *A Place on the Corner: A Study of Black Street Corner Men,* and numerous articles and publications on the black experience. Dr. Anderson is director of the Philadelphia Ethnography Project and associate editor of *Qualitative Sociology* and other professional journals. He is a member of the Board of Directors of the American Academy of Political and Social Science, and vice president-elect of the American Sociological Association.

Pade Badru is associate professor of Pan African Studies and Sociology, and director for the Center of Educational and Social Policy Research, University of Louisville, Kentucky. His research interests focus on international economic development with emphasis on Sub-Saharan Africa, political and economic history of Africa, the political economy of underdevelopment, historiography, and the sociology of race and ethnicity. He has authored *Imperialism and Ethnic Politics in Nigeria, 1960–1996* and *International Banking and Rural Development in the Third World: The World Bank in Sub-Saharan Africa.*

Roy Bryce-LaPorte is the John D. and Catherine T. MacArthur Professor of Sociology and Anthropology Emeritus at Colgate University. His research and teaching interests emphasize sociological and historical studies of new non-white immigration and comparative and ethno-historical studies of Afro-American, Afro-Caribbean, Afro-Hispanic, and other "New World" black experiences, particularly in institutional and communal settings. Professor La-Porte has edited four books including *Voluntary Immigration and Continuing Encounters between Blacks (The Annals of the American Academy of Political and Social Science)* and other articles and book contributions.

Patricia Hill-Collins is department chair and associate professor of the Department of African American Studies at the University of Cincinnati, Ohio. She is also the Charles Phelps Taft Distinguished Professor of Sociology and associate professor of Sociology. Dr. Hill-Collins has numerous publications and articles including *Black Feminist Thought: Knowledge, Consciousness, and the Politics of Empowerment* and *Race, Class and Gender: An Anthology*, edited with Margaret Anderson.

Jeanette Covington is associate professor in the Department of Sociology at Rutgers University in New Brunswick, New Jersey. Her research and publications have focused on the social ecology of crime, neighborhood change and crime, and fear of crime. She has also written and conducted research on the causes of drug use, the links between drug use and crime, and an examination of current drug policies. She is currently considering how academic criminologists construct the variable of "race" when analyzing data on both crime and drugs.

Donald Cunnigen is associate professor in the Department of Sociology-Anthropology at the University of Rhode Island, Kingston. He is president-elect of the Association of Black Sociologists and 2001 program chairperson. He has contributed chapters and articles to and is a reviewer for a number of sociological journals such as *Sociological Spectrum* and *Teaching Sociology*.

Edgar G. Epps is professor of Educational Policy and Community Studies at the University of Wisconsin-Milwaukee and Marshall Field IV Professor of Urban Education Emeritus at the University of Chicago. His current research interests include race/ethnic relations, minority access to higher education, faculty diversity in higher education, and educational reform in urban school districts. Dr. Epps is coauthor (with Patricia Gurin) of *Black Consciousness, Identity and Achievement* and most recently coedited with John J. Lane *Restructuring the Schools: Problems and Prospects.*

Bruce R. Hare is professor and former department chair of the Department of African American Studies in the College of Arts and Sciences, and professor of sociology in the Maxwell School of Citizenship and Public Affairs, Syracuse University, Syracuse, New York. He has written numerous articles and publications in refereed journals such as *Sociological Forum, American Journal of Psychiatry, Journal of Negro Education,* and *Journal of Black Psychology.* Professor Hare's renowned "Hare General and Area-Specific (School, Peer and Home) Self-Esteem Scale," published in *Measures for Clinical Practice* (Vol. 1), is sought after by educators and researchers of children throughout the country. He was founding chair of the Black Studies Department at the University of Massachusetts at Boston in 1976.

Paget Henry is professor of sociology and Afro-American Studies at Brown University. His research focus includes dependency theory, Caribbean political economy, sociology of religion, Africana philosophy and religion, race and ethnic relations, and poststructuralism and critical theory. He is the author of *Caliban's Reason: Introducing Afro-Caribbean Philosophy and Peripheral Capitalism* and *Underdevelopment in Antigua,* as well as numerous articles, essays, and reviews. He is the editor of the *C.L.R. James Journal* and the Routledge series *Africana Thought.*

Aldon D. Morris is professor in the Department of Sociology at Northwestern University, Evanston, Illinois. He is the editor of *Frontiers in Social Movement Theory,* which is being translated into Chinese by the Peking University Press; *The Origins of the Civil Rights Movement: Black Communities Organizing for Change;* and is coedtior of *Oppositional Consciousness: Subjective Roots of Social Protest.* He has contributed book chapters and articles to refereed journals in sociology.

S. N. Sangmpam is associate professor in the Department of African American Studies and Political Science at Syracuse University, Syracuse, New York. His research and teaching interests focus on cross-national comparative politics:

developing countries vs. Western democracies, empirical theory, state, state-society relations, ideology, democracy, capitalism, modes of production, systems analysis, political development, international politics/political, economy, and North-South relations. Professor Sangmpam is the author of *Comparing Apples and Mangoes: The Overpoliticized State and Integrated Comparative Politics* and *Pseudocapitalism and the Overpoliticized State: Reconciling Politics and Anthropology in Zaire*, in The Making of Modern Africa series.

Joseph Walter Scott is professor of sociology, University of Washington. He has published more than forty research articles and chapters in such journals as the *American Sociological Review, American Journal of Sociology, National Journal of Sociology, Sociological Focus, Phylon, The Western Journal of Black Studies*, and the *Journal of Criminology*.

Howard F. Taylor is professor in the Department of Sociology at Princeton University, Princeton, New Jersey. His research interests encompass social psychology, the IQ heritability controversy, and race and ethnic relations. He has recently completed a nationwide study of the network structure of America's black leadership. Professor Taylor has published numerous scholarly articles in the major professional journals in the fields of sociology, social psychology, race relations, and education. His books include *Balance in Small Groups*, and his *IQ Game: The Black Elite Network in America* is in process.

Charles Vert Willie, a sociologist, is the Charles William Elliot Professor of Education Emeritus at the Graduate School of Education, Harvard University. Prior to his Harvard appointment, Professor Willie was affiliated with Syracuse University for twenty-five years as a graduate student, sociology professor, department chair, and university vice president. His research interests are race relations, urban education, public health, community development, and family life. He has authored or edited twenty-three books and more than one hundred articles and book chapters. His most recent books are *Controlled Choice, a New Approach to School Desegregation and School Improvement* (1996) and *Mental Health, Racism and Sexism*.

Sarah Susannah Willie is associate professor of sociology and chairperson of the Black Studies Program at Swarthmore College, Swarthmore, Pennsylvania.

She writes and teaches on race, identity, knowledge, and American culture. Dr. Willie is the author of "Playing the Devil's Advocate: Defending a Multicultural Identity in Fractured Community," in Thompson and Tyagi's *Names We Call Home,* and of "Outing the Blackness in Whiteness: Race, Class, and Sex in Everyday Life," in *Annals of Scholarship.*

Overview

CHAPTER I

Toward Cultural Pluralism and Economic Justice

Bruce R. Hare

> What good is the right to sit at the counter if you can't afford the meal?
> —Martin Luther King, Jr.

Overview

Twentieth-century America, it may be argued, has been dominated by two ongoing social movements, the quests for cultural pluralism and for economic justice. The Civil Rights movement for desegregation has sought the inclusion of African Americans in the center of American life by removing the barrier to inclusion forwarded by the separate-but-equal doctrine codified in the *Plessey vs. Ferguson* United States Supreme Court decision of 1896. This idea of a just form of segregation was subsequently declared unconstitutional by the Supreme Court in the case of *Brown vs. the Board of Education* in 1954.

The labor movement has simultaneously spearheaded the ongoing drive to advance labor rights through higher wages, increased job security, and safer working conditions. These two movements have, for the most part, been parallel rather than coordinated, even as they both pursued aspects of social and economic justice. The two movements were, for a brief moment, set on the same track toward the end of the Civil Rights movement when Martin Luther King, Jr. and others mobilized the Poor People's Campaign before it was aborted by King's assassination. Thus King's support for a multiethnic garbage workers strike represented a banner moment toward the unifying goals of cultural pluralism and economic justice. It may be argued that the King assassination and the subsequent decline of the labor movement, under continuing

3

attacks during the Reagan era, forestalled the emerging alliance of these parallel movements at great cost to both causes.

In this chapter I offer an analysis of the relationship between the dual goals of cultural pluralism through desegregation and economic justice through labor movements. It is argued that neither movement can fully achieve its goal without the other, since both ideally assume acceptance and fairness. In also recognizing that these two concepts (cultural pluralism and economic justice) are frequently treated as distinct social goals because they have historically sought to advance different populations (African Americans and laborers), it is posited that they must each be separately understood in order to be made simultaneously present.

On Cultural Pluralism

For the purposes of this discourse, cultural pluralism is defined as the simultaneous existence of cultural diversity and national unity. Model 1 offers a cultural, rather than racialized, view of an America composed of Native Americans as well as Americans of African, Asian, Latino, and European descent (fig. 1.1). Rather than calling for homogenization or melting into some Eurocentric paradigm, it calls for an acceptance and celebration of cultural diversity as the true fabric of an emerging pluralistic America. The advantage of such a paradigm shift is that the pluralism concept de-centers the European American, deracializes the discourse, and offers equal standing for all America's cultural and ethnic groups, as represented by the pie, under an umbrella of national unity, as represented by the circle of inclusion.

On Economic Justice

For purposes of this discourse, economic justice is defined as a condition that seeks the greatest good for the greatest number of people. Such an ideal would pursue a class-based, rather than simply gender- or "race"-based, "affirmative action" program to challenge the continuing inequitable distribution of wealth, power, and privilege in the society as a consequence of current taxation, inheritance, wage, social service, criminal justice, and educational opportunity policies.

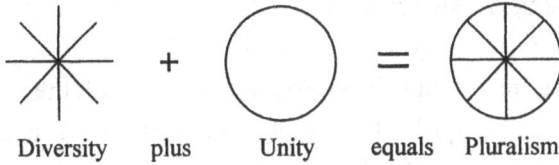

Diversity   plus   Unity   equals   Pluralism

Fig. 1.1 Cultural Pluralism

Cultural Pluralism and Economic Justice

Assuming the argument that the concerns for pluralism and justice can be theoretically separate, the following two-by-two model offers four possible paired social systems characteristics (fig. 1.2). The horizontal "cultural pluralism axis" divides segregated from desegregated settings. The vertical "economic justice axis" divides economically just from unjust systems. Thus, the four system types are posited: (1) Unjust Segregation, (2) Just Segregation, (3) Unjust Pluralism, and (4) Just Pluralism. Each will be explained in turn.

Box 1. Unjust Segregated Systems

This is the box no one wants to be in. It is characterized by an absence of multiethnic, multi-"racial" or multicultural exposure and by economic oppression. It is economically distasteful both to the segregationist on economic grounds and to the pluralist on economic and cultural grounds. It is a condition overwhelmingly experienced by poor "white" people although stereotyped as the province of poor "minorities."

	Just	Unjust
Desegregation	(4) Just Pluralism	(3) Unjust Pluralism
Segregation	(2) Just Segregation	(1) Unjust Segregation

(Cultural Pluralism Axis) →

↑
(Economic Justice Axis)

Fig. 1.2 Cultural Pluralism/Economic Justice

Box 2. Just Segregated Systems

This box, advocated as "just" by segregationists, forwards the notion that separate but equal can be equal. This school of thought was affirmed by the United States Supreme Court in the *Plessey vs. Ferguson* decision of 1896 and reversed by the same court in the landmark *Brown vs. Board of Education* decision of 1954. While arguments about whether justice and segregation can exist simultaneously persist, the Supreme Court in the 1954 decision, in rejecting the promises to build parallel and identical, separate, black and white school systems to avoid desegregation, affirmed its view that separate but equal is inherently unequal. The Court found that the psychological costs of segregation to segregated minorities were present and unacceptable, even if the facilities were identical.

Box 3. Unjust Pluralism

Rather than arriving directly from "unjust segregation" to "just pluralism," which would include both a significant reduction in segregation and economic inequality, I posit that, while unjust segregation is being successfully challenged, we have entered a period of vulnerability to unjust pluralism, a situation in which gender and "race" desegregation are falsely assumed to be evidence of "just pluralism."

Symbolically represented by the Supreme Court appointments of Sandra Day O'Connor, who evidences that you can get gender without the (feminist) agenda, and Clarence Thomas, who evidences that you can get the complexion without the (civil rights) direction, the door to "unjust pluralism" has thus been opened.

This desegregation of the visible elites will be discussed later as domestic neocolonialism. It presents a new challenge in the quest for social and economic justice. The recent gender and "race" desegregation of the cabinets of American presidents, including President George W. Bush's appointments of Colin Powell, Condi Rice, and Kristy Whitman among others, is further evidence of this phenomenon.

It appears that the emergence of a few highly visible selected women and "minority" individuals is being perceived as evidence of group progress. This form of pluralism is considered unjust because it does not significantly address the gross economic inequality between classes, through a more equitable distribution of wealth, even as the gender and complexion of the political elites have desegregated significantly.

Box 4. Just Pluralism

This box represents what I consider the ideal type. It combines both cultural pluralism and a just economic order. It has historically been the goal of activists who have seen both desegregation and economic justice as the necessary conditions of a just society. Martin Luther King, Jr. was among the early members of the Human Rights movement who recognized this need to simultaneously pursue cultural pluralism through desegregation and economic justice through a Poor People's Campaign. He symbolically signaled this combining of goals in his evolution from Civil Rights to Human Rights when he asked, "What good is the right to sit at the counter, if you can't afford the meal?"

This discussion is divided into four parts. The first part discusses American racism and the challenge it presents to the pursuit of cultural pluralism. The second part discusses the special dilemmas of the Native Americans and the endangered status of recent "black" immigrants and visitors. The third part of this discourse elaborates a thesis regarding why affirmative action, even if maximally attained, is not guaranteed to deliver economic justice, since merely desegregating the complexion and gender of the elite does not necessarily change the structure of economic relations, but may result in a form of domestic neocolonial administration. The last part presents an argument for a paradigm shift from better race relations to deracialization as the solution to American racism. It presents an argument for "deracialization" as the solution to American racism through the transforming of the American discourse from one about color to one about culture and ethnicity. This paradigm shift, it is argued, is essential to transcending the current "race relations" paradigm that has dominated American societal and sociological discourse for over a century and that, in my view, has taken us as far as it can.

Part 1

The Idea of "Race": America's Mental Illness Distorts Us All

A poor rural Mississippi "white" man was asked by a New Orleans newspaper reporter, "What is white?" After musing for a little while, the man responded,

"Well, I don't know a lot about that. But, I'll tell you one thing . . . it's not black!"

Early in the 1900s, the famous African American scholar and activist W. E. B. DuBois defined the problem of the twentieth century as the problem of the color line. He proved to be tragically correct. And yet, this statement itself offers hope as it imports, however softly, that perhaps the twenty-first century would bring a solution.

Despite the enormous progress made in "race" relations, as through the desegregation of schools and sports, and the emergence of African American political elites, racism is alive and well in America. It continues to soil the minds of our citizens and, occasionally, spills embarrassingly out of the mouths of the David Dukes, Kalid Muhammads, and John Rockers of America. As a social psychologist, I am convinced that these voices are more than the individual random rantings of rabid racists. In my view, they represent the tip of a deep-seated collective mental illness as old as the nation.

This illness is grounded in the denial of thousands of glorious years of Native American history on this continent in favor of the 1492 Columbus "discovery myth." It is also founded in the failure to discuss the genocide committed against the aboriginal Americans in expanding this nation. This national illness also originated in the retention of enslaved Africans and the legalized oppression of women at the moment of the founding of this nation in 1776.

It seems that too many Americans are more embarrassed than truly indignant about racist discourse, not so much by what is said, but that such things, when said in public, reveal the private contempt with which America's "races" are encouraged to view each other. This part of the discourse thus offers an analysis of the psychological dimensions of this problem and its consequences for interethnic and intercultural interaction. Psychologists have long argued that the first step to recovery is the acknowledgment of the problem. What follows is an elaboration of the problem and a possible twenty-first-century solution.

When asked why there was resistance to a "mixed race" category's being included in the 2000 census that would allow people to check multiple identities, as might Tiger Woods, a fellow sociologist responded, "We need these categories to do our work." I suggested that the use of ethnic heritage identities such as Italian American, Japanese American, and Nigerian American, and continental identities such as African American, Asian American, Latin American, Native American, and, heaven forbid, European American, would still allow for studies of ethnicity, culture, and legal recourse against discrimination.

It also would allow for the use of multiethnic rather than "multi-racial" categories. Such a change has the additional benefit of "deracializing" the conversation, reaffirming the aboriginal/original status of the Native American/American Indian, and reminding us all that the so-called "white" is actually more accurately described as European American with a racialized identity.

James Baldwin, the famous writer, most eloquently addressed this conversion to white-ness as a racist identity when he noted that "white-ness is a state of mind, not a complexion." He told a largely European American audience at the State University of New York at Stony Brook, "It is a strange quirk of history that in England they were English; in France, French; in Germany, German; Italy, Italian; in Ireland, Irish . . . but that by some strange symbolic miracle, somewhere between the Statue of Liberty and Ellis Island, they all turned into 'white' people."

As quiet as it has been kept by black and white nationalists alike, Malcolm X also shared the Baldwin position in noting upon return from Mecca that, "I prayed with blue-eyed soul brothers and blond-haired soul brothers and have come to the conclusion that white-ness is a state of mind, not a complexion."

Prizes in the White Box

The emerging knowledge that there are privileges connected to "white-ness" both for career advancement and for self-esteem makes European Americans reluctant to give up being white.

Thus, there appears to be a conspiracy of silence, particularly in educational and clinical circles, where the anthropologists, geneticists, biologists, sociologists, psychologists, and psychiatrists, among others, *know* that there is no objective evidence to support the belief in human "races."

More recently, the genome projects, in tracing human evolution and migration through DNA studies, have further confirmed the existence of but one human race and the probable African roots of all, including European, civilization. Evidence of the commonality of human origins profoundly challenges the social belief in races and the prototyping of "races" as black and white or Negroid, Mongoloid, and Caucasoid. Thus, there is increasing evidence that the very idea of "white-ness" itself is an "Aryanism" and a pathological invitation to a superiority complex based simply on the lightness of one's complexion. Socially speaking, one simply needs to be "white" to acquire superior standing. No scientific genetic evidence or evidence of accomplishment need be presented. Because whiteness is neither an ethnic nor national identity, it may be argued that "white-ness" has no meaning outside its oppositional relationship to "black-ness." The idea, nevertheless, persists because it provides psychological and material rewards to those who are lighter than a temporary tan and who identify with the notion.

The benefit to the "white" ego derives from the invitation to base the ego, at least in part, on opposition modeling rather than on one's own accomplishments. Rather than "I think, therefore I am," it offers "You ain't, therefore I is." Thus, racism allows any unaccomplished poor "white" to consider himself automatically superior to Secretary of State Colin Powell, Jesse Jackson, Rosa Parks, Oprah Winfrey, or any other "black." This is the self-esteem prize in the "white" box.

There are also material rewards in the "white" box. In fact, increased awareness of the advantages of declaring the self "white" has produced a phenomenon that scholars refer to as the emergence of "unhyphenated" white people. Such folks may be recent or older immigrants who have learned to voluntarily give up low-prestige European ethnic identity such as Polish, Bulgarian, and so forth in favor of "white." Put differently, European immigrants are invited to trade in inferior status in the European ethnic community for superior standing in the American racist community.

High-prestige European Americans such as those of English and German background identify themselves as "white" while retaining public pride in their European ethnic heritage as well. Increasingly, American Jews such as former mayor Ed Koch are identifying themselves as white, while retaining their Jewish ethnic identity. In fact, when Mayor Koch announced a few years ago that "Jews and other white people believe," I wondered what the Ethiopian Jews were to make of the equating of Jewishness and whiteness.

On the Problematic Status of the "White" Liberal

In the American racist discourse, the "white liberal" holds a peculiar position. He or she seeks to simultaneously hold superior standing in the white community and leadership in the progressive community. This dual status has been perplexing to both camps across the racist divide where both black and white nationalists hold this "go-between" posture as suspect. It is indeed a strange dance to want to be "white" in racialized identity and deny being racist.

Both Martin Luther King, Jr. and Malcolm X among others have questioned the legitimacy of this dual claim and noted that such persons, who, paternalistically or maternalistically, often call for patience, tolerance, and harmony, are beneficiaries of the status quo. They often appear less predictable than the Klansman and harder to figure out than white nationalists. Perhaps they experience a conflict of interest between their superior standing as "whites" and their alleged liberalness. It may be that the only realistic resolution to these conflicting identities would be the abandonment of either the "white" or "liberal" labels.

One might argue that the claim of white liberal standing is an oxymoron in need of critique and solution. After all, how can one be both a part of the problem and simultaneously part of the progressive solution? True European American liberals, in my view, are challenged to give up being "white" or to run the risk of being seen as race brokers.

It may be argued that the perpetuation of the notion of the "white" liberal has come to do more in perpetuating the notion of human races, as opposed to one human race, than in solving the problem of American racism. Put differently, were it not for the notion of the "white liberal" who brings legitimacy to the idea of whiteness, it would be clear that the ideology of whiteness centrally belongs to the Ku Klux Klan, the White Citizen Council, the Aryan Nation, the skinheads, and other out-of-the-closet racists.

It is important to note, in understanding the extreme racist nature of overt white nationalists, that many of these groups idealize and revere Adolph Hitler as the greatest white nationalist of all. Ultimately, there is nothing liberal about the idea of whiteness.

American racism has also contorted world religions such that both Southern "White" Baptists and "Black" Muslims defy the universal principle of brotherhood and sisterhood in Christianity and Islam by superimposing racialized domestic politics on world religions, as both, in principle, reject the notion of human races. Finally, American racism leaves Asian Americans perceived as "forever foreign."

Sanctions in the Black Box

Just as there are prizes in the white box, conversely, there are strong and known sanctions in the "black" box, which, for example, encourage some darker-complexioned Latin Americans to utilize their Spanish accent as a marker of non-blackness. It also causes many dark-complexioned immigrants to make their "foreign" identities immediately known in order to hopefully avoid the negative stereotype and contempt that automatically comes with being identified as "black."

Racism also forwards color prejudice within the larger "black" community, where "light-ness" provides limited material and ego enhancement rewards. Racism also encourages some Caribbean and African immigrants, with encouragement from "white" America, to develop a superiority complex over African Americans. On the basis of their English or French colonial connection, such persons seem to be saying, "My master is better than your master. Therefore, I am better than you."

The failure to understand racism can be life-threatening. Such was the case when a naïve and innocent brown-complexioned Haitian man found himself trapped in South Boston during the busing crisis in 1974 by a group of irate and racialized/racist Irish youth. An Irish American police officer appeared and probably saved the Haitian man's life. While hiding behind the officer, the Haitian man kept desperately yelling, "I'm not black; I'm Haitian! I'm not black, I'm Haitian!" in a futile attempt to escape the black box.

It is important to note that the brave Irish American police officer who put his life at risk to save the Haitian man, in the context of this discussion, was not "white," since white cops, as in the case of Rodney King, Johnny Gammage, and Amadou Diallo, are known for endangering or taking, rather than saving, "black" lives. This officer thus offers additional evidence, behaviorally speaking, that not everyone light is "white," as Clarence Thomas offers evidence, politically speaking, that not everyone brown is "black."

Children offer additional evidence that racism is learned behavior by their initial resistance to the notion of blacks and whites. For example, in a preschool classroom, a four-year-old when called black by another child said, "no, I'm brown," and then, pointing to the back of his brown hand, said, "see, see, see." At another moment I overheard a conversation between my then three- and five-year-old sons, in which the three-year-old, having learned his Crayola colors, said to his brother, "I just figured something out." His five-year-old brother answered, "What?" and the three-year-old said, "They (meaning we racist adults) call pink people white." His brother responded, "Yeah, and they call brown people black." It unfortunately occurred to me that it would not be long before the children first adapted to and then subsequently adopted our definition of the situation. Having been appropriately socialized and racialized, they would inevitably become normal and pathological like the rest of us. Surely the children see that this "race" emperor has no clothes on.

Part 2

The Special Case of the Native/American Indian

With regard to issues of racism and stereotyping, it is clear that Americans also suffer from "selective indignation." We retain the amazing ability to be protective of our own group's image while simultaneously tolerating or forwarding disrespectful stereotypes of other groups. There are no greater victims of this phenomenon than the American Indian/Native Americans.

From the earliest years of our lives we are told a "Eurocentric" story. We are socialized to romanticize, celebrate, and enjoy a Native American image that has nothing to do with how Native Americans want to be seen. We are programmed from childhood to wear feathers and dance in circles in crude imitation of their culture. In a "big lie" crime of commission, a deliberate distortion of historical fact, we are led to believe that in 1492 a lost European named Columbus could still "discover" the land that they had occupied for thousands of years. In an equally significant crime of omission, we are not told that Columbus enslaved them and, in fact, took some of them involuntarily back to Spain with him. We are also denied knowledge of the genocide that the cowboys and cavalry and "settlers" committed against them in conquering this land.

Because the Native Americans are a relatively small and powerless population and segregated on reservations/territories, they are not a threat to the larger society. Unlike African Americans, who are heard because we are strategically located in significant numbers in the major cities of this nation and are known to have the collective power to disrupt the nation, the Native American is in no position to demand respect.

Thus the image of the Native Americans as "Indians" is contorted and distorted at will by the rest of the American people, despite the fact that they would not tolerate such an assault on their particular cultural/ethnic group image and despite the continuing plea of the Native Americans that others not continue to distort their image. This ability to be protective of one's own group image, while exploiting another's, is the stuff of selective indignation.

There were simultaneous telecasts of distorted Native American images on Columbus Day a few years ago when both the Cleveland Indians baseball team and the Washington Redskins football team were playing. The Native Americans made it clear that they find the name "redskins" and the Cleveland Indians' toothy, red-faced logo highly offensive. They have protested outside of the team stadiums to no avail. They have also unsuccessfully sought to have the Atlanta Braves change their name and logo and cease promoting the tomahawk chop cheer.

Were the American people not selectively indignant, they would know that these images are disrespectful and harmful. Were the Native Americans as powerful as other American ethnic groups, their request would be respected, if only out of fear of retaliation. For example, were the toothy red-faced caricature on the Cleveland Indians uniforms and hats black-faced, yellow-faced, or otherwise "ethnic-ed" as Irish, Italian, or Jewish, all hell would break loose.

Those who would dismiss this issue as trivial or "political correctness" should note that this is psychological warfare. These negative images are nationally and internationally projected when these teams travel the nation and are televised around the world. It is shameful and hypocritical that the athletes who passively wear and thus forward these "Indian" stereotypes would be protesting rigorously were their group contorted similarly.

As I see it, the task of actively fighting racism, prejudice, and discrimination belongs to every person even when his or her group is not the target. We should treat others as we would have them treat us; give up the names, logos, and practices that the aboriginal Americans find offensive; and cease being selectively indignant.

The Special Endangerment of the "Black" Visitor or Recent Immigrant to America: The Case of Amadou Diallo

Many years ago Richard Pryor joked, in one of his not-just-funny comic skits, about being stopped by the police and loudly announcing before making any move, "I am reaching for my wallet." This sarcastic joke caused great nervous laughter and simultaneously offered important advice to an African American Harlem audience that understood, all too well, the danger that black people may find themselves in when confronted by white cops, not because of the content of their characters, but because of the color of their skin.

This advice might have saved Amadou Diallo's life. Like many incoming "blacks," this African immigrant may not have understood that at the same time and in the same symbolic place between the Statue of Liberty and Ellis Island, where James Baldwin noted that light-complexioned European ethnics from England, France, Germany, Ireland, and Italy turn miraculously into "white" people, he turned into "black" people. Mr. Diallo may not have understood that while the European immigrants experience an automatic promotion to "whiteness" in racist America with all the attending rights and privileges, he acquired the duties and obligations of his demotion to "blackness" in America.

The absence of this African American cultural knowledge may explain why these conflicts between "white" cops and "black" men are too frequently with foreign-born black men. Mr. Diallo failed in his new obligation not to appear suspicious-while-black (SWB). It seems to me that immigrants darker than a temporary tan may be disproportionately victimized by white police because they fail to understand the racist rules of the American game.

Because neither the U.S. State Department nor the National Association for the Advancement of Colored People issues travel advisories, as perhaps they should, on the expected behavior of incoming "blacks," African and Caribbean immigrants may believe, on the basis of their own home experiences, that the police may be reasoned with, challenged, or even shown adequate ID. Like the Haitian man in Boston, Mr. Diallo failed to understand the American racist rules. As new immigrants, many of these brown newcomers may even naïvely believe that they will be treated differently, as exotic visitors rather than domestic "blacks."

We Americans remain tragically far from the moment when "black" people will be treated according to the content of their character rather than the color of their skin, no matter where they are from. Anyone visiting or immigrating to America who is darker than a temporary tan, beware.

The third part of this discourse elaborates a thesis regarding why affirmative action, even if maximally attained, is not guaranteed to deliver economic justice, since merely desegregating the complexion and gender of the elite does not necessarily change the structure of economic relations, but may result in a form of domestic neocolonial administration.

Part 3

On the Desegregation of the Visible Elite, or, Beware of the Emperor's
New Helpers: He or She May Look Like You or Me!

This section presents an analysis of what I believe to be a significant transition
in race and gender relations in the United States. While one might argue with
the notion of the "declining significance of race," there is reason to suspect an
increasing significance of class within the black community. The same forces
that have served to decrease the level of collective commitment among African
American/black people, through assassination, harassment, and incarceration
of black leadership, have also freed upwardly mobile black individuals to pursue
personal reward without community reprisal. Just as the Africans spoke of "sellouts" that would work as neocolonial administrators overseeing their fellow
Africans for the colonialists, we also have an emerging group of such individuals, although we believe them to be in the minority. Nevertheless, we currently
have "black" professionals sitting atop educational systems, police departments,
and welfare departments that do not work in the community's interest, as well
as politicians, religious, and business leaders who are not responsive to the real
needs of the masses.

Having recently emerged from an era of black nationalism, in which all
whites were enemies and all blacks friends, we fall subject to the residual ploy of
assuming that the elevation of black persons to decision-making positions in
such institutions as government, education, social services, and criminal justice
constitutes automatic progress.

The danger of such an assumption might best be expressed by imagining that
one day a group of Africans, during the latter stage of the colonization of Africa,
sat around in a circle and legitimately agreed that they had all been given a hard
way to go that day by the "white" people. That day symbolically became their day
of defining white people as the enemy. The oppressing whites had subsequently
heard the news, were wise enough to realize that they could no longer *directly* ad-
minister. The logical solution became to recruit "some" blacks to act in their
place in exchange for limited privileges. The effectiveness of such a strategy rests
on the initial inability of the group to recognize a foe of the same characteristic
on the heels of a struggle initially, logically, based on color. The consequence
then, becomes *a period of vulnerability to exploitation by "one's own kind."*

An excellent example of this vulnerability was the ability of an African

American "black" mayor to get away with the bombing of a row house in Philadelphia in 1988 to remove the "black" MOVE members. His actions resulted in the burning down of over sixty houses and the deaths of twelve people including five African American children. Those who protested the event argued that he would not have dropped the C-4 bomb if it had been a "white" neighborhood." While I concur with that notion, I am also convinced that had a "white" mayor done the same thing, the African Americans would have burned the rest of Philadelphia and other significant parts of America, instead of being stumped by the retort, "but, he's a brother."

It should be noted that the traditional elites, who are largely "white males," continue in large measure to successfully oppress the masses of "white men," who remain vulnerable to similar oppression by these look-alike elites because poor "white men" identify with them on the basis of shared gender and complexion. This "false consciousness" and commensurate invitation to scapegoating is, in my view, increasingly successful, given the decline of the labor movement. It is the labor movement that has traditionally been the (psycho-political) place from which such men have received an alternative definition of the causes of their exploitation and the place where they may also most likely learn that not everyone who looks like them is their friend nor is everyone who does not, their enemy.

As indicated in Model 3 (fig. 1.3), our domestic translation of such a scenario posits the analogous emergence of "black" elites who, while identified as friends by the general black population, in fact serve at the pleasure and in the place of the white domestic elites in administering the black domestic colony. It should be noted that such administrator status could refer to business, political, or even religious leadership that acts in the interest of the traditional elites. Such persons are also sometimes elevated to the status of "community leader." They are, most often, selected by the elites, rather than elected by the people.

In the absence of community accountability, such false leadership has been known to flourish, especially in a climate in which community charismatic leadership is less likely to rise and challenge for fear of assassination. This development presents the challenge of learning to distinguish between foes and friends of the same group.

It should also be noted that such a model, while presented here regarding white/black superordinate/subordinate relationships, is generally applicable to any situation in which some members of an identifiably distinct subordinate group are absorbed into the identifiably distinct superordinate group in its attempt to maintain control. At stage one, the mode of control was direct: whites

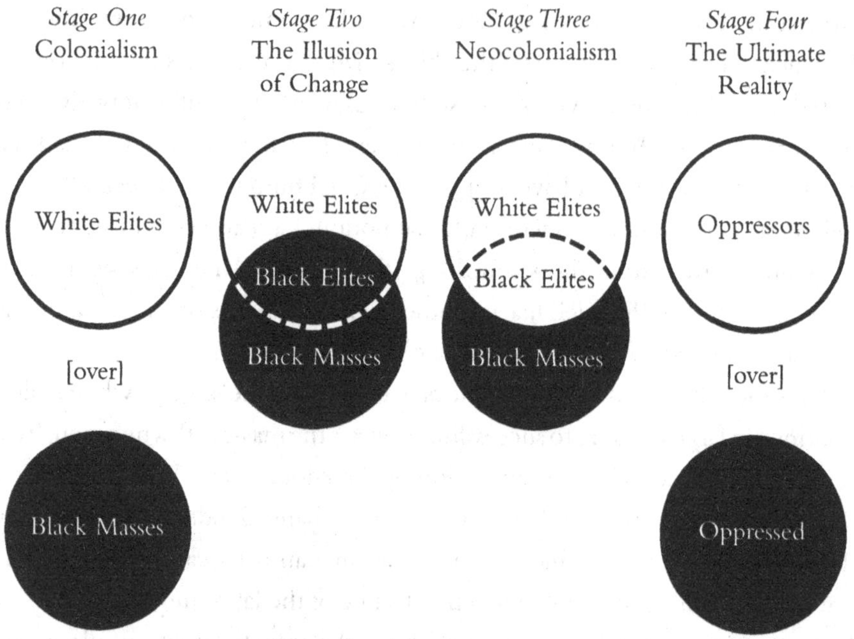

Fig. 1.3 Evolution from Domestic Colonialism to Domestic Neocolonialism

ruling blacks. At stage two, the recognition of collective oppressed status results in the reorganization of structure such that a class of black elites is created, who, while viewed as members of the oppressed group by the masses, as a consequence of stage one nationalism become in fact aligned with the oppressing white elites as indicated in stage three. Stage four represents a possible point of convergence for oppressed people under the broader understanding that, for example, not "all light people are your enemy, nor are all dark people your friend." These two notions, although little noted, were left to us by Martin Luther King, Jr., among others, as he strove to develop the bases of a *poor people's movement*. The failure to understand this separation of complexion from direction precludes the ability to form progressive coalitions across purported "race" lines.

It should be pointed out, however, that the acquisition of status does not by definition create an enemy either. As should be the case with any high-status occupant, it is at the point of action that such people should be judged, recognizing that inaction is also a form of action. W. E. B. DuBois's ultimate disillusionment with the notion of the "talented tenth" as possible sellouts reflects the depth of this crisis, and speaks to the need to develop mechanisms of accountability within the African American community.

It is nevertheless worth pointing out both some good news and bad news about this development. First, I would argue that this desegregation would not have occurred had the historical forces of the Civil Rights movement and the women's movement not succeeded in opening the door. Second, as is the case with the Supreme Court appointments of Justices O'Connor and Thomas, the very presence of a woman and a "black"/African American person on the Court serves to inspire children, ideology aside. The court is no longer "nine old men" nor "nine white men" and thus forwards the image of inclusion. Third, however evolutionary this development, it can be argued that it hastens the arrival of the day when people will have to judge others on the basis of actions rather than gender or complexion, because stereotypic assumptions will increasingly prove less accurate. On the other hand, this "desegregation," like "affirmative action," even if maximally successful, will not solve the problem of social and economic injustice because it does not reorganize the structure of economic and class relations.

For example, theoretically speaking, assuming equal distribution of talent, the implementation of maximum affirmative action would have women as 51 percent of the rich, the middle class, and the poor. African Americans would similarly be approximately 15 percent of the rich, the middle class, and the poor. This desegregated result would approximately match the proportion of each group in the general population. This result would not eliminate, but merely desegregate, the rich, middle-class, and poor boxes.

The desegregation of the visible elite is, nevertheless, a phenomenon in urgent need of further study, since it represents a significant shift in the intergroup and intragroup relations and has implications that transcend the traditionally dichotomous male/female gender and black/white "race" relations paradigms.

Part 4

> When you believe in things that you don't understand then you suffer, superstition ain't the way.—Stevie Wonder

Beyond Better Race Relations

In my view, the traditional race relations approach to American racism leaves us stuck with limiting our aspirations to better race relations, racial healing, and racial harmony. It is paradoxical that the traditional "race relations" approach may do more to reaffirm the belief in the "objective" existence of races than to migrate us toward a deracialization campaign to end racism.

It is worth noting that President Nelson Mandela, when faced with the question of how to address the new status of the Afrikaners, the previously ruling light-complexioned "white" South Africans of recent European descent, noted that this group would never be absorbed into a newly democratic South Africa as a breed apart. It is interesting to note that these "white" South Africans are roughly the same proportion —15 percent—of the South African population as so-called "black" Americans are of the U.S. population.

President Mandela called for a public campaign to resocialize the South African people, so they might be encouraged to see the Afrikaners as an additional cultural group rather than as a different color group. He thus called for deracialization rather than better race relations. It is unfortunate that in 1997, President Clinton's Initiative on Race, titled, *One America in the 21st Century*, failed to take this track, but merely renewed the traditional calls for racial harmony and healing.

As hard as it may be for us to see, to believe, belief systems, like the belief in "whites" and "blacks," are temporary and ever-changing. Notions of automatic superiority come and go. Kings have had to give up believing in serfs, masters have had to give up believing in slaves, and Brahmans have had to give up in believing in Untouchables.

In recent history, the Germans and the Afrikaners of South Africa have had to give up their "Aryan" notion of automatic superiority. Racialized Americans would be wise to do the same by giving up the belief in "whites" and "blacks."

We might start by challenging ourselves to approach each person as an *individual* rather than as a representative of a stereotyped group. A new cultural and ethnic conversation with pluralistic goals among African Americans, Asians Americans, Latino Americans, Native Americans, and European Americans may prove more fruitful than another harmony discourse across purported "race" lines and still allow for addressing matters of ethnic and cultural discrimination.

Attempting to solve this problem through the use of the race relations paradigm has been tried for over 100 years, and in my view has taken us as far as it can. *The pursuit of a noble goal with a flawed approach is still doomed to failure.*

If, as W. E. B. DuBois told us, the problem of the twentieth century is the problem of the color line, it is my view that the solution is deracialization rather than racial harmony, racial healing, or better "race relations." To solve the problem of racism, we need a paradigm shift.

We, the people of the United States, in order to form a more perfect union, need to reframe the conversation, think differently about the problem, and migrate from calling for better race relations to calling for deracialization, in the quest for cultural pluralism and economic justice.

CHAPTER 2

Performing Blackness

What African Americans Can Teach Sociology About Race

Sarah Susannah Willie

Introduction

Despite the challenges that postmodernism has levied against uniform notions of identity (Calhoun 1995), many sociologists continue to talk about groups and individuals as if their racial identities are immutable, monolithic, and non-negotiable. This legacy persists for at least two reasons. The first has to do with the definition of race itself. Most people use "race" to refer to categories of human differences, each category being a combination of ancestry, phenotype, and cultural tradition.[1] But Howard Winant cautions against seeing race merely as human difference without understanding its history. Winant argues that race is neither apolitical nor commonsensical, having its genesis in the modern world.

> Although some forms of racial awareness preceded the rise of Europe, it was the European conquest of the Americas, Africa, and Asia and the introduction of the imperial forms of rule associated with capitalism that ushered in the consolidation of racial divisions in society. [This] is the historical context in which racial concepts of difference have attained their present status as fundamental components of human identity and inequality. (Winant 1994)

I wish to thank the Spencer Foundation in Education and Colby College as a member of the Consortium of Liberal Arts Colleges for a Strong Minority Presence for generous fellowships that allowed me to write my dissertation, from which material is drawn for this chapter.

1. As philosopher Lucius Outlaw notes, well before the advent of racial categories, human beings noted each other's differences, answering the "general need to account for the unfamiliar [and] to organize the life world" (1990, 62).

Since the definition of race itself has a politically loaded history and has slightly different meanings depending on the nation, culture, and time period one is studying, its definition remains contested by scholars and laypeople alike. In short then, one reason for treating race as if it is monolithic and unchanging is because its diversity seems overwhelming and its mutability so difficult to capture conceptually.

A second reason that sociologists have tended to mistreat the concept has to do with the way the discipline looks at the world. The most popular units of analysis in sociology are groups and institutions, rather than interpersonal dynamics where challenges to uniform identity are most likely to appear.

In this chapter, I briefly explore sociology's take on race and describe the three paradigms through which the discipline in the United States has tended to conceptualize it. Then, drawing on interview data from my own study of college-educated African Americans,[2] I suggest the addition of another paradigm to capture more fully what race has meant and can mean. I allude to the work of scholars in sociology, women's studies, and gay and lesbian studies, engaging Davis (1991), Waters (1990), Hughes (1945), and Butler (1991) as my interlocutors.

Three Paradigms

Over the past century, mainstream sociology has provided three overarching paradigms beyond primordial biological distinctions between people (Montagu 1964; van de Berghe 1967; Osborne 1971) to talk about race: stratification, economics, and social constructionism.[3]

Stratification theorists assume the hierarchical arrangement of society by ascriptive and acquired characteristics such as sex, class, and age. For these theorists, race is usually understood as a signifier of status or group membership,

---

2. From 1989 to 1991, I have interviewed more than sixty African Americans who had been undergraduates at one predominately black university, Howard, and one predominately white university, Northwestern. Participants in the study were all alumni and had been enrolled for at least two years at one of the two colleges between 1968 and 1988. Interviews ranged from twenty minutes to two and one-half hours and took place face to face or over the phone. I reached participants referred to in this article by pseudonym through the method of snowball sampling.

3. The sociologists who have used race in these ways are too numerous to list.

which either advantages or disadvantages individuals (Lieberson 1961; Wilson 1973; Blau 1977).

Sociologists who explain race economically have tended to follow conflict theories. Race is understood as an invention of emergent capitalism—together with an appropriation of Darwinism applied to the social world—that justified the treatment of some people as commodities and others as owners of commodities for the generation of profit. Or race is understood as a social fact that emerges from class conflict, like its correlates racial antagonism and race consciousness. Edna Bonacich's (1972) theory of split labor markets is an example of the latter.

Just as the approaches to race in the first quarter of the twentieth century synthesized biologic paradigms with stratification and economic ones (DuBois 1965; Park 1924), in the last quarter of the century, there were those approaches that synthesized stratification and economic paradigms treating race relations, racial expectations, and racial consciousness as a function of caste (Willie 1989) or class status (Wilson 1978). The theory of domestic colonialism, articulated by Blauner (1969), is an example of such a synthesis.

The third overarching paradigm is social constructionism, which can include stratification and economic paradigms insofar as race is assumed to be differently understood and defined across space and time. The meaning of race, these social constructionists argue, changes depending on the social context (Frankenberg 1993; Berger and Luckmann 1966; Gossett 1963). Symbolic interactions is one example of social constructionism. Here interaction between individuals and groups is the focus. Much of the time, symbolic interactionists have shown, individuals treat the race of a person or a group as a proxy for a range of things from danger or kinship to low status or trustworthiness. Within this paradigm, the meaning people give to each other's behavior is always understood symbolically and influences their interactions with each other (Thio 1994).

Although more sociologists are combining these paradigms for understanding race (Ansell 1997; Omi and Winant 1986; Winant 1994; Gilroy 1993; Gallagher 1998), for most of this century race has been given much more careful sociological consideration as a determinant, discrete, and intractable characteristic that either helps or hurts one.[4] This tendency to see race as a variable

---

4. The explicit, if limited, way race is treated by sociology is interesting since it contrasts so sharply with the tendency of most Americans to dismiss the concept formally, even as they are

with fixed meaning runs the risk of obscuring how individuals and groups are also proactive agents and how race can play a positive role in group and individual identity.[5] As scholarship from that of James Scott (1985) to Charles Payne (1995) demonstrates, people are not only acted upon, they also act.

Theorizing the Experiences of Black Alumni

The black college alumni I interviewed who came of age in the twenty years immediately following the heyday of the American Civil Rights movement—1968 through 1988—offer multiple descriptions of race and racial identity. They recollect that what it meant to be black changed over time; they refer to their racial identity as bestowing upon them insider as well as outsider status; they relay stories of how class, gender, and social exposure shaped their sense of themselves racially; and finally they recall feeling at different times the sense of racial constraint, possibility, or malleability.

The words of my respondents go beyond the idea advanced by social constructionists that race is understood differently across cultures and time to suggest that simply having as one's primary reference group or being physically surrounded by persons of one's own racial group is not sufficient to guarantee a similar understanding of or way of talking about race.

Henry and Robert provide examples of African Americans who are not in agreement about what it means to be black. In discussing the idea of "blackness" by behavior, Henry redefines blackness for the interviewer so that she will not confuse his behavior with a repudiation of his African heritage, and he distances himself from those African Americans whom he perceives as materialistic.

---

distracted by and preoccupied with it informally. This paradoxical behavior is the result of the fact that, since the 1964 Civil Rights Act, race has been treated as a marker that can only be understood negatively in a democratic society attempting to achieve racial justice, where justice is equated with equal treatment. The national embrace of color-blindness, for example, is not only a backlash of the Right against gains made by people of color, it also expresses the desire of many Americans to heal the racial pain of the past with the misplaced belief that such healing can only happen by refusing to acknowledge the differences that once set people apart. Stuart Hall discusses a new and more positive understanding of ethnicity: "What is involved is the splitting of ... ethnicity between ... the dominant notion which connects it to nation and 'race' and ... a positive conception of the ethnicity of the margins, of the periphery" (1992, 258).

5. Each pseudonym is followed by the abbreviation HU for Howard University or NU for Northwestern University and the class in which the alum entered.

I'm not a bona fide buppie; I don't have no BMW. I drive a Volkswagen. . . . I
don't need a BMW. All I want is to be happy and have peace of mind. And
that's what I have and school gave me that. School gave me my lifestyle.
Everyone has to do it their own way. . . . There's something for everybody. I
know people who get lost in the school. And I guess they happy, but I don't
think they are 'cause it's like they're puttin' on. They're not real to me. I have
this thing about being real. That's why I work on my lawn. I have to touch the
earth. Because it's real. It's some substance. And you go and take a good look
at it and you think it's just dirt, but this is life. This is what life is really about,
believe it or not. It's not about the *Wall Street Journal* and what the stock market is doing. Life is in the ground. This is dirt. This is the base, where everything comes from and where we all will return. And we miss that sometimes;
we forget about it. I try and stay in touch with that. I come home sometimes
and cut my grass and dig in the lawn to keep my roots and know who I am. It's
just like being black is not just wearing your hair a certain way or changing
your name or going on different marches or reading this or caring about what
they did in South Africa. That is not the basis of being black. We have a culture and a way we talk at times, what's more important to me is where we're
going. You now, I think my definition of the black race is a certain pride: I am
a black man and I can achieve. I am doing my best and I'm still black. I'm still
black. I was very radical in school—I mean sandals, dashikis, I didn't cut my
hair for three years. I cut it during my junior year and I didn't cut it again until
I was working. That was the way it was. I'm a corporate soldier now. I won't
lie. I have the uniform. I mean, I will admit it if anybody asks me: I'm a corporate soldier. (Henry, NU 1977)

What counts in Henry's definition of racial identity is less who his parents
were or where he grew up and more who he is in the present. Using lawn care
metaphorically, he describes what it means to be black and human, importantly
indistinguishable for Henry. His analogy provides him with the space to do
three things: one, to define who he is now; two, to include race in that definition; and three, to avoid an explicit rejection of his past. His description suggests a desire to move away from historical, behavioral, or ideological
definitions of race.

While some African Americans may move toward all-encompassing economic definitions of race, such definitions are indistinguishable from how middle-class whites would talk about themselves racially. Psychologist Signithia
Fordham's work suggests that Henry may be "constructing an identity that, on

the one hand, enhancing [his] sense of 'Self,' while, on the other hand, enhancing [his] sense of fit within a given context" (1993, 12). Similar to other post-Civil Rights era African Americans, Henry wants to be seen as an individual.[6] And although he is not yet willing to give up the concept of racial identity—"my definition of the black race is a certain price"—if "blackness" means owning property with a lawn and tending to that, here its meaning has been subsumed within the rubric of class.

In contrast, Northwestern graduate Robert defines racial identity by his past associations: parents, neighborhood, high school, and friends:

> [M]y freshman year it was not the thing to go to University Theater productions. And there was a group of us who were really into music and theater. Freshman year I never went to a University theater production. I didn't go to [the annual variety show], didn't go to concerts or anything. But sophomore year I started saying, "well, wait a minute, I know I'm black. I went to a black high school, I lived in a black neighborhood all my life, I really can do this without risking my blackness." (Robert, NU 1980)

Robert separates his racial identity from his broader, extraracial interests. Confident that his ties to the black community are clear to self and others, he considers his past an arsenal to respond to any accusation of not being authentically black. Robert's background conforms to the expectations of others enough to allow him to participate in unexpected activities without threatening either blacks or whites.

Henry is similarly conscious, and he understands that his contemporary decisions to own a house in a predominately white suburb, live the life of a "corporate soldier," and spend his leisure time tending his lawn make him vulnerable to attacks by both blacks and whites that he just wants to be white, does not know his place, or has forgotten where he comes from. It is precisely his awareness of the potential for being ill-received that leads to the somewhat par-

---

6. Fordham's work shows how more and more young blacks who have come of age in the post-Civil Rights era believe "that American society is truly democratic and that the individual makes it or fails based solely on ability. In the school context [they are] committed to the meritocratic ideas promulgated there and [do] not want to have any information around [them] that might suggest that what [they have] learned, and perhaps [are] learning . . . is misleading or even untrue" (Fordham 1993, 17).

adoxical descriptions of his behavior as both beyond race and examples of racial pride.

As the quotations from Robert and Henry both show, the expectations of others play an important role in how we see ourselves and each other. As Everett C. Hughes argues, "[P]eople carry in their minds a set of expectations concerning the auxiliary traits properly associated with many of the specific positions available in our society" (1945, 144). Several alumni mentioned high school guidance counselors and teachers who expressed low expectations of them. Hannah, for example, remembers:

> The [counselor] in my high school told me I should go to beauty school. . . . That was her advice . . . and my English teacher was the same way. She was like, "You'll never make it through your freshman year in college. Your writing skills are terrible." And they were. Freshman English was the hardest class in my life, but I mean it really wasn't encouraging. . . . [The guidance counselors] kind of pushed along their few favorites, and the rest of the people [were on their own]. (Hannah, HU 1988)

With the help of their parents or their own willpower, students like Hannah had to fight others' expectations that they would not succeed in college.

During the college years, expectations combined with exposure and socialization were crucial elements for alumni's being able to see possibilities for themselves and, by extension, to expand their ideas of what it meant to be black:

> I had an opportunity to do an internship with IBM . . . and it was just a tremendous experience because it introduced me to things I'd never seen. . . . It put me in touch with minorities that owned sailboats and had prestigious jobs and lived a suburban, traditional kind of lifestyle, earning great sums of money—certainly by my standards. . . . [I]t just gave me a different sense of what one could truly accomplish. (Adam, NU 1974)

While Adam notes the possibility of being black and wealthy, Jennifer notes the experience of being introduced to corporate culture:

> I was an intern at [a Fortune 500] corporation downtown in their corporate affairs department. . . . I got to go to the annual meeting, and got to go out to

dinner several times, and I got to go on a boat ride—I had never been on a boat, sailing—. . . . And I got to see how you're supposed to act when you're standing around human resource people; how to make small talk with people you could care less about. So it was enlightening. (Jennifer, NU 1988)

The findings of Zweigenhaft and Domhoff (1991) confirm the experiences of my respondents. The people whom they interviewed for *Blacks in the White Establishment* gained similar knowledge: "[I]n addition to the formal education they had received, many had acquired at least two skills that became part of their culture and social capital: the ability to talk with anyone about anything, and the ability to benefit from the access to influential people they had gained as a result of attending elite schools" (107).

Not all of my respondents described success in economic terms. Especially for those individuals who had grown up in situations where they saw limited options for their lives, the chance to go to college provided them with ideas about pursuits and occupations they had never considered.

[At college,] I just realized . . . There's really no limit to what I can do. . . . I think I got a real good idea [at Howard] of what it is to be black in a lot of different parts of the country, you can aspire to be something. (Karl, HU 1989)

Lydia's testimony below complements Karl's above, showing the importance of social context to how one sees oneself.

[I]n the ghetto in New Jersey . . . you'll always hear "niggers can't do this and niggers can't do that," and "Niggers ain't this and niggers ain't that." [I was always] looking up there and [seeing] them standing around on the corner. And it was just so uplifting to go to a black institution that has been there for over one hundred years. And it's still standing and it's operating day to day and you're turning out the *crème de la crème* of black society. . . . [I]t's very positive and uplifting. . . . And it was good to be a part of that. . . . I was excited to be a part of history, because I felt connected to everybody that had been through there. (Lydia, HU 1997)

In her explanation of why she loves Howard University, Lydia shows us three conceptualizations of race: how race operates as a status, how blacks suffer the effects of domestic colonialism, and how race is symbolically interpreted.

Clearly, race operates at several levels. If one is a member of a subdominant racial group, in this case black in a culture dominated by whites, fluency in both the subculture and the dominant culture is a matter of survival. Howard alum Joseph advises: "if a black student has a black background, he should probably experience a white environment. And if a black student has a white background, [he should probably experience a black environment]" (Joseph, HU 1971). Sally had gone to a predominately white private school, and she confirms Joseph's advice:

[T]here's no question there's a lot to be gained from a black cultural experience. . . . There are sort of black traditions in [the] closed system [of black culture] that are acceptable [and others] that are not acceptable. . . . [College] was probably the first time in my life that I really got to know all these black folks. And so it was learning a lot about the culture, but it was learning by doing. I had never really been in a system that was predominately black. . . . And so, for that reason, I would certainly try to advocate to send my children to Howard or to a Howard-like school. (Sally, HU 1974)

Like Sally, Matthew had grown up in a predominately white environment, and he was "absolutely petrified" of being exposed as not "black enough" at Howard. He made some discoveries his first year:

[Y]ou grow up around all white people and none of them are going to Howard. In high school, my biggest problems came from black people, because I was class president and the [black students] saw me as being too white. . . . And I'm like, Oh, my god, I'm gonna go to a black school and these people are gonna harass me and I'm gonna hate it. And then I got there—and Howard is in a lower income area—and I was petrified. I had never even seen a project before. . . . I guess I had very low expectations in terms of me getting along with people. I thought that everyone was going to, like, hate me, and that everyone was gonna tell me that I talk like I was white. . . . It was a lot easier than I thought it was gonna be, because, I'd say, probably about half the students came from similar backgrounds [to my own]. . . . I thought American Top 40 [mainstream popular music] was gonna be laughed out of the dormitory, and you know, I'd walk down the hall and hear [the rock group] AC/DC and I was like, Oh, maybe I'm not that weird after all. Or you

know [some] people would assume I was from California or something. And
I was like, no, that's [just] how people talk in suburbia. You know, it's not just
a "valley" kind of a thing. (Matthew, HU 1986)

Matthew's reminiscence suggests that he was successful in convincing other
African Americans of his own authentic—if different—black experience. In
this example, it's clear that race is socially constructed even at the level of individual interaction.

Lucy, however, is not as sanguine as Matthew. Although she remembers
that the Howard experience allowed her to see the diversity of black identities,
she was disappointed that those identities did not live up to her expectation:

[A]ll the black people [are] . . . not unified in any one course or under our
skin color; we are not going in the same direction . . . there are as many view-
points as there are people . . . that's how [Howard] was. But I thought that if
we were "the talented tenth," we're suppose to know better than to buy into
all that other social [hierarchy] stuff. (Lucy, HU 1985)

Invoking DuBois's idealistic characterization of black leadership, Lucy expected blacks at Howard to be less cliquish and more politically unified. Finally,
however, Lucy explains the discontinuity between her expectations and the reality of what she found as a personal problem. When asked if she would like to
return, she says: "I'd like to go back and change me, not change anything about
Howard" (Lucy, HU 1985).

As the Black Freedom movement came to a close in the last of the 1960s
and early 1970s, definitions of blackness were changing and contested. But,
Joseph continues, racial expectations are not just influenced by the racial mix in
which one grows up, but also by the era:

[U]p until very, very shortly before [I arrived at college], it was an insult to be
called black. . . . I was on both sides. I remember when you couldn't call me
black. You know, Negro was acceptable; nigger was okay. Negro was just a
nicer way of saying it. But we went from that to black, and everybody had to
accept black. And black was cool. (Joseph, HU 1971)

As the 1970s gave way to the 1980s, not everyone could risk defining black
identity for themselves with impunity, especially not Northwestern students

who had grown up in predominately white environments. When I asked, "As for . . . the [members of the] black community who never sat at the black tables?" Robert responded, "Everyone talked about them, everyone. They were snubbed" (Robert, NU 1980).

Katrina, Northwestern class of 1981, was one of those black students who was snubbed. Having grown up surrounded by white people, she entered college ignorant of the fact, she says, that from the start, her blackness was in question. Trying to make sense of her marginality, she recalls her disappointment at not having been invited to the pre-freshman summer program that Northwestern sponsored for many of its entering black students:

> I wasn't ever invited. I didn't know anything about it, which I still get a crick in my neck about it because I don't know how they determine who goes to [it] exactly. So you get up here and the black people are already cliqued off. . . . And I had made these [white] friends and so I like ate with my friends. And I guess it took me a while before I realized what a big deal some of the rules were. (Katrina, NU 1985)

Katrina was expecting to find a niche more easily than she did in the black community at Northwestern. Her friendships with whites were negatively judged by some of her black classmates. It is only in retrospect, she says, that she is aware of the expectations that her black classmates had of her; and she now understands that without having spent a certain amount of time with them, she was ostracized. And, although she spent the majority of her time with white women friends, she was never pursued romantically by white men.

Beyond symbolic interaction, the concepts of performance and status help us to understand Katrina's position. Socialized in an affluent and highly educated family and surrounded by white people as a high school student, Katrina entered college to a confusing reception. As a high school student, her advanced academic placement and family's affluence allowed her an elevated status. As she entered adulthood at Northwestern, she discovered her status at home was not necessarily consistent with the status of being black at college, or at least not a good fit with the racially polarized campus she joined. She eventually found another "outsider" to date, a black student who pledged a white fraternity but soon deactivated.

To a certain extent, then, Katrina faced what Hughes describes as the dilemma of the contradiction of status: "[T]he more [the] individual, acquires of those elements of American culture which bring to others the higher rewards of success, the greater is his dilemma" (1945, 221). Hughes offers the example of the woman (whom he implies is white) or the Negro (whom he implies is male) who becomes a physician: "[T]he question arises whether to treat her or him as physician or as woman or Negro. Likewise, on their part, there is the problem whether, in a given troublesome situation, to act completely as physician or in the other role. This is their dilemma" (1984, 223).

Hughes mentioned five ways—two dependent upon the actions of the marginal individual, three dependent upon the society—for the marginality of such people to be reduced. First, the individual may "give up the struggle" and live according to the status or role that the dominant society assiduously has assigned him or her. Secondly, the individual may attempt to "resign from" the lower status to which the society would assign them. In such a case, she defines herself only as physician, for example, and works hard to avoid playing the role of "woman." This, Hughes admits, is a "tragic theme of human drama. The temptation to resign, and even to repudiate, is put heavily upon marginal people" (1984, 224).

The three ways in which the society might change include, first, that one of the statuses might simply "disappear," ceasing to have social meaning; second, "[o]ne or both of the statuses might . . . be so broadened and redefined" that formerly marginal people no longer face a dilemma; or third, the society might designate additional and discrete categories for people who occupy such marginal statuses (1984, 223–24).

The limitation of Hughes's analysis is that he did not carefully examine how people negotiate their statuses. Some people—even in 1949 when he authored this essay—no doubt negotiated with certain amounts of success such "contradictory class locations" (Wright 1985). A close analysis of their situations would have revealed the extent to which their statuses were malleable and performative. But Hughes does point us in the right direction:

> [W]e might distinguish between that kind of protest which is merely a squirming within the harness, and that which is a questioning of the very terms and dimensions of the prevailing status definitions. . . . [T]here is still much work to be done . . . on the processes by which the human biological individual is integrated . . . into a status system. (Hughes 1984, 228)

Considering how Hughes uses the language of roles and status, it is striking that he did not bring us closer to a serious questioning of race and sex roles as well as discussion of their performative nature.[7]

It is further interesting that for Hughes, the only choices open to the so-called marginal man or woman are to embrace the degraded status, to reject the degraded status, or to wait for the society to change. There is no middle ground in Hughes's schema, no place where the individual may negotiate his status, temporarily turning it off, creating with his colleagues, family, or friends new definitions of reality.

Other sociologists, however, have taken the metaphors of performance and dramaturgy further (Mead 1934; Berger and Luckmann 1966). "Constructing an identity" and "playing" that identity out have been twin themes in the scholarship of many twentieth-century sociologists. Erving Goffman (1959), for example, uses performance as a central organizing theme around which he proposes a theory of human action.

Most people do not think of themselves as *acting* when they behave in ways that feel natural and normal, and for this reason, the analogy of human behavior to drama makes most of us uncomfortable. It forces us to face the inevitability of confronting the labels, status, or behaviors with which we identify as invented, fake, and insubstantial. One of Goffman's most radical claims and helpful observations is that we are all performing all of the time. For him, performance has a broader meaning than simply living out a role or attempting to deceive others; performance need not convey insincerity or deception. He argues that we are always living for an audience simply because we cannot escape the presence of the social world; it is always with us, even if only in our minds.

Those scholars who have taken the fluidity of race seriously have often done so under the rubric of ethnicity. In *Ethnic Options* (1990), Mary Waters offers an excellent analysis of ethnicity's shifting boundaries with her study of U.S. census and other survey data. While confining her observations to white ethnics, she argues that, "[E]thnic identification is . . . a dynamic and complex social phenomenon" (Waters 1990, 16). Her findings reveal that European Americans treat ethnic affiliation as provisional and assumable. Her observation that white Americans conflate race with ethnicity is one of her most important

7. At the same time, Hughes's assumption appears to have been that the status system itself was beyond question. His focus, therefore, was how individuals are integrated in and respond to such systems rather than questioning the validity of the systems themselves.

contributions. One implication of this conflation is that white Americans "put on" and "take off" their ethnicity while remaining angry with people who claim ethnic oppression but cannot similarly "disrobe." Implicit in Waters' statement, however, is its complement that for African Americans, ethnic identification involves only constraint. Although the constraints are still much greater for any American dweller who appears to have African ancestry, I argue that constraint alone does not adequately describe the racial or ethnic identities of black Americans.

Most scholars have used the concepts of race and ethnicity in the same breath and yet alternately attribute distinctive meanings to them. Davis (1991) suggests that a racial group refers to people who share obvious *physical* characteristics while an ethnic group refers to people who share a sense of *cultural* identity (1991, 18). Although he admits that many people who identify as black have more European than African ancestry (1991, 13), in the final analysis, Davis's own reason for noting that "most blacks are physically distinguishable from whites" rests on a socially specific, and often biologically inconsistent, agreement of what constitutes "physically distinguishable" or "black." He argues further that people can belong to an ethnic group without belonging to the same racial group and vice versa. Then, despite the increasing economic, religious, and socioeconomic diversity among Americans of African ancestry, Davis proclaims that all black Americans belong to both the same racial and ethnic group (1991, 18). Davis is not alone when he decides to assert who is black and what that means. Another example of other-aspiration is the United States's "one drop rule" and the very different implications it has for blacks than it does for whites.

Likewise, pushing against the constraints that narrow biological definitions have offered for more complicated definitions of social life, women's studies and gay/lesbian scholars argue that masculinity, femininity, and androgyny are each a set of social expectations that are distinct from the biological sexes (Anderson, Connell, Stoltenberg, Kimmel, Caplan). The concept of gender, for example, has been successful in helping many people differentiate between role and biology.

Judith Butler (1991) provides us with a model for understanding that racial identity, too, is continuously reinstituted and reinvented by emphasizing the ways in which sexual identity is also continuously reinstituted and reinvented. Implicit in Butler's argument are two tenets: first, that changes in anyone's routine depend on the audience, and second, that an uncertainty exists in the mind of the actor that betrays the instability of the identity, racial or sexual, at which the actor is "playing."

By referring to sexual orientation, Butler makes these ideas concrete. She discusses heterosexuality as a role and an institution that is compulsively played out, rather than always or only as biologically determined. In the very need or decision to repeat the performance for others, she argues that the actor betrays the nature of the characteristic in question as at most unreal and at least incoherent and unstable. The characteristic in question might be straightness, masculinity, or whiteness; it might also be gayness, femininity, or blackness. Butler's point here is that the people with dominant characteristics—which also enjoy higher status—are compelled to remind others of them again and again in order to prove themselves to be more real, in other words, more worthy of that high status.

Clearly, to embrace the understanding that identity is always changing, in fact, must be repeated in order to (re)affirm itself, is one of the primary dilemmas for the postmodern black. Every person who has so recently learned to embrace a previously degraded identity now finds her- or himself in a world where racial identity is regularly contested and clearly not fixed.

Several Northwestern alumni remember taking advantage of this historical moment where identity was regularly contested and clearly not fixed. They admitted playing with or against the expectations that white people had of black behavior. Deborah explains, "[Y]ou know, when you had a 'fro out to here [she stretches her hands six inches away from her head] and your hat on and sunglasses, I mean nobody was messin' with you!" (Debbie, NU 1975).

Another Northwestern alum remembers mimicking white expectations. This was one way to undermine their construction of blackness:

[O]ne of my [sorority sisters] had a [white] roommate: she was extremely rich. Her name was Sally, and Pat [my soro] was her roommate. . . . Sally was flexible [and she realized that the whole time while she was growing up] her parents told her that blacks were this and black were that. The whole stereotypical [thing]. So when she came, it was like [she was] smart, you know. [She realized] "You're just like me." She had a car, [and] you weren't supposed to have a car freshman year, but she knew somebody [in the administration] at Northwestern so she was able to have a car. Her mom and her sister and them came up, so what we did is we gave them the stereotypical black. And Sally pretended like she was assimilated so well [to her black roommate] that now she was like us. . . . Her parents ran out. [And then] she said, "Oh my gosh!" So we had to [run after them,] grab 'em, and bring 'em back. And then finally we became very good friends with her mom and dad. And we laugh about it to this day. (NU female alum)

The ability to "play" with stereotypes or assume them for a specific purpose tells us about the malleability of race and racial stereotypes. Unlike "passing," this is less about pretending to be something one is not and more about pretending to be something one is thought to be.

Below, John characterizes living in a predominately white world as "a game" or performance, albeit a very serious one, that does not necessarily demand twenty-four-hour attention:

[T]here's a game that gets played from 9 to 5. And if you realize it's a game, then you win the game. Because then you play from 9 to 5 and after 5 o'clock you don't play it anymore. And unless you realize that, and that teaching, I think, comes from being around white people and realizing that there's a certain time when you can click this shit off. 'Cause they don't want to be at your parties either, okay? (John, NU 1980)

What characterizes both of the two examples immediately above, even more than the examples of Henry and Robert that opened this chapter, is the explicit awareness of manipulating one's audience.

Conclusion

A closer examination of the experiences of African Americans reveals that a 1950s paradigm performance is useful for sociologists who attempt to capture more completely what we mean when talking about the social construction of race. If we combine Erving Goffman's idea of dramaturgy with DuBois's awareness of the double consciousness, and incorporate work on sexuality and gender roles from women's studies and gay/lesbian studies, performance is a logical addition to sociology's understanding of race. Furthermore, using performance to understand race reminds us that agency has always been present in many of the sociological musings on race, but rarely taken further. Listening carefully to how African Americans talk about their own racial identity reveals that they do not see race as only something that *happens to* people, but as a dynamic that is negotiated, resisted, embraced, and performed with each interaction. This more fluid understanding of race is important to acknowledge, not just so we are reminded that people in subordinate positions have agency, but so that we are reminded that persons in subordinate positions have racial agency as well as racial responsibility.

CHAPTER 3

Myrdal, Park, and Second-Generation African American Sociologists

Donald Cunnigen

A merican sociology has produced a variety of scholars over the years who have contributed a unique perspective to the discipline. Within the community of African American sociologists, the generation of scholars produced between 1930 and 1960 offered an original worldview. Unlike two highly recognized volumes on African American sociologists (Blackwell and Janowitz 1974; Bracey, Meier, and Rudwick 1971) that provide an interesting historical overview of African American sociologists with special attention to the works of prominent scholars such as W. E. B. DuBois, Charles S. Johnson, and E. Franklin Frazier, the goal of this chapter is to focus on an African American sociological worldview within a specific generation. The chapter will analyze their worldview as being constructed through the analytical placement of African American sociologists in the context of their theoretical growth and contributions to the discipline. It is an inquiry into "academic sociology" through the generational prism of African American scholars.

As Alvin Gouldner (1970) suggested in his history of American sociology, a multidimensional critique of the sociology of second-generation African American sociologists is essential for examining the rise and decline of mainstream theoretical influences. The multidimensional critique would include influences on their work such as functionalism, Park's race relations cycle, the caste-class school, and Gunnar Myrdal's classic race study; the impact of the

A version of this chapter, "An Association of Black Sociologists Silver Anniversary Retrospective: The Legacy of the Second Generation African American Sociological Tradition," was presented at the 25th Anniversary Meeting of the Association of Black Sociologists, Washington, D.C., August 17–19, 1995.

shifting character of American society during the Great Depression in their adoption of a liberal perspective; the structure of the American university, with emphasis on the African American college and university milieu; the significance of sociology's development as a professional academic discipline on the careers of African American sociologists; and the consequence of African American sociologists' training in elite intellectual centers. By using the multi-dimensional critique, the African American sociological tradition may be explored in the context of Richard J. Bernstein's two critical questions (1972, 70): (1) How are we to tell to what extent a [second-generation African American sociologist] was shaped by preconceptions? (2) What extent did [second-generation African American sociologists'] research and work shape their understanding? The answers to these questions are related to an understanding of second-generation African American sociologists as social actors located in a specific time and place with regard to the academic community.

As Douglas Davidson (1977, 46) suggested, the impact and influence of African American sociologists would be "impossible to assess critically without assessing critically the larger society and the politics of the discipline." Therefore, an essential element in an analytical construction of the African American intellectual community's development is its relationship to "mainstream" sociological scholarship and popular culture.

The Four Periods of African American Sociology

Four distinct periods have existed in the African American sociological tradition, each influenced by the broader social system: first generation, 1905 through 1930; second generation, 1931 through 1951; third generation, 1960 through 1975; and fourth generation, 1976 through present. These periods were based on the production of Ph.D. recipients. In recent works, scholars in different disciplines have suggested that the Ph.D. production of African American scholars has significance in the study of African American scholarship.[1]

Within recent years, four separate attempts have been made by Butler A.

---

1. The attempt at periodization by scholars of an African American historical tradition has had similar problems. According to Robert L. Harris, Jr., the historical periodization of African American scholars has been influenced by the interests and racial emphasis of scholars. John Hope Franklin provided four generations of historical scholarship that corresponded closely with the sociological periods, that is, first generation 1882–1915; second generation 1915–1935; third

Jones, Gordon D. Morgan, R. Charles Key, and Jacquelyne Johnson Jackson to catalog and classify African American sociologists according to generation. Jones (1974) and Morgan (1973) provided imprecise periods for the first and second generations of African American sociologists. Morgan lists the first generation as containing Horace Mann Bond, Horace Clayton, Oliver Cromwell Cox, Allison Davis, Bertram W. Doyle, St. Clair Drake, W. E. B. DuBois, G. Franklin Edwards, E. Franklin Frazier, George Edmund Haynes, Charles S. Johnson, Hylan Lewis, and Ira de Augustine Reid. Thus, Morgan's first-generation list included African American social scientists from the 1890s through the 1950s.

Jones used the period from 1897 to 1955 for his discussion, beginning with early African American college sociology courses. His first generation cited Cox, Doyle, DuBois, Frazier, Haynes, Johnson, Reid, Henry Bullock, Walter Chivers, Vattel Daniel, E. Horace Fitchett, Charles G. Gomillion, Henry McGuinn, Kelly Miller, R. Clyde Miner, Earl Moses, Charles Parrish, Eugene Richards, and Harry Roberts. His second generation listed Lewis, John C. Alston, John T. Blue, Tilman C. Cothran, Sarah Curwood, Joseph Himes, Lewis Wade Jones, Charles E. King, Charles R. Lawrence, James Moss, Lionel Newsome, Leonard Robinson, Alvin Rose, Preston Valien, Albert Whiting, and Raytha Yokely.

Key (1978) suggested three distinct periods: (1) The Beginning School: Exclusion-Segregation, 1885 through 1930; (2) The New School: The Accommodation-Assimilationist Orientation, 1931 through 1964; and (3) The New Black Sociologists: Co-optation and Containment, 1965 to present. Key's first generation included names such as DuBois, Haynes, Issacs T. Brown, Henderson H. Daniel, James R. Diggs, and Richard R. Wright. His second generation included names such as Cox, Davis, Doyle, Drake, Edwards, Frazier, Himes, Johnson, Lewis, Reid, Rose, Valien, Daniel C. Thompson, Mozell C. Hill, Butler A. Jones, and Charles U. Smith. Despite the exhaustive character of these lists, many names were still omitted, as indicated from James Conyers' (1968), Charles V. Willie's (1982), and Lewis M. Killian's (1994) references to

---

generation 1935–1950; and fourth and current generation 1950 to present. On the other hand, August Meier and Elliott Rudwick began their periodization with 1915. The Meier and Rudwick periods placed emphasis on historians with earned doctorates and significant published works. Robert L. Harris, Jr., "Review Article—The Flowering of Afro American History," *The American Historical Review* 92 (1987): 1150–61.

William Henri Hale, Richard Hope, Jerome Holland, Robert Johnson, John Reid, James Rollins, Harry Walker, and Sadie Yancey.

Unfortunately, Jacquelyne Johnson Jackson (1974) failed to offer a similar periodization of African American women. She does provide a brief list of dissertation authors. The list includes Curwood, Wilmoth Carter, Mary Diggs, Joan Gordon, Anna Hardin, and Adelaide Hill, receiving degrees between 1945 and 1956. Surprisingly, Anna Roselle Johnson-Julian, the first African American female sociologist, was not listed among the early Ph.D. recipients.[2]

The lists above contain scholars trained in a variety of disciplines as well as individuals whose chronological ages were quite different. However, their training and research during a specific time period influenced their work. The problems associated with the process of identifying participants in periods of scholarly endeavors are not limited to sociologists.

Within contemporary scholarship, the method of periodicity used by scholars has often been the subject of great debate. In artistic fields, normative categories based on time and specific artistic influences have surfaced. Yet Jerry Ward has taken exception to this method by suggesting that the African American poet has subverted the nice paradigmatic structuring of works. The subversion in African American poetry was attributable to their work's having features which "may or may not conform to the dominant ideas of a period" (Ward 1997, xxi). Ward's notion of African American artists creating an origi-

---

2. Anna Roselle Johnson Julian (1904–94) received her doctorate in 1937 from the University of Pennsylvania, where she had earlier received her bachelor's and master's degrees. Her Penn years included numerous institutionalized on- and off-campus racial slights such as campus prohibitions against African Americans using swimming pools, eating in restaurants, and living in dormitories.

Through this haze of institutional and cultural racism, she became the first African American inducted into Penn's Phi Beta Kappa chapter. She was a recipient of the prestigious Moore Fellowship, the highest Penn award for women. With the receipt of her Ph.D., she became the first African American female in the world to receive a doctorate in sociology. Despite her outstanding achievement, her first job was a teaching post in a New Jersey high school. She worked as a statistician for the Washington, D.C. public schools.

Later, she married the prominent research chemist Dr. Percy L. Julian, who was credited with the discovery of cortisone. Her social activism included serving as a national president of Delta Sigma Theta Sorority, Inc. and as national vice president of the Links, a women's civil organization.

It took Penn fifty-two years to award a Ph.D. to another African American female, Simona Hill. Paula Giddings, *In Search of Sisterhood—Delta Sigma Theta and the Challenge of the Black Sorority Movement* (New York: William Morrow and Company, 1988), 83, 124–25.

nal poetic space provides an interesting approach to understanding the complexity of describing an intellectual group's generational experiences. It was this complexity that led some historical scholars to debate the legitimacy of methods used to define periods of African American scholarship in the field of history.

In a review of recent works on African American historiography, Robert L. Harris takes August Meier and Elliott Rudwick to task for their arbitrary use of five periods. Their periodicity was based on three primary documentation forms: interviews, monographs, and books. In addition, they utilized the "relations between the evolution of Afro-American historiography and changes within the society in general and historical profession in particular" (Harris 1987, 1153). It resulted in the exclusion of scholars who had not published "significant" works and were not doctorate holders.

Realizing the pitfalls of using a specific period, I have decided to use second-generation African American sociologists as an appropriate descriptor for the individuals discussed in these pages because the sociologists shared many of the common experiences and perspectives of African American sociologists schooled from 1930 to 1950. With the important exceptions of Chivers and Clayton, I focus on scholars who received the Ph.D. and published scholarly work during and after the period. Their scholarly production and graduate study reflected a generational experience, which makes them distinctive. The scholars in this generation were trained in many disciplines, and they often did interdisciplinary research.

Unlike Ward, we cannot make a claim to a subversive subtext in second-generation African American sociologists' work. Their acceptance of an assimilationist stance counteracted subversiveness. Yet, the second-generation African American sociologists maintained a distinct worldview from previous and subsequent generations.

Their worldview was formed by a configuration of sociocultural historical events that shaped the American intellectual discourse. In this discussion, the focus will be on the intersection of the following: (1) The development of the sociological discipline; (2) the contemporaneous patterns of race relations and the mainstream sociological community's response; (3) the development of basic sociological assumptions; (4) the unique isolation of the second-generation African American sociological tradition vis-à-vis the relationship of African American sociologists with mainstream sociological research institutions from the perspective of the Myrdal study.

Race and American Sociology: The Influence
of Domain Assumptions

The development of the sociological discipline and the convergence of racial and ethnic crises including the proliferation of lynchings occurred simultaneously in 1890s America. The period of American history from 1895 to 1910 was labeled as the "Nadir" by Rayford W. Logan (1956), who said the period was noted for the mistreatment of African Americans. While Logan's nadir may have signaled a particular period of racial animosity, white Americans' antipathy toward African Americans in popular culture has persisted throughout the twentieth century. The best examples of the anti-African American sentiments were highlighted by the lynching of 2,789 African Americans between 1889 and 1931, the maintenance of *de jure* and *de facto* segregation throughout the country, and the unpleasant frequent occurrence of race riots in urban areas.

As American race relations crystallized in the events listed above, a cadre of white male scholars attempted to define the discipline of sociology in the halls of academe. Simultaneously, the founders of sociology attempted to develop a theoretically informed praxis for the discipline. Many early white sociologists came out of the disciplines of history, philosophy, and economics. Consequently, the earlier theoretical discussions of sociologists and the discipline reflected the burning issues related to their perceptual views of society. Many scholars in the new discipline examined the social world from the perspective of a European confrontation between a dying *gemeinschaft* social order and an emerging *gesellschaft* order.

Within their examination, they developed the domain assumptions of sociology, which Gouldner (1970, 52) has described as, "[a]cademic sociology's emphasis on the potency of society and the subordination of [people] to it [as] an historical product that contains an historical truth."

Gouldner suggested that sociology developed the concepts of society and culture when the world was changing as a consequence of revolution. People were able to see the social changes they created and the contradictions of their inability to control the world in which they lived. The concepts of society and culture developed as ambiguous terms related to human invention. As an emerging academic discipline, sociology attempted to fill the European need for expression of what Gouldner (1970, 53) described as "their estrangement of themselves," which had previously been filled through religion and metaphysics. As these intellectual, social, and political changes in concert with the

Industrial Revolution shaped the modern world, sociology took halting steps at defining itself with a particular European point of view.

The 1800s were critical years for the development of sociology as a discipline. The first sociology courses were offered at Yale University and Colby College in the 1800s. The first department of sociology was established at the University of Chicago in 1892. The first sociology textbook was published in 1894. The first sociological journal, the *American Journal of Sociology,* was published in 1894. In the early 1900s, sociology continued to add elements that would give it legitimacy in academic circles. In 1905, sociologists organized the American Sociological Association.

Throughout these early years, sociologists were challenged with a critical dilemma. In simple terms, the sociologists were trying to develop credibility as a legitimate academic discipline while being social critics. According to Thomas F. Pettigrew (1980, xiii–xxxiii), the insider/outsider roles of sociologists such as William Graham Sumner, Albion Small, and W. I. Thomas were ordained clergy, sons of missionaries and/or ministers. The religious influences in their lives led many early sociologists to seek answers to social problems in the discipline of sociology. The religious influence made them interested in finding answers to humanity's pressing problems. They were interested in understanding their social worlds.

As sociology developed into an academic discipline, early sociologists emphasized policy-oriented research, which provided answers to pressing social problems. Despite the impact of race on American society, the new discipline of sociology failed to take a major role in developing policy-oriented research that would have shattered many of the racist assumptions permeating American life. The focus of white sociologists was on racial problems vis-à-vis a very limited prism, which was defined narrowly in a "racist" context.

The perspective of white sociologists mirrored the society's view on race. Sidney M. Wilhelm (1971, 247) suggested that American society has been racist from its incipient stages. According to Wilhelm (1971, 247), white American society's problem "for the better part of four hundred years has been the necessity to make racism palatable to [whites]." According to Rhett Jones (1992, 16), the failure of white society has been its inability to consider African Americans' awareness of the knowledge that "their experiences were different from whites." In addition, Jones (1992, 16) believed white sociology "failed to effectively grapple with [African American] life because of its preoccupation with organizations not individuals." While the Jones perspective provided an

intriguing interpretation of the African American experience, its greatest utility was its application to the understanding of the domain assumptions that
generate white sociological scholarship. The domain assumptions related to
what John H. Stanfield (1985, 3) described as the "societal conditioning factors
which shape the origins and development of social science disciplines, communities, and institutions" [and reproduce] the "societal patterns of class, gender, and racial inequality." Jones's description of white sociology's essential
failure highlighted the domain assumptions' influence in the creation of
methodological flaws that became critical elements of mainstream research.

Similarly, Steven J. Rosenthal (1976, 1) suggested sociology, as a discipline,
was embedded deeply with racist assumptions through the development of its
intellectual discourse. According to Rosenthal (1976, 1), the first American sociology texts by Henry Hughes and George Fitzhugh "were Comtean pre-
Civil War defenses of the morality of [African] slavery." Rosenthal also stated
that Sumner (1906) introduced American sociologists to the concept that "legislation cannot make mores [a method] to combat Reconstruction and racial
equality." Thus, leading American sociologists provided an intellectual rationale for the perspective that "government[al] protection of civil rights [was] futile 'interference.' "

According to Rosenthal (1976, 1), sociologists gave legitimacy to "Social
Darwinism" in race relations through the "re-imposition of slave-like conditions on [African Americans] and on the working class as a whole." Similarly,
Key (1975) said, "the expression of racism among the 'pioneering sociologists'
[was] so subtle it [was] difficult to recognize." Sumner's commitment to the
conservative role of mores and his discussion of their use to justify anything
provided one example of the powerful influence of the discipline's founding fathers' views regarding race.

The conservative views of William Graham Sumner on mores provided an
illustrative example of the dominant group's influence on sociological thought.
In *Folkways—A Study of the Sociological Importance of Usages, Manners, Customs,
Mores, and Morals* (1956, 77–78), he made the following statement:

> In our southern states, before the Civil War, whites and blacks had formed
> habits of action and feeling toward each other. They lived in peace and con-
> cord, and grew up in the ways which were traditional and customary. The
> Civil War abolished legal rights and left the two races to learn how to live to-
> gether under other relations than before. The whites have never been con-

verted from the old mores. Those who still survive look back with regret and affection to old social usages and customary sentiments and feelings. The two races have not yet made new mores. Vain attempts have been made to control the new order by legislation. The only result is the proof that legislation cannot control mores . . . some are anxious to interfere and try to control. They take their stands on ethical views of what is going on. It is evidently impossible for anyone to interfere. We are like spectators at a great natural convulsion.

In Sumner's view, mores were important aspects of the traditional customs of social interaction between African Americans and whites. He described the racial mores of the antebellum southern domination and exploitation of slaves as a social arrangement in which the races "lived in peace and accord." In a society of frozen heterogeneity such as the American southern slave community, the peace was maintained through violence. This point is not a minor consequence in southern race relations. Yet Sumner chose to describe the region's race relations as derivative of tradition and custom.

Given Sumner's benign description of slavery and its impact on society, it was not surprising to read his commentary regarding the imposition of change from outside the region as being an impossibility. He felt moral decrees would not have an impact on the deeply embedded racial habits and practices.

As an early sociological text, Sumner provided many young sociologists with a particular view of the African American that highlighted an institutional arrangement of "traditional and customary" racial inferiority. Sumner's commentary provided a legitimate intellectual cover for some scholars to assume cultural racism in their view, that is, that the southern white culture was superior to the African slave's previous cultural experiences. This cultural racism became an implicit part of the discourse that shaped American sociology's domain assumptions.

Similarly, Franklin H. Giddings provided his own racial perspective vis-à-vis the development of a theoretical perspective that examined "consciousness of kind." In Giddings' theoretical perspective, emphasis was placed on the following:

In its widest extension the consciousness of kind marks off the animate from the inanimate. Within the wide class of animate it next marks off species and races. Within racial lines, the consciousness of kind underlies the more definite ethnic and political groupings. It is the basis of class distinctions of innumerable forms of alliance, of rules, of intercourse and of peculiarities of policy. Our conduct towards those whom we feel to be more like ourselves is instinctively and rationally different from our conduct towards others, whom we believe to be less like ourselves. (Giddings 1921, 18)

Giddings' theoretical perspective highlighted a stable homogeneous population that reflected the racial sentiments of the time. When *The Principles of Sociology* was published in 1921, America maintained de facto and de jure segregation against African Americans, based on the assumption of their racial inferiority. African Americans were deemed by social scientists as an unstable and dysfunctional social group. Thus, Giddings' perspective suggested these groups should continue as separate entities. In the following, he explained his position:

It is sometimes said that we ought not to assert that the lower races have not the capacity for social evolution, because we do not know what they could do if they had the opportunity. They have been in existence, however, much longer than the European races, and have accomplished immeasurably less. We are therefore, warranted in saying that they have not the same inherent abilities. (Giddings 1921, 328–29)

According to Smith and Killian, the views of Sumner and Giddings reflected the fact that "sociologists in the white mainstream were debating whether blacks were even assimilable." (Smith and Killian 1990, 110).

According to Herman and Julia Schwendinger (1977, 100), "the founders of American sociology adopted social Darwinian ideas in order to buttress their own racist and imperialist doctrines." Thus, Giddings' notion of inferior races was a reflection of a reductionist ideological interpretation of the differences among people around the world. The Schwendingers stated that early American and European social scientists maintained "simple racial schemes of gradation." The top of the racial schema consisted of the more "evolved" Anglo-Saxon and Germanic races. The very bottom of the racial schema consisted of the "savage" races such as Africans, Asians, Indians, and Mexicans. These views had a profound impact on the participants in the discipline. As members of one of the so-called "savage" races, second-generation African American sociologists became participants in a discipline grounded by the racist domain assumptions of its founders.

The influence of sociological pioneers' views became an integral part of the sociological discourse. According to Key, the discourse shaped the values of most white or mainstream sociologists. He suggested the values included normative theories of race that influenced their sociological inquiry. White sociological inquiry was developed with little regard for the scholarly production of African Americans, especially nontraditional views. Consequently, mainstream sociologists' discourse focused on the problems of European groups with greater interest. As sociology took fledgling steps to define itself, America experienced a rapidly changing racial dynamic. Mainstream sociologists' interest in Euro-American social problems took precedence over the study of other groups, especially African Americans.

Not surprisingly, sociology's development at a critical juncture in American race relations had a negligible impact on the study of race relations. According to Pettigrew (1980, xiii–xxxiii), little research was conducted on race relations because of a lack of interest, a lack of resources, and the use of old analytical models. Similarly, the disinterest of the discipline's leaders in the study of race relations extended to attitudes regarding their African American colleagues' scholarship.

Sociology in African American Colleges and Universities

As "mainstream" sociologists developed the discipline in their racially exclusive academic community, parallel developments occurred in the African American social science community. As early as 1894, Morgan College (now Morgan State University) had a course of eight lectures on social science. In 1897, Atlanta University (AU) had sociology courses. Concomitantly, DuBois began his AU sociological studies of African American life. By 1917, sociology courses were reportedly offered by twenty-three African American institutions of higher learning (Himes 1949, 17–32). In 1931, a survey of departments found 232 different sociology courses listed as curricular offerings. The most popular courses were rural sociology, educational sociology, and race (Doyle 1933, 11–13).

As African American college and university sociology programs were developing, individual African American scholars were receiving degrees in the field. James Robert Lincoln Diggs received the first Ph.D. in sociology from Illinois Wesleyan University in 1906 (Green 1946, 561). Although Diggs has been acknowledged as the first recipient, George Edmund Haynes's doctorate from Columbia University in 1912 has been singled out by some scholars as significant because of his pivotal role in the development of the sociology department at his alma mater, Fisk University (Himes 1949, 21).

While some young African American scholars received training as sociologists, other African Americans were making substantive research contributions to the discipline. In 1899, DuBois published his classic community study, *The Philadelphia Negro*. DuBois's study was the first major sociological study of an African American community directed by an African American and funded by a significant philanthropic foundation. At Tuskegee Institute (now Tuskegee University), Monroe Nathan Work became the director of the Bureau of Records in 1911. Through his work, the Bureau of Records published a series of statistical volumes on African American life, *Negro Yearbook* (Himes 1949, 19–21; McMurry 1985).

It was during this period that the first generation of African American sociologists made their mark on the discipline. The first generation of African American sociologists was trained and practiced their craft in an America that blatantly did not acknowledge African American intellectuals. The early founders of the African American sociological tradition consisted of individuals who took Ph.D.s and a variety of master's-level scholars. Like their white counterparts, many first-generation African American scholars received Ph.D.s in other disciplines. Many of these scholars were employed in the premiere segregated African American institutions of higher learning such as Howard University, Fisk, and Atlanta University. Their scholarship was ignored by all but a small segment of the white sociological community. They received little research support from their colleges and universities and no substantial research support from the major philanthropic sources.

By the 1930s and the 1940s, the African American intellectual community shared the following characteristics: (1) it embraced ideologies, theories, and philosophies that were not reflective of the African American community; (2) it embraced uncritically liberal integrationist ideology and methodology; (3) it was alienated from the African American community; and (4) it accepted liberal ideology because of "Jim Crow's" pernicious hold on the popular culture of American society through law and social custom (Davidson 1977, 45–51).

Although leading white sociologists such as Chicago's William Ogburn publicly opposed the hiring of African American faculty during the period from the 1930s through the 1950s, it was a time of stellar scholarship among African American sociologists (Banks 1996, 121). During this period, significant scholarly publications appeared such as E. Franklin Frazier's *Negro Family in Chicago* (1932) and *Negro Family in the United States* (1939), Allison Davis and John Dollard's *Children of Bondage: The Personality Development of Urban Youth in the Urban South* (1940), Charles S. Johnson's *Shadow of the Plantation* (1934) and *Growing Up in the Black Belt* (1941), Ira de Augustine Reid's *In A Minor Key* (1940), St. Clair Drake and Horace Cayton's *Black Metropolis: A Study of Negro Life in a Northern City* (1948), Oliver C. Cox's *Caste, Class and Race* (1945), and Hylan Lewis's *Blackways of Kent* (1955).

This period was an important time for the second-generation African American sociologists. According to James E. Conyers (1986, 77–93), two of the top four African American sociologists were produced in this generation, Oliver Cromwell Cox and Frazier. During the period, a network of second-generation African American sociologists provided links between earlier generations as well as cross-racial lines. The sociopolitical currents of the African American intellectual community had a profound impact on the second generation. Carl Jorgensen has provided an intricate diagram of the intellectual influences of African American sociologists. By examining a modified version of the Jorgensen diagram in reference to several scholars, the intricacy of the second-generation African American sociological network may be highlighted in miniature (fig. 3.1).

The network was linked by the interaction and influence of older and younger African American scholars. The Atlanta University scholars played a significant role in the cross-fertilization of African American scholarship, especially W. E. B. DuBois. Butler A. Jones was influenced moderately by W. E. B. DuBois as an AU student. As a student, he was also influenced strongly by Morehouse College faculty member Walter Chives. During his professional life, he interacted with Cox, Hill, and other members of the generation.

In addition to the AU network, the Chicago School had an important impact on African American scholars. St. Clair Drake was influenced strongly by W. Lloyd Warner, Robert Redfield, Everett C. Hughes, and Louis Wirth. Through his Hampton Institute (now Hampton University) years and later Chicago School days, Allison Davis became a strong influence on Drake. Davis was influenced by Gunnar Myrdal. He collaborated on research with Horace Clayton and interacted with other second-generation scholars. Horace Clayton was influenced strongly by Robert E. Park and Louis Wirth.

Like their AU and Chicago colleagues, African Americans who studied at Harvard University and Columbia comprised a social network within the second generation. Daniel C. Thompson was influenced strongly by Robert K.

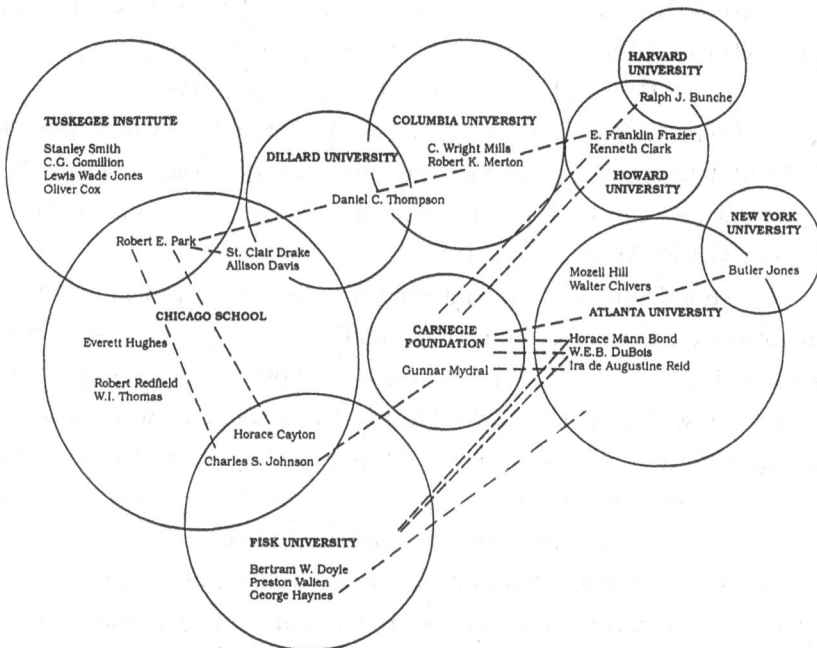

Fig. 3.1 African American Scholars

Merton as a Columbia student. Gunnar Myrdal's influence, through funding and the production of *An American Dilemma*, had an indirect and direct effect on the network. Similarly, the overarching influence of African American political figures such as Booker T. Washington had a strong influence on scholarship. The complex network of influences was derivative of an intellectual community that exhibited four basic characteristics.

Within the African American intellectual community, sociologists had the following characteristics: (1) they were a privileged minority whose high-status occupational membership and racial status gave them advantages and disadvantages; (2) they were a group who suffered ambiguity regarding the confluence of their racial status with their professional/occupational status; (3) they were a group who "directed all of [their] energies and attention to problems of race relations"; and (4) they were a group whose training and intellectual views were influenced greatly by the liberal views of scholars such as Robert E. Park (Hines 1967, 30–35).

In addition, Key (1978, 35–48) identified seven unique characteristics of the second-generation African American sociologists: (1) their professional careers usually began after 1931; (2) they were not very concerned about professionally refuting the racist assumptions present in the intellectual discourse of the late nineteenth and early twentieth centuries; (3) they focused their research on the conditions that immediately affected the African American community and larger society; (4) their work more effectively utilized sociological methods and was better documented than that of the first generation; (5) they attempted to be more objective and scientifically oriented; (6) they were not very much engaged in social action; and (7) they had greater acceptance from some segments of the white sociological community. Key's suggestion of the generation's greater acceptance by white scholars reflects the second generation's acceptance of particular white scholars' theoretical models.

One of the dominant models used by white sociologists of the period to explain race relations was the assimilationist model. Because many of the second-generation sociologists studied under University of Chicago's Park, a leading proponent of the assimilationist model, they incorporated the model or elements of the model in their research. The acceptance of the assimilationist perspective by many second-generation sociologists was part of their accommodationist stance in relationship to the discipline.

The Chicago School's tradition had a significant impact on their perspective. Although Andrew Abbott suggested the Chicago School was "a body of work produced by students and faculty of the department between the First World War and the mid 1930s," the tradition extended well beyond the 1930s, for African American sociologists utilized elements of the Chicago School's methods. According to Abbott, the Chicago School of thought "felt that no social fact makes any sense abstracted from its context in social (and often geographic) space and social time" (Abbott 1997, 115). This view was shared by many second-generation African American sociologists as they examined racial issues of the 1930s through the 1950s. Thus, many of the second-generation sociologists combined the Park assimilationist model with the Chicago School of thought.

As Alford Young (1993, 107) has noted in his study of Frazier and Johnson, the publications of many African American sociologists of this period were influenced by Park. Park's "views on the culture of Afro-Americans and Africans as well as his race relations cycle" had a strong impact on Johnson and Frazier (Young 1993, 109). In Young's opinion, Frazier's body of work represented a methodological and theoretical extension and revision of Park's ideas. Morgan (1973, 106–19) suggested that the entire second generation of African American sociologists was influenced by Park and/or the caste and class school of thought. In both analyses, the scholars support Key's basic assumption that second-generation African American sociologists operated under an assimilationist-accommodationist model that did not challenge profoundly the domain assumptions of sociology. As marginalized scholars, they viewed their commitment to the discipline's shibboleths as a mark of being well trained and a requirement for full acceptance by their mainstream peers. Despite their attachment to the discipline's assumptions, their lives as members of the African American community created personal tensions.

The second generation best represented DuBois's concept of "dual-consciousness" as African American intellectuals. Their dual consciousness was based on the conflictual nature of their commitment to sociology's domain assumptions, the myth of objectivity by which they were trained in white graduate schools, and their personal commitment to a racially just society. Anthony Platt (1990, 51–52) has suggested that Frazier resolved the conflict in his written work by affecting two diverging writing styles, a scholarly style that was "a sociological language in his academic publications" and an advocacy style that was "[a] polemical language . . . [used] in [popular] journals like the *Messenger*." The Frazier writing technique for ideological conflict resolution was evident in the written work of other sociologists during the period. Their ability to devise an intellectual stance, which made their ideas acceptable to mainstream sociologists, meant the difference between success and failure in the small liberal circle of mainstream sociological scholarship's funding sources.

Gunnar Myrdal and the African American

Within "mainstream" sociology, the Carnegie Foundation's research project on the African American community of the 1930s provided a telling glimpse of second-generation African American sociological scholars' relationship with white sociologists and white research institutes. Gunnar Myrdal's classic study of American race relations, *An American Dilemma—The Negro Problem and Modern Democracy* (1944), provides an excellent example of mainstream sociologists' role behavior in relationship to their African American colleagues. Myrdal's study helped to launch young white scholars' careers and to enhance established white scholars' careers, including Arnold Rose, Richard Sterner, Edward Shils, Donald Young, Samuel Stouffer, William Ogburn, Herbert Goldhammer, and Louis Wirth. Although Martin Bulmer has suggested the years between World War I and World War II provided a "means of illuminating the conditions of [African] Americans and also an avenue of upward mobility for a small number of [African American] scholars" through the Myrdal study (Bulmer 1992), the participation of second-generation African American sociologists and other social scientists was circumscribed rigidly by Myrdal through a controlled participation selection process.

In the early planning of the Carnegie-funded study, Melville Herskovits insisted on including African American scholars (Walter Jackson 1990, 26–31). While Walter A. Jackson (1990) and David Southern (1987) have heralded Myrdal's selection and inclusion of African American scholars for the project, their inclusion was preplanned by the foundation, which considered the presence of "one colored social scientist" as the appropriate level of representation. The critical issue for Myrdal was the selection of a "colored social scientist." Henry (1999, 93) suggested that Ralph J. Bunche, the noted Howard political scientist, fulfilled Myrdal's expectations of a competent "colored social scientist." Although Jackson (1990) and Southern (1987) cited Myrdal's early suggestion to have Charles S. Johnson as a coauthor to the Carnegie Foundation study, Stanfield (1985, 181 n. 95) has suggested that Myrdal chose Bunche over the more eminent Charles S. Johnson or E. Franklin Frazier because "[Myrdal] was interest[ed] in controlling the interpretations of the Afro-American experience."

According to Jackson, Bunche's selection was critical because of his pivotal role in recruiting unknown young African American scholars to conduct research and prepare memoranda. Very often, his contacts were established through the insular network of the African American intellectual community.[3] While Bunche's selection of scholars reflected the ambiguities present in the African American intellectual community, it highlighted his personal intellectual idiosyncrasies and the fluidity of the African American social scientific community during this period. He provided Myrdal with a special entrée into the African American community.

---

3. Jones to Bunche, Nov. 11, 1939 (Jones 1939); Jackson to Jones, Nov. 15, 1939 (Jackson 1939); Jones to Bunche, Jan. 14, 1940 (Jones 1940f); Bunche to Jones, Jan. 17, 1940 (Bunch 1940f); Jones to Bunche, Jan. 22, 1940 (Jones 1940d); Bunche to Jones, Jan. 27, 1940 (Bunch 1940e); Bunche to Jones, Feb. 20, 1940 (Bunch 1940d); Jones to Bunche, Feb. 25, 1940 (Jones 1940c); Bunche to Jones, Mar. 19, 1940 (Bunch 1940c); Bunche to Jones, May 7, 1940 (Bunch 1940b); Jones to Bunche, May 15, 1940; Bunche to Jones, May 27, 1940 (Bunch 1940a).

Myrdal and Bunche had a very close relationship, which gave the latter privileges and insights unavailable to any other African American social scientists (Jones 1993). Their unique relationship was solidified on a 1939 southern tour during which Bunche often passed for white as the two scholars occasionally violated the color bar. Bunche's scholarly sophistication, light complexion, and rugged handsomeness were characteristics that made him an attractive companion for Myrdal (Jackson 1990, 121–34).

While their personalities were compatible, Myrdal and Bunche disagreed on a key intellectual concept: the validity of Marxism in contemporary society. In a recent work, Bunche was described as a "neo-Marxist" who eschewed DuBois's ideas of "race barriers" for a class analysis of the social problems facing African Americans (Banks 1996, 106–7). As indicated in *An American Dilemma*, Myrdal (1944, 67–72) thought Marxism was a "fatalistic theory." Unlike Bunche, he was not very optimistic about the possibility of an interracial working-class alliance. According to Charles P. Henry (1990, 50–67; 1999, 47–64), Bunche maintained a "Marxist-oriented approach to racial problems" between 1929 and 1940. Bunche believed imperialism and capitalism were the main reasons for "racial oppression" (Henry 1990, 50). According to Henry (1990, 52), Bunche viewed the caste status of African Americans as a "pre-capitalist survival [or] relic of feudalism which found a happy home in the decaying structure of capitalism in its final imperialist monopolistic epoch." He viewed race prejudice as a critical idea of America's ruling class. In Bunche's words, "race prejudice established its hegemony and is absorbed by the other classes of society" (Henry 1990, 52). Thus, the white American working class was reproducing the racial prejudices of those in power.

Bunche's optimistic perspective reflected the idealism of a radical intellectual circle of Howard scholars who included E. Franklin Frazier, Alain Locke, Eric Williams, W. O. Brown, Charles Wesley, Ernest Just, Charles Thompson, Emmett Dorsey, and Abram Harris. According to Henry (1990, 52–53); Meier and Rudwick (1986, 102), and G. Franklin Edwards (1980, 109–29), Howard in the 1930 and 1940s had a particularly progressive and talented social science faculty. As a group, the "Howard Circle" made an invaluable contribution to scholarship on the African American experience. The radical perspective of the younger generation of African American scholars appealed to Myrdal.

Myrdal felt the younger generation of African American social scientists would search forthrightly for innovative data on the society's racial issues. He ignored senior African American sociological scholars, with the exception of early conferences with Monroe Nathan Work and W. E. B. DuBois (Jackson 1990, 990). Similarly, senior African American historians such as Carter G. Woodson (Jackson 1990, 11) were not a main part of his extensive research group, which consisted of a primary staff of Bunche, Guy B. Johnson, Dorothy S. Thomas, Doxey Wilkerson, Paul Norgren, and Richard Sterner, thirty-one independent scholars, and thirty-six assistants (Henry 1999, 93). According to Jackson (1990, 114), Charles S. Johnson also became a part of Myrdal's primary staff.

As a result of Myrdal's perspective, the African American social scientists who participated in the study included sociologists and Communists such as Wilkerson, Lyonel Florant, and James E. Jackson; sociologists such as E. Franklin Frazier, Ira de Augustine Reid, St. Clair Drake, Charles S. Johnson, Butler A. Jones, Horace Clayton, and Allison Davis; and a young graduate research assistant, Kenneth B. Clark. Myrdal worked closely with African American scholars on an individual basis rather than as a group (Jackson 1990, 116; Kelley 1990, 205). Consequently, one's ability to get along with him and appeal to his idiosyncrasies became an important aspect of the African American scholars' participation in the study.

Drake, Jones, and Clayton were only three of the second-generation African American sociologists who participated in Myrdal's classic study on race relations. While the presence of a sizable African American scholarly group as participants in the research project presented a departure from traditional foundation-funded race studies, the Myrdal study reflected the major methodological and theoretical biases held by mainstream sociologists against African American sociologists and their scholarship. According to Key (1975, 76–77), mainstream sociologists have had monopolistic access "to the sociological enterprise on both [the individual and group] levels, since their preferences and prejudices, theories, notions, and facts and figures are in effect interconnected and interdependent." Key suggested their monopolistic access was presented in biases that included the following: (1) their adherence to a particular school of thought and orientations spawned by their monopoly of the discipline; (2) the congruence of the school and orientations with their social location and styles of life; and (3) the adaptation and reconciliation of their school and orientations with the dominant social forces of the prevailing social order, especially the cultural, institutional, and individual racist assumptions in American society (Key 1975, 76–77).

Despite the discipline's biases, Drake, Jones, and Clayton prepared memoranda for the Myrdal study. In the case of Clayton, the memorandum was never completed because of intellectual differences and remunerative conflicts between the men (Bracey 1994; Stanfield 1985, 164–74). Jones's "The Political Status of the Negro" (1940) memorandum and Drake's collaborative monograph with Allison Davis, "Negro Churches and Associations in Chicago" (1940), were used by Myrdal. In the case of Jones's memorandum, the entire document was included verbatim in the posthumously published work of Ralph J. Bunche. Unfortunately, Dewey Grantham, the editor, referenced Jones's valuable contribution in a single footnote (Bunche 1973, 485–91). The participation of African American sociologists in Myrdal's study provided recognition for their scholarship, which few first- or second-generation scholars ever experienced in their professional careers. While it did not boost their academic careers like those of their white counterparts, it gave them exposure that aided them during the advent of integration. Jones became a member of a select group of African American sociologists hired by white institutions (Winston 1971, 678–719).

The participation of African American sociologists in the study's research effort served them in far more practical ways. Since the Great Depression was a very lean financial time for African American scholars, the prospect of participating in a major research project with "unlimited" philanthropic funding was a golden financial and scholarly opportunity. As Stanfield (1985, 89) has indicated, the employment options for newly minted master's and doctorate holders among African American sociologists were very limited during this period. Within the African American social scientific community, the Bunch/Myrdal connection became an important means for the acquisition of scholarly recognition and financial reward. It would not be an exaggeration to describe the Myrdal project as a major "welfare program for many white and African American race relations scholars, with Bunche serving as his primary 'colored' conduit." However, Stanfield's (1985, 163) description of African American participants' role as "field hands" was an apt description of Myrdal's approach to some of their contributions.

Conclusion

The Myrdal study highlighted the marginality of second-generation African American sociologists. Although they received greater professional recognition than their first-generation predecessors, they were exploited easily by mainstream sociologists because of disciplinary assumptions that perpetuated cultural, institutional, and individual racism. Since the period of the second generation spanned World War II and the 1954 *Brown vs. Board of Education* decision, the experiences of the generation may be categorized as having two phases—an early phase and a latter phase—because of the postwar changes in civil rights.

The latter phase of second-generation African American sociologists provided the gradual opening of opportunities at white colleges and universities. While these opportunities were offered to an extremely lucky few (often in or near the twilight of their professional careers) who were situated in the right place at the right time, they marked a shift in the institutional dynamics of the discipline. Similarly, the election of second-generation scholars to the presidencies of several professional organizations during this phase signaled a level of intellectual recognition found in very few American academic communities. Yet the legacy of the second-generation African American sociologists can be described appropriately as one scarred by "Jim Crow" and shaped by the participants' personal desires to be recognized as sociologists through traditional patterns of scholarly productivity.

If their generational weakness could be categorized in a single problem, it would be their reliance on the assimilationist theoretical model. However, their training and the limited ideological options—disciplinary restraints on radicalism—provided few alternatives in academia. Most second-generation African American sociologists were southerners who received their undergraduate degrees from African American colleges and universities. They received graduate degrees from northern white graduate schools, with Chicago and Ohio State producing the lion's share. As suggested by Robert K. Merton (1972), they specialized in race and education. These group variables influenced their careers as much as segregation.

According to Key (1975, 33–37), the "dominant group [of sociologists were] not compelled to question or make sense of most of their values. Many [took them] for granted, as normative, and therefore correct. It [was] only by opposing or competing values that many of their own values [were] recognized." The discipline's leaders provided no ideological outlets for nontraditional views. The African American sociologists' very presence in the field was viewed by many as nontraditional. To that extent, they were marginalized by the mainstream sociologists. Their marginalization and the institutional dynamics of the African American college and university environment made their objective almost insurmountable.

CHAPTER 4

Deconstructing the Bell Curve

Racism, Classism, and Intelligence in America

Howard F. Taylor

One of the biggest sets of problems facing African Americans at the turn of the millennium involves the structure of the education institution in America and the education, achievement, and assessment of consistently oppressed groups such as African Americans, women (especially African American women), Native Americans, Latinas/os, and other working-class persons. Without homogenizing these groups, and without homogenizing any particular group, it is nonetheless evident that certain dimensions of oppressive treatment in society exist as common for such groups. I wish to focus this chapter primarily, though not exclusively, on African Americans.

Periodically, since the mid-nineteenth century (which witnessed the beginning of scientific racism with Sir Francis Galton), and about once every twenty to twenty-five years or so from the 1920s on, a statement is made via the scientific journals and other scientific writing that some particular oppressed group (Blacks, Jews, Greeks, the Irish, the Polish, and several other groups at various historical periods) is intellectually inferior to the dominant white Anglo-Saxon (that is, ethnically English) Protestant group. It is argued, once every twenty to twenty-five years or so, that the reasons for this are largely genetic, and that differences among people in intelligence, talents, and achievements are thus less caused by differences in their social, educational, home, and other socializing environments. It has also since been argued, though consistently rather than only every twenty-five years, that women simply do not possess the genes for mathematical and scientific thinking, and that is the reason they have performed less well than men for the last sixty to eighty years on the quantitative portions of standardized intelligence tests. One can hypothesize, as some have, that the attribution of genetic intellectual inferiority to a group, including women, is a mechanism by which the institutions controlling society justify the oppression of the group in question, and thereby justify the status quo. Racism, sexism, and classism are thereby given scientific justification.

During the Great Black Migration from South to North early in the twentieth century, (Marks 1989) blacks were described in some of the *scientific literature* of the day as genetically intellectually inferior and as a "fungus growth" in need of "extermination." The late 1960s and the early 1970s saw William Shockley, co-inventor of the transistor, argue for genetic causation of racial differences in intelligence, and for the systematic sterilization of low-IQ blacks. This period also saw Arthur Jensen of Berkeley and Richard Herrnstein of Harvard argue that *within*-race genetic causation of intelligence was extremely high (with a within-group "heritability" of around 80 percent) and (thus) between-race genetic differences in intellect were a very real possibility.

Right on schedule (twenty-five years later), the very same Richard Herrnstein, joining forces with Charles Murray, published in 1994 the now notorious *The Bell Curve* (Herrnstein and Murray 1994), in which they argue, using elaborate yet flawed statistical arguments, first, that currently used standardized tests (IQ tests as well as academic assessment tests such as the SAT and ACT) validly measure something called "intelligence," and further, that they measure intelligence *equally validly* for whites, blacks, Hispanics, Native Americans, and also Asians; second, that intelligence is strongly genetically heritable within any given racial-ethnic group, showing a within-group heritability coefficient of around 70 percent; third, that different social classes differ in intelligence, and since intelligence is primarily genetic, then it follows that America contains a "cognitive elite" upper class of individuals who are there primarily on the basis of their intelligence genes and who consist mainly of those who are white, upper class, and male, and that the lower classes (consisting of those who are minority, female, and of working-class origins) are of lesser station in life because of their genes for low intelligence; fourth, that success in society (high income, impressive education, and a prestigious job) is caused by good intelligence genes, and that failure in society (crime, welfare dependency, and several other behaviors) is caused by having genes for low intelligence. Consequently, Herrnstein and Murray argue (as did Herrnstein himself in a verbatim argument twenty-three years earlier [Herrnstein 1971 and 1973]) for a society wherein one's opportunities for upward social mobility are constrained not by racial or class discrimination and oppression and other social environmental ills, but by one's intellectual genetic makeup. Those who are downtrodden and poor and oppressed (and in prison) are there because of bad genes. Case closed.

There are policy references that were around just prior to the publication of the *Bell Curve* (and for which the publication of the work might be seen as justification), and further, its publication may have stimulated—or at least fallen consistent with—at least two major national social policy developments since its publication. The book argues for the abolishment of affirmative action in education and jobs based on race, on the grounds that African Americans have been denied a good education and good jobs because of their genes, and not on the basis of forces in the social environment such as discrimination and racism. The argument is that affirmative action is a manipulation of the social environment and thus would have little resulting effect on the educational and occupational success of blacks. The end of race-based affirmative action is now a reality in the University of California system of higher education, and at the University of Texas School of Law as well. Murray had argued earlier (Murray 1984) that welfare should be abolished, and he and Herrnstein argued in *The Bell Curve* that since being on welfare is likely caused by low-intelligence genes, that manipulation of the social environment (as by welfare payments to single mothers—who are disproportionately though not exclusively minority and lower class) will not solve the problem.

It is therefore unfortunate that *The Bell Curve*, like the works of Shockley and Jensen earlier, is so methodologically flawed—with faulty reasoning, faulty inferences, incorrect data analysis, out-and-out incorrect arithmetic calculations, selective citing of literature, and arbitrary and implausible assumptions used in certain calculations, particularly those cited in estimating the heritability of intelligence. Let us then have a look at not only the errors in *The Bell Curve* work, but in related work and argument and thinking in the behavioral sciences as well. We seek here to methodologically deconstruct the entire "bell curve" construction, and not only the particular work that bears the name.

"Intelligence"

"Intelligence" is a hypothetical concept, or latent variable, on which individuals are presumed to differ or vary from each other. The concept of intelligence is not itself directly observable or measurable. Intelligence, an abstract continuum, is distinct from its non-abstract presumed indicators or measures; "intelligence" (concept) is distinct from "intelligence test" (presumed indicator). The accuracy of the indicator—that is, its validity and reliability—is a matter of how accurately it measures observable phenomena presumed to reflect differing amounts of intelligence in the individual. For example, the *predictive validity* of a presumed indicator of intelligence in the individual (such as an IQ test, or the "assessment" as opposed to the "achievement" sections of the popular SAT) is the extent to which it accurately predicts some later measures criterion (such as college grades obtained after taking the SAT; or, likelihood of graduation; or, even occupation and/or income after graduation). The *differential predictive validity* of the presumed indicator (the test) is the degree to which it predicts differently, test-to-criterion, for different racial groups, different ethnic/cultural groups, different social classes or socioeconomic strata, and/or different genders.

To the extent that a comparison of different racial groups (such as black versus white, or any comparison of racial-ethnic groups) embodies also at the same time a comparison of cultures, then to that extent the assessment of differential predictive validity between black and white samples of individuals will capture at least part of what would be called a *cultural* difference between these two racial groups. This includes, but is not limited to, differences between racial groups that are linguistic, aesthetic, musical, nutritional, even cognitive, and many others. (Recent research by Nisbett [1998] regarding cultural cognitive differences suggests that individuals of different ethnic cultures not only "think about different things," but in fact "think differently"—not inferior, just different.) Such a comparison will capture between-race cultural differences but not within-racial cultural differences. (We do not want to be guilty of culturally homogenizing a given racial group.) Any comparison between black and white also involves a host of other differences, such as differences in family socialization, neighborhood residence, and parental education, parental occupation, parental income, and many other such variables usually subsumed under the heading of social structural differences. A test (independent variable) is said to be *unbiased* if it predicts the same, in slope and size of correlation, a given criterion (dependent variable) for any two or more groups compared. Thus if a test shows the same slope and correlation in its relationship to later college grades for both blacks and whites, then by definition that test is "unbiased"—*even if* blacks score on average less on the test itself than whites. But it is upon this matter that standardized tests are suspect, frequently showing different slopes and/or correlations. More about this below.

The overall distribution of intelligence in a population (all races, classes, and genders included) is still to this day presumed by most researchers to closely approximate the theoretical normal (Caussian) distribution, a symmetric bell-shaped distribution—the name "bell curve." Yet the distribution of intelligence test scores in the population in fact has a distinct skew, due to a clustering of scores at one end of the distribution. It is thus not a symmetric "bell" at all, but instead a distinctly lopsided curve. Nonetheless, many researchers—notably the authors of *The Bell Curve*—still insist that the distribution of intelligence scores, across all races, ethnicities, social classes, and both genders, closely approximates the normal bell distribution, which it does not. Finally, few researchers ever bother to compare the shape of the distribution of test scores for two or more groups; it is generally assumed, without much evidence, that the distribution is bell normal for any given groups as well as for the overall population as a whole.

Various definitions of intelligence have appeared in the literature since the idea of a unitary coordinating "mental" faculty was used by the ancient Greek philosophers. The principle formulation of the modern notion of intelligence as some kind of mental capacity began in 1850 with Herbert Spencer and—guess who—Francis Galton! It was, after all, Galton who coined the term "eugenics," a term he used to mean "improving stock" by having "the more suitable" races prevail in both mental capacity as well as accomplishment over the "less suitable" races. The notion of "mental capacity" was central to Galton's formulation. Since then definitions of intelligence have varied only somewhat, and generally involved the notion of "potential," "ability," or "capacity" as distinct from actual achievement, attainment, or accomplishment. Louis Terman (1916), inventor of the still-used 1916 version of the Stanford-Binet IQ test, defined intelligence as "the ability to carry on abstract thinking." Interestingly, E. L. Thorndike (1905) defined intelligence as "the ability to adapt to the environment." Applying this definition to a contemporary example, a streetwise African American who better navigates the ghetto environment is by this definition "smarter" than (more intelligent than) the non-streetwise middle-class white who is less likely to survive the street. It seems that Thorndike's ninety-five-year-old definition, clearly a cultural/social/environmental definition of intelligence, has long since been forgotten, particularly by the likes of Jensen, Herrnstein, Murray, and many contemporary researchers.

Measurement and Measurement Error

Measurement accuracy—or, conversely, measurement error—is the degree to which presumed indicators of intelligence (the test) accurately reflect or measure the extent to which an individual possesses intellectual ability. It subsumes both the reliability as well as the validity of a test. Reliability is the stability or consistency of the indicators across, for example, different times (test-retest reliability), different forms or wordings of the same test (equivalent forms reliability—done, for example, by Educational Testing Service [ETS] in administering two forms, forms "A" and "B," of the SAT), or different researchers. Validity is the degree to which a score on the indicator reflects the unobserved, unknown score on the concept of "intelligence." Generally, validity can be of several types, for example convergent validity (do several different indicators of some subtype of intelligence, say, mathematical ability, all intercorrelate with each other?), discriminant validity (do different indicators or different subtypes of intelligence correlate somewhat less with each other?), content validity (do the indicators being used represent a wide sampling from a possible universe of indicators?), and as already noted above, predictive validity (do the indicators, treated as independent variables, accurately correlate with some "outside" criterion measure, treated as dependent, such as freshman college grades?). Predictive validity is the most widely employed form of validity assessment.

A closely allied issue of measurement is whether the concept of intelligence is unidimensional or multidimensional. In 1904, Charles Spearman maintained that there was a statistical dimension, or *factor*, called simply "g" for "general intelligence," and that this factor accounted for, and correlated very highly with, specific separate abilities or performances on tests (Spearman 1904). This would mean that one single dimension of intelligence, "g," correlates highly with a large range of specific test questions, and thus, a single "dimension" of intelligence underlies a large range of indicators. This is the unidimensional view. This antiquated view—that intelligence is fundamentally reducible to one basic master capacity—is still quite popular today. It has been perpetuated over the years, under the name of "g-theory," by the well-known investigators of group differences in intelligence such as Arthur Jensen, William Stockley, and Richard Herrnstein and Charles Murray of *Bell Curve* fame (cf. Gottfredson 1998). This would mean that persons who score high on one type of ability (say mathematics) would tend to score high on other abilities as well (such as reading comprehension, vocabulary, verbal analogies, and so on); and that persons who score low on one ability would also tend to score low on others. In fact, modern-day factor analysis, especially that variety known as principle component analysis (Harman 1960; Jensen 1980), a "data reduction" technique for assessing the extent to which many indicators may be parsimoniously accounted for by their relationship to (correlation with) a fewer number of variables called *factors,* began with Spearman. (This is not the case with so-called confirmatory factor techniques, most notably that of Joreskog and Sorbom [1993]). Despite considerable contemporary evidence—in fact, overwhelming evidence—that intelligence is very probably multidimensional, containing several to many distinct abilities, and that the number and type of dimensions *may differ by race,* the unidimensional conceptualization is nonetheless slavishly adhered to by quite a few, most notably Jensen, Herrnstein, and Murray.

In the late 1960s and early 1970s, important contributions to the multidimensional view were made by J. P. Guilford (1968), who theorized that intelligence was so multidimensional that it could be broken down into as many as 120 specific abilities. Most recently, the multidimensional formulation of Howard Gardner (1993, 1998; cf. Sternberg 1988, 1998) posits seven or eight different independent abilities: Logical-mathematical; linguistic; spatial; musical (for example, skill at musical composition); interpersonal (for example, skill at "politicking"); intrapersonal (for example, introspective abilities); and body-kinesthetic (athletic skill, thus arguing that such skill is indeed a type of "intelligence" as such). Current standardized ability tests such as the SAT or ACT (and certainly IQ tests as well, such as the Stanford-Binet, Lorge-Thorndike, Wechsler, or Raven's) for the most part measure only the first two (mathematical and linguistic) and a small amount of the third (spatial), and even these measures probably carry a significant cultural bias.

Some of these abilities may encompass what has come to be called creative intelligence. While the unidimensional view stresses individual abilities such as inductive and deductive reasoning, creative intelligence stresses "divergent" reasoning, or the ability to draw new and unanticipated conclusions or inferences. There is some limited evidence that black children may score higher than white children on certain types of creative and divergent reasoning (Shade 1992; Willis 1992). Debates in the professional literature now center on the question of whether creativity is a separate trait itself or whether it bears some relationship or overlap to unidimensional general intelligence.

It has been noted that while measures of general intelligence may correlate moderately with creativity for individuals in the low to normal ranges on both, the two types of abilities differ markedly and are virtually independent at the extreme upper ranges, namely, among uniquely gifted individuals. Sadly, giftedness and exceptionally high achievement among African Americans has been *grossly* understudied. Indeed, in the past, it has been difficult to obtain funding for such research, and our knowledge about class and particularly racial differences in giftedness and exceptional achievement (and gender differences as well) is extremely limited.

Attempts to increase ability test scores by specific coaching programs (such as the well-known Kaplan seminars and the Princeton Review seminars; cf. Lemann 1999) have met with some limited success. In general, such attempts to increase one's SAT score are more successful for individuals in the middle ranges than for individuals who score either very high or very low (Messick 1983; Powers and Rock 1998). Programs geared to increasing specific abilities (such as increasing specific math skills) are more likely to result in an increase in that particular ability rather than in other abilities not addressed by the program. Studies of the effect of coaching to increase SAT scores show that after removing the effect of test experience—that is, subtracting out the average differences between first and subsequent test scores for matched control individuals who have not had an intervening coaching seminar (most people score higher the second time they take the SAT than on their first attempt)—some increase in SAT score results, depending upon the length and type of coaching program. For example, some studies show score gains of 50 or more points (on a 200 to 800 scale)—which is itself a large part of the *entire* so-called black-white test score gap—whereas others show reliable increases only in the neighborhood of 10 points on the verbal and 15 to 20 points on the math, thus 25 to 30 points overall (Powers and Rock 1998). There is recent evidence (Neisser 1998) that some long-term gains in ability scores can be obtained, thus getting around earlier assertions by Jensen, Herrnstein, and Murray that ability test as well as IQ scores could only be increased over the short term (for no more than two or three months), and could not be increased for over the long term (a year or more) by coaching seminars.

Very little is known about whether different racial-ethnic groups (and different social classes) respond differently to such coaching than whites, or even whether women respond differently than men. In fact, there are those who wonder why such a question would ever be asked. "Of course there would be no reason to expect a difference in how they respond," many might say. But such would (again) ignore the reality of cultural differences. It may be that such cultural differences produce different *sensitivities* to such coaching seminars. Yet virtually no well-defined and large-scale research on this question has ever been done. It is the kind of question that Jensen, Herrnstein, and Murray never ask.

Despite this there is some limited evidence that minorities, including blacks and also women, are somewhat more sensitive to coaching-produced score gains on the verbal section of the SAT than are whites and males. Powers and Rock (1998) present evidence that test-takers of color (African Americans, Native Americans, Mexican Americans, Puerto Ricans and other Latinos/as— all, unfortunately, lumped together for analysis, thus in effect presuming their cultural and structural homogeneity) do show somewhat more score gain (a 10-point increase) than whites or Asians (who in turn show a 6-point score gain) on the verbal section of the SAT, but not on the math section. On the math section, score gains for whites and Asians were slightly more (19 and 16 points respectively) than for persons of color (14 points)—although everyone on the average gained to some degree, rather than remain unchanged or decrease. Regarding female-male differences, males reveal somewhat more score gain (up to 14 points change) than women (9 points or less) on the SAT verbal section, but women show slightly more score gain (up to 26 points) than men (20–24 points) on the math section. (In general, women score lower than men initially on the math section and thus have more "room" to increase.)

It appears that no study has ever been conducted on race X gender *interaction* on score gain. For example, do black women (a race X gender combination) show a greater gain than others on the math section? Specifically, do black women show a gain greater than what would be expected on the basis of race alone and gender alone (thus showing an interaction effect as such)? We do not know. All this serves to highlight is the lack of research on what some (Collins 1998) have aptly identified as *intersectionalities* in the study of oppression.

Finally, it must be noted that partly because of the expense, those groups who are in relatively greater need of coaching seminars are the very ones who are less likely to take them: blacks and Latinas/os (Asians are the most likely to take a coaching seminar); those with parents of less formal education and income; and those with lower high school grades to begin with (Powers and Rock 1998). Such seminars are expensive ($800–$1,000 and more) and are thus less likely to be taken by minorities and individuals from lower income families. In this respect, coaching seminars are discriminatory. To counteract this discrimination, some coaching programs offer scholarship funds for some high school students to take them, but only a very few such scholarships have been offered.

More on Group and Cultural Differences

It has been generally found on whatever it is that standardized tests either measure or do not measure, that *on the average* whites tend to score about one standard deviation higher than blacks and Latinas/os on IQ tests (amounting to about 15 IQ points) and on the ability portions of the SAT (amounting to about 50 to 100 SAT points on their 200–800 scale). These differences have, however, been decreasing somewhat in recent years (College Board 1999; Jencks and Phillips 1998)—a trend incidentally utterly ignored by *Bell Curve* authors Herrnstein and Murray (1994).

Herrnstein and Murray argue that one's IQ score as well as one's SAT score have high predictive validity; namely, that these scores accurately predict such criterion measures as one's freshman college grades, one's overall grade point average for four or more years in college, the likelihood that one will graduate, and even the kind of job one gets after graduation. Ignored or downgraded by them is the overwhelming evidence that test scores are only moderately predictive of freshman grades, and virtually not predictive at all for sophomore, junior, and senior grades. This is generally true for everyone—regardless of race, class or gender. Meta-analyses involving *hundreds* of separate studies show test-to-grade correlations of only about .40 (for example, Manning and Jackson 1984), but such studies are ignored by Herrnstein and Murray. These correlations are roughly the same in magnitude that one finds for correlations between high school grade average and freshman college grades. In other words, your SAT scores predict your college freshman grade average only about as well as does your high school grade average—which is to say, not very well. And test scores predict sophomore, junior, and senior grades progressively less well than they do freshman grades. Predictions are not improved much when an index combining both test scores and high school grades (or high school class rank) is used. All this shows only modest predictive validity of the tests for blacks, whites, and everyone else as well.

Anemic as they are in predicting various criterion measures (college grades) for everyone in general, there is still the matter of whether the predictions are worse for blacks and others of color (and for working-class persons) than for middle- and upper-class whites; that is, the prediction slopes and/or correlations are lower for blacks and people of color. If so, this is by definition test bias (bias in predictive validity). Herrnstein and Murray, and Jensen before them, state outright—and blatantly incorrectly—that researchers "unanimously accept the conclusion that no bias against blacks in educational or occupational prediction has been found." Yet studies they list in the references of their own book present strong evidence against this claim. There are analyses even in Jensen (1980) that clearly show significantly different slopes *and* correlations for whites versus blacks and Latinas/os, with whites showing the higher slopes and correlations. This is evidence of measurement bias against blacks and Latinos/as.

They cite Crouse and Trusheim (1988), but totally ignore these very same researchers' detailed account of greatly differing predictions of dichotomized freshmen GPA (grade point average) predicted from dichotomized score ("high," or admit, versus "low," or reject) on an index that combined high school class rank and SAT score. While 52 percent of the high-scoring whites got higher grades (>2.5), only 25 percent of the high-scoring blacks did so, while roughly the same percent of each group (4.4 versus 6.5 percent respectively) who would have scored as "reject" on the SAT and class rank actually got above a 2.5 GPA (the so-called "false negative"). This constitutes a much better prediction for whites, thus measurement bias against blacks. The recent analyses of Bowen and Bok (1998) show that black graduates of Ivy League universities who were admitted twenty-five years earlier under affirmative action guidelines actually had a *higher* rate of admission to graduate and professional schools than did whites who were admitted to college twenty-five years earlier with them. On average, these black students had lower SAT scores than did the whites but *higher* "scores" on the criterion measures—graduate and professional school admissions—thus clearly showing lack of predictive validity for the SATs for blacks.

All such differences in predictive validity of blacks and whites point to considerably greater measurement error for blacks than for whites. (This generalization differs somewhat from that of Jencks and Phillips, 1998, who attribute a relatively small portion of the black-white test gap to measurement error as such, and relatively more directly to disadvantages in the education and other environment.) Yet another source of measurement error has been revealed in the recent research of Claude Steele and colleagues at Stanford University on what they call *stereotype vulnerability* (Steele 1999, 196; Steele 1992; Steele and

Aronson 1995). To what extent can a negative stereotype one may have about *one's self* affect one's own actual behavior and test performances? Steele notes that two common stereotypes exist in the United States: That since, on the average, blacks perform less well on tests of math and verbal ability than whites, blacks must have, so it is believed, some "inherent" deficiency in math and verbal abilities relative to whites. (The attribution of this presumed difference in abilities to genetics is what the Jensens, Shockleys, Herrnsteins, and Murrays, along no doubt with many in the general public, do.) Second, that since women perform less well than men on tests of math ability, women must therefore have some inherent deficiency in math ability relative to men. (The attribution of this *gender* difference to genetics is not explicitly made in Herrnstein and Murray, but it is very, very clearly concluded by them.)

To the extent that black students in high school or college may actually believe (internalize) such stereotypes, then to that extent they may perform less well on a test if they were told that "this is a genuine test of your true ability," even though "race" as such is *not* mentioned in what they are told. This can activate the stereotype in the mind of the person so informed and thus increase test anxiety, with the result of lowered actual test performance. White students who are told this would be less likely to have the stereotype activated (since the stereotype is not *about* whites) and thus be less likely to have their test performance lowered; they would be less vulnerable to the stereotype. If the black students are not told this, their test performance would be less likely to be lowered; the stereotype is not activated, and thus they are less vulnerable to it.

Results show that this is just what happens on the GRE (Graduate Record Examination, a test similar to the SAT for college students who contemplate graduate school). Black college students who are simply told that the test is a "genuine" test of their true verbal ability (called the *diagnostic condition*) perform less well than whites who are also told the same thing. Note that nothing is actually said to the students about black and white test performance specifically, nor is anything said about "race," nor are the terms "race" or "ethnic" mentioned in any way.

What happened when the test taker—whether black or white—is told nothing (the nondiagnostic condition)? This condition reveals *no difference at all* between blacks and whites in test performance! Both got the same average number of test items correct. There is no more black-white test gap. These results cannot be attributed to differences in "ability" amongst the students, since the effects of any actual SAT-score differences were subtracted out. Furthermore, the study was done on college students who all had relatively high SAT scores to begin with. The differences cannot be attributed to unmeasured or unknown differences between the diagnostic and the nondiagnostic conditions since the black students as well as the white students were randomly assigned beforehand to either the diagnostic or nondiagnostic conditions.

There is some evidence that stereotype vulnerability may operate in the same or similar way with regard to the presumed male-female differences in math ability test performance. It remains to be seen whether a similar effect occurs with respect to social class differences, for example, whether working-class persons may be more vulnerable to common stereotypes about the working class relative to the middle or upper class. Finally, there is some evidence that stereotype vulnerability can be a *positive* effect: Preliminary results show that Asians (about whom stereotypes exist concerning high test performance) actually perform *better* when told that the test is a "genuine" test of their abilities (Shih 1999). Further results will clearly be of interest.

Nature versus Nurture and the "Cognitive Elite"

Are human differences in intelligence, to the extent that intelligence is measurable, influenced more by biological heredity (nature), by social environment (nurture), or by the interactions (combinations) of both? The contemporary approach to the issue, which has arisen in part from the field of population genetics, has been to attempt to estimate empirically what is called the *heritability coefficient,* defined as the proportion of the total differences (total variance) in intelligence in a population that is causally attributable to genetic factors. Equivalently, it is the proportion of variance in intelligence that is accounted for by the genetic similarity between pairs of biological relatives. Consequently, if heritability in a population is 30 percent, then statistically speaking 30 percent of the differences in (the variance in) intelligence among individuals in that population is due to genetic factors, assuming that intelligence is validly and reliably measured to begin with—a highly questionable assumption, as we have already noted in some detail. A 30 percent heritability would mean that 70 percent of the differences in intelligence in the population would be due to environment or to combinations or interactions of genes and environment.

The environment includes a large range of variables such as education, social class, cultural advantages or disadvantages, childhood socialization, nutrition, and many others. Virtually all heritability estimates made to date are based on white populations and are thus not generalizable to black populations; nor does the heritability coefficient, gotten on a given population, allow one to conclude or generalize about differences between populations, as between blacks and whites. Thus, the heritability coefficient does not permit conclusions about between-group differences, although the Jensens and Murrays persist in attempting in effect to do so.

Authors Herrnstein and Murray argue that the genetic heritability of intelligence is high, at around .70, or 70 percent. This conclusion is based on their reading of past studies of intelligence heritability that are based on pairs of biological relatives. They note that identical twins raised together correlate higher in their test scores (for IQ) than pairs of fraternal twins raised together and also pairs of ordinary siblings, and these in turn reveal a higher pair correlation than, say, first cousins. Thus higher genetic similarity or overlap of a pair of individuals shows a proportionately higher intelligence similarity (a higher pair-correlation for the measure of intelligence being used)—suggesting strong genetic causation for the pair's similarity in intelligence. However, the more similar a pair is biologically, then the more similar they are as well in their environments, and so both genetic similarity as well as environmental similarity are confounded in such analyses, and estimates of heritability versus environmental effects upon intelligence are thus suspect.

One way around this problem, as noted correctly by Herrnstein and Murray as well as the others, is to study identical twins (who are by definition genetic clones of each other) who have been separated early in life and raised in different environments. They argue that such studies produce a heritability of about .70, or 70 percent. But, many of the twins in the studies to which they refer were not really separated at all, since many of the pairs were not separated until late in life, were raised in different branches of the same family. The intelligence correlation (the estimate of heritability) for the remaining truly separated twins is only about .25 to .24 (Taylor 1980, 1992; Kamin 1974). Similarly, the degree of separation of pairs of twins is suspect in the recent Bouchard "Minnesota Twins" study cited by Herrnstein and Murray, which yielded a heritability estimate of .75 (Bouchard et al. 1990). In general, evidence suggesting a heritability of less than .40, lower-bound estimate, is unused and uncited by Herrnstein and Murray. Further, the authors completely ignore estimation techniques that incorporate several kinships simultaneously and that systematically vary a quantity for degree of separation of identical twins, and these techniques have shown heritability estimates of as low as .25 under plausible assumptions (Chipuer et al. 1990; Taylor 1995, 1988, and 1980; Gold-berger 1979).

Because *The Bell Curve* authors argue that intelligence is largely genetically heritable, it follows for them that different groups in society, such as different social classes, are likely to differ in genes for intelligence. Thus, or so they reason, social classes very probably differ on the average in inherited intelligence, such that the higher one's social class origins, the more favorably one is endowed with intelligence genes. Lower social classes, as well as those trapped in poverty and the underclass, are in possession of genes for lower intelligence, on average. By similar logic, the authors argue that since certain racial or ethnic groups differ in average intelligence (as revealed by test scores), it is entirely possible that they differ as well in intelligence genes. The authors strongly imply, but do not state outright, that blacks, Latinas/os, Native Americans, and other U.S. minorities therefore have on average lower intelligence genes, while other groups (such as Asians, some Jews, and whites in general) possess on average genes for higher intelligence. Furthermore, the authors imply that males and females probably differ in intelligence genes as well, at least for any genes for quantitative or mathematical abilities, since women consistently score lower than men on the quantitative portions of standardized ability and IQ tests. They assert further that since criminals score lower in average intelligence than non-criminals (and the evidence even for this is relatively weak, though present), even controlling for social class, given that IQ is highly heritable, then criminals—like lower-class persons, minorities, and women—are less genetically intellectually endowed than are non-criminals, middle- and upper-class persons, non-minorities (whites), and males.

America now contains what Herrnstein and Murray call a *cognitive elite*, consisting of those with high IQ and prestigious jobs, given the moderately strong correlations between IQ and occupational prestige rank. This cognitive elite is hence more likely, though not exclusively, to consist of upper-class white males, and this elite is on average more likely to possess the genes for higher or superior intelligence. This argument is virtually identical to the nineteenth-century eugenics argument of Galton and others who asserted that society's elites are elite because their genes (their "inherent constitutions," according to Galton) compel them to be so, and that the downtrodden non-elite masses are such because *their* genes doom *them* to be so.

Herrnstein and Murray argue that these conditions in American society are all linked via the following syllogism—a syllogism introduced by Herrnstein way back in 1971 (Herrnstein 1971 and 1973) and that is stated, utterly unchanged and verbatim, twenty-three years later in *The Bell Curve:*

> *First Premise:* That intelligence is largely genetically inherited.
>
> *Second Premise:* Measured intelligence (via test scores) is correlated positively with a variety of measures of socioeconomic success in society, such as a prestigious job, high annual income, and high educational attainment; and inversely, with certain indicators of failure in society, such as criminality, chronic unemployment, welfare dependency, and other ills.
>
> *Conclusion:* Therefore, it follows that these kinds of successes (and failures) in society have a strong genetic basis and are largely genetically caused. Thus, these stratified distinctions among people, as well as (by implication) racial and some gender distinctions, are genetically based.

The structure of their entire argument, which is at the center of their entire book, is that if variable(s) *A* (intelligence genes; intelligence genotypes) and *B* (intelligence test scores) are correlated, and if variable(s) *B* and *C* (measures of success) are correlated, then we can predict the *direction* (the sign, positive or negative; namely, direct or inverse) of the correlation of *A* with *C*. This all sounds quite logical. That is why *The Bell Curve's* arguments appear upon superficial examination to be valid and convincing. But what Herrnstein and Murray do not tell us is that one may predict the sign of the correlation of *A and C* only under certain statistical conditions—conditions that their analyses do not meet. Namely, it is entirely possible to have a positive correlation between *A and B,* yet still have a *negative or zero* correlation between *A and C.*

In general, one can statistically predict the sign (direction of the A-to-C correlation) only if, without further assumptions (and assuming linearity):

$$r^2(AB) + r^2(BC) > 1.00.$$

The vast majority of the analyses presented in the book do not even come close to meeting this condition. Thus even using their overly inflated heritability estimate of .70 for $r^2(AB)$, that means that the test score-to-success correlation must be .54 [$=r(BC)$] or greater [the squared correlation $r^2(BC)$ must be .30 or greater] in order to infer that there is a positive correlation between (unmeasured) intelligence genes *(A),* on the one hand, and success *(C),* on the other. Only some of the authors' intelligence-to-success correlations are .54 or greater; in fact, many are considerably less. So, statistically, the relationship between intelligence genes and success (the conclusion to the syllogism) could very well be zero, or even slightly negative. Given a more plausible heritability estimate, say .40, then the test score-to-success correlation would have to be the square root of .60 or about .78, quite high, in order to conclude a positive relationship between intelligence genes and success. Very few if any of the test score-to-success correlations given in the entire book are this high.

Their inferences pertaining to crime are even less valid. We are led by them in the text to believe that the negative correlation between test score and crime is quite high. This is not the case, even from their own data. Buried in appendix 4 of the book are the authors' own obtained multiple correlations between criminality (self-reported crime, no less!) and test score as well as socioeconomic status (SES) as the two independent variables. These multiple correlations range from a *very* low .02 to .10 (thus .14 and .32 unsquared). Substantiating these correlations in place of the (bivariate) test score-to-crime correlation, we see immediately that no inference at all can be legitimately made about the supposed connection between genes and crime. Note also that heritability would have to be implausibly high (1−.90) or .90 to conclude any gene-to-crime connection, even using the *highest* squared multiple correlation of .10 given in their analysis. Clearly, then, the authors' conclusions that success and failure in society are genetically intellectually based are unsupported, as are their conclusions regarding an upper-class white professional male "cognitive elite."

CHAPTER 5

Sociology

After the Linguistic and Multicultural Turns

Paget Henry

The Linguistic Turn

The linguistic turn refers to a fundamental shift in the relationship between language and the disciplines of humanities and social sciences, and hence between language and the explanation of human behavior (Levi-Strauss 1963, 1–97; Rorty 1967).[[FR 1]] We can describe this shift as the gradual releasing of language from imprisonment in its communicative role, as modern cultural systems continue the process of internal differentiation. In its communicative role, language has been severely restricted by the communicative needs of everyday speech and specialized discourses like sociology. Now that it is able to do more, language is emerging as a powerful explanatory principle of human behavior. As these new capabilities of language emerge, different aspects have been appropriated as founding analogies for new explanatory or interpretive strategies. Thus the communicative (Habermas 1984), the semiotic (Derrida 1984), the categorical (Foucault 1973), and semantic (Austin 1962) aspects of language have been employed in this way. Exploring the possibilities inherent in these strategies slowly secured this turn to languages not just as a theory of texts, but also as a theory of social behavior.

The gradual solidifying of the linguistic turn produced a number of new discourses that have changed the composition and social organization of disciplines in the academy. Among the more important of these new discourses are

The author would like to thank Martin Martel, Richard Williams, and Jens Nielsen for their helpful comments on an earlier draft of this chapter. This article was originally published in *Sociological Forum* 10, no. 4 (Dec. 1995) and is reprinted with permission.

semiotics, cultural studies, critical legal studies, and postcolonial studies. These new fields employ one or more of the above linguistically based approaches to theory. They offer new explanations that compete with those coming from sociological subfields such as interpretive theory, sociology of mass culture, sociology of law and development. In these fields, sociological explanations now find themselves in competition with linguistic explanations from these new discourses and the older humanities, such as literature and philosophy, that have also been influenced by the linguistic turn.

In addition to the rise of these new discourses, the linguistic turn has also produced two important epistemological shifts that have significantly affected sociology's competitive position. The first of these was its contribution to the decline of the neopositivist philosophy of science that had its roots in Popper and extended to Lakatos and declined with Feyerabend. In the current postpositivist environment, epistemological and methodological pluralism has become more the norm. As a result, the nonscientific epistemic claims of the new linguistic theories of the humanities have found a much more receptive audience than they might have in the high days of positivism. Thus the edge that our scientific techniques gave us in the past vis-à-vis the humanities has declined in the postpositivist period.

Second and closely related was the contribution of the linguistic turn to the dethroning of rational, Cartesian models of the knowing subject in which language was confined to its communicative role. Many subfields in sociology made use of these Cartesian models. They have now been replaced by more linguistically inscribed models that are closer to the assumptions of ethnomethodologists, who have been marginal to the sociological enterprise. In these new models, thinking is shaped by logic as well as language. Consequently, social action is not only institutionally but also linguistically determined. With this conceptual shift, language emerges as a relatively autonomous domain of human self-formation and behavior regulation. As with the first epistemological shift, the decline of the rational subject has lowered the epistemic advantage that sociology derived in the past from its overdependence upon rationalism.

In short, the linguistic turn has given rise to new discourses that have changed the division of intellectual labor within the academy. It has also changed relations with old ones such as philosophy and literature that have decreased the edge sociology had because of its more rational and scientific orientation.

The Multicultural Turn

The multicultural turn is also grounded in an important discursive shift. This time it is between ethnic discourses and the established disciplines of social sciences and humanities. As in the case of the linguistic turn, we can also describe this shift as a process of discursive differentiation that has given rise to new discourses, programs, and departments within the academy. Unlike the linguistic turn, this is not a case of differentiation that is driven by the adaptive needs of basic institutions but by changes in patterns of racial and ethnic inequality.

The ethnic hierarchy of American society has been and continues to be a primary source of the personal troubles and public issue of dominated racial and ethnic groups. Since the 1950s, the most important changes in those hierarchies were produced by the period of African American resistance known as the Civil Rights era. This resistance changed not only the institutional framework of white/black domination, but also most of its discursive representation. As we will see, this would also bring to an end sociology's quasi-monopoly on race within the academy.

In addition to the above changes, African American resistance produced an outbreak of what Stephen Steinberg has called "ethnic fever" (1989, 50). Since that outbreak, the demand for ethnic information has been growing steadily. An increasing number of social groups have reclaimed suppressed ethnic heritages and have been demanding space within the academy. These demands have dramatically increased the number of ethnic discourses seeking academic recognition. As a result, we now have programs or departments of Afro-American Studies, Asian American Studies, Latino Studies, or Ethnic Studies in many universities. Programs of race and ethnicity are also being housed in English and American Studies departments. It is the institutionalizing of these ethnic discourses that has multiculturalized the study of race and ethnicity. These new discourses have posed a competitive challenge to the sociology of race that is comparable to the challenges from the new linguistically oriented discourses and from economic theory. Similar shifts and related processes of differentiation have supported the institutionalization of feminist discourses within the academy.

These ethnic and gender discourses have also made unique contribution to the epistemological pluralism of the present period. Along with the linguistic turn, they have contributed to dethroning of the artesian subject by exposing his concealed white and male identities. From their perspective, the knowing subject is particularized not only by language, but also by gender and ethnicity. These concrete identities do not disappear in moments of abstract universalism. As an always gendered or ethnic agent, the knowing subject brings the special hermeneutic of an insider to the tasks of ethnic or gender knowledge production. Discursive recognition for such gendered or ethnically marked hermeneutic processes has increased in this period of epistemological pluralism. The true claims of these insider hermeneutics, of course, are contested and offer no absolute guarantees. But this increase in philosophical legitimacy for ethnic and gender discourses also means increased competition for the sociology of race, whose quasi-monopoly rested in part on more abstract models of the epistemological subject.

The New Competitive Challenges

If the above interpretations are correct, then the new competitive challenges confronting sociology are at least partially the result of the new discourses that have found place in the academy because of the linguistic and multicultural turns. Whether it is Afro-American studies, semiotics, postcolonial studies, or women's studies, these programs are attracting students and producing explanations that compete with those of sociology. It is important to note that these discourses are not offering propositions that have been produced with greater scientific or technical rigor. It is not their technical or empirical power that is making them competitive. Theirs is not the instrumental challenge of economic theory. Rather it is their ability to deconstruct identities, to interpret, and to explain behavior in terms of systems of linguistically structured meanings that provide them with influence.

More than disciplines like economics or political science, these changes in the academic marketplace have been particularly hard on sociology. The primary reason for this is that sociology has no exclusive institutional or social property. That is, there is no institutional or social process that it can claim in the way that economists claim the economy, political scientists the state, or psychologists the psyche. Because sociology has no such protected area to provide a buffer against market competition, the rise of the new linguistic, gender, and ethnic discourses have been pretty hard on us. As a discipline, we survive and grow by entering already occupied markets with explanations that both producers and consumers in these markets find useful. The impact of political sociology on political science is a good case in point. Whenever our share of these external markets contracts sharply, we enter into a state of crisis.

Because of its special market conditions, sociological practice often takes place at the interface of two or more analytically distinct discourses. Thus whether it is the sociology of race, literature, science, or religion, sociological explanations must compete with the accounts that producers of works in these fields have as their own production. The continuing crisis in sociology is the outcome of changes in patterns of cooperation and competition in areas where sociology has been sharing a market with another discipline or set of disciplines. The resulting tensions between the sociological and nonsociological accounts will necessarily produce periodic swings in the evaluation of sociological explanations in particular markets.

For example, in the fine arts, the Marxist revival of the late 1960s brought a renewed interest in sociological explanations of art. This revival competed successfully with the formalism of the "new critics" and peaked in the works of Arnold Hauser, Theodore Adorno, George Lukacs, and Lucien Goldman. However, the subsequent rise of structuralism and post-structuralism has produced a new formalism that has led one historian of ideas to the following observation: "The trend has been always from psychological and sociological theories . . . and toward theories that recognize language in all its density and opacity as the place where meaning is constituted, and that have their own more general theoretical articulation in linguistics, philosophy and literary criticism" (Loews 1987, 881).

This swing back to formalism in the fine arts is a good example of the competitive challenges we have been facing.

In short, the linguistic and multicultural turns have dramatically altered the nature of the marketplace for interpretive sociology. They have changed its organization, the major players, and the level of competition. As new theoretical and interpretive products enter these markets, ours are being pushed out. This is the meaning I attach to Horowitz's "post-sociological environment" (1993, 169) rather than that of "decomposition." To continue this development analogy, our exports to important markets are falling, and our products are finding buyers only in our small domestic market. The latter is small precisely because of our lack of exclusive institutional or social property. Here lies the primary source of our private troubles and public issues. These are the larger forces of history and social structure that have deposited them in our laps. Here is our new challenge. We are not beyond the reach of these forces because we study them. No, the only advantage sociology gives us is the ability to understand our unease in terms of our location at "minute points of intersection of biography and history within society" (Mills 1977, 7). However, before dealing with our responses to this larger set of interpretive challenges, I will examine more closely the case of the sociology of race.

The Sociological Discourse on Race

During the decade of the 1920s, sociology gradually replaced biology as the home of race/ethnic studies in the academy. The securing of this quasi-monopoly was facilitated by the failure of biologists to find genetic support for white supremacist claims regarding African American inferiority. It was also facilitated by the exclusion of African Americans and African American discourses from the classrooms of the academy. However, emerging when it did, the new subfield interfaced with biology, anthropology, psychology, African American scholarly discourses, and the everyday discourses of both European and African Americans. The parameters of the sociology of race were also shaped by increasing conflicts between blacks and whites, and the tensions that accompanied the arrival of large numbers of European ethnics.

Between the 1920s and the early 1960s, we can distinguish at least four distinct theoretical approaches to race and ethnicity by sociologists: the social Darwinist, the assimilationist, the intergroup relations, and the culture of poverty approaches. Although some of these theories were progressive in their day, as a group their constructions of the African American sociopolitical identity and their policy recommendations have left a lot to be desired. In these theories, African Americans did not find revealing reflections of their personal troubles or their public issues. Consequently, it is not difficult to understand why these theories were surpassed by the multicultural turn.

Social Darwinism was sociology's first theoretical offering on race as it moved to replace biology. Although critical of biological claims, this approach was heavily indebted to biology. It did not change the basic way in which the race problem had been formulated. It was still cast in terms of what to do with an inassimilable, inferior population that was now a permanent part of the American landscape. To explain the differences between European and African Americans, sociologists resorted to the principle of natural selection. The inferiority of African Americans was the result of the limited mental capacities that life in Africa required that they develop—capacities that were seen as inadequate for the American terrain. Sociologists such as Ross, Cooley, Giddings, Summer, and Ellwood were of this level; Jerome Dowd sanctioned the status quo by declaring the race problem insoluble (1926, 360). Thus, at a time when African Americans were proposing full civil rights, Black Nationalism, or an end of apartheid, sociologists were declaring them to be unrealizable solutions.

In contrast to the bipolar, black/white world of the social Darwinists was the broader framework of culture contact and assimilation formulated by Robert Park (1950). Applied to the experiences of European immigrants in America, Park saw two possibilities: Anglo-conformity or a melting pot of mutual influencing. Along with this theoretical shift came Park's open involvement with African Americans and his reformism. But in spite of these significant moves, his policy recommendations were in the main noninterventionist. Reform was reform within the racist sociopolitical order of American society. Only hard work and education were useful activities in the face of white domination. It was for this reason that Gunnar Myrdal placed Park and other assimilationists in the category of "do nothing" liberals.

The more interventionist stance of the intergroup relations approach derives from two sources: its association with the New Deal of the Roosevelt administration and the increasing militancy of African Americans as evidenced by the organizing activities of A. Phillip Randolph and the Detroit riot of 1943. The theoretical center of this approach was the work of Robin M. Williams, who shifted the conceptual framework from Anglo-conformity to ethnic pluralism with a system of shared values (1947). Williams attempted to formulate a dynamic theory of the tensions that signifiers of difference such as race and ethnicity created within this system of shared values. Propositions for reducing such intergroup tensions were generated and tested. Education emerged as the primary instrument of intervention. Whites needed to be educated about their attitudes, and blacks needed education for social mobility. Thus, in spite of the revolt that was partly responsible for the heightened interest in reducing racial tensions, there was no serious discussion of the persistent insurrectionary consciousness that distinguished the African American experience from that of European ethnics.

Finally, we have the culture of poverty approach. Essentially, this is the social Darwinist approach with a twist. Instead of defects being located in the specific adaptations of national cultures, this approach hypothesizes a universal culture that emerges whenever a human group adapts to poverty. This culture makes mobility, integration, or assimilation into the mainstream extremely difficult. Originating with the work of Oscar Lewis, this approach has been most influential in sociology through the work of Moynihan and Glazer (1970). For these authors, the melting pot was an existing reality. Thus, the problem becomes "why haven't groups like African Americans and Puerto Rican Americans made it into the mainstream?" The answer is the culture of poverty, with its peculiar patterns of family disorganization. Because in the view of the authors this culture reproduces itself independently of the order of domination that produces it, state intervention and political resistance are of little help here. The more helpful strategies were the "bootstrap" activities of family reorganization and the acquiring of achievement values.

From this brief view, it should be clear that the intellectual and institutional space created by the sociology of race was a cramped one for African Americans. Access was limited. The discourse was controlled by white males. Its policy recommendations were weak. Its representations of Africa and its culture remained unsatisfactory, and so, also, were its representations of African Americans and their political capabilities. These representations contrasted sharply with the portrayals of African Americans in works of W. E. B. DuBois, C. L. R. James, or Oliver Cox. For James, African Americans represented "potentially the most revolutionary section of the population" (1939, 3).

In short, African Americans did not find illuminating reflections of their unease about identity misrepresentation and institutional exclusion in the sociological imagination of these four decades. This failure was both interpretive and political in nature. One result of this failure was the attempt to establish a "black sociology" that was distinct from "white sociology." Joyce Ladner's *Death of the White Sociology* was the manifesto of this movement. In her introduction, Ladner links the rise of black sociology to the claim that white sociology "had seldom advocated the kinds of progressive changes that would ensure that blacks no longer experience the subjugated status in American society to which they have been subjected" (1973). Thus, dissatisfaction with the white identity of sociology and its conservative policy recommendations were major stimuli to the rise of the black sociological movement of the 1960s.

The political failures of the sociological discourse on race point to dimensions of the ideological issue that do not fit the paradigms of Lipset and Horwitz. They suggest that ideology, like the empirical factors, can contribute to the rise or the decline of a field. Which of these two possibilities will be realized depends on the competitive context. As we will see, it is not just the technical propositions of the new discourses that have made them competitive. It is also their ideological stances and their interpretive or cultural capabilities.

Afro-American Studies, Multiculturalism, and Poststructuralism

The Civil Rights movement significantly changed the discursive representation and institutional organization of race/ethnic studies in the academy. Segregated schools and universities were forced to desegregate, while those that discriminated informally came under pressure to increase enrollments of African Americans and other excluded groups. In addition to these quantitative issues, there was the qualitative impact on various academic disciplines. This impact manifested itself in the greater representation of African American contributions in courses, in the growth of studies of race in English and American Studies departments, in the growth of black sociology, and in the rise of programs and departments in Afro-American studies.

For sociology, these shifts produced significant changes in the competitive and intertextual dynamics of its discourse on race. The highly restricted border relations with African American scholarly discourses were replaced by more open ones. Long-ignored African American intellectuals such as DuBois, Johnson, Frazier, Reid, and Cox experienced a rebirth. This more cooperative attitude in textual production also changed sociology's relations with the everyday discourses of African Americans. The racial or insider hermeneutics of these discourses joined those of European Americans to become a basic stock of predefined meanings that guided the sociological analysis of race.

In the short run, these shifts strengthened sociology's competitive positions as the home of race relations within the academy. They provided African Americans and other excluded ethnic groups with new opportunities to articulate, confirm, or disconfirm the central claims of their scholarly traditions and everyday discourses. In other words, both the discursive space and the institutional framework that sociology provided for the study of race were now less cramped.

One important indication of these changed intertextual relations was Robert Blauner's 1972 *Racial Oppression in America*. Reflecting also the Marxist revival of the period, this work took the analysis of American race relations outside the framework of existing theories and placed it squarely within an internal colonial framework. It rejected the claim that African Americans were just another ethnic group by thematizing a history of oppression that made their experiences comparable to those of external colonies. This change of framework reflected tendencies in a number of black scholarly and everyday discourses. Thus, the initial impact of the Civil Rights movement was a strengthening of sociology's dominant position in the field of race and ethnic studies.

However, the above strengthening of sociology's competitive position did not last very long. By the early 1980s, the rise of newly formed Afro-American and other ethnic studies departments brought new suppliers of race/ethnic knowledge to this market. Increasing competition from these departments, the linguistic turn in the humanities, and a political shift to the right have all combined to erode sociology's position. Until this period, race relations was as close as sociology came to owning exclusive social property. The institutionalizing of the multicultural turn transformed this de facto monopoly into the more competitive pattern that holds for most of sociology's subfields. Thus, conditions of textual production in the sociology of race have moved closer to conditions in the sociology of literature, the sociology of religion, or political sociology.

The increased competition in the sociology of race derives from the qualitatively different nature of Afro-American and other ethnic studies departments. In the case of Afro-American studies, departments are usually interdisciplinary and focus more exclusively on the experiences of continental and diaspora Africans; intertextual relations with the wide variety of black scholarly and everyday discourses are more open, and faculty are often predominately African American. These differences have resulted in distinct contexts for studying race. Consequently, students now have choices that did not exist before.

Another important factor that currently distinguishes the Afro-American Studies approach to race is its greater openness to the linguistic turn than to the sociological approach. Because of its interdisciplinary nature, Afro-American Studies registers with equal weight important shifts in both the humanities and the social sciences. In the 1960s and early 1970s, it was the sociopolitical writings of African Americans that dominated the discourses in Afro-American Studies departments. They were also the texts that were important for sociologists like Blauner, Ladner, Nathan Hare, and Robert Stapes. Hence the strong social science influence on Afro-American studies, and the significant parallels with the sociology of race.

However, by the early 1980s, the spectacular growth in African American fiction and its criticism turned many Afro-American Studies departments in the direction of the humanities. It was the search for interpretive tools to analyze this body of fiction that opened Afro-American Studies departments to poststructuralist theory. Evidence of this linguistic turn in Afro-American criticism can be seen in the works of Houston Baker, Cornel West, and Henry Louis Gates. In the area of popular culture, it can be seen in the works of Michael Eric Dyson, Trisha Rose, and Wahneema Lubiano. From these sites it was spread to others, creating tensions with older Pan-Africanists or Black Nationalist approaches. The work of the Jamaican/British sociologist Stuart Hall (1992) provides us with interesting locations where these currents have intersected. This shift toward poststructuralist theory might have been avoided had African American critics made the sociology of literature their theoretical point of departure. But in literature, the sociological approach was being eclipse by the new formalism of poststructuralist theory. Hence the linguistic turn in Afro-American studies.

Many of the features and trends I described above also hold for Hispanic and Asian American studies programs and the more inclusive ethnic studies departments. These institutional and discursive changes are increasing the disciplinary choices available to the student of race/ethnic relations. In other words, the multicultural turn has dramatically changed the nature of competition in this field. It has divested sociology of its disciplinary monopoly and has transformed the field into a more interdisciplinary market, in which many players have more specialized interests. To survive under these changed conditions, sociologists must now do more than write for each other. We must make available texts that producers and consumers in this now interdisciplinary market will find useful.

Sociology's Response to the New Challenges

As I see it, the roots of sociology's continuing crisis are to be found in the inadequacy of its response to changes in its competitive situation. These changes are not confined to sociology of race. They have also affected areas such as theory, the sociology of the arts, and social change and development. Our loss of shares in these markets is due primarily to a theoretical challenge that is hermeneutic in nature. The new discourses are not offering propositions that are more ideologically neutral or logically rigorous. Rather, what they are offering are propositions that make good use of linguistic theories of meaning and difference.

With regard to the multicultural turn, sociology's response has been ambivalent without being genuinely innovative. Some sociologists have embraced multiculturalism, but in ways that do not adequately address basic sociological concerns. The recent volume edited by Margaret Anderson and Patricia Hill-Collins, *Race, Class and Gender* (1995), is a good case in point. The editors situate race in a general theory of difference that is broader than Robin Williams's and that rejects his emphasis on common values. In Derridian fashion, this theory draws analogically on linguistic notions of difference that polarize binary oppositions such as male/female, sacred/profane, or white/black. Racism or sexism thus becomes a categorical difference that is projected onto a group. However, this categorical orientation opens a cleavage with the institutional aspects of racial or gender domination that Anderson and Hill-Collins do not successfully negotiate (1995, 1–9). Achieving such a sociolinguistic or sociosemiotic synthesis would constitute an important advance over what currently exists.

However, not all sociologists have been this open to the multicultural turn. Some, such as Glazer (1983), have responded by defensively reasserting the claim of the culture of poverty or assimilation paradigms. These conservative responses have gained significant support from the political shift to the right. The retreat from the position of the 1960s that this shift has produced is also evident in William Julius Wilson's *The Truly Disadvantaged* (1987).

As a response to multiculturalism and the rise of Afro-American and other ethnic studies departments, this ambivalence is inadequate. For those who embrace the multicultural theory of difference, they need to tailor it more specifically to the institutional concerns of sociology. The link between semiolinguistic and social structures must be more fully theorized, so that contributions not derivable from the semiolinguistic alone can be made. Without such distinct contributions, we will not get the full theoretical benefits from this linguistic import.

To compete with the particularizing of the modern subject that ethnic departments have institutionalized, race needs to be more centrally located within the sociological discourse on modernity. The latter has been centered on processes of rationalization and industrialization. This focus is too narrow as it excludes the complex processes of racializing, cultural mixing, and creolization that have been such basic parts of the modern experiences of nonwhites. Like India and other Asian countries, Africa needs to be included in the classical analyses of modernity. African modernization needs to be freed from its ethnographic construction as the quintessential site of pre-modernity and included in Weberian and Marxian accounts of modernizing processes. We now need to be ethnically and racially specific in our accounts of the rise of the modern world. To resist these processes of diversification and particularization in the face of the increasing differentiation of race/ethnic discourses will only decrease our capacity to survive in this increasingly complex market.

Finally, to deal with the experiential and organizational difference between sociology and ethnic studies departments, we will have to examine more carefully the institutional and discursive spaces that we offer to nonwhites. This is still a major problem. Afro-American students and faculty still do not feel quite at ease in sociology departments or in the subfield of race and ethnicity. The persistence of a black sociology suggests this unease. Sociology's record in historically and empirically documenting the reality of racism remains very strong. However, it has been lacking in bold policy recommendations, innovative institutional changes, and illuminating interpretive mirrors for African Americans and other ethnic groups. Dealing with these issues will be critical to our survival in the field of race/ethnic relations.

With regard to the linguistic turn, our responses have been even less adequate. We have not appropriated the strength of this discursive event to maintain or widen the appeal of sociological theory, nor have we successfully deployed sociological theory to gauge the limits of this turn. For the most part, we have ignored it, hoping that this specter would soon go away. But it has not, because behind it is a process of institutional differentiation within the academy. This process has been more difficult to see because its institutional patterns have been more fragmented and dispersed than those of the multicultural turn. Linguistics, the basic locus for the study of languages, continues to study them as detached systems of communication. However, the behavior-regulating and identity-forming consequences of language have found institutional space in programs such as cultural studies, postcolonial studies, and literary criticism. As the dust settles on these specific programs, it becomes clear that the current hermeneutic challenge is not rooted in them specifically, but in the new explanatory power of language (made available by linguistics) that brought these programs into being. In other words, the institutional separation between linguistics and the study of linguistically coordinated social action has made the increasing differentiation of language and its intellectual consequences for sociology difficult to see.

In addition to this ambiguity, sociology's response was further complicated by the fact that the linguistic turn peaked at a time when interpretive sociology had entered a period of decline. As the most linguistically oriented styles of sociology, symbolic interactionism, ethnomethodology, and Schutzian phenomenological sociology would have been the likely sites of creative engagements with the linguistic turn. Alfred Schultz attempted to outline a phenomenological semiotics (1964, 287–356). Berger and Luckman's (1966) principles of social constructionism have been central to poststructuralist applications of linguistic theory. So also have been the conversational strategies of ethnomethodology. This was the group of sociologists who were best positioned by interest and training to engage the linguistic turn. They were the ones to respond to it, the way rational choice theorists responded to the technical/instrumental challenge from economic theory. However, it was at this time that they began to disintegrate.

Among the earliest responses to the linguistic turn was Charles Lemert's. Lemert very clearly perceived the changing role of language in the academy. "Sociology," he noted, "has never produced a forthright theory of language-practiced, of discourse" (1979, 14). However, addressing this gap was not Lemert's concern. Rather, it was the implication of Foucault's critique of homocentrism for sociological theory.

The work of Richard Brown is indicative of the affinity between interpretive sociology and the linguistic turn that I noted earlier. Brown very successfully used the new linguistic theories to enrich his interpretive sociology (1987). However, his polemical use of the category of rhetoric reinforced rather than weakened tensions with empirical and historical sociologists. Nevertheless, it is primarily from these two sociologists that the interpretive response to the linguistic turn has come.

Responses have also come from outside of the interpretive tradition. Among the functionalists there was Talcott Parsons' attempt to engage the thought of Levi-Strauss. However, Parsons' systemic interests pushed him to conceive language in instrumental terms that make it analogous to "steering media" like money and power (1967). This orientation took it away from his theory of symbolism (1981) and contained the new linguistic possibilities that Levi-Strauss was exploring. In the Loubser et al. volume *Explorations in General Theory in Social Science,* several Parsonian scholars took up the problem of language in functionalist theory, and how it could be used to supplement the analysis of meaning (Loubser 1976). However, the push in this direction was eclipsed by the rise of neofunctionalism.

From the neofunctionalists we have Jeffrey Alexander's clear recognition of "the hermeneutic challenge" (1987, 281). However, the challenge was perceived primarily in relation to Parsonian theory and not to the competitive position of sociology as a whole. In this context, Alexander characterized the turn as a form of sociological idealism that reduced everything to meaning. Thus, caught up in the search for a post-Parsonian multidimensional synthesis, Alexander missed the new explanatory powers of language before they reached the condition of sociological idealism.

By far and away, Jürgen Habermas has provided sociology's most innovative response to the linguistic turn. He has perceived with great clarity the increasing differentiation of language in modern societies, and the challenge it poses to theories of meaning that are grounded in intentional subjects. Choosing the pragmatic/communicative aspects of language over the semiotic and semantic, Habermas attempts to reformulate the development of sociological theory in relation to this process of linguistic differentiation. His re-reading of Marx, Weber, Durkheim, Mead, and Parsons have all been shaped by this linguistic turn (1989). However, the more Habermas has moved in this direction the less influential has been his work on sociology. The dissatisfaction appears to be with the degree to which linguistic/communicative structures have eclipsed social structures in Habermas's work. His formulation of the dialectical interplay between these two has not won the approval of most sociologists. On this particular issue, Pierre Bourdieu with his notion of cultural capital seems to be closer to the mark, even though his synthesis is not as explicitly worked out. However, Habermas's reformulation remains our most innovative response to the linguistic turn. It has clearly stimulated the work of Ben Agger (1989) in this area.

Finally, from the rational choice theorists we have had little or no response. In Coleman's *Foundations of Social Theory*, we have a highly instrumental and economical model of sociology that expands the technical/empirical dimensions. Coleman's legal reconstruction of norms is particularly indicative of this will to instrumentalization (1990, 241–55). With such a strong turn in the direction of economics and away from the humanities, it is understandable why rational choice theorists have had so little to say about the linguistic turn.

Given the wide influence of this turn on both the humanities and the social sciences, it should be clear that ours has indeed been an inadequate response. The resulting decline in theoretical influence has not been restricted to interpretive sociology. On the contrary, it has been a disciplinary-wide decline.

This decline points to the interconnected nature of the three dimensions that make up the sociological imagination. In *Knowledge and Human Interests,* Habermas reinforced this three-dimensional view from an epistemic perspective. If, in spite of the tendencies to diverge and fragment in three separate directions, we accept this integrated view, then it should be no surprise that a major crisis for interpretive sociology has become a crisis for the discipline as a whole. All need to be concerned even when only one of these three pillars of our imagination is confronted by an external challenge of this magnitude. At such times, we need to put internal differences on the back burner and face the challenge together.

Although a little late, sociology needs a strategy to address the long-term changes in academic markets that have come with the linguistic turn. These changes are indicated by the claims that are being made for language by the producers of linguistic theories of social behavior. In his recent book, *The Construction of Social Reality,* John Searle makes the argument for the linguistic nature of institutions. If we are to meet this challenge, two processes of differentiation within sociology must be more firmly institutionalized.

First, we need to encourage the growth of the sociology of language. This particular interface has become extremely important, but this subfield has not experienced a corresponding boom. This is a measure of inflexibility that we cannot afford, given our particular mode of market insertion. More resources must be put in this subfield and graduate students encouraged to enter it. In these times, we must not only be politically and ethnically correct, we must also be linguistically correct.

Second, we must institutionalize more firmly the slowly emerging division of labor between theory construction and metatheory. Our metatheorists would be largely responsible for the general models of societies that derive from the classical tradition and their relationships to new models arising in other social sciences or the humanities. The stream of ideas that gave birth to the classical tradition has not stopped. The linguistic turn demonstrates clearly the need for a group of theoretical sociologists whose primary responsibility is indeed the impact of movements in this stream of sociological theory. If we want to regain our position as net exporters of theory, this is a market in which we must be competitive. The metatheoretical field would then have a relationship to the history of ideas that the sociology of religion or literature has to religious or literary studies. In this case, we would have a very special interest in a particular set of ideas. In the past, we have relied too heavily on the big theorists to do this work. The time has come for us to train more ordinary graduate students in metatheory, just as we do in all other subfields. As a group, they should be able to respond to sociology's interpretive, empirical, and historical interests vis-à-vis new developments in the history of ideas.

Without this capacity, we will not be able to respond effectively to new theoretical challenges, hermeneutic or otherwise. Internal fragmentation will continue and so will the loss of market shares. At some point on this path, we would have to redefine ourselves on a more restricted model, such as Cole's. But such contractions would be particularly costly for sociology, as we have no distinct institutional property. Because the social dimension cuts across all institutions, being competitive in these institutional markets that are dominated by specific disciplines is extremely important for sociology. We are at our best when we can hold our own in these markets. And to do our best, we need all three cylinders working together.

To keep all three cylinders working, there must be significant changes in our patterns of resource allocations. The contrast between our inadequate response to the hermeneutic challenge and the more credible response to the instrumental challenge points to a structural imbalance in need of correction. The inadequacy of the interpretive response reflects a lack of personnel, resources, and internal organization. Between Lemert and Habermas are the fragments of a response that were never mobilized. To respond, more attention and more institutional support must be given to the interpretive wing of our discipline. To the extent that ideological factors maintain this imbalance, they will be contributors to this and other crises.

Conclusion

I have argued that the continuing crisis in sociology is the result of our inadequate responses to new competitive challenges that have been produced by the multicultural and linguistic turns. This position reflects the troubles I have had in reconciling the increasing appeal of Afro-American studies and postcolonial studies over the sociology of race and the sociology of development in the minds of many of my students. Although I am primarily a historical sociologist, the impact of these changes has moved me to look more closely at the state of interpretive sociology. I am convinced that these changes have increased the competitive pressure most directly on the interpretive pillar of sociological explanations that is especially in need of revitalization, not the empirical, the historical, or the ideological. If there are problems with these, they are in how we relate them to each other. This revitalization can only take place if there are shifts in resource distribution and a greater sense of collective responsibility among sociologists as a whole.

As C. Wright Mills often reminded us, the cultural significance of sociology is realized when through its lenses people see their personal troubles and public issues in a new and more familiar light. As a result, they gain a new understanding of themselves; they experience a change of identity or a transvaluation of values. These are the cultural, interpretive gifts of the sociological imagination. It is in this area that we are being surpassed by Afro-American studies, postcolonial studies, and other new discourses. We cannot be content with the production of empirical and historical generalizations. As Max Weber suggests, it must be the primary responsibility of some sociologists to employ these generalizations in the understanding of particular situations. Only then is the cultural significance of sociology realized. Consequently, the more immediate challenge confronting us is the revitalizing of this cultural function in an era in which the multicultural and linguistic imaginations are also changing identities and trans-valuing values.

PART TWO

Area Studies

CHAPTER 6

Black Youth at Risk

Bruce R. Hare

Introduction

There comes a period in every person's life when the tasks of moving from childhood dependence to adult independence are to be accomplished. It is ideally at this time that a fusion of mental readiness and structural opportunity makes this passage possible. The continuous and smooth movement of youth from childhood to adulthood, from school to work, from parents' abode to their own abode, is essential to the future well-being of both the individual and society. Thus, it is in the interest of a society to provide its young people both the training (aptitude) and the opportunities (structures) necessary to accomplish these tasks.

Were such conditions being optimally accomplished for African American/black youth, they would be demonstrating a pattern of self-development at the very least commensurate with that of their "white" and more likely middle-class counterparts.[1] They would be raised in psychologically and economically stable homes, successful in school, optimistic about their progress and their futures, and successfully transitioning from school to work. They would furthermore as black youth demonstrate patterns of self-discipline and commitment to self, family, and community, reflecting the legacy of struggle for equality and justice of which they are a part. Such does not, however, appear to be the case. Not only do our youth remain "disadvantaged" in comparison to other youth,

1. It should be noted that for purposes of this discourse the term "black" is used in recognizing the caste-like social and political status and stereotypic consequences that African American children face. This use of "black" is also consistent with the term used by the National Black Urban League in publishing annual reports. For most purposes, I prefer the term "African American."

but also they are at greater risk than at any other time in recent history. Not only are they being denied their structural opportunity, as reflected in their highest high school dropout and eviction rates, but they are also reflecting alarming attitudinal formations as well.

These youth reflect a lower sense of control over their destinies and an absence of political and collective consciousness, as would be unfortunately expected of children of the post-Civil Rights and Black Nationalism era. They are subsequently short on mentors, and long on rugged individualism. The soaring rates of out-of-wedlock birth, "babies having babies" among increasingly younger black girls with irresponsible and abandoning black boys, the rising crime and drug abuse rates, and the increasing violence committed by our youth against each other and our elders also speak to a rising despair and declining discipline among our black youth.

While we recognize the role of dramatic change in the American economy and psychological climate in general that are causal to this shift, we cannot afford to be content with system blame and allow an entire generation of our youth to go down the drain. It is within this context that this detailed analysis of the state of black youth will be undertaken. Such an analysis, however, could not be undertaken in a theoretical vacuum and thus will be accompanied by an analysis of the workings of the American social system and the state of black people within America. Policy recommendations for increasing the life-chances of our youth will be suggested in the conclusion of this chapter.

Overview: On Being Black in America

It should be stated from the outset that this overview of the condition of black Americans begins from the premise that it is largely the environmental, rather than any mystical, within-group, biological, or cultural, disorder that is responsible for the overrepresentation of black Americans among the losers in the society. Much as a slave may have been defined as ill-adaptive or maladaptive for failing to adjust to slavery, we have failed to adjust to poverty, racism, and discrimination.

For as long as recognition of the "disadvantaged" status of black Americans has existed, an assortment of explanations has been advanced to justify their disproportionate location in the lower slots of the social system. The notion of biological (genetic) inferiority is an example of the "bad genes" explanation for the inferior social position of African Americans. A revised and more liberal, although equally devastating, argument appeared with the emergence of cultural inferiority explanations. This justification of discrimination shifts the blame from the genes of the group to the culture of the group, while subtly retaining a victim-blame focus. While the second explanation does represent a kind of progress, under the assumption that culture can be improved, both perspectives serve to maintain the locus of blame within the group itself, while leaving the system unchallenged. In neither mode has it been posited as a tenable hypothesis that differential attainment is a requirement of the American social order and that processes are operative within the system that increase the probability that African Americans will be disproportionately allocated to the lower slots.

While acknowledging the relative underattainment of "black" Americans, I adopt a third ideological perspective in search of an explanation: that the relative academic and economic failure of black Americans in the American social order is functional, if not intended, given racism and the differential distribution of wealth, power, and privilege in the social structure. It is posited that both the biological and cultural explanations serve largely to justify current race, class, and gender inequalities. Furthermore, it is argued that the myth of equal opportunity serves as a smoke screen through which the losers will be led to blame themselves, and be seen by others as getting what they deserve. One might simply ask, for example, how can both inheritance of wealth for some and equal opportunity for all exist in the same social system?

Bowles and Gintis (1976) posit that the unequal distribution of wealth, power, and privilege is, and historically has been, the reality of American capitalism and that such a system must produce educational and occupational losers. I further argue, in what I term a "class-plus" analysis, with classism as the engine and racism as the caboose, that black Americans have simply been chosen to absorb an unfair share of an unfair burden in a structurally unfair system.

As indicated in figure 6.1, our structural determinism approach assumes that the character of the social system is preponderant as the determiner of the hierarchical arrangement of people within it, over either their biological predisposition or cultural dispositions. It is further argued that, in addition to the inherent intergenerational inequality legitimized by inheritance, the educational system, through its unequal skill-giving, grading, routing, and credentialing procedures, plays a critical role in legitimating structural inequality in the American social system. The triangles in figure 6.1 represent the following: triangle 1, the assumed hierarchical distribution of intelligence—many low, few high; triangle 2, the assumed similar distribution of cultural readiness; triangle 3, the actual stratifying function of schools—many enter, few make it to the top; and triangle 4, the actual distribution of occupation, prestige, and power—many low, few high.

The biological and cultural deterministic traditions have argued that schools merely respond to innate genetic or cultural differences in ability when they receive and stratify youngsters. The occupational structure is further assumed simply to respond to the schools when it slots people into hierarchical positions on the basis of credentials and skills given in schools. The structural argument goes from right to left instead of left to right, and charges that the social system needs people to replenish its ranks at all levels of skill and credentials, and that in producing such differences the schools respond to structural needs rather than to innate differences. It is further assumed that such ascribed characteristics as one's "race," sex, and social-class background deliver differential treatment, consequently increasing the probability of lower educational attainment and lower occupational placement among "people of color," women, and people of lower-class origin. The amount of inequality explained by biology or culture becomes notably minor in such an analysis, since such a system would theoretically be compelled to stratify a population of identical culture and biological characteristics.

Given the structural issues presented, and the already known precarious state of the adults, one might wonder specifically how a people of equal innate childhood potential arrive at such a disadvantaged youth status. To be sure, early indicators do exist in the over 45 percent unemployment rate of black youth, but the process of structuring differential perceptions, access, and attainment among black youngsters is begun early on.

The cornerstone of the health of an adult is the capacity to take care of one's own, and of one's own self. The mechanism through which this task is made possible is employment. As we enter this new millennium, not only do black Americans remain twice as likely to be unemployed as whites, but when they are employed they can expect to hold lower-status positions and to be paid less even if holding the same occupational positions as their white counterparts. The social and psychological consequences of job discrimination remain enor-

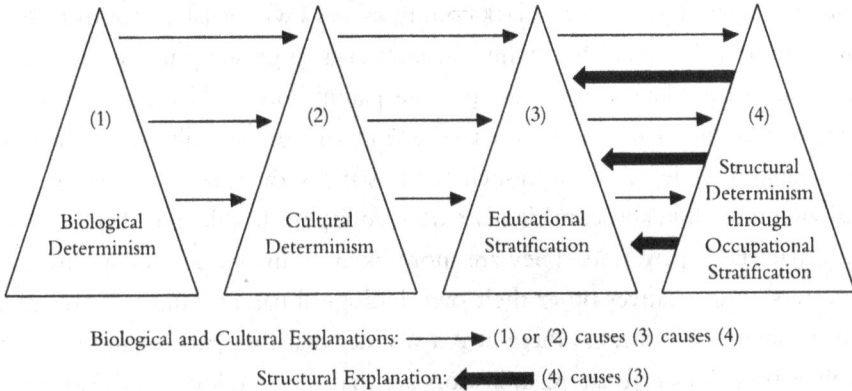

Biological and Cultural Explanations: ——————▶ (1) or (2) causes (3) causes (4)

Structural Explanation: ◀———— (4) causes (3)

Figure 6.1 Alternative Explanations of Inequality

mous both for the individuals and the relationships within the community and its families.

Environmental Influences

The Role of Home

Ideally, the homes in which black children would blossom would consist of stable and successful parents who were capable of meeting their material and spiritual needs, providing discipline, and interceding on their behalf in the outside worlds of school, work, and community. They would be parents who would confidentially challenge the school to teach their children. They would do the kinds of things that would facilitate their children's learning, such as reading to them, helping them with their homework, rewarding their successes, and exposing them to experiences and the world of knowledge. In short, such parents would provide their children with a safe, secure, and protected environment in which they would flourish with positive role models and develop both the skills and optimism necessary for a successful future.

While there are many black youth who, in fact, are blessed with such conditions, a significantly larger number find themselves in quite the opposite situation. It is important to emphasize that the existence of some privileged black individuals, be they children or adults, does not contradict or deny the aggregate endangered status of the black community as a whole. Black youth are four times more likely than their white counterparts to grow up in a poor household and are as likely to grow up in a one-parent household as not.[2] They are, therefore, at high risk of exposure to the kinds of family instability and turmoil associated with deprivation. In such circumstances, they are also more likely to fall victim to child abuse, inadequate nutrition, poor health care, drugs, crime, and material deprivation. They are more likely to live in below-par crowded quarters, with relatives other their own biological parents, and in foster care. Given such possibilities as these, it is a wonder that they survive and thrive as well as they do. Fortunately, indicators are that they are loved and feel loved, but there is no denying that many black youth must also suffer the consequences of the pressure under which they and their parents live.

The significant absence of fathers both as successful role models and as partners in the socialization of these youth is likely to have profound, although different, effects on both boys and girls. For example, there is evidence that this absence of fathers may be partially causal to reported differences in academic achievement, favoring black girls over black boys. Allen (1979) suggests that since black parents are role models for their children and are harder on their same-sex children, the boys lose both the model and disciplinarian. Lewis (1975) reports that black mothers are in fact harder disciplinarians on their daughters. Thus, to the extent that adolescent development requires boys to break from their mother's control, the absence of fathers is posited to contribute significantly to a loss of control as well as to the increased probability that such boys will also reject, or be rejected by, school and subsequently recruitable to, and controlled by, exploitive males of the peer and street cultures.

To the extent that some poor, academically failing young girls see their mothers coping "successfully" as single parents, they are led to believe that they can do the same. Mayfield (1986) suggests "motherhood" may become an alternative road to recognized adult status. The rapid rise in the "illegitimacy" rate among young black girls, which is as high as 50 percent in some cities, who are literally abandoned by their children's young fathers and left to rear their children in poverty, speaks to the seriousness of this issue. In my view there may be illegitimate parents, but there are no illegitimate children.

It is worth emphasizing that acknowledging these negative possibilities neither denies existing strengths of black families nor removes the system from

2. *Crisis,* 93 (Mar. 1986), entire issue on the topic "Black Males in Jeopardy."

its responsibility for creating the conditions that are causal to these patterns. The fact, however, remains that socialization and control problems do exist among black youth, and particularly poor black youth.

The Role of School

It has been said that schools are places that people attend most and know the least about. Education to black Americans remains the symbolic key to advancement. The historic 1954 Supreme Court decision[3] declaring segregated schools inherently unequal represented what many hoped would be the turning point. Many believed it would bring an end to inferior education. However, over forty years later the dream of the *Brown* decision remains to be realized, particularly in our cities. The underlying twin desegregation notions, that sprinkling a few black children in a predominately white school would not depreciate the assumed higher quality of education and that sprinkling a few white children in a predominately black school would appreciate the quality, are both racist and questionable. However, the fact that the wait for desegregation has allowed for significant "in the meantime" declines in predominately black urban school systems is unquestionable. The education of our youth in urban systems has largely become an exercise in social control and babysitting by outsiders.

While much has been written about the achievement gap between blacks and other groups on standardized tests, as through suggestions concerning the innate ability and motivational problems of the youngsters, less has been offered about the possible role of the school and teachers in the creation and forwarding of such differences. Nevertheless, there exists a body of literature on teacher expectations and differential treatment of children of different characteristics that might shed alternative light on the causes of these achievement differences (Hare 1977; Boykin, Franklin, and Yates 1979; Spencer, Brookins, and Allen 1985).

While conventional wisdom would have us believe that every child begins the greater quest for status at the same starting line, with the same track shoes, with only aptitude determining placement at the finishing line, there is ample evidence to suggest that such egalitarian theories are myths and distortions of facts. For example, Cicourel and Kitsuse, examining the egalitarian assumption

3. *Brown vs. Board of Education of Topeka*, 347 US 483 (1954).

in a study of educational decision-makers, concluded that quite the opposite is true. They reported that their research "supports the view that the student's progress in this sequence of transitions is contingent upon the student's biography, social and personal adjustment, appearance and demeanor, social class, and 'social type' as well as his demonstrated ability and performance," and they concluded that "the professed ideal of equal access to educational opportunities for those of equal ability is not necessarily served by such procedures" (Cicourel and Kitsuse 1963). Lavin, in a study on predicting academic performance, concluded, "some evidence suggested that implicit subjective criteria are involved in teacher grading practices. We refer here to the possibility that certain characteristics of the student, such as his sex, 'race' and social class background, affect the quality of the relationship between the student and the teacher" (Lavin 1963).

Katz concluded, in an analytic study of teacher attitude, that "the meaning of these teacher differences is that on the average, children from low-income homes, most of whom are Negro, get more than their fair share of classroom exposure to teachers who really are unqualified for their role, who basically resent teaching them, and who therefore behave in ways that foster, in the more dependent students, tendencies toward debilitating, self criticism" (Katz 1967).

While older research has attempted to attribute the lower attainment of black youth to low self-esteem, more recent studies, when controlling for economic background, have found no significant race differences in general or area-specific (school, peer, and home) self-esteem. Nevertheless, consistent with the hypothesis of differential treatment, achievement differences remain even when economic background is controlled (Hare 1980).

As previously noted, the school plays a unique role in allocating people to different positions in the division of labor through routing and grading practices. Relative success in school is, in fact, the major avenue through which discrimination in the job market is justified. Given racism as well as sexism and classism in a stratified America, it has been posited that the disproportional allocation of black Americans, women, and people of lower-class origin to the lowest labor slots is functional, and that their relative academic failure is essential to getting the job done.

For example, such traditional procedures as differentially allocating girls to home economics and sewing courses, lower-class youngsters to slower tracks, and black children to compensatory programs are common school practices with long-term educational and occupational implications. *Thus, it is argued that structured educational failure legitimizes job discrimination while eliminating legal recourse.* One cannot successfully sue an employer for failing to give a desired job if one arrives relatively unqualified.

It should be noted that such a process does not require a conscious conspiracy to operate; rather it is posited that Newton's law of inertia regarding material objects is also applicable to notions. Begging the issue of origins, continued educational discriminatory practices merely require that school personnel, like other people, act on socialized unconscious beliefs in established stereotypes, which then require a conspiracy to stop, not to continue (Hare 1984). There is little reason to assume that if such processes and attitudes exist in the general culture, they would not be operative in the schools. The fact that the schools simultaneously homogenize attitudes while differentiating skills increases the probability that the youngsters themselves will accept their outcomes as the consequence of their own attributes or deficiencies.

This discussion, while not denying the existence of achievement gaps, has attempted to offer a structural alternative to conventional victim-based explanations. Such a notion appears not at all inconsistent with reported findings of gross "race" differences in academic achievement.

The Role of Peers

As early as preadolescence, black children show a trend toward higher peer self-esteem than white children, and higher ratings of the importance of such social abilities as being popular and good at sports and games. The fact that they do not differ from white children in general self-esteem or home self-esteem, but tend toward lower school self-esteem, as well as significantly lower standardized reading and mathematics performance, suggests that a shift from school to peers may already be beginning to take place (Hare 1985).

It may be theorized that as black children age and progressively lose in school evaluations, they may shift toward peer evaluations in search of higher possibilities of success and ego enhancement. As stated by Castenell in a 1983 study of area-specific achievement motivation, if an adolescent is "discouraged by significant others, or through repeated failure, to perceive achievement [as possible] within the school environment, then that adolescent may choose to achieve in another arena." Cummings and others (1977) have reported evidence that as black children grow older, their values are more influenced by peers than by other groups, and that the maintenance of ego and self-respect increasingly requires peer solidarity.

These authors further support the possible existence of a progressive shift in motivation and attachment from the school to the peers among black youth, and particularly poor black youth. More importantly, they suggest that such a shift is a logical pursuit of "achievement" and positive strokes, and a flight from failure and ego-damaging experiences. Since the benefits are short-term in that they are unlikely to pay off in the adult occupational structure, the poor black adolescent peer culture may also be viewed as a long-term "wash-out" arena although a short-term achievement arena.

Consistent with Castenell's area-specific achievement motivation notion, Maehr and Lysy (1979) question traditional restricted cultural and academic notions of achievement motivation. They posit that contextual conditions are important in expressions of achievement motivations, and that the particular form in which achievement is expressed is determined by the definition that culture gives to it. They further indicate that their definition suggests that motivation is manifest in a broad range of activities, and that motivational questions are ultimately about the ways in which, rather than whether, people are motivated. In some communities, such abilities as mastering street-wiseness, playground sports, sexuality, domestic and child-rearing chores, supplementing family income, and taking on other aspects of adult roles at an early age provide youth opportunities to demonstrate competence. It should be noted that although the larger cultural milieu decries these adaptations, they are perfectly realistic, adaptive, and expected responses to reality.

The black youth peer culture may be regarded as a long-term failure arena because even though it succeeds in providing alternative outlets of achievement through the demonstration of competence, as through street, athletic, and social activities, it offers little hope of long-term legitimate success. It carries the real dangers of drafting young people into the self-destructive worlds of drugs, crime, and sexual promiscuity.

The notion of "peer solidarity," with its oppositional flavor, also suggests an anti-intellectual strain between the peers and the schooling experience. It should be emphasized, however, that it is more likely that the collectively negative schooling experience of black youth produces this anti-school sentiment than the reverse, and that to whatever degree such a sentiment does exist within the culture, it is dependent upon the schools to produce the negative experiences that feed it new recruits.

In summary, given the presence of negative schooling experiences, the availability of positive peer experiences, and the inability of youth to perceive the long-term consequences of adolescent decisions, many of these youth can be said to be making what appears to them to be a logical decision in shifting from the school to the peers. In the long run, of course, they are disproportionately excluded from legitimate occupational success possibilities. *They are also subsequently blamed, as adults, for the consequences of school-system-induced self-protection decisions made during adolescence.* In this context, the rising crime, drugs, and out-of-wedlock pregnancy rates among black youth may be seen as a consequence of the interplay of negative schooling experiences as provided by incompetent outsiders, a decline of parental control, and a significant rise in the independence of an attractive peer culture that offers positive strokes and ego-enhancement to a vulnerable population.

The Political Context

The political context in which these youth are found is quite different from what it was forty years ago. The era of Black Nationalism and Civil Rights is not a conscious part of their experience, and they are consequently deprived of the kinds of political socialization that was available to those of us who grew up prior to and during the era of Martin Luther King, Jr. and Malcolm X. They are more likely to blame themselves for their condition in the absence of political mentors, and less likely to understand the workings of the American social system. This knowledge void is further enhanced by youth attendance in schools we do not control in which they will more likely be taught "his-story" rather than "our-story." Since we provide no alternative structured ways for them to come to know, they are also likely to believe what they are taught.

The downside of desegregation is that in many urban centers we have given our children to people who do not like us and are curiously surprised at what we get back. For example, African American/Black History was a normal part of what we taught our children in our segregated schools. Our children thus learned *our* story from us in the regular process of the school year as they now learn the European/white story in the public schools. Because we no longer have our time with them, our history is relegated to a month (February) and told with their Eurocentric distortions. The need to establish our time with our children as the Muslims require their children to be taught at the mosque and the Jews require their children to be taught at the temple is urgent.

The Catholics also require religious instruction for their children. Each of these groups requires their moment with their children under their tutor, after school if necessary, to guarantee their cultural knowledge and pride. The black church, in my view, is the only place positioned to serve this function and has been negligent on this issue of urgency.

The absence of movements has also served to deny these youth the opportunity to develop the sense of community and "collective consciousness" that provided ego-protection enhancement and a sense of mission to many of us who were aware in the sixties. Such movements not only provided a shift from self-blame to system-blame, but also encouraged doing something about the group condition.

The consequences of the absence of such leadership and movements cannot be overestimated, since such spokespersons and actions provide a "redefinition of the situation" to the population, along with increased pride, discipline, and willingness to work collectively toward problem resolution. Not only was this true in the political arena proper, but it was true of other community-affecting institutions as well.

Black music, for example, which used to give our youth such collective political messages as, "Say it loud, I'm black and I'm proud," and "ain't no stoppin' us now," now instead provides materialistic and individualistic messages of sexual prowess and promiscuity that demean ourselves, our women, and our community, while reducing our men to dogs. For example, I was recently confronted by a young crude gangsta rapper who asked why I was so hard on rap music. I told the young man that I did indeed like some of it, but was offended by some of the language. I then asked him, "Young man, do you think we had a revolution in the 1960s so that you could go on TV and hold your personal parts? Do you think we had a revolution so that you could go on TV and radio and call our mothers, daughters, and sisters pussies, bitches, and hoes? Do you think we had a revolution so that you could make records for the world and call yourself a 'nigger'? When your granddaddy would have died before he let a 'cracker' get away with that?"

The young man responded, "Professor Hare, we don't mean 'nigger' the way you mean 'nigger.' " I responded, "Listen, nigger, you ain't been on this planet long enough to rehabilitate that word. That word has history." He smirked and walked away, and I felt that we adults were responsible for not having oriented and educated him better.

The black church, which has historically been a fertile source of child socialization, leadership, and moral development, appears to have slipped in its
ability to generate community solidarity and progressive leadership.

Black business remains largely what E. Franklin Frazier (1957a) describes as
an economic myth in terms of its ability to employ a significant number of
black people and willingness to play a philanthropic role in the community.
The black press appears less willing to fill the information void regarding the
true state of the community than it is in forwarding gossip and sensationalism.
If the black church can be accused of deferring gratification more than raising
indignation, the black press can be accused of providing vicarious living experiences through the presentation of lifestyles of selected "successful" blacks,
most of whom are either athletes or entertainers.

This assessment is not intended to romanticize the sixties, but merely to
describe the probable declines in community activism and responsibility and
their likely effect on this generation.

On Mass Media Intrusion

There is an undeniable symbolic truth to George Orwell's prediction in *1984*.
His error simply resided in direction when he predicted that "Big Brother" is
watching you. The truth is that you are watching "Big Brother!" The average
eighteen-year-old today has watched over 22,000 hours of television and
350,000 commercials. Aside from the exploitation of youthful insecurities by
commercials, creating diseases to sell cures, such as perpetuating the need to
"relax" one's hair, prevent chapped lips, and wear designer jeans, the tube serves
to condition the population. Television tells youth what to want, whom to like,
how to be, and what to think. It romanticizes greed, crime, infidelity, material-
ism, and individualism. Furthermore, it not only provides white America with
distorted images of black people and black communities, but creates gross mis-
conceptions of the world for black America as well. While comic treatment of
whites on the tube is counterbalanced by serious treatment, it is hard for a
viewer to conclude that the black family, for example, is anything other than a
joke. It creates people who confuse reality and illusion, desensitizes people to
violence, and programs all populations to a pro-male, "white," and upper-class
imitation pattern.

To be sure the occasional presentations of serious black programs and sporadic appearances of uniquely talented black personalities, such as Oprah Winfrey, do occur, but the dominant message to black youth remains illusionary possibilities of star status as through athletics or entertainment. The futility of such programmed aspirations as star status in the NBA (National Basketball Association) or NFL (National Football League) was aptly indicated by sociologist Harry Edwards, when he noted that black youth were twice as likely to be hit by a star (a falling meteorite) as they were to become one in professional sports.

One might wonder what such program exposure does to condition young black children toward the deification of "white" men. Most importantly, however, one might simply wonder what else might have been done to, or for, a mind, had it not spent this amount of time (22,000 hours) sitting in front of the tube. The point here is that, however subtle, the television is the most massive programming and socializing instrument ever created, and cannot be expected to do anything more than deactivate our youth.

While it is true that television previously served to bring the news of marches, protests, rallies, and so forth into the home and the American conscience, it appears that the lesson has been learned and that such events are intentionally being played down, if covered at all. The management of news has become more sophisticated, and a shift from straight news to sensationalistic entertainment is evident. The danger of television's raising consciousness is declining.

The American population generally, and the black population specifically, have yet to measure or understand the degree to which this cable and MTV television generation has been affected. People have only begun to investigate, for example, the connection between television crime and street crime, and even less has been done to assess the long-term consequences of television addiction for interaction skills or moral development. It is clear, however, that we do not control the tube and thus are surely giving strangers access to our children's minds when we fail to police their watching habits.

On Street Models

To the extent that role models are significant, poor black youth run a high probability of exposure to successful participants in what has been called "the underground economy." While short on doctors, lawyers, engineers, and other legitimized professionals to emulate, they are differentially exposed to numbers runners, drug dealers, pimps, prostitutes, and other assortments of creative and innovative characters with apparent money, cars, and fine clothes. To the extent that models of legitimate success become unavailable and legitimate opportunities become scarce, these youth also become vulnerable to and recruitable to such activities. This becomes even more likely when one further considers that the professionals working in their communities such as teachers, police, firefighters, and so on are not likely to live there, and that their local religious and political leaders are also less likely to have meaningful contact with them.

Thus, black youth can be said to be in a community context that is simultaneously less effective in protecting, organizing, and socializing them, while more vulnerable to negative influences. The combined facts of mass media intrusion, an absence of control over local schools, and exposure to alternative lifestyles provide increased opportunity for our youth to be programmed contrary to our, or their, interests.

The Psychology of Social Control

As pointed out long ago by Carter G. Woodson (1969), when you control a man's thinking you do not have to worry about his actions. One does not have to accept the Grier and Cobbs (1968) or Kardiner and Ovesey (1951) arguments about self-hatred to acknowledge that *living under constant psychological and material abuse does have its price.* For example, some black people are successfully socialized into internationalizing negative messages about themselves. Others are brought to believe that what is said about the group is true, while viewing themselves as the exception. Still others, in overzealous defense of the group, deny that there is any effect on any group members.

Just as it would be unwise to claim that nothing is wrong with the lowerclass black family, and thereby remove the system from any responsibility for the economic strains such families suffer, it would be foolish to fail to acknowledge the special pressures affecting black people. Rather than denying effects, I relocate the causes from the group to the system, while simultaneously recognizing both *our* responsibilities and societal responsibilities for change. Frederick Douglas noted "that no matter how accurate our claim to blame 'white' America for our plight, nobody can save us from us but us."

The combination of racism, poverty, a psychologically hostile environment, and negative schooling experience has a profoundly negative effect on the psychological and academic adjustment of our black youth. Amazingly, however, they are also creative and talented in the development of survival skills, and in utilizing mechanisms to protect and enhance their self-imagery even if it means the reorganization of self-definition. They are therefore capable of change and can be saved.

It is toward this last capability that we must direct our energies. It is in this context that the following policy recommendations are offered.

Policy Recommendations

Inform the black communities and others concerned of the true endangered status of the youth. In addition to meetings, utilization of mass media (television, press, radio, and so forth) should be sought.

Work with other organizations, community groups, and parents to organize programs to assist the youth in developing:

A stronger sense of self-worth and self-discipline

A commitment to academic achievement

A stronger sense of commitment to family

A stronger sense of commitment to local community

A stronger sense of commitment to the general black community

A stronger sense of connectedness to all other oppressed people

Work with black business persons, politicians, clergy, and So Forth to provide opportunities for black youth to be exposed to mentors and role models, as well as to understand the workings of business, government, and so forth.

Provide organized collective activities for youth. The black church, for example, is the essential location for the recreational, educational, and political socialization of our youth.

Develop mechanisms of accountability for black professional business persons, politicians, clergy, and so forth.

Organize and demand of the federal government:

Enforcement of our rights in general

Services delivery, such as health care, housing, employment, and child nutrition programs

Voting rights protection

Civil rights protection

Organize and demand of local government:

Quality education for our youth, as distinguished from, but not as opposed to, desegregated education

Services delivery, such as better drug enforcement, police service, sanita-
tion services, fire protection, housing code enforcement, and so forth

Organize, register, and vote

Such an analysis and action list is not intended to be all-inclusive, but does
represent a possible point of departure. It *acknowledges our* as well as the system's
responsibilities, and suggests the need to move ahead collectively for ourselves,
for oppressed peoples, and most importantly, for our youth.

Concluding Remarks

Given the inequality-reproducing structure of the American social system,
there are limits to the amount of progress we can expect to make short of radical change. There are reforms, however, that can be pursued in order to
decrease the probability that black youth will continue to suffer disproportionately as "class-plus" victims in a racist class system.

We must assist youth to organize and, in some cases reorganize, in such a
way as to maximize their self-image, self-discipline, and attainment. As previously indicated, it would seem that the black church is the ideal site for the academic and political socialization of our youth. It is through such institutions
that other ethnic groups have guaranteed the moral and political socialization
of their youth necessary to the integrity and continuance of the community.
Historically, it is from the black church that many of our leaders and movements have emerged. This child socialization task becomes increasingly important since we are not in charge of the schools our youngsters attend.

We must be aware, however, that to raise the expectations and efforts of our
youth without also placing additional pressures on the institutions, agencies,
and individuals (particularly teachers) who serve them would be grossly unfair.
We must, in fact, seek control of the environment in which our youth are located. If we do not, we will not only have wasted human resources, but will
have an increasing population of embittered and dangerous adults.

CHAPTER 7

Work, Family, and Black Women's Oppression

Patricia Hill-Collins

> Honey, de white man is the de ruler of everything as fur as Ah been
> able tuh find out. Maybe it's some place way off in de ocean where de
> black man is in power, but we don't know nothin' but what we see. So
> de white man throw down de load and tell de nigger man tuh pick it
> up. He pick it up because he have to, but he don't tote it. He hand it
> to his womenfolks. De nigger woman is de mule uh de world so fur as
> Ah can see.
>
> —Zora Neale Hurston, *Their Eyes Were Watching God*

With these words, Nanny, an elderly African American woman in Zora Neale Hurston's *Their Eyes Were Watching God,* explains black women's "place" to her young, impressionable granddaughter. Nanny knows that being treated as "mules uh de world" lies at the heart of black women's oppression. As mill worker Corine Cannon observes, "your work, and this goes for white people, and black, is what you are . . . your work is your life" (Byerly 1986, 156).

One core theme in black feminist thought consists of analyzing black women's work; especially black women's labor market victimization as "mules." As dehumanized objects, mules are living machines and can be treated as part of the scenery. Fully human women are less easily exploited. Documenting black women's labor market status in order to see the general patterns of race and gender inequality is one primary area of analysis (Wallace 1980; Higginbotham 1983, 1985; Glenn 1985; Jones 1985). This research is supplemented by studies of black women's positions in specific occupational niches, such as the attention devoted to black women domestic workers (Dill 1980, 1988a; Rollins 1985), and during specific historical eras, such as slavery (Jones 1985; D. White 1985) and the urbanizing south (Clark-Lewis 1985). This emerging scholarship provides convincing evidence for Maria Stewart's deft claim that "let our girls possess whatever amiable qualities of soul they may . . . it is impossible for scarce an individual of them to rise above the condition of servants" (Richardson 1987, 46).

More recent scholarship supplements this initial emphasis on oppression by presenting African American women as constrained but often empowered figures, even in extremely difficult labor market settings (Terborg-Penn 1985). Black women's organizational role in unions (Lerner 1972; Sacks 1988) and black women's characteristic forms of everyday resistance (Rollins 1985; Byerly 1986; Dill 1988a) are also receiving increased attention.

Black women intellectuals demonstrate a sustained effort to examine the connections between race and gender oppression in analyzing black women's work in capitalist political economies (Davis 1981; Higginbotham 1983; Mullings 1986b; Collins 1986a; Brewer 1988). African American women certainly are not the only group taking this position (see, for example, Brittan and Maynard 1984; Glenn 1985), but they have consistently done so the longest. While the concept of the interlocking nature of oppression is proposed as a premise, efforts at untangling the nature of the relationships themselves typically yield uneven outcomes (King 1988). As a result, we have a better sense of what these relationships are *not* than of what they are in a political economy of domination.[1]

Research on black women's unpaid labor within extended families remains less fully developed in black feminist thought than does that on black women's paid work. By emphasizing black women's contributions to black family well-being, such as keeping families together and teaching children survival skills (Martin and Martin 1978; McCray 1980; Davis 1981), such scholarship suggests

1. Elizabeth Spelman (1982) rejects additive approaches to conceptualizing oppression:"An additive analysis treats the oppression of a black woman in a sexist and racist society as if it were a *further* burden than her oppression in a sexist but non-racist society, when, in fact, it is a *different* burden" (43). Similarly, Brittan and Maynard (1984) argue that separate oppressions cannot be merged under one "grand theory of oppression." Omi and Winant (1986) warn against the tendency to subsume one type of oppression under another—for example, of seeing everything as stemming from class structure. For an incisive discussion of multiple jeopardy as an alternative model, see King (1988).

that black women see their unpaid domestic work more as a form of resistance to oppression than as a form of exploitation by men. Less attention is given to ways that black women's domestic labor is exploited within African American families, an omission that obscures investigations of families as contradictory locations that simultaneously confine yet allow black women to develop cultures of resistance.

Afrocentric feminist analyses of black women's work investigate both the interlocking nature of black women's oppression in the paid labor market and the dialectical nature of black women's unpaid family labor. Such analyses stimulate a better appreciation of the powerful and complex interplay between black women's position as "de mule uh de world" and patterns of capitalist development, racial oppression, and gender subordination.

Afrocentric feminist analyses of black women's work also promise to shed some light on ongoing debates concerning social class. Black women's experiences have not been adequately explained by the two primary models of social class. In the status attainment model, class sorts out positions in society along a continuum of economic success and social prestige. Social classes become relative rankings and people engage in relative amounts of ascending or descending the ladder of social class. In the class conflict model, class divides society into two or more groups, each of which has vested class interests and contends for control of society. Social classes are defined by the social relations of domination and subordination, usually economic and political, and social class always requires a power relation (Vanneman and Cannon 1987).

Neither status attainment nor class conflict models adequately explain black women's experiences with social class. Status attainment research has relied heavily on occupational prestige of traditionally male jobs. Women's social class position was thought to derive from that of their fathers and husbands. But the higher rates of black male unemployment, the racial discrimination that has crowded all African Americans into a narrow set of occupations, and the existence of household arrangements other than two-parent nuclear families among African Americans have all combined to make status attainment models less suitable for explaining black social class dynamics. Moreover, the emphasis on *paid* labor and the exclusion of *unpaid* domestic labor have severely limited the ability of status attainment models to explain black women's social class experiences.

Conflict models have also failed to capture the intersection of race and gender in explaining black women's social class location. By focusing on paid labor, they too obscure the full range of black women's work. Moreover, the type of paid work that has long preoccupied conflict theorists—namely, industrial factory jobs, especially unionized jobs—is problematic. African American women have traditionally worked in agricultural labor or as domestic workers, two occupations resistant to unionization. The result is that black women's paid work has been neglected in class conflict models.

Placing black women's work and family experiences at the center of analysis suggests a view of social class other than that offered by status attainment or conflict models. Moreover, understanding the intersection of work and family in black women's lives is key to clarifying the overarching political economy of domination. Black women's work remains a fundamental location where the dialectical relationship of oppression and activism occurs.

Family and Work: Challenging the Definitions

Racially segmented labor markets, gender ideologies in both segmented labor markets and family units, and the overarching capitalist class structure in which black women's specific race, gender, and social class positions are embedded all structure black women's work. And yet traditional social science research assesses African American women's experiences in families using the normative yardstick developed from the experiences of middle-class American and European nuclear families (Billingsley 1968; Ladner 1972; Johnson 1981; Brewer 1988). Three elements of this approach are especially problematic for African American families. First, this model posits a dichotomous split between the public sphere of economic and political discourse and the private sphere of family and household responsibilities. Contrasting a public political economy to a private, non-economic, and apolitical domestic sphere creates a distinction between the paid labor of the public sphere and the unpaid labor of the domestic sphere. Work and family emerge as separate, discreet spheres, with paid work done outside the household deemed more valuable than unpaid work performed for families. Within the public sphere gradations of pay correspond with differences of status, prestige, and power. For the private sphere, household residency and the family are treated as synonymous. The normative family becomes defined as a heterosexual couple who live together with their dependent children in a self-contained, economically independent household.

Second, under this model the public sphere of political and economic discourse is reserved for men as a "male" domain. In spite of claims that the two spheres are separate but equal, in capitalist settings the "female" sphere of family has long been subordinated to the "male" sphere of paid work and political authority. Gender roles are tied to the dichotomous constructions of these two basic societal institutions: men work and women take care of families.

Finally, this public/private dichotomy separating the family/household from the paid labor market shapes sex-segregated gender roles within the private sphere of the family. The archetypal white, middle-class nuclear family divides family life into two oppositional spheres: the "male" sphere of economic providing and the "female" sphere of affective nurturing. This normative family household ideally consists of a working father who earns enough to allow his spouse and dependent children to withdraw from the paid labor force. As head of the household, the father presides over the intimate, private affairs of his own sphere of influence. Guided by the moral influence of the mother, the household/family serves as a haven from the pressures and demands of the impersonal, public sector. All members of the household/family should be glad to retreat from the impersonal public sphere to the warm, supportive environment of "home" (Dill 1988b; Mullings 1986a, 1986b).

Black women's experiences and those of other women of color have never fit this model (Higginbotham 1983; Glenn 1985; Mullings 1986b). Rather than trying to explain why black women's work and family patterns deviate from the alleged norm, a more fruitful approach lies in challenging the very constructs of work and family themselves. Because household and kin arrangements vary tremendously cross-culturally, the family as described earlier is not a universal institution but is better seen as arising only in particular political and economic contexts (Collier et al. 1983; Oppong 1982; Rapp 1982). Sociologist Rose Brewer (1988) points out that "the nuclear family imperative is rooted in upper-class, white patriarchal prerogatives that are unevenly shared across race and class lines" (332). Because the construct of family/household emerged with the growth of the modern state and is rooted in assumptions about discrete public and private spheres, nuclear families characterized by sex-segregated gender roles are less likely to be found in African American communities, where political life is radically different.

The family life of poor people challenges these assumptions about universal nuclear family forms because poor families do not exhibit the radical split equating private with home and public with work (Rapp 1982, 179). In order to survive, the family network must share the costs of providing for children. Privatization is less likely when survival depends on rapid circulation of limited

resources. African American families exhibit these fluid public/private boundaries because racial oppression has impoverished disproportionate numbers of
black families (Stack 1974). But they also invoke the Afrocentric worldview
that offers alternative definitions of family and community (Surdarkasa 1981a,
1981b).

Like family, work is a highly contested category. In the following discussion of the distinction between work and measures of self, May Madison, a par-
ticipant in John Gwaltney's study of inner-city African Americans, alludes to
the difference between work as an instrumental activity and work as something
for self:

> One very important difference between white people and black people is that
> white people think you are your work . . . Now, a black person has more
> sense than that because he knows that what I am doing doesn't have anything
> to do with what I want to do or what I do when I am doing for myself. Now,
> black people think that my work is just what I have to do to get what I want.
> (Gwaltney 1980, 174)

Ms. Madison's perspective deconstructs definitions of work that grant white
men more status and human worth because they are employed in better-paid
occupations. She recognizes that work is a contested construct and that evaluating individual worth by the type of work performed is a questionable practice in systems based on race and gender inequality within segmented labor
markets.

Work might be better conceptualized by examining the range of work that
black women actually perform. Work as alienated labor can be economically
exploitative, physically demanding, and intellectually deadening—the type of
work long associated with black women's status as "mule." Alienated labor can
be either paid, as was the case of domestic service, or unpaid, as was black
woman's work under slavery or as is some work within families. But work can
also be empowering and creative, even if it is physically challenging and appears
to be demeaning. Exploitative wages that black women were allowed to keep
and use for their own benefit or work done out of love for the members of
one's family can represent work that is empowering and/or creative. Again, this
type of work can be either paid or unpaid.

What is the connection between black women's work both in the labor
market and in African American family networks? Addressing this question for

four key historical periods in black political economy uses the lens of black women's work to further an Afrocentric feminist analysis of social class and oppression.

The Process of Enslavement

Historically, African American families have had a different relationship to capitalist political economies than have middle-class, white families (Cox 1948; Davis 1981; Hogan 1984). This difference provides a context for understanding black women's work in kin networks and in the wider political economy (Mullings 1986b).

During the transition from competitive to industrial capitalism, which characterized the early nineteenth century, white urban middle-class families adopted self-contained nuclear household units. In contrast, the majority of African American families were enslaved. These families had great difficulty maintaining private households in public spheres controlled by white slave-owners. Enslaved Africans were property (Burnham 1987), and they resisted the dehumanizing effects of slavery by recreating African notions of family as extended kin units (Web 1978; Sobel 1979). Bloodlines carefully monitored in West Africa were replaced by a notion of "blood" whereby enslaved Africans thought of themselves as part of an extended family/community consisting of their black "brothers" and "sisters" (Gutman 1976). The entire slave community/family stood in opposition to the public sphere of a capitalist political economy controlled by elite white men. For black women the domestic sphere encompassed a broad range of kin and community relations beyond the nuclear family household. The line separating the black community from whites served as a more accurate boundary delineating public and private spheres for African Americans than that separating black households from the surrounding black community.

Before enslavement, African women combined work and family without seeing a conflict between the two. In West African societies, women routinely joined child care with their contributions to pre-capitalist political economics (Schildkrout 1983; Ware 1983). In agricultural societies dependent on female farmers, children accompanied their mothers to the fields. Women entrepreneurs took their children with them when conducting business in the marketplace. When old enough, children contributed to family-based production by caring for siblings, running errands, and generally helping out. Working did not detract from West African women's mothering. Instead, being economically productive and contributing to the family-based economy was an integral part of motherhood (Sudarkasa 1981a).

For enslaved African women in the United States, this basic relationship linking work and motherhood was retained, but with two fundamental changes. First, whereas African women worked on behalf of their families and children, enslaved African American women's labor benefited their owners. Second, the nature of work performed was altered. Women did not retain authority over their time, technology, work mates, or type or amount of work they performed. In essence, the fundamental shift economically exploited politically powerless units of labor.

Gender roles were similarly shaped under slavery. Black women generally performed the same work as men. This enabled them to continue West African traditions whereby women were not limited to devalued domestic labor (Davis 1981; Jones 1985; D. White 1985). This similarity of work coupled with the harshness of racial oppression for all African Americans suggests that a general equality existed between black men and women (Webber 1978; Davis 1981).

Unlike African political economies, where women's labor benefited their lineage group and their children, under slavery neither men nor women got to keep what they produced. Slavery also established the racial division of labor whereby African Americans were relegated to dirty, manual, nonintellectual jobs. As Maria Stewart pointed out, "the Americans have practiced nothing but head-work these 200 years, and we have done their drudgery. And it is now high time for us to imitate their examples, and practice head-work too, and keep what we have got, and get what we can" (Richardson 1987, 38). In spite of slavery's burdens, African Americans did not perceive work as the problem but, rather, the exploitation inherent in the work they performed. A saying among enslaved Africans, "it's a poor dog that won't wag its own tail," alluded to popular perceptions among blacks that whites were lazy and did not value work as much as African Americans themselves.

Black women's work affected the organization of child care. Perceptions of motherhood and child care as an occupation in the home comparable to male occupations in the public sector popularized by the cult of domesticity never became widespread among the majority of African women (Mullings 1986b). Instead, women organized communal child care arrangements such that a few women were responsible for caring for all children too young to work, and women as a group felt accountable for one another's children (D. White 1985).

African American women's experiences as mothers have been shaped by the dominant group's efforts to harness black women's sexuality and fertility to a system of capitalist exploitation. Efforts to control black women's reproduction were important to the maintenance of the race, class, and gender inequality characterizing the slave order in at least three ways. First, the biological notions of race underpinning the racial subordination of the slave system required so-called racial purity in order to be effective. Since children followed the condition of their mothers, children born of enslaved black women were slaves. Forbidding black men to have sexual relations with white women eliminated the possibility that children of African descent would be born to white mothers. Motherhood and racism were symbolically intertwined, and controlling the sexuality and fertility of both African American and white women was essential in reproduction notions of "race" as a social and cultural entity (King 1973; Hoch 1970; Mosse 1985).

Second, motherhood as an institution occupies a special place in transmitting values to children about their proper place. On one hand, a mother can foster her children's oppression if she teaches them to believe in their own inferiority. As noted African American educator Carter G. Woodson contends, "if you can control a man's thinking you do not have to worry about his actions" (1933, 84). On the other hand, the relationship between mothers and children can serve as a private sphere in which cultures of resistance and everyday forms of resistance are learned (Caulfield 1974; Scott 1985). When black slave mothers taught their children to trust their own self-definition and value themselves, they offered a powerful tool for resisting oppression.

Finally, controlling black women's reproduction was essential to the creation and perpetuation of capitalist class relations. Slavery benefited certain segments of the population by economically exploiting others. As black feminist intellectual Frances Ellen Watkins-Harper argued, "How can we paper our appetites upon luxuries drawn from reluctant fingers. Oh, could slavery exist long if it did not sit on a commercial throne?" (Sterling 1984, 160). Under such a system in which the control of property is fundamental, enslaved African women were valuable commodities. Slaveowners controlled black women's labor and commodified black women's bodies as units of capital. Moreover, as mothers, black women's fertility produced the children who increased their owners' property and labor force (Davis 1981; Burnham 1987).

Efforts to control black women's sexuality were tied directly to slaveowners' efforts to increase the fertility of their female slaves. Historian Deborah

Gray White (1985) claims that "slave masters wanted adolescent girls to have children, and to this end they practiced a passive, though insidious kind of breeding" (98). Techniques such as assigning pregnant women lighter workloads, giving pregnant women more attention and rations, and rewarding prolific women with bonuses were all employed to increase black women's fertility. Punitive measures were also used. Infertile women could expect to be treated "like barren sows and be passed from one unsuspecting buyer to the next" (D. White 1985, 101).

The relative security that often accompanied motherhood served to reinforce its importance. Childbearing was a way for enslaved black women to anchor themselves in a given location for an extended period and to maintain enduring relationships with husbands, family, and friends. Given the short life expectancy of slave women—33.6 years—and the high mortality rates of black children—from 1850 to 1860 fewer than two of three black children survived to the age of ten—the enslaved woman's ability to bear many healthy children was often the critical element in the length and stability of slave marriages (Giddings 1984). Similarly, the refusal of women to bear children and cases of black infanticide can be interpreted as acts of resistance (Hines and Wittenstein 1981).

Deborah Gray White contends that slaveholders' efforts to increase fertility elevated motherhood over marriage and fostered the continued centrality of women in African American family networks: "Relationships between mother and child . . . superseded those between husband and wife. Slaveholder practice encouraged the primacy of the mother–child relationship, and in the mores of the slave community motherhood ranked above marriage. . . . Women in their roles as mothers were the central figures in the nuclear slave family" (1985, 159).

Black women's centrality in black family networks should not be confused with matriarchal or female-dominated family units (Collins 1989). The conceptual assumption of the matriarchy thesis is that someone must "rule" the household in order for it to function effectively. Neither black men nor black women ruled black family networks (Davis 1981; Burnham 1987). Rather, African Americans' relationship to the slave political economy made it unlikely that either patriarchal or matriarchal domination could take root.

The Transition to "Free" Labor

For African Americans the period between emancipation and subsequent migrations to southern and northern cities was characterized by two distinct models of community. Each offered a different version of the connections between work and family. Within dominant white society the model of community reflected capitalist market economies of competitive, industrial, and monopoly capitalism (Baran and Sweezy 1966; Braverman 1974). Firmly rooted in an exchange-based marketplace with its accompanying assumptions of rational economic decision-making and white male control of the marketplace, this model of community stresses the rights of individuals to make decisions in their own self-interest, regardless of the impact on the larger society. Composed of a collection of unequal individuals who compete for greater shares of money as the medium of exchange, this model of community legitimates relations of domination either by denying they exist or by treating them as inevitable but unimportant (Hartsock 1983b).

While enslaved, African Americans paradoxically were central to yet existed largely outside the market economy and its version of community. Upon emancipation, blacks became wage laborers and were thrust into these exchange relationships in which individual gain was placed ahead of collective good. Anna Julia Cooper describes this larger setting in which African Americans found themselves as the Accumulative Period, and challenged its basic assumptions about community and women's role in it:

> At the most trying time of what we have called the Accumulation Period, when internecine war, originated through man's love of gain and his determination to subordinate national interests and black men's rights alike to the considerations of personal profit and loss, was drenching our country with its own best blood, who shall recount the name and fame of the women on both sides of the senseless strife. (Cooper 1892)

Cooper's ideas are key in that they not only link racism, economic exploitation after emancipation, and the violence needed to maintain both, but they clearly label the public sphere and its community as a male-defined arena. By asking, "who shall recount the name and fame of the women?" she questions the role of gender in structuring women's subordination generally, and black women's work and family roles in particular.

During this period, revitalized political and economic oppression of African Americans in the South influenced black actions and ideas about family and community. Notions such as equating family with extended family, of treating community as family, and of seeing dealings with whites as elements of public discourse and dealings with blacks as part of family business endured. As a result, African American definitions of community were distinct from public, market-driven, exchange-based community models. Whether adhered to as a remnant of the African past or responding to the exigencies of political and economic disenfranchisement in the post-Reconstruction South, black communities as places of collective effort and will stood in contrast to the public, market-driven, exchange-based dominant political economy in which they were situated (Bethel 1981).

For African American women the issue was less one of economic equality with husbands and more the adequacy of overall family income. Denying black men a family wage meant that women continued working and that motherhood as a privatized, female "occupation" never predominated in the African American communities (Dill 1988b). Communal child care within extended families continued (Martin and Martin 1978; Jones 1985). Segregation fostered rigid boundaries between African Americans and whites such that the public/private oppositional dichotomy characterizing racial discourse hardened while fluid boundaries among black households in the black family/community continued. Within African American communities social class-specific gender ideology developed during this period (Higginbotham 1989).

For at least seventy-five years after emancipation, the vast majority of black families worked in southern agriculture (Jones 1985). Black women's work in the public, male-defined sphere of exchange relations took two types. The majority of black women worked in the fields, with the male head of the extended family unit receiving the wages earned by the family unit. Such work was hard and exhausting and represented little change from the work done by enslaved African American women. Sara Brooks began full-time work in the fields at age eleven and remembers, "we never was lazy cause we used to really work. We used to work like mens. Oh, fight sometimes, fuss sometime, but worked on" (Simonsen 1986, 39).

The other primary occupation for black women's wage labor was domestic work. Young black girls were prepared by their families for domestic work. An eighty-seven-year-old North Carolina woman remembers her training: "No girl I know wasn't trained for work out by ten. You washed, watched, and whipped somebody the day you stopped crawling. From the time a girl can stand, she's being made to work" (Clark-Lewis 1985, 7). Such work was low paid and exposed black girls and women to the constant threat of sexual harassment. One African American woman describes the lack of protection for black women domestic workers in the South: "I remember . . . I lost my place because I refused to let the madam's husband kiss me . . . when my husband went to the man who had insulted me, the man cursed him, and slapped him and—had him arrested!" (Lerner 1972, 155–56). Even though she testified in court, her husband was fined $25.00 and was told by the presiding judge, "this court will never take the word of a nigger against the word of a white man" (156).

The sexual harassment of African American women by white men contributed to images of black women as fair game for all men. The difficulty of the environment prompted one southern black woman to remonstrate:

> We poor colored women wage earners in the south are fighting a terrible battle. . . . On the one hand, we are assailed by white men, and on the other hand, we are assailed by black men, who should be our natural protectors; and, whether in the cook kitchen, at the washtub, over the sewing machine, behind the baby carriage, or at the ironing board, we are little more than pack horses, beasts of burden, slaves! (Lerner 1972, 157)

African American women who were the wives and daughters of able-bodied men withdrew from both field and domestic service in order to concentrate on domestic duties in their own homes. In doing so, they were "severely criticized by whites for removing themselves from field labor because they were seen to be aspiring to a model of womanhood that was inappropriate to them" (Dill 1988b, 422). Black women wanted to withdraw from the labor force, not to duplicate middle-class white women's cult of domesticity but, rather, to strengthen the political and economic position of their families. Their actions can be seen as a sustained effort to remove themselves from the exploited labor force in order to return the value of their labor to their families and to find relief from the sexual harassment they endured in the marketplace. While many women tried to leave the paid labor force, the limited opportunities available to African American men made it virtually impossible for the majority of black families to survive on black male wages alone. Even though she was offered work only as a maid, Elsa Barkley Brown's college-educated mother was fortunate. From Brown's standpoint, her mother's "decision to be a wife and mother first in a world which defined black women in so many other ways, the decision to make her family the most important priority, was an act of resistance" (1986, 11). Far too many black women could not make this choice—they continued to work, and their work profoundly affected African

American family life, communities, and the women themselves (Bethel 1981; Jones 1985).

Urbanization and Domestic Work

Black women's move to southern and northern cities in the early 1900s continued virtually unabated until after World War II. Migration stimulated substantial shifts in black women's labor market activities as well as changes in African American family patterns and community organization. While racial segregation delimited African Americans from white physical space, gender relations within black communities delimited female from male space. Male space included the streets, barber shops, and pool halls; female arenas consisted of households and churches. "Women, who blurred the physical boundaries of gender, did so at the jeopardy of respectability within their communities (Higginbotham 1989, 59).

Black women migrants encouraged urban labor markets segmented along lines of race and gender (Gordon et al. 1982). For the vast majority of African American women, urbanization meant migration out of agricultural work and into domestic work. In 1910, 38.5 percent of all employed black women were domestic workers. By 1940, that number had risen to 59.9 percent (Higginbotham 1983).

Black women's confinement in domestic service has attracted the attention of black women intellectuals who have investigated key dimensions of this special occupational niche. Unlike the life histories of the countless enslaved and emancipated black women who worked in the fields, black feminist research on black domestic workers allows a closer view both of how African American women perceived their work and of the actions they undertook to resist its exploitative and dehumanizing aspects.

One benefit of urbanization was that it allowed black domestic workers to shift the conditions of their work from that of live-in servant to day work. A common migration pattern was for black girls to train for domestic work in the South by doing chores and taking care of siblings and then go to cities of the North around age ten to assist working relatives (Clark-Lewis 1985). At first girls might take care of their relatives' children. Although it often took years to accomplish, young women eventually found employment in day work. Moving to a larger marketplace where domestics could leave employers when demands were inappropriate allowed African American women to make the transition from live-in to day work. One eighty-three-year-old respondent in Elizabeth Clark-Lewis's study recounts how she viewed this shift as a move toward better working conditions: "The living-in jobs just kept you running; never stopped. Day or night you'd be getting something for somebody. You'd serve them. It was never a minute's peace. . . . But, when I went out days on my jobs, I'd get my work done and be gone. I guess that's it. This work had a end" (Clark-Lewis 1985, 1).

While an improvement, the shift to day work maintained some of the more negative features of the employer/employee relationship. In spite of their removal from the particular form control took in the South, domestic workers in the northern cities were economically exploited even under the best of circumstances. At its worst, domestic work approximated conditions the women left behind in the South. Florence Rice describes how the 1930s New York City "Bronx slave market" operated, where women stood in an assigned spot and waited for employers to drive by and offer them day work: "I always remember my domestic days. Some of the women, when they didn't want to pay, they'd accuse you of stealing . . . it was like intimidation" (Lerner 1972, 275). Although sexual harassment was less pervasive, it too remained a problem. Ms. Rice remembers another male employer who "picked me up and said his wife was ill and then when I got there his wife wasn't there and he wanted to have an affair" (275).

Judith Rollins (1985) contends that what makes domestic work more "profoundly exploitative than other comparable occupations" is the precise element that makes it unique: the personal relationship between employer and employee. Rollins reports that employers do not rank work performance as their highest priority in evaluating domestic workers. Rather, the "personality of the worker and the kinds of relationships employers were able to establish with them were as or more important considerations" (156).

Deference mattered, and those women who were submissive or who most successfully played the role of obedient servant were most highly valued by their employers, regardless of the quality of the work performed. When domestic worker Hannah Nelson reports, "most people who have worked in service have to learn to talk at great length about nothing," she identified the roles domestics must play in order to satisfy their employers' perceptions of a good black domestic. She continues, "I never have been very good at that, so I don't speak, normally. . . . Some people I have worked for think I am slow-witted because I talk very little on the job" (Gwaltney 1980, 6).

Employers used a variety of means to structure domestic work's power relationship and solicit the deference behavior they desired in their domestic employees. Techniques in linguistic deference included addressing domestics by their first names, calling them "girls," and requiring that the domestic call the employer "Ma'am." Employers routinely questioned domestics about their lifestyle, questions they would hesitate to ask members of their own social circle. Gifts of used clothes and other household items highlighted the economic inequality separating domestic and employer. Employers used domestics as confidantes, another behavior that reinforced the notion that domestics were outsiders (Rollins 1985).

Physical markers reinforced the deference relationship. One technique was to require that domestics wear uniforms. One respondent in Clark-Lewis's study explains why her employers liked uniforms: "Them uniforms just seemed to make them know you was theirs. Some say you wore them to show different jobs you was doing. This in gray, other serving in black. But mostly them things just showed you was always at they beck and call. Really tha's all them things means!" (Clark-Lewis 1985, 16). The use of space was also a major device in structuring deference behaviors. Domestics were confined to one area of the house, usually the kitchen, and were expected to make themselves invisible when caught in other areas of the house by members of the employer's family. Judith Rollins recounts her reactions to being objectified in this fashion, to being treated as invisible while her employers had a conversation around her:

> It was this aspect of servitude I found to be one of the strongest affronts to my dignity as a human being. To Mrs. Thomas and her son, I became invisible; their conversation was private with me, the black servant, in the room, as it would have been with no one in the room. . . . These gestures of ignoring my presence were not, I think, intended as insults; they were expressions of the employer's ability to annihilate the humanness and even, at times, the very existence of me, a servant and a black woman. (Rollins 1985, 209)

Some African American women were fortunate enough to locate work in manufacturing. In the South, black women entered tobacco factories, cotton mills, and flower manufacturing. Some of the dirtiest jobs in these industries were offered to African American women. In the cotton mills black women were employed as common laborers in the yards, as waste gathers, and as scrubbers of machinery (Glenn 1985). With northern migration, some black women entered factory employment, primarily in steam laundries and the rest in nonmechanical jobs as sweepers, cleaners, and ragpickers. Regardless of their location, African American women faced discrimination (Terborg-Penn 1985). For example, Luanna Cooper, an employee for the Winston Leaf To-bacco Storage Company, described her reactions to the effort to organize seg-regated unions in her plant: "They're trying to have jimcrow unions. But I'm telling you jimcrow unions aren't good. They wanted me to join. I told them 'I get jimcrow free. I won't pay for that' " (Lerner 1972, 268).

The shift to day work among domestic workers and the incorporation of some black women into the manufacturing sector paralleled changes in African American family and community structures. Even though the hours were long and the pay low in the majority of occupations held by black women, they did have more time to devote to their families and communities than that available to live-in domestic workers. During the first wave of urbanization, African Americans recreated the types of communities they had known in their south-ern rural communities (Gutman 1976). De facto segregation in housing and in the labor market meant that African Americans continued to live in self-contained communities even after migration to northern cities. As a result, the public/private split separating black communities from what were frequently hostile white neighborhoods remained a salient feature framing black women's work and family relationships. The cooperation networks among African American women, which were created under slavery and sustained in the rural South, endured. Black women domestic workers who rode buses together shared vital information essential to their survival as domestic workers and, on occasion, attempted unionization (Terborg-Penn 1985). Neighbors took care of one another's children, and churches typically formed the core of many black women's community activities (Clark-Lewis 1985; Dill 1988a).

Black Women's Work and the Post-World War II Political Economy

As long as African Americans lived in self-contained, segregated communities, Afrocentric notions of family and community endured. In the mid-twentieth century, the post-World War II period brought a shift in this relationship be-tween work and family (Collins 1986a; Brewer 1988).

Dramatic changes in the post-World War II political economy of African American communities have been stimulated by several factors. One is the restructuring of urban labor markets that has accompanied such areas as job export to nonunionized American locations and foreign markets, job deskilling, the shift from manufacturing to service occupations, and job creation in suburban communities (Baran and Sweezy 1966; Braverman 1974; Gordon et al., 1982; Wilson 1987). Another is the increasing economic marginalization of African Americans in urban economies, as evidenced in black unemployment rates double those of whites, and by the increasing dependence of black households on Aid to Families with Dependent Children (Hogan 1984; Wilson 1987). Changing attitudes in wider society toward the normative nuclear family as expressed in higher divorce rates, more single-parent households, and a rising number of out-of-wedlock births for all groups in the society represent yet another factor (Burnham 1985; Collins 1986a; Claude 1986; Wilson 1987; Brewer 1988).

As a result of these factors, the black community has become more stratified by social class.[2] A comfortable yet vulnerable black middle class and a sizable working class segmented by the ability to find steady, well-paying work has emerged. Best estimates place between 25 and 30 percent of African American families in the middle class (Pinkney 1984, 102). This leaves approximately 70 to 75 percent of African Americans in the working class. The one-third of African Americans identified as living below the official poverty line represents the most economically marginalized segment of the black working class. Each social class has a distinctive relationship to the advanced capitalist welfare state. These relationships frame the changing nature of work and family for African American women.

These dramatic changes in how racial inequality has been structured should not obscure the overall stability of racial oppression. In 1987, the median black family income of $18,100 represented 56 percent of the median white income of $32,270 (U.S. Department of Commerce 1989). In 1985, approximately one of every three African Americans lived below the official poverty line, as compared with one of every ten whites (U.S. Department of Commerce 1986). These measures of inequality remain constant in spite of emerging social class differences.

2. The definition of social class that I use in this section derives from class conflict models, especially those based in labor market segmentation theory (Braverman 1974; Gordon et al. 1982; Vanneman and Cannon 1987). For an extended discussion of labor market segmentation and black social class structure, see Collins (1986a).

Historically, the classic pattern of employment for African American men and women has been higher-paying yet less secure work for black men as contrasting with lower-paying, more plentiful work for black women. For example, black men employed in low-skilled manufacturing occupations typically receive higher wages than their wives working in domestic service do. But, black men are more vulnerable to layoffs, and although they make higher wages, few guarantees exist that their wages will be consistently available to their families. In contrast, black women receive substantially lower wages, but can count on receiving them. This classic pattern of exploitation, differentiated by gender, has often been misrepresented in arguments suggesting that black women or black men have a labor market "advantage" over the other. What these approaches fail to realize is that both African American women and men have been disadvantaged in the labor market, with gender differences in employment structuring distinctive patterns of economic vulnerability.

Increased access to managerial and professional positions enabled sizable numbers of African American individuals and families to move into the middle class. In the post-World War II political economy, owners of capital and labor, the two groups originally forwarded in class conflict theories, have been joined by a new middle class. Members of the new middle class work for owners of productive property just as blue-collar workers do, but they earn generous incomes and enjoy substantial prestige. This new middle class is not merely an arbitrary range along a status scale—it is a genuine class with interests in opposition to those of the working class (Vanneman and Cannon 1987).

The emerging black middle class occupies a contradictory location in the American political economy. As is the case for their white counterparts, being middle class requires black professionals and managers to enter into specific social relations with owners of capital and with workers. In particular, the middle class dominates labor and is itself subordinate to capital. It is this simultaneous dominance and subordination that puts it in the "middle" (Vanneman and Cannon 1987, 57). Like owners, it exercises economic control. Professionals and managers also exercise political controls over the conditions of their own work and that of other workers. Finally, members of the new middle class exercise ideological control of knowledge: they are the planners of work and framers of society's ideas.

On all three dimensions of middle-class power—economic, political, and ideological—the black middle class differs from its white counterpart. Persistent racial discrimination means that black middle-class families are less economically secure than members of the white middle class (Pinkney 1984). Members of the black middle class, most of whom became middle class through social mobility from working-class origins, may express more ambivalence concerning their function as controllers of working-class blacks. While some aspire to manage working-class blacks, others aim to liberate them from racial oppression and poverty. Similarly, though many middle-class blacks defend the ideological constructions of the dominant group, others, such as many black feminist intellectuals, use their minds to challenge race, gender, and class ideologies.

When the traditional gender differences in black employment patterns are combined with the economic, political, and ideological vulnerability of the black middle class caused by race, some interesting patterns emerge for African American women. Black women and men both share the employment vulnerability of being more excluded than whites from these occupations. Fewer black men have such positions, but when they do get them they acquire higher-paying, higher-status positions. In contrast, greater numbers of black women than men work in professional and managerial positions, but in lower-paying, lower-status occupations.

For black women, most of whom are not born into the black middle class, but who have recently arrived in it through social class mobility, dealing with the demands of work and family can be unsettling (Dumas 1980). Consider the case of Leanie McClain, a black woman journalist raised in segregated Chicago public housing who eventually became a feature writer for a major Chicago newspaper (McCllaurin-Allen 1989). In a widely cited piece entitled "The Middle Class Black's Burden," Ms. McClain lamented, "I am not comfortably middle class; I am not uncomfortably middle class. I have made it, but where? (186, 13). A substantial source of Ms. McClain's frustration stemmed from her marginal status in a range of settings. She notes, "my life abounds in incongruities . . . sometimes when I wait at the bus stop with my attaché case, I meet my aunt getting off the bus with other cleaning ladies on their way to do my neighbor's floors" (13). No wonder Ms. McClain felt compelled to say, "I am a member of the black middle class who has had it with being patted on the head by white hands and slapped in the face by black hands for my success" (12).

Black women's employment patterns may have significant effects on black middle-class families, especially single-parent households. The smaller number of black men than black women in professional and managerial positions represents one important issue facing black heterosexual women interested in interracial marriage. This sex ratio imbalance may contribute to an increase in female-headed households among middle-class black women. Given that separated and divorced black women professionals are much less likely to remarry than their white counterparts, higher rates of separation and divorce may become a special problem for married black women professionals. Other factors may also influence the growth of single-parent households among black professional women. One issue concerns whether African American women will choose to become mothers when faced with the absence of a suitable marital partner. Another factor is the likely decline in marriages between black women in professional and managerial jobs and black men in other segments of the labor market. Another factor may be an increasing tendency by both black heterosexual women and black lesbians to head their own households and create alternative family arrangements.

Black working-class families are similarly affected by changing employment patterns. Black women are heavily concentrated in clerical work (50.1 percent), whereas black men are clustered in factory work (43.2 percent). One of every four African American women and men in this sector is a skilled craft worker. The projected patterns of growth for these occupational categories are quite different. Factory work is declining, a trend that is especially problematic for black men. In contrast, black women clerical workers are in a growing occupational area.

Studies examining the interaction of race and gender in structuring the work experiences of working-class black women are sorely needed. Clerical work and other administrative support positions often involve different relationships reminiscent of Judith Rollins' (1985) study of black domestic workers. Consider Alice Walker's experiences when trying to visit Dessie Woods, a black woman incarcerated in the Georgia penal system for defending herself against a white rapist. Walker describes her arrival at the prison, where she was turned away, not by white male guards, but by a black woman very much like herself:

> We look at each other hard. And I "recognize" her, too. She is very black and her neck is stiff and her countenance has been softened by the blows. All day long, while her children are supported by earnings here, she sits isolated in this tiny glass entranceway, surrounded by white people who have hired her, as they always have, to do their dirty work for them. It is no accident that she is in this prison, too. (Walker 1988, 23)

The disappearance of well-paying manufacturing jobs for black working-class men suggests that the dual-income, working-class family is becoming less of an option for young African Americans. The alternative open to past generations of blacks—intact marriages based on reasonably steady, adequately paid jobs for black men and reliable yet lesser-paid jobs for black women—is less available in the advanced capitalist welfare state.

While black working-class women, especially those in clerical work, are more likely to find steady employment, the income of black working-class wives cannot compensate for the loss of black men's incomes. Black working-class families may experience an increase in female-headed households, but for very different reasons from those stimulating a similar trend in the black middle class. Aggravated by black men's inability to find well-paying work, rates of separation and divorce may increase, or young blacks may not be able to marry in the first place. For many black working-class families, the economic vulnerability of black men is one fundamental factor spurring increasing poverty among black working-class women (Burnham 1985; Claude 1986).

Low-income black families form the economically marginalized, vulnerable segment of the black working class. Labor market trends as well as changes in federal policies toward the poor have affected this group (Zinn 1989). Ironically, occupational gender differences between black women and black men are becoming less pronounced among poor African Americans. In 1980, 32 percent of black women and 29 percent of black men worked in jobs characterized by low wages, job instability, and poor working conditions. These jobs are growing rapidly, with an increasing need for cooks, waitresses, waiters, laundry workers, health aides, and domestic servants to serve the needs of affluent middle-class families. While plentiful, many of these jobs are in neighborhoods far from the inner-city communities where poor black women live. Moreover, few of these jobs offer the wage, stability, or advancement potential of disappearing manufacturing jobs.

The work performed by employed poor black women parallels their traditional duties in domestic service. In contrast to prior eras, when domestic service was confined to private households, contemporary cooking, cleaning, and child care have been routinized and decentralized in the growing service industry of fast food, cleaning services, and day care centers. Black women perform similar work, but in different settings. The location may have changed, but the treatment of black women parallels relationships of dominance reminiscent of private domestic work. Mabel Lincoln, an inner-city resident, describes how the world looks at her as a working woman:

> If you are a women slinging somebody's hash and busting somebody else's suds or doing whatsoever you might do to keep yourself from being a tramp or a willing slave, you will be called out of your name and asked out of your clothes. In this world most people will take whatever they think you can give. It don't matter whether they want it or nor, whether they need it or not, or how wrong it is for them to ask for it. (Gwaltney, 1980, 68)

Many black women turn to the informal labor market and to government transfer payments to avoid being called out of their names and asked out of their clothes. In 1980, approximately one-half of all black women age sixteen and over were not in the formal labor force. School attendance, child care responsibilities, retirement, and poor health are all factors affecting non-working women (McGhee 1984). A considerable proportion supported themselves through varying combinations of low-wage jobs and government transfer payments such as Social Security and Aid to Families with Dependent Children, payments that reduced their dependence on the informal economy.

The employment vulnerability of working-class African Americans in the post–World War II political economy, the relative employment equality of poor black women and men, and the gender-specific patterns of dependence on the informal economy all have substantial implications for female-headed households. That such households are increasing in low-income black communities (Pinkney 1984) suggests that as much as 70 percent of low-income black households are headed by women) is commonly accepted. But the more alarming trend is the increasing poverty of African American women and children living in such households. In 1985, 50 percent of black families headed by women were below the official poverty line (U.S. Department of Commerce 1986). The situation is more extreme for young African American women. In 1986, 86 percent of families headed by black women between the ages of fifteen and twenty-four lived below the poverty line (Simms 1988).

It is important to distinguish explanations of the growing poverty of black women that stress their preexisting social class position under advanced capitalism (see, for example, Blumberg and Garcia 1977, and Steady 1981, 1987), from explanations such as "feminization of poverty" analyses prominent in feminist thought.[3] As Linda Burnham (1985) points out, "while poverty has not been 'feminized,' it is true that increasing numbers of working class and minority women are sinking into impoverishment. This is a subtle but crucial distinction" (18). Growing poverty among black women is attributable less to being a divorce away from poverty and more to the "transformation of the economy and conservative social policies leading to a dismantling of the welfare state" (Ladner 1986, 14). Effects of welfare policies on poor black women are especially troublesome (Valentine 1981; Pearce 1983; Zinn 1989).

The increase in unmarried black adolescent parents is only one indication of the effects that changes in the broader political economy are having on work and family patterns of poor black women. Rates of adolescent pregnancy are actually *decreasing* among young black women. The real change has been a parallel decrease in marital rates of black adolescents, a decision linked directly to perceived opportunities to support and sustain an independent household (Simms 1988). A sizable proportion of black female-headed households are created by unmarried adolescent mothers. This decline in marital rates, a post-World War II trend that accelerated after 1960, is part of the changes in African American community structures overall (Wilson 1987). The communal child care networks of the slave era, the extended family arrangements of the rural South, the importance of grandmothers in child care, and even the re-creation of black community structures during the first wave of urbanization appear to be eroding for poor black women. These shifts portend major problems for African American women and point to a continuation of black women's oppression, but structured through new institutional arrangements.

The effects of these changes are convincingly demonstrated in a replication study conducted by Ladner and Gourdine (1984) of *Tomorrow's Tomorrow*, Joyce

3. Linda Burnham (1985) suggests that the "idea that poverty is being 'feminized' presents a highly distorted picture of the general dynamics that are at the source of poverty in the United States" (14). By taking an additive approach to oppression, such approaches view poverty as a female problem that is quantitatively intensified for black women. But as part of a racial group that has experienced traditional racial oppression, the social class patterns of black women are quite distinct from those of white women. This class difference is key to understanding the statistical disparity between white and black women, and black women's poverty is not simply an additional measure of women's oppression. Claude (1986), equally critical of the feminization of poverty thesis, points out that black female-headed households are not newly poor and that the origins of poverty for white women are profoundly different from those for black women.

Ladner's (1972) groundbreaking study of black women adolescents. The earlier study examined poor black teenaged women's values toward motherhood and black womanhood. The women in the original study encountered the common experiences of urban poverty—they became mothers quite young, lived in substandard housing, attended inferior schools, and generally had to grow up quickly in order to survive. But in spite of the harshness of their environments, the girls in the earlier sample still "had high hopes and dreams that their futures would be positive and productive" (Ladner and Gourdine 1984, 24).

The findings from the replication study are quite different. Ladner and Gourdine maintain that "the assessments the teenagers and their mothers made of the socioeconomic conditions and their futures are harsher and bleaker than a similar population a generation ago" (24). In talking with young grandmothers, all of whom looked older than they were even though the majority were in their thirties and the youngest was twenty-nine, Ladner and Gourdine found that all became single parents through divorce or never being married. The strong black mothers of prior generations of black women were not in evidence. Instead, Ladner and Gourdine found that the grandmothers complained about their own unmet emotional and social needs. They appeared to feel "powerless in coping with the demands made by their children. They comment frequently that their children show them no respect, do not listen to their advice, and place little value on their role as parents" (23).

Unlike prior eras when black women's work as "mules uh de world" more uniformly structured black women's oppression, social class differences increasingly distinguish black women's experiences with race and gender oppression in the post–World War II era. All African American women encounter the common theme of having their work and family experiences shaped by the interlocking nature of race, gender, and class oppression. But this commonality is experienced differently by middle-class women such as Leanita McClain and by working-class women such as Mabel Lincoln. Even more ominous are the potentially negative relationships that may develop among black women of different social classes because of these changes. In prior eras the precarious political and social position of the small numbers of middle-class black women encouraged all African American women. Will middle-class black women continue to value racial solidarity with their working-class sisters, especially those in poverty, or will they use their newly acquired positions to perpetuate inequality of social class? Large numbers of poor black women working as cooks and laundry workers and in other service occupations serve not only white middle-class individuals but black ones as well. Countless others living in inner-city neighborhoods are isolated and encounter few middle-class black women in their daily lives. How will these poor black women view their more privileged sisters?

There has never been a uniformity of experience among African American women, and there is less uniformity today. What remains as a challenge to black feminist scholars is to rearticulate these new and emerging patterns of institutional oppression that differentially affect middle-class and working-class black women. If this rearticulation does not occur, each group may in fact become instrumental in fostering the other's oppression.

CHAPTER 8

African American Family Life in Societal Context

Walter R. Allen

S ince 1965 hundreds of articles and books have been published about African American families. Nevertheless, our understanding of these families continues to be limited. There is a tendency to gloss over important within-group differences; thus monolithic, stereotypic, and inaccurate portrayals of black family life are common. This chapter sets aside debates of black family pathology or viability, focusing instead on these families' essential character. The chapter seeks to understand black families on their own terms, locating them in relevant social, historical, political, and cultural contexts. Key empirical patterns and trends reveal dramatic changes in black family geographic location, headship, quality of life, and socioeconomic status since 1950.

A complex picture is revealed. There has been gradual but steady overall improvement alongside persistent, extreme racial disparities and pronounced class disparities among black families. The proposed Black Family Socio-Ecological Context model specifies and connects institutional, interpersonal environmental, temporal, and cultural facts that shape the essential character of black family life in such a way as to produce characteristics simultaneously shared and idiosyncratic. The model also provides an organized, systematic accounting of research and public policy issues relevant to the study of African American families.

Introduction

During the past thirty years, well over a thousand publications have been added to the research record on African American families in the United States. The

This article was originally published in *Sociological Forum* 10, no. 4 (Dec. 1995) and is reprinted with permission.

count would be much higher if we adopted a broader interpretation of what qualifies as systematic, scientific study of African American families. To do so would require the inclusion of additional sources from a wide range of scholarly, literary, popular, and religious writings (Allen et al. 1986).

Despite the voluminous research on black family life, students of the area are uneasy. This uneasiness is caused by continued references to "the black family." Such references ignore the extensive regional, ethnic, value, and income differences among black families. It is an uneasiness with the theoretical and methodological shoddiness, bordering on suspension of the scientific method, apparent in so many published, widely circulated studies of black families. This uneasiness is bred by entrenched, stereotypic portrayals of black family life that not only persist, but dominate. It is uneasiness due to a frequently demonstrated ignorance concerning the internal dynamics and motives of black family life in this society.

Diversity and Stereotypes in the Study of Black Family Life

Much that is written about black American families is flawed by the tendency of researchers to gloss over within-group differences. While prior research has explored black/white family differences, information is relatively sparse regarding differences among African American families of different incomes, regions, life-cycle stages, and value orientations. As a result, monolithic, stereotypic characterizations of black families abound. The black family headed by a single mother with numerous children and living in a roach-infested tenement is a familiar stereotype. This image has been reinforced in the hallowed halls of universities, on the frenetic sets of movie and television shows, as well as in the august halls of Congress. This stereotype represents but a limited slice of black family life in the United States. It distorts the truth about female-headed households in the black community. Such stereotypes leave the genuinely curious searching for the true face(s) of black family life in this country.

As a society, the United States is comfortable with stereotypes. Indeed, we revel in them. Stereotypes serve a useful function: They help reduce the complexity, nuances, and dilemmas of life to manageable proportions. In this respect, Americans are no different from other people. Generally speaking, humans seek to organize reality by extracting neat categories of meaning(s). Thus, we become accustomed to loose usage of terms charged with unstated implications in order to summarize our day-to-day experiences. Designations such as "liberal," "born-again Christians," "fascists," "feminists," and "racists" are commonplace in our daily discourse. Rarely, in the next breath, are the intricacies of meaning apparent in such terms clarified. Why should they be? We all know what is meant by them . . . or do we?

Race is an area of inquiry in the social and behavioral sciences that is particularly affected by our willingness to accept simplistic, unsupported, and stereotypic statements at face value. Such scientific confusion may have complex explanations, such as the difficulty of disentangling race from culture from history; or the explanations may be more simple, as in the failure to recognize that race is not a perfect predictor of a person's psyche, values, or even experiences. Therefore, for both complex and simple reasons, race continues to be one of the most widely studied, yet most poorly understood, areas of scientific inquiry. As Frazier noted, and DuBois before him, ours is a society obsessed with color. How we think about and interact around race therefore exerts profound influence on the broader realities of individuals, groups, and institutions who are black. These are topics requiring further study.

Predictably, black family studies share many problems with the related area of race relations research. Writers in the area obscure much of the richness, complexity, and subtleties of African American family systems through their use of crude categories, poorly defined concepts, and negative stereotypes. Apparent in the literature are abundant references to "family disorganization," "the underclass," "culture of poverty," and "the black matriarchy." Such terms are offered, picked up, and repeated as if they effectively summarized the reality of black family life in this society. They do not. Unfortunately, with successive repetition, such concepts and the myths that they represent become more palatable and more believable. Equally dissatisfying are terms offered from the "other side" in the ongoing debate over pathology and well-being among black American families. For me, the issue is not wholly reducible to whether black families should be cast as good or bad, positive or negative. Both views pursued to an extreme tamper with reality, become stereotypic, and ultimately dehumanize black families. In the most fundamental sense, life is a collage of good, bad, and indifferent; so, too, is black family life.

I wish to set aside debates over black family wellness or illness. The record of these families in ensuring the survival and development of black Americans on these shores since 1619 is sufficient evidence of their adaptability and viability. Instead, I am concerned with seeing the core of black family life, with exploring their essential character. To this extent, the research question is recast, from "wellness" or "illness" to "is-ness." What are the significant qualities, characteristics, and dimensions of black family life revealed in the research record from 1965 to the present? What environmental and historical conditions determine whether the tenor of black families' experiences is favorable? What are the distinctive features of Afro-American family life? In sum, the need is to understand black families for who and what they are on their own terms.

Definition and Current Statuses of Black Families

Before we undertake to examine the experiences of black American families, we must first decide how best to define these families. Properly, the criteria for definition will vary in accordance with the definition(s) used by authors whose research is being examined. Readers should therefore expect to see, and not be put off by, shifts in the parameters used to define black family life. In some cases, location will be the emphasis, thus defining family as coterminous with household. In other cases, blood ties will be relied on to define the boundaries of a given black family. At still other points, functional ties such as shared emotional support or economic responsibilities will be used to define families. In our thinking, emphasis of shared location over, say, affiliations, as the criterion for defining family relationships, is an *analytic decision*. Such decisions do not alter the fact that black families are defined by complicated overlaps between location, functional relations, shared values, affiliations, and blood ties. As such, black families represent complex systems of relationships that transcend any one of these areas of life. Accommodation to multiple definitions of black family life simply admits the current limitations in social science theory and methods, requiring that researchers restrict their focus to smaller parcels of the family system that they seek to understand. However, a consistent feature across researcher definitions is the primacy assigned to blood ties. At root, black families are seen as institutions whose most enduring relationships are biological.

Systematic examination of significant trends and patterns in black American family life offer useful lessons for evaluating scientific research in the area. The history of black Americans, like any other people, is marked by change. Black Americans have experienced four major transitions over their history, and each left legacies that influence contemporary black family life. The first and most obvious transition involved bringing captured Africans to this country as slaves. For enslaved Africans, this transition involved both gross (for example, the loss of personal freedom) and subtle (for example, exposure to plantation agriculture) redefinitions. Out of these redefinitions was created a new people, African Americans, who represented cultural, social, and yes, biological hybrids. The second major transition in African American history involved emancipation: blacks were freed from slavery. This status change was accompanied, however, by the equally demeaning and restrictive redefinition of blacks as an "untouchable"-like caste group in American society. It is worth noting that, while over time the terms of reference (for example, Negro, Colored, Black, African American, Afrikan) have changed, the degrading caste status of black people has been an immutable constant.

On the heels of this evolution of blacks from slavery to caste status came the geographic, socioeconomic, and cultural transition of black America from a southern, rural, agrarian folk society to a northern, western, and midwestern industrial society. In four generations, or roughly three hundred years, African Americans had moved from agrarian slavery into the industrial and urban heartland of this country. They had been hybrids, combining the heritages of their African and American experiences.

The fourth major transition for African Americans involved the desegregation of U.S. society. This transition was most notably signaled by the string of presidential orders and Supreme Court decisions banning racial segregation in public life (for example, the 1949 presidential order desegregating the military, the 1954 Court decision outlawing segregated public schools). A major impetus for the desegregation of American society was the activities and actors associated with the Civil Rights movement. However, efforts to desegregate U.S. institutional, corporate, and community life at all levels have so far proven to be only partially successful. Vestiges of past disadvantages and persistent discrimination in the present continue to restrict black equality and participation in this society (Farley and Allen 1989; Jaynes and Williams 1989).

The Empirical Picture: Patterns and Trends

Government statistics convey valuable information about the contemporary faces of black families. Such statistics are admittedly limited in what they reveal concerning the nuances of black family life. However, these statistics do provide valuable insight into the broad patterns characteristic of black families currently. By 1991, the black presence in this country had grown to roughly 31 million, representing 13 percent of the total U.S. population and some 7.7 million households. A massive geographic redistribution had also occurred. Since

1945, there has been a sizable drop in the percentages of black residents or born natives of the South (the figure declined from 80 percent to 50 percent); contemporary blacks and their households are overwhelmingly located in urban areas (nearly 85 percent). Recent statistics suggest sizable modifications in historically observed patterns: increasing numbers of blacks will likely return to the South and/or move to suburbs or small towns (U.S. Census Bureau 1992).

The trend toward increased numbers of female-headed black households continued. By 1992, 46 percent of all black households had female heads; in addition, the percentage of dual-parent households had declined to 47 percent (respectively, 18 percent and 77 percent in 1940). Consistent with shifts in family headship were declines in the percentage of black children residing with both parents, from 75 percent in 1960 to 36 percent in 1992. Black childbearing rates continued their steady drop toward replacement levels, reaching an all-time low total fertility rate of an estimated 2.28 children per woman by 1975 (as compared to 2.62 in 1940). Finally, rates of marital dissolution and lifelong singlehood continued to rise among black Americans during the period. The latter statistic certainly reflects, in part, the great imbalance between men and women in the critical marriage and childbearing years (in 1974, there were 100 men for every 116 women aged twenty to fifty-four, not adjusting for men lost from the pool of eligibility for reasons of imprisonment, interracial preferences, homosexuality, and so forth). By 1992, fewer than three of four black women would eventually marry compared to nine out of ten white women (U.S. Census Bureau 1992).

Along with shifts in geography and structure of family life among blacks came important changes in the socioeconomic status. Median family income levels have been rising since 1947. By 1991, the real median income of black families was $33,310 compared to $41,510 for white families. The 1991 real median income for black female-headed households was substantially lower ($11,410). The percentage of black family incomes below the poverty level also dropped steadily, from 41 percent in 1959 to 15 percent in 1974. By 1991, however, the number of black families below the poverty line has risen to 32 percent.

Accompanying changes in family income levels were changes in the educational and occupational attainment of black Americans. Since 1940, the median years of school completed by blacks has doubled to 12.6 percent from 6.3 percent. Some 83 percent of blacks have four or more years of high school, and 11 percent have four or more years of college. Both of the latter figures represent a sixfold increase from 1940 to 1975. In the world of work, contradictory trends are observed. On the one hand, black representation in higher-status occupations has increased dramatically. From 1960 to 1972, the percentage of black workers in white-collar jobs grew from 16 percent to 45 percent. On the other hand, since 1978, black labor force participation rates have declined steadily, down to 70 percent for men and 58 percent for women by the year 1992. Unemployment rates have continued to rise, reaching crisis levels in many black communities across the country (U.S. Census Bureau 1992; Jaynes and Williams 1989).

When attention turns to health, morbidity, and mortality statistics, major improvements are again noted for African Americans. Life expectancies for black men and black women are now respectively 65 and 74 years versus 51 and 55 years in 1940. The infant mortality rate has been cut from 80 to 18 per 1,000 live births, while maternal deaths in childbirth have been reduced eightfold (to fewer than 0.2 per 1,000 live births). Black deaths due to so-called poverty diseases (for example, tuberculosis, venereal disease, cirrhosis of the liver, and contagious disease) have also been drastically curtailed. Offsetting these declines, however, are the rising numbers of blacks contracting and dying from AIDS (Catania et al. 1995, 1497–98). Moreover, the percentage of black families residing in substandard housing dropped from over 50 percent in 1940 to less than 25 percent by 1970 (U.S. Census Bureau 1992).

The picture conveyed by this overview of key government statistics is one of gradual but steady improvement in the life circumstances of black families. During the African American's transition from the rural South into the urban North, significant improvements have occurred in health, education, income, occupation, and housing. Lest a false sense of complacency result, however, it must be pointed out that deprivation and disadvantage are relative concepts. Black families continue to be extremely disadvantaged relative to white families in this society. Now, as earlier in this country's history, the occupational and educational attainment, health status, housing conditions, incomes, and life opportunities of white Americans are far superior to those of their black brethren. When select subcategories of black families (for example, urban, low income, aged, and so forth) are compared to black families in the general case, another level of inequality is revealed. Vast differences in resources, opportunities, and quality of life are often found among black families of different incomes, regions, and headship status (for example, two-parent vs. single-parent).

The aggregate statistics discussed above conceal a complex array of underlying relationships. For this reason, what a particular statistical pattern reveals about the nature of black family life in this society is not always clear. Undoubtedly, poor health, chronic unemployment, teen parenthood, paternal absence, and poverty have potentially negative consequences for black family organization and functions. However, the relative impact of these factors on particular families is mediated by those families' resources, values, and situations. It is thus important to recognize that individual and family characteristics help determine whether certain conditions are positive or negative in their effects, and to what degree. We can now turn our attention to a consideration of the complicated interaction between class and culture in African American families.

Conceptual Issues: Class, Culture, and Black Family Life

Researchers have long debated the importance of economics and culture in the determination of black family organization and dynamics. E. Franklin Frazier, University of Chicago, profoundly influenced our thinking about the interplay of class and race in black family life (1966). Writing in an era of social concern with the consequences of industrialization and rapid urbanization for families, Frazier focuses his attention on black families. He rejects explanations attributing high rates of marital instability, desertion, and illegitimacy among urban black families to innate, biological deficiencies. Rather, Frazier believes these disrupted family patterns were caused by a unique historical experience that left some black Americans ill-prepared to cope with the exigencies of life in modern industrial society. Briefly, he argues that personal and institutional discrimination in society placed blacks at a severe economic disadvantage, with ruinous consequences for their family life. Denied the skills necessary to insure economic viability, black men fell short in the performance of their provider roles, thereby contributing to the breakup of families. Hence, Frazier largely attributes family disorganization among blacks to economic factors, suggesting in the process that as black families achieved higher economic status, their rates of disorganization would drop.

Certain features in Frazier's research make its application to the analysis of contemporary black family life problematic. First is his failure to specify the societal-level processes thought to determine black family patterns. At best, readers are left with vague impressions of such processes and their casual operation.

Second is his consistent denial of legitimacy to aspects of black family life representing departures from normative white family patterns. Third is his implicit attribution of cultural consequences to economic deprivation, such that the idea of continuities in family disorganization is advanced. Black family disorganization, he argues, results from a self-perpetuating tradition of fragmented, pathological interaction within lower-class black urban communities. A culture of poverty, if you will, is said to develop. Frazier basically proposes a socioeconomic/cultural deprivation model for interpretation of black family life, as an alternative to then-current biological deficit models. Unfortunately, Frazier's perspective is sometimes equally injurious to the image and understanding of black family life. By treating racial discrimination in vague historic terms, denying the legitimacy of black cultural forms, and fostering deterministic views of poverty and its consequences, his perspective lends itself to interpretations of black families as pathological. Where black families exhibit signs of disorganization, the tendency is to seek internal rather than external causes, or for that matter, to not question the ethnocentric (and patriarchal) connotations of the family disorganization concept. Vivid illustration of this point is provided by Moynihan's (whose work is closely patterned after Frazier's) grim portrayal of black family life and conclusion:

> At the heart of the deterioration of the fabric of Negro society is the deterioration of the Negro family. It is the fundamental source of weakness in the Negro community at the present time . . . the white family has achieved a high degree of stability and is maintaining that stability. By contrast, the family structure of lower class Negroes is highly unstable and in many urban centers is approaching complete breakdown. (Moynihan 1965, 5)

While criticisms of Moynihan's conclusions were widespread (Allen 1978a, 1978b; Gutman 1976; Staples 1971), perhaps the most penetrating and thought-provoking criticism was offered by Nathan Hare (1976, 5). Hare suggested that Moynihan, by neglecting Frazier's crucial linkage of black family pathologies with racial oppression, "had stood Frazier's analysis on its head and made family instability the source of black occupational and economic degradation." Again, African Americans were blamed for their depressed status in society (as well as for any negative consequences deriving from this status), only in this instance, learned cultural, rather than innate biological, deficiencies were alluded to as causes. Rainwater (1970) and Bernard (1966) essentially concur with Moynihan's conclusions on the issue of culture and disorganization in black family life. They also see an intergenerational "tangle of pathology" founded on historical racial oppression *but* perpetuated by present-day destructive, cultural, and interactional patterns within black family life. However, Rainwater, Bernard, and other adherents (Glazer 1966; Schulz 1969) to the "sociocultural determinism" perspective tend more so than Moynihan to explicitly restrict their generalizations to lower-class, urban blacks.

In contrast to proponents of sociocultural determinism, Billingsley (1968) and others emphasize facets of Frazier's writings dealing with the economic determinates of black family organization. Writing from the socioeconomic determinism perspective, Billingsley and others argue that black families—indeed black communities—are economically dependent on and subordinate to the larger society. Recognizing the inextricable dependence of black families on the society for resources linked to their sustenance and survival, Billingsley expands Frazier's original thesis, linking economics with family organization and function (Billingsley 1992). The result is a typology outlining various structural adjustments that black families make in response to economic imperatives threatening their ability to provide for family member needs. The idea of differential susceptibility to economic and social discrimination is integral to Billingsley's argument; thus, more severe resource limitations cause low-income black families to display higher rates of disorganization than middle- and upper-income black families. To buttress this point, he presents case studies of middle-class black families and their accomplishments. In each instance, the long-term economic stability of these families enhanced their ability to maintain conventional patterns of organization, fulfill member needs, and conform to societal norms. Ladner (1971), Rodman (1971), Scanzoni (1971), and Stack (1974) share this perspective through their stress on the primacy of immediate economic factors over historic cultural factors in the determination of black family organization. This perspective, it should also be noted, views lower-class, urban black family departures—where these occur—from normative family patterns as valid, sensible adaptations to the attendant circumstances of racial and economic oppression.

In summary, two competing perspectives, both derived from Frazier's earlier work, tend to dominate our thinking about relationships obtaining between class, culture, and black family life. Sociocultural determinism attributes disorganization in black family life to what were initially adaptive responses to economic deprivation, but over time have ingrained self-perpetuating cultural traits. By contrast, socioeconomics views black family disorganization as an out-growth of immediate economic deprivation. Quite simply, the question concerns the relative importance of class and culture in the determination of black family organization. Are black family organization patterns most effectively explained in terms of current economic circumstances or persistent cultural values? In my view, it is wisest to assume that where rates of family disorganization (measured by conventional indices, for example, divorce, desertion, illegitimacy, and nonsupport rates) are high among African Americans, it is more often due to economic deprivation than to values that esteem such conditions.

Toward a Comprehensive Model of Black Family Experience

Many problems associated with distortions of African American family life in the literature owe to the inability or refusal of researchers to locate their findings within the settings experienced by these families (Hill et al. 1993; Billingsley 1992). Black family patterns and outcomes are best understood when viewed in larger context. Historically, family researchers have tended to analyze and interpret black family life from perspectives of white middle-class families. The conclusions reached about black families, not surprisingly, have been wrong. Seen outside rather than through the lenses provided by their special circumstances and experiences, African American family values, behaviors, and styles have been alternately misrepresented and misunderstood. Without the perspective that attention to context provides, researchers who study black families have mistakenly portrayed the positive as negative, the patterned as chaotic, and the normative as deviant.

The model proposed here responds to a felt need for systematic approaches that unravel the effects of sociocultural and economic-ecological context on African families in the United States. The necessity of developing models and strategies to assess the consequences of context for family functions and structure is obvious. In many ways, however, research on African American families offers unique opportunities for pursuing such questions. As even casual perusal of the literature will attest, few other areas compare in terms of the sheer magnitude of vehement and prevalent disagreements over data and interpretations. The special circumstances that characterize black family life in the United States, both historically and today, warrant—indeed require—that these families be examined in relation to their environments. Where this is done, one can expect clearer understandings of black family experiences. African American families display an incredible diversity of value orientations, goals, behavioral patterns, structural arrangements, geographic locations, and socioeconomic statuses. This is not to ignore the elements that are common to all African American families—those qualities that join them and distinguish them from other families in the society. Rather, I seek to identify significant factors that combine to define the essential character of the family life of Africans born and raised in the United States.

The model emphasizes two themes, stressing first the black family's socioecological contexts and second, the dynamic nature of black family experiences. These important themes are incorporated into the model through the use of multiple perspectives. The four perspectives used in combination are Social Systems Theory, the Ecological Perspective, the Developmental Conceptual Framework, and the Multiple Social Realities Perspective.

Social Systems Theory and the Ecological Perspective are used jointly to incorporate a focus on family environment. The model derives partially from a social system view of African American family life. While Social Systems Theory as an approach to the study of family life was articulated and proposed much earlier (Parsons 1951; Parsons and Bales, 1955), its most systematic application to the analysis of black families came in 1968. Billingsley argues that the Social Systems approach to the study of black families was necessary "precisely because Negro families have been so conspicuously shaped by social forces in the American environment" (Billingsley 1968). He defines African American families as social systems that contain aggregations of people and their accompanying social roles, bound together by patterns of mutual interaction and interdependence. Billingsley sees these families as embedded in networks of relationships that were both larger and smaller than themselves. Social Systems Theory is useful to the emerging model because it acknowledges the interdependent nature of black family life in this society. It shows that black families—and black individuals—depend on systematic linkages with societal institutions for sustenance and support.

The Human Ecology Perspective is best articulated in the work of Amos Hawley (1950, 1971). This approach encourages the interpretation of family structure and process in relation to environmental constraints. Family organization and functioning are believed to represent adaptations that allow for the maximum exploitation of the physical and social environment. I was not able to identify contemporary research that explicitly applies the Ecological Perspective to the analysis of black family life. However, Bronfenbrenner's (1979) research on child development using an ecological perspective provides a useful illustration. In this work, "the ecological environment is conceived as a set of nested structures, each inside the next" (1979, 3). Bronfenbrenner identifies four levels of ecological environments: (1) the microsystem, a developing person's immediate setting; (2) the mesosystem, settings where the developing person participates; (3) the exosystem, settings that the person may never enter but where events occur to affect his immediate environment; and (4) the macrosystem, patterns of ideology and social organization characteristic of a particular society or culture. He places major stress on the interconnectedness occurring not only within, but also between, the different system levels. The Ecological Perspective's potential value for illuminating black family experiences is embodied in Bronfenbrenner's assertion that:

> by analyzing and comparing the micro-, meso- and exosystems characterizing different social classes, ethnic and religious groups, or entire societies, it becomes possible to describe systematically and to distinguish the ecological properties of these larger social contexts as environments for human development. (1979, 8)

The comprehensive black family model incorporates dynamism by merging elements of the Developmental Conceptual Framework and the Multiple Social Realities Perspective. The Developmental approach provides a framework for viewing family structure and process over the family life cycle. Families are viewed as traversing several developmental stages from their initial organization in marriage to their ultimate disintegration in divorce or physical death. Associated with each stage in the family life cycle are distinct family tasks and resources to accomplish these tasks. Once more, I encountered difficulties identifying examples where this perspective was specifically applied to the analysis of black family life. Nevertheless, this model's emphasis on the changes black families and their members undergo over the family life cycle is drawn from the Developmental Perspective.

The remaining dynamic component of the model comes from the incorporation of the Multiple Social Realities Perspective. The root of this perspective dates back to Durkheim's discussion of social reality's multiple levels. He argues that there are five strata, or levels, apparent in social organization: (1) geographic/demographic bases; (2) institutions and collective behavior; (3) symbols; (4) values, ideas, and ideals; and (5) states of the collective mind (Durkheim 1964). George Gurvitch, the French sociologist, provides a useful modification of Durkheim's ideas for our purposes. Arguing that "in order to integrate the various aspects of social reality, sociological theory must provide a systematic account of the dialectical inter-relations of micro-social processes, groups, classes and societies and their interpretation at different levels of social reality: (1971, xxi), Gurvitch presents an excellent framework with which to approach the analysis of black family dynamics (see Bosserman 1968 for detailed elaboration of Gurvitch's framework). His framework speaks to the whole of social reality, differentiating these among two main axes, one horizontal and the other vertical. The horizontal axis corresponds to types of social frameworks, or categories, of which Gurvitch identifies three: *forms of sociality* (that is, interpersonal interactions), *groups* (that is, institutionalized forms of sociality, such as families or unions), and *global societies* (that is, large combinations of diverse groups, such as nations). The vertical axis corresponds to levels of depth in social reality. Depth is determined by the accessibility of phenomena at each level to direct external observation. The tenth and deepest level is the collective consciousness (that is, shared collective mentality), while the surface or first level is represented by social morphology or ecology (geographic or demographic characteristics). Of paramount importance here is the implication that families will maintain dynamic, ever-changing relationships with agents, groups, and institutions at various levels in the society.

In sum, the proposed comprehensive model of African American family life combines elements from various perspectives. The model is intended to reflect the ecological-environmental contingencies, as well as dynamic processes, of black family realities in this country. Thus, the nature of African American family systemic relations, their responses to environmental factors, how they change over the life course, and their ongoing exchanges with other societal bodies are all emphasized.

The Black Family Social-Ecological Context Model

The Black Family Social-Ecological Context Model seeks to specify and interrelate the variety of institutional, interpersonal, environmental, temporal, and cultural factors that merge to determine the essential character of black family life in this society. While figure 8.3 provides a full-blown presentation of this model, it is important to illustrate systematically the steps through which this final model was derived. Thus two figures, with accompanying discussion, precede our consideration of the model. The model seeks to be widely encom-passing of variables and relationships, from the myriad of factors believed to in-fluence African American family experiences. Although the model certainly fails to achieve this ideal goal, it does effectively outline the major parameters from which truly comprehensive approaches to the study of black family expe-riences can result. Bronfenbrenner qualifies his attempt to develop an encom-passing perspective on child development as follows: "It is necessary to emphasize in this connection that it is neither necessary nor possible to meet all the criteria for ecological research within a single investigation" (1979, 4). In this same spirit, what is presented here is a best approximation of the most comprehensive model possible, given unavoidable limitations in resources and perspective.

A schematic representation of Billingsley's social systems perspective of black family life is provided in figure 8.1. The concentric circles represent the embeddedness of African American families in this society. Individuals exist in the context provided by their families; families exist in the contexts provided by their communities; and communities exist in the contexts provided by the larger society. Central to this model are the twin notions of interdependence and in-terpenetration. In essence, the perspective views black families as subsystems that are embedded in successively larger nested systems. The conceptual model takes this sequential subsystem's view as the fundamental point of departure. The next step was to "telescope" the concentric circles of the social system model outward. Then, the telescoped subsystems are inverted in order to illustrate the increasingly restricted space and spheres of reference encountered as one moves from the wider macro-systems toward the innermost, smaller micro-subsystems (fig. 8.2). Here, the emerging model represents the different levels of social real-ity and demonstrates the fact that these levels are dynamically connected by their interdependence and interpenetration. Finally, figure 8.3 provides an elabora-tion and a systematic presentation of mechanisms and linkages through which the entire system of hypothesized relationships is tied into a codified whole.

The black family Social-Ecological Context Model summarizes the system of relationships believed to determine the nature of black family life in the United States (fig. 8.3). As an approximation of these causal relationships, the model is flawed in many important respects. For example, it suggests that ob-served relationships are unidirectional, when in fact we know that these rela-tionships are bi-directional, mutually influencing. By the same token, in its present form the model lacks the detail and specificity normally associated with

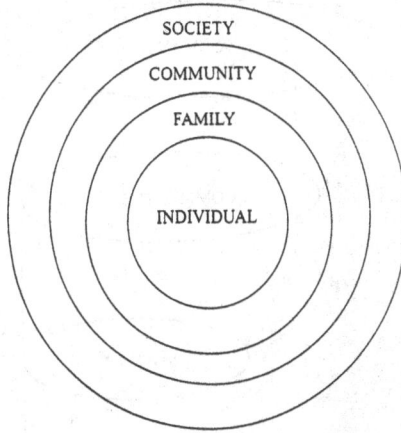

Fig. 8.1 Billingsley's "Social Systems Theory of Black Family Life"

predictive models. In short, the model is at best a gross approximation of complex linkages, direct and indirect relationships, situational factors, and interpersonal exchanges that form the experiential basis of black family life. Nevertheless, this model serves effectively to organize and to orient our thinking about the black family experience along more systematic and encompassing lines. The model also provides a framework within which these complex relationships can be examined.

This model of African American family life represents causal linkages as moving from larger systems down through successively smaller subsystems. Thus, it suggests that societal institutions (dichotomized into those that perform normative functions and those that perform maintenance functions) influence community settings. Further, community settings influence kinship networks, which in turn influence the family units. Finally, individual outcomes are seen as direct products of family units. Clearly, the family realities abstracted in this model are much more involved than is shown. There is considerable interpenetration *between* levels, there are elaborate causal relationships *within* each level, and there is wide variation *across* families in terms of how strongly each of the different causal factors influences observed outcomes. Nevertheless, the general patterns outlined can be expected to assert themselves consistently in the construction of black family outcomes. For all families, and for black families in particular, one expects to find societal institution effects being mediated by community setting, that, in turn, is mediated by dual levels of the family system (kinship network and family unit).

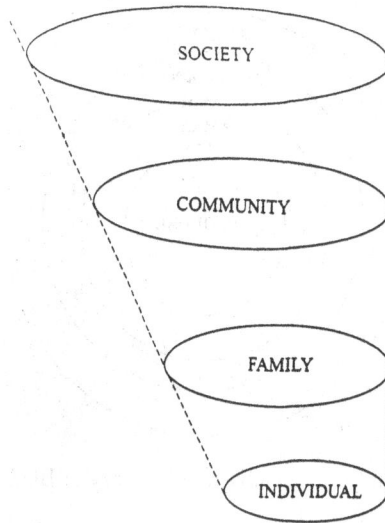

Fig. 8.2 Telescopic Inversion of the Concentric Circles (Systems) in Model

Once all of the linkages expressed (and implied) in this model have been taken into account, several additional determinants of black family experiences would need to be addressed. These additional factors particularly involve the variation one expects, and indeed finds, to be characteristic of black family experiences across different settings represented by economic status, time, space, and value orientation. Dependent on the historical period, economic class, spatial location, and value position of the black families in question, one should expect to see the components in the model combining in distinctive ways and producing different outcomes.

Implications for Social Policy

Black children and their families currently face social and economic crises of such magnitude that their very survival is threatened (Hill et al. 1993). Spiraling inflation, economic restructuring, and changing societal priorities greatly diminish the opportunities and quality of life for black families and their children. Social scientists therefore have a special obligation to offer practical recommendations aimed at alleviating the crises currently experienced by too many black (and minority and poor) families and children in this society. I offer these recommendations not as a disinterested, dispassionate, detached scholar,

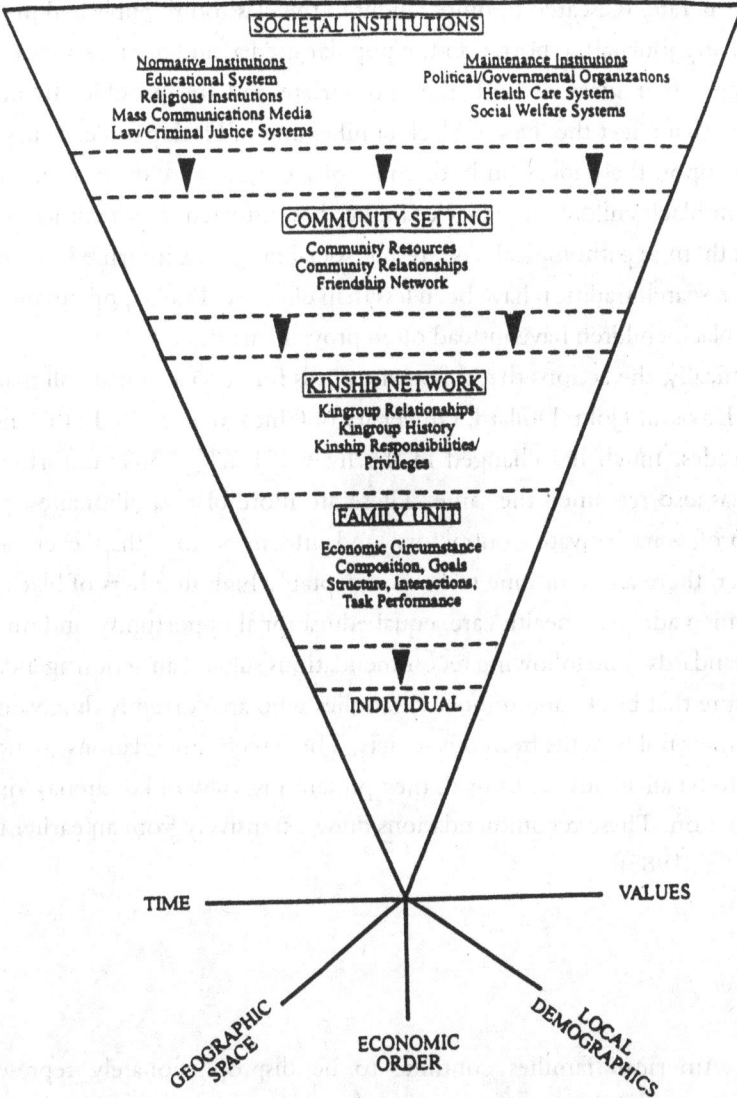

SOCIETAL INSTITUTIONS

Normative Institutions
Educational System
Religious Institutions
Mass Communications Media
Law/Criminal Justice Systems

Maintenance Institutions
Political/Governmental Organizations
Health Care System
Social Welfare Systems

COMMUNITY SETTING

Community Resources
Community Relationships
Friendship Network

KINSHIP NETWORK

Kingroup Relationships
Kingroup History
Kinship Responsibilities/
Privileges

FAMILY UNIT

Economic Circumstance
Composition, Goals
Structure, Interactions,
Task Performance

INDIVIDUAL

TIME — VALUES

GEOGRAPHIC SPACE   ECONOMIC ORDER   LOCAL DEMOGRAPHICS

Fig. 8.3 The "Black Family Ecological Context" Model

but rather as an African American professional who is concerned about the futures of our children and of our communities.

Social and behavioral research findings exert profound influence on public policy, which shapes the lives of an inordinate number of black families and children. Too often, this simple connection is overlooked. It would be naïve to think that research findings have no consequences for how key decision-makers operate. Research findings taught in the classroom, published in popular scholarly journals, reported in the popular media, and discussed over cocktails shape their ideas of both the appropriate and the possible. In making decisions that affect the lives of black families and of black people, policymakers draw upon these ideas (in both conscious and unconscious ways). Past research on black children and black families has distorted their realities and has defined them as pathological. As a result, social programs informed by this pejorative research tradition have been less than effective. Public policies intended to help black children have instead often proven harmful.

Ironically, the actions that this agenda calls for echo a similar call made by Allison Davis and John Dollard, University of Chicago, in 1940. In the ensuing five decades, much has changed in the lives of black people; unfortunately, much has also remained the same. There are more black millionaires, physicians, professors, private contractors, and attorneys now than ever before. However, there also continue to be unacceptably high numbers of black children denied adequate health care, equal educational opportunity, and minimal living standards. The following recommendations suggest an action agenda that will ensure that black (and minority) families who are currently disadvantaged receive their full benefits from this society. These recommendations are not intended to be all-inclusive. Instead, they present my view of key arenas for corrective action. These recommendations draw extensively from an earlier paper (Allen et al. 1985).

Poverty

African American families continue to be disproportionately represented among this country's poor. From generation to generation, blacks—compared to whites—earn less, have fewer capital resources, and are caught in systems of economic deprivation. Poverty conditions the life chances and experiences of black children in a variety of ways. In this society, the basic necessities of life—and any frills—are for sale. Those with limited or nonexistent purchasing power are therefore placed at a great disadvantage. Action is required to improve the economic circumstances of black children and their families. Among the actions to be taken are the following: Institution of an adequate guaranteed family income; institution of a program of full employment involving the public and private sectors; and the equalization of worker salaries and earnings potential.

Health Care

African American children and their families are deprived of adequate health care in this, the world's most medically advanced society. Disproportionate numbers of black children die in infancy, suffer poor nutrition, are not immunized, and die from accidents. Poor access to health care ends many young black lives prematurely and diminishes the quality of existence for others. Action is required to improve the health status and health care access of African American families. The specific needs include the following: alternative financing of medical and health care services to ensure their availability, regardless of ability to pay; expansion of health care outlets, including the location of health care facilities in inner-city areas and increased recruitment/training of African American physicians and health care professionals; and the establishment of comprehensive, preventive health programs emphasizing early and periodic screening/intervention.

Education

Educational attainment has steadily risen among African Americans. There is reason to believe, however, that the qualitative gains in their education have been less pronounced—certainly the economic returns on the whites on most objective measures of achievement are higher, and black college entrance rates are lower. The educational experiences of black children are impaired through their enrollment at schools with larger numbers of underachieving students, more frequent violence, fewer experienced teachers, and substandard facilities. In order to improve the school experience and educational outcomes for black children, there is a need for alternative financial approaches to eliminate current economic inequities between school districts, the development and implementation of individualized remedial/instructional programs, and the implementation of school accountability systems that establish target achievement goals and assess progress toward these goals.

Media

The electronic media in the form of television and radio exert an influence over African American children that at times exceeds the influence of parents. Children spend substantial amounts of time absorbing the content of the most recent television programs and the most popular songs. Yet parents and the black community exert at best minimal influence over the content of these messages. There is ample evidence that media messages are often detrimental to black children's healthy development. The negative effects include advocacy of violence, sexual indiscriminations, and conspicuous consumerism.

Steps must be taken to maximize the positive effects of media and to minimize any negative effects. There is need for parents to regulate their children's media habits and exposure and for the community to monitor media broadcasts so as to encourage positive programming.

Child Care

If the model of a full-time homemaker/wife ever had applicability in African American communities, that time has long since passed. The majority of black mothers who can find jobs are employed outside the home. At the same time, the character of extended family involvement has changed so as to lessen the viability of these as child-care alternatives. The result has been an increased need for child care alternatives. Limited availability of child care options, high costs where these are available, and large numbers of black children in foster care make the provision of child-care services to black families necessary. Recognizing the facts, this requires the following: the expansion of low-cost/community-based child care programs to serve the needs of working parents; the institution of training programs and referral resources for child care providers, and the revision of guidelines regulating black child placement in foster homes or group-care facilities.

These are but a few of the many public policy initiatives to be pursued. If implemented, these social policies and other related initiatives should vastly improve the circumstances of African American families in the United States. To the extent that family circumstances are improved, we can reasonably expect to see improvements in the quality of life and outcomes for African American families. This social policy agenda speaks mostly to the responsibility of government for improving black family life. Beyond this lies another set of initiatives that are more properly the responsibility of the black community.

Responsibilities of the African American Community

African American communities have responsibilities extending to and beyond each of the problem areas above. African Americans must pool and organize resources to ensure that, even where the government and larger society fail to fulfill their commitments, the needs of black children and of black families do not go unmet. Self-help activities based in churches, social clubs, private homes, and available public meeting places must become the rule rather than the exception. This is a call for the creation and expansion of community-based tutorial programs, social welfare cooperatives, and mutual support organizations of the sort commonly found in black communities at an earlier point in our history. It is a terrible irony that African Americans possess economic resources, educational achievements, and technical skills that would place us among the top fifteen countries in the world were we an independent nation. Yet, we mobilize the merest fraction of these vast resources in cooperative activities aimed at self-benefit. We continue to depend far too much on others for the fulfillment of our needs and for the protection of our young.

Conclusion and Implications

Thirty years ago, Daniel Patrick Moynihan issued a call for national action to respond to real threats to African American family life. Citing the declining fraction of households headed by married couples, he forecasted the destruction of African American family and community life unless the government took drastic action. The trends identified by Moynihan have continued; now, nearly half of all black families are headed by a single female. More often than not, these families are mired in poverty and beset by the social problems associated with severe economic deprivation.

Time has proven the trends in African American family life to be much more complex and elusive than Moynihan predicted. In fact, what has happened since 1965 is a hastening of two currents in black family life and the black communities. On the one hand, many black families have sunk deeper into abject poverty. Associated with their impoverishment is their isolation from the societal mainstream. They and their members are increasingly outside the educational system, without jobs, cosigned to high-crime areas, leading dead-end lives, and facing limited futures. On the other hand is the group of black families who were able to escape the cycle of deprivation and destruction forecasted by Moynihan. These families and their members have moved into areas of American life previously off-limits to black people. With their fantastic success and unrestricted access has come unrivaled social and economic mobility.

Hence, two contrasting realities are presented for contemporary African American families. Middle-class blacks require little more than the continued commitment of the society to equal opportunity. Given a fair chance, they are, by virtue of their educational, economic, social, and political resources, able to compete successfully. At the other end of the continuum are the poor urban black families, whose needs are legion. Denied or deprived of gainful employment, adequate educational preparation, and safe, healthy, productive communities, these families find it challenging to maintain even a semblance of normal family life.

The case for national action on behalf of urban poor African American families is indisputable. The nation must mobilize its resources and resolve first to ease and then ultimately to erase the frightening deterioration of viable family and community life among poor urban African Americans. The problems contributing to this deterioration are not entirely—or sizably—of black people's making; therefore, these problems cannot be left solely to black people to solve. Industrial decline, the proliferation of guns and illegal drugs, the failure of the public school system, and massive unemployment loom large in the equation of black family crisis. African American families face problems of epic proportions and, unless these problems are solved, the negative effects will continue to be felt by the whole nation. Black families have historically nurtured and sustained African Americans under extreme conditions, ranging from enslavement to impoverishment (Billingsley 1992). With critical assistance from government and the rest of society, these families will continue to produce citizens who are able to help this society advance.

While the case for concerted action concerning research on African American families is not so sharply drawn, it is nevertheless of weighty importance. The empirical record cries out for correction. Time and time again, it has shown how researchers have distorted black family life and misinformed society about its essential elements. The result of these flawed studies has been to cripple society's understanding of African American families and to hobble attempts to address the problems that confront these families. It is imperative that additional, more sensitive empirical studies of African American families be undertaken. Further, these studies need to employ alternative theoretical, methodological, and ideological approaches that will help clarify the socioecological context within which African American families function and illustrate how these families respond to such constraints. A period of revisionist scholarship is required in order to challenge and to supplant a literature that portrays African

American families as pathological. The strategy will not be to replace this literature with one that says all is well; it will be to show not only the obvious characteristics of the African American family but also its subtle variations. From such research will come reliable information to guide attempts to shape social policy that improves the circumstances of African American families.

Faith is the substance of things hoped for, the evidence of things not seen.—St. Paul

CHAPTER 9

Race, Class, and Educational Opportunity

Edgar G. Epps

This chapter examines some of the trends in educational, sociological, and social psychological research on inequality of educational opportunity for African Americans in the United States. A review of theoretical approaches and methodological developments is followed by an overview of research and theory in selecting substantive areas: social allocation processes in schools (ability grouping, tracking, and so forth), the relationship of poverty to academic achievement, and educational attainment. This chapter concludes with recommendations for future research.

Introduction

The persistence of racism and racial stereotypes has a profound effect on the educational opportunities of African American children. Recent popular books by Cose (1993), Hacker (1992), Kotlowitz (1991), and Kozol (1991) highlight the intensity of racial conflicts, and the enormity of the gaps between African Americans and whites in access to decent housing, lifestyles, and high-quality education in America during the 1990s. To paraphrase Kozol: It is possible to imagine the continued existence of the conditions described in *Savage Inequalities* and *There Are No Children Here* in a "color-blind" society.

Research focusing specifically on African Americans strongly suggests that, while African American families view education as a major avenue of social mobility, schooling has generally not operated to equalize opportunity for African Americans. Allen and Jewell (1995) report that African Americans have

This article was originally published in *Sociological Forum* 10, no. 4 (Dec. 1995) and is reprinted with permission.

made dramatic educational progress during the past fifty years, but they are still disadvantaged in the quantity and quality of education that is available to them over the span of their lives. Findings from *The Condition of Education 1994* (U.S. Department of Education 1995) show the following:

Black children start elementary school with less preschool experience than white children, and a gap in preschool enrollment rates has developed;

Gaps in the academic performance of black and white students appear as early as age nine and persist through age seventeen;

At age thirteen, black children are more likely than white children to be below the modal grade for their age;

Students who repeat grades are at greater risk of dropping out of school;

Black students are more likely than their peers to face a disorderly learning environment, but black and white students have similar attitudes about teaching quality in their schools;

Black students are no less likely than white students to have their parents involved in their schooling;

Both black and white high school graduates are following a more rigorous curriculum than a decade ago;

Black high school graduates are still less likely than white graduates to take advanced science and math courses or study a foreign language;

The educational aspirations of black and white students are similar;

Blacks are less likely than whites to make an immediate transition from high school to college;

In 1971, black twenty-five to twenty-nine year-olds were only about half as likely as their white peers to have completed four years of college, and this gap has not *diminished* (emphasis added);

Blacks take longer than whites to complete college on average;

Black women earn substantially more bachelor's degrees than black men, and the *difference doubled between 1977 and 1991* (emphasis added);

Employment and earnings rates rise with educational attainment of both blacks and whites, *but are lower for blacks than for whites with the same amount of education* (emphasis added).

This chapter begins with a brief overview of research concerned with issues of equality of educational opportunity. Hallinan (1988) identified four bodies of empirical work related to the concept of social equality: status attainment studies, research on educational effects, studies of school and classroom organization, and research on school and classroom processes. Other reviews (for example, Epps and Smith 1984; Gordon et al. 1994; Slaughter and Epps 1987) have examined research on the school environment, outcomes (effects) of schooling, the relationship of family background (socioeconomic status and race/ethnicity) to outcomes of schooling, family structure, and relations, culture, and socialization.

Carter and Goodwin (1994) concur with Hacker (1992) that race has historically and continues to serve as a barrier to African Americans' educational and occupational mobility. Carter and Goodwin describe three paradigms that have defined educational research on African Americans and members of other racial/ethnic groups in this country:

> The inferiority, cultural deprivation, and cultural difference paradigm . . . each is associated with a particular period in the nation's educational history. None of the three is confined by that period. [They] have been used simultaneously, and the assumptions undergirding each are embedded, to varying degrees in current political and educational structures and practices. (294)

The educational proposals supported by the inferiority paradigm are based on the assumption that African Americans are incapable of learning complex abstract subject matter. The cultural deprivation paradigm gave rise to compensatory education programs such as Head Start and Title I of the Elementary and Secondary Education Act designed to supplement deficiencies in the culture and socialization practices of low-income African Americans and other poor people. The cultural difference perspective is the basis for the multicultural education movement and the notion of "culturally responsive/responsible pedagogy."

Gordon et al. (1994) observe that between 1940 and 1970 studies and commentary focus on the problems and ills of the African American family and the impact of slavery. More recently, unemployment, lack of educational opportunity, and institutional racism (reflected in segregated housing, concentrated poverty and social isolation, problems of substance abuse, crime and violence, welfare dependency, teenage parenthood, and affirmative action) have become the focus of debate. What has not changed in the past fifty years is the tendency to "blame the victim."

Maxine Greene, an educational historian and philosopher, contends that "white people have constructed black people as 'other' and defined them in the light of what whites deny, repress, or exclude" (1994, 447). She also states,

[I]t is all too likely that, in many research laboratories and centers, the plight of the children described in Jonathan Kozol's *Savage Inequalities* (1991) is set aside either as irrelevant to the concerns of researchers or as "political" or "extreme." (448)

Implicit in many of the dominant rationales was a presumption of study body homogeneity, overlooking racial/ethnic, gender, and sometimes social class. The ability to generalize to some "universal" (white/male) norm was viewed as the ultimate in research standards. While increasing attention is currently being paid to ethnographic and other qualitative methods that focus on the diversity of racial, ethnic, demographic, social class, and gender roles and status in America, the quantitative mode still dominates as increasingly sophisticated statistical methodological approaches are generated by improved data storage and retrieval capacity and the ready availability of statistical software for personal computers.

In this chapter, I will focus on social background as it relates to schooling and on explanations of the racial gap in educational opportunity. The question to be addressed is, to what extent is the persistence of racism and racial discrimination a determining factor in limiting equal access to educational opportunity for African Americans? Alternatively, to what extent is social class (poverty) the major barrier?

Schools and Society

Although varying in content and purpose across countries, the most universally recognized function of schools is to impart knowledge and skills that will enable the learned to participate successfully in the society's institutions. Schools also facilitate normative outcomes. Schooling occurs in the context of the society at large; therefore, its academic and normative functions are not independent of other societal institutions. Socialization into gender, class, and racial/ethnic roles is a primary function of the schools. The school's success as a socializing agent depends upon its ability to teach students to see themselves as the school and the society define themselves. That is, African American children in public schools frequently encounter attitudes and social arrangements that communicate to them that they are not valued as persons and that they are expected to fail (Steele 1992). This is especially true for African American males (Hare and Castenell 1985). Linda Grant (1985), in her observations of

African American and white elementary school children in racially desegregated classrooms in a midwestern city, has provided clear descriptions of the different types of expectations educators have for students based on race and gender identification. She concluded that schooling experience seems to contribute to socialization of boys and girls of each race in a manner consistent with prevailing societal norms about appropriate roles for adults of their race and gender.

Social Background and Schooling

In the past several decades, researchers have studied the relationship of family life to educational outcomes. Socioeconomic status (SES), family structures, and race/ethnicity are assumed to influence educational outcomes. In much of this research the measure of family background is some combination of occupation, education, income, and family structure. The consistent finding is that the higher the family's social status the more likely the child is to be successful in school. These relationships vary in strength for different populations and for different outcome variables (Duncan 1994; Epps 1969; Epps and Jackson 1988). For example, Rumberger (1995) found that SES predicts dropout rates for Latinos and whites but not for African Americans; misbehavior, changing schools, and low grades all increased the odds of dropping out for African Americans and whites, but not for Hispanics; high absenteeism predicted dropping out for all groups.

With regard to family structure, other things being equal, children from stable (two-parent) families tend to be more successful than those from disrupted families. Children who live in single-parent families or stepfamilies during adolescence tend to have lower grade point averages, poorer attendance, and lower high school completion rates (Astone and McLanahan 1994). However, Duncan (1994), using data from the *Panel Study of Income Dynamics,* an ongoing longitudinal survey of U.S. households begun in 1968, found that female headship of families had a positive association with completed schooling for African American females. He also found that, contrary to expectations, maternal employment had a detrimental effect on educational attainment for both African American males and females. Such inconsistencies are difficult to explain with survey data. Ethnographic studies of families in specific settings are needed to provide more detailed analysis of the socioemotional and structural factors that may cause similar family structures to yield different results. While there are conflicting perspectives on the influence of family structure on adolescent adjustment, it is widely accepted that academic achievement is influenced by parental involvement in, support of, and expectations for their children's educational experience.

Research using the National Longitudinal Study of 1972 and the sophomore and senior sample of High School and Beyond, which focused specifically on the status attainment process among African Americans (Epps and Jackson 1988), suggests that SES had little direct influence on educational attainment. However, SES does influence educational aspirations, which, in turn, strongly influence educational attainment. SES is also associated with track placement in high school, and therefore with the types of courses students take. Finally, SES influences the types of high school students attend (public or private). Overall, however, the status attainment model does not explain African Americans' educational attainment as well as it does that of whites. Perhaps this occurs because, as Ogbu (1994) points out, African Americans' educational opportunities are constrained by race more than by class.

Neighborhood Poverty

Wilson (1987) incorporates structural and cultural arguments in his theoretical approach to understanding urban poverty. He shows how African Americans in areas characterized by concentrated poverty are especially vulnerable to structural economic changes that reduce the proportion of relatively high-paying manufacturing jobs that require few academic credentials, and increase the number of service jobs that require high levels of academic skills. The polarization of the labor market into low-wage and high-wage sectors, and the relocation of manufacturing jobs out of central cities, have created new barriers that increasingly undermine poor people's faith in education as a path out of poverty.

Lee and Croninger (1994), in a multilevel analysis of poor (largely African American and Latino) and middle-class (white) eighth graders from the *National Longitudinal Study* of 1988 (NELS:88), found that poverty had a strong effect on reading achievement. They also found that:

> If the home and school identified here [home support for learning; presence
> of reading materials in the home; family discussions about school experiences
> and educational plans; positive teacher-student relations; teacher cooperation;

teacher absenteeism; more book assignments in English classes; and authentic instruction (teachers' efforts to encourage students to construct knowledge)] were somehow made equivalent for young adolescents living in poverty and their middle-class counterparts, the disparity in reading, achievement levels between groups would diminish substantially.... However, even if these conditions were completely equalized, the achievement disparity would not disappear completely. (311)

The results of this quantitative study are in agreement with results of Clark's (1983) qualitative study of high- and low-achieving African American students from low-income backgrounds with respect to the importance of family support for learning, social capital (that is, parents knowing their children's school friends and the parents of these friends), and family discussions about school experiences and educational plans. As Clark points out, it is important to look beyond such gross classifications as race and socioeconomic status to the specific family dynamics that are associated with high and low achievement.

Another study using NELS:88 data (Davis and Jordan 1994) investigated school and contextual factors affecting African American males' success in middle and high school. They observed three important results in middle school: first, males in urban schools have poorer performance than those in other contexts; second, an emphasis on discipline at school is associated with lower achievement (perhaps because schools with a high proportion of poverty-level African American students also have high levels of disruption and student nonconformity with rules, or perhaps because teachers are not prepared to function effectively in troubled school environments); and third, teachers who assign more work seem also to issue higher course grades (perhaps because they have higher expectations for their students and therefore demand more from their students).

At the high school level, the only major school context effect was that teachers' locus of control was related to students' achievement; for example, teachers who believe in their own efficacy, that is, teachers who take responsibility for the quality of education they provide for their students—and for these students' failure as well as success—more often than not produce students who achieve.

In terms of student personal characteristics, school experiences and personal practices were found to be the major determinants of success for African

American males. Remediation, retention, and suspension were all shown to be negatively linked to academic failure among African American males.

Mickelson's (1984) research in nine Los Angeles, California, high schools found that students simultaneously hold two different kinds of attitudes toward education. Abstract attitudes reflect the dominant ideology; students who are able, ambitious, and hard working can use schooling as an avenue for social and economic mobility. Abstract attitudes are uniformly endorsed by students of all backgrounds, but do not predict performance (high school grades).

Concrete attitudes, however, reflect the race-, class-, and gender-specific social and cultural experiences that people have in the opportunity structure. African Americans and people from lower-class backgrounds have concrete attitudes that are more cynical about the occupational and economic benefits of education than are those of middle-class whites. It is these concrete attitudes based on life experiences that predict high school grades. This finding supports Ogbu's (1990) conclusion that for African Americans who have not gone to college, the perceived linkage between schooling, work experiences, and earnings is relatively weak. Ogbu uses "job ceilings" as a concept to explain how economic barriers work against African Americans. In a racially stratified society with a job ceiling, the type of schooling provided for African Americans has, historically, been structured to prepare them educationally for "their place" below the job ceiling.

Explaining the Racial Gap in Education

In response to questions about why racial inequality still exists, and why African Americans continue to lag in school performance and educational attainment in spite of the changes attributed to the civil rights movement, Ogbu (1994) argues that the cause of the inequality is not class stratification, but racial stratification, which created the gap in the first place, and continues to maintain it to some degree. He rejects the traditional social class (socioeconomic status) explanation of racial difference in achievement because it does not explain why African American children from middle-class homes do not achieve at levels equal to those of comparable whites. The social class explanation also fails to account for high levels of achievement by Asians from working-class families. Ogbu concludes that the interplay of "white treatments" of African America in economic, political, social, and educational spheres, and African Americans' responses to those treatments, is the real cause of the persistence of racial inequality. He contends that improving the economic condition of African Americans, even those classified as members of the "underclass," will not be sufficient to eliminate the achievement gap. The barriers to equality caused by racial stratification go beyond those of jobs, income, housing, and the like. The obstacles from society and within the schools must be transformed into "effort optimism" that motivates students to work hard to achieve at high levels.

Macleod (1995), drawing upon knowledge gained in his qualitative study of aspirations and attainment in a low-income neighborhood, contends that schools actually maintain and legitimate social inequality for working-class white males as well as comparable African Americans.

> The familiar refrain of "behave yourself, study hard, earn good grades, graduate with your class, go on to college, get a good job, and make a lot of money" reinforces the feelings of personal failure and inadequacy that working-class students are likely to bear as a matter of course. By this logic, those who have not made it have only themselves to blame. Because it shrouds class, race, and gender barriers to success, the achievement ideology promulgates a lie, one that some students come to recognize as such. (Macleod 1995, 262)

In Macleod's study, the working-class white "hallway hangers" exhibited overt rejection of school values and rules (and explicitly racist attitudes), while the African American "brothers" displayed conformity and compliance. This appears to contradict Ogbu's argument that racial stratification is the genesis of oppositional stances among adolescents. However, Ogbu does acknowledge that a similar phenomenon occurs among the "lads" in Willis's research in England. Perhaps it is a matter of class barriers for whites, but both race and class barriers for African Americans. In his follow-up of the "hallway hangers" and the "brothers," when they were approximately twenty-four years old, Macleod found that the strategies of both groups had failed to provide access to good jobs and economic success.

Social Context of Schools

From one perspective, the school can be seen as a cultural system of social relationships among family, teachers, students, and peers. Studies with this focus examine how the various components in the "cultural systems" of schools interact to influence both cognitive and normative outcomes. Focal variables include ability groupings, classroom organization, and teacher-student relationships.

African American children begin to fall behind white children on standardized tests as early as kindergarten. The assumption that home-based disadvantages contribute to the early academic difficulty of African American children provided a rationale for the development of Head Start and other preschool intervention programs. However, the benefits of Head Start appeared to be transitory and did not prevent low achievement in the primary grades (Slaughter-Defoe 1995). Slaughter-Defoe contends that the transition into schools is a significant point of discontinuity for poor African American children. Because in her conceptualization the long-term outcomes of schooling depend on student self-perception, both as a learner and as a person, the opinions of educators become paramount as students progress throughout elementary school. Slaughter-Defoe's research findings, based on a longitudinal study that continued from 1965 to 1978 (Slaughter 1977), suggested that the self-perceptions of the African Americans in her study about their academic capabilities and potential were strongly influenced by the grades their teachers gave them, and that these grades also influenced mothers' opinions. Slaughter-Defoe concludes that the social context of the school is an important variable that mediates the family's ability to promote high aspirations and expectations for academic success.

What is it about the context of schools that impedes the progress of African American children? African American scholars have attributed much of the responsibility for the academic problems of African American children to the attitudes and expectations of school personnel. For example, Kenneth Clark (1965) contended that a key factor leading to the academic failure of African American children was the fact that generally their teachers did not expect them to learn, and adopted, as their concept of their function, custodial care and discipline. Irving and York (1993) report that teachers have more negative expectations for African American students than for whites. Results from a survey of 474 teachers in elementary schools in a metropolitan school district in the Southeast suggest that teachers do not take any responsibility for the school failure of the African American, Hispanic, and Vietnamese students in this district. Teachers also give different explanations for the failure of students in the three ethnic groups.

Teachers explained African American students' academic failure as a function of their parents' inadequacies and deficiencies in the students' personal traits and characteristics—lack of motivation and discipline and negative self-concept. For the Vietnamese and Hispanic students, teachers explained academic failure primarily as a function of language difficulties. (169)

Nonetheless, survey research by Stevenson et al. (1990) found that the achievement level of African American and Hispanic elementary school children is not substantially lower than that of white children of similar socioeconomic status, and that the beliefs of African American and Latino children and their mothers are similar to those typically associated with middle-class white mothers. Why, then, do high rates of school failure and school dropout occur in junior and senior high school? Perhaps the gap between home and school cultures becomes more important as students progress through the various layers of the educational system.

Battistich et al. (1995) used hierarchical linear modeling to examine relationships between students' sense of school community, poverty level, and student attitudes, beliefs, and behavior in twenty-four elementary schools. They found that individual students' sense of the school/community relationship is positively associated with academic attitudes and motives. Thus, the authors concluded "that the school experience is less pleasant and rewarding, on the whole, for students in poor than in affluent communities" (649).

Heyns (1978) and Entwisle and Alexander (1992) examined "summer-learning-loss." Heyns found that the rate of learning drops off for all students during the summer if they are not enrolled in school. However, her study also showed that the decline is greater for "disadvantaged" children. Summer school programs also appeared to benefit advantaged children more than disadvantaged students. Entwisle and Alexander (1992), in a very well designed study, looked for family and school factors that contributed to the increasing difference in mathematics performance between African American and white children. They tracked the progress of a cohort of Baltimore, Maryland, children from the beginning of first grade in the fall of 1982 into the fall of their third year of school. They found that differences in children's mathematics achievement were more strongly associated with family economic level than with school racial composition. The design of the study enabled the researchers to determine the following:

For children in poverty, every summer meant a loss; for those not in poverty, every summer meant a gain. The telling point is that being in poverty hurts all children . . . summer gains or losses were not very different by race when poverty status was [statistically] controlled. Also, any advantage to two-parent homes disappeared when economic status was considered. These are powerful clues that it is not race or family status that controls summer gains—it is economic status, i.e., children in poverty do well in winter [when they are in school] but suffer losses in summer. (82)

The effect of ability grouping on achievement of African American students is widely perceived to be negative (Braddock and Dawkins 1993; Oakes and Guiton 1995). African American children tend to be located disproportionately in low-ability tracks that provide fewer challenging learning opportunities than average- or high-ability tracks. Braddock and Dawkins (1993) found that eighth graders' plans to enroll in high school college preparatory classes differed markedly by the ability level of their current classes even when socioeconomic status and prior achievements were accounted for. They also found that track arrangements impact students' future schooling opportunities.

Oakes and Guiton (1995) suggest that tracking decisions are shaped by the following: the way schools view students' abilities, motivation, and aspirations (as fixed); curriculum that seeks to accommodate, not alter, student characteristics; curriculum tailored to accommodate (advantage) high-achieving students; and the way race, ethnicity, and social class signal ability and motivation. They found that differences in course participation flowed, in large part, from educators' perceptions about race and social class differences in academic abilities and motivations. Schools rarely pressed African American or Latino students to stretch beyond their own or others' low expectations. Weinstein et al. (1995), using qualitative methods, found that perceived deficits in students and lack of support for mixed-ability teaching were among the factors that prevented the raising of expectations in schooling.

Discussion

There are some research traditions that are important for understanding African Americans' educational experiences and approaches to solutions to academic and developmental concerns that can only be mentioned here. These include the following: social psychological factors in adjustment and achievement (Epps 1969; Gurin and Epps 1975); racial/ethnic identity as it affects adaptation to school and achievement attitudes (Spencer et al. 1985); Afrocentric models of education (Asante 1988); African Americans' access to and attainment in higher education (Allen et al. 1991); African American educational history (J. Anderson 1988; Franklin 1984); mentoring African American graduate students (Blackwell 1986); African American male immersion schools (Leake and Leake 1992); parental involvement in their children's schooling (Epstein 1995); and systematic school reform. However, there is one subject that I will briefly address in the conclusion: the neglected African American middle class.

The Neglected African American Middle Class

Most of the attention in research and policy has targeted the African American urban poor (for example, Wilson 1987). African American males are now the focus of special attention from African American scholars and members of helping communities (for example, Polite and Davis 1994). Whether the linguistic, family, socialization, and other cultural and social characteristics that attract so much attention (Kotlowitz 1991; Lemann 1991; Wilson 1987) and that are currently the focus of qualitative dissertation (O'Connor 1995; Young 1993a) are new patterns of adjustment that have arisen from the pressures of social isolation and urban poverty (Wilson 1987), or extensions of patterns that developed in the rural South and were brought north during the "great migration" (Lemann 1991), is still a matter of debate. However, the African American middle class has both antebellum northern and southern roots, and both heritages have comingled (intermarried) through a long history of segregated education when most college-educated African Americans attended historically black colleges because they had no other options (J. Anderson 1988).

Because of the "caste-like" system of racial stratification (see Ogbu 1994), African Americans developed a parallel, but occupationally different, social class structure. From the 1970s to the present, there has been a rapid increase in upward social mobility, a new professional and technical job increase in upward social mobility as new professional and technical job opportunities developed. Thus, many of the members of the African American middle class, perhaps the majority, are first-generation, upwardly mobile from working-class or lower-class backgrounds. Research on this growing population, and on the way it socializes its children to try to pass on its status to its offspring, would present a very different picture than that which is popularly associated with African Americans. A synopsis of one such study is presented as my conclusion.

In a study of African American students in private schools, Slaughter-Defoe and Schneider (1986) found that middle-income African American children were able to adapt successfully to a wide range of educational programs and options. The key factor involved, in terms of family-school relations, was a fit between the formally stated mission and goals of the schools, and the beliefs and values held by the parents about their children's education and learning. That these families had chosen the schools and paid tuition casts them in a very different position as consumers of education than poor parents who must send their children to the neighborhood school whatever its quality.

> Thus, when parents can be influential and actively involved in their children's education, when schools engage in responsible teaching and in an organization and management consistent with their stated educational philosophies, and when parents and schools share mutual respect and an agreement upon educational philosophy, black children, just like all children, are educable. After the preschool years, the nature of the continuity in these children's development depends on how families and schools cooperate in childhood socialization. (Slaughter-Defoe 1995, 282)

I conclude that the race versus class question is too simplistic. Obviously, both factors are at work and they interact in different ways depending upon the person's or family's position in the race/class structure. Additional research on this interaction is very much needed to facilitate understanding of a very complex set of issues.

CHAPTER 10

Racial Classification in Criminology

The Reproduction of Racialized Crime

Jeanette Covington

Sociologists of crime have long observed that there are race differences in crime, with African Americans having much higher crime rates than whites. Unfortunately, in attempting to explain the differences in crime rates between racial aggregates, they have run the risk of racializing crime. Crime can be said to be racialized when the criminal behaviors of individual black offenders are understood in terms of "racial traits," "racial motives," or "racial experiences." Because these traits, motives, and experiences are described as the properties of entire race or race-class categories, the predisposition to get involved in crime gets generalized beyond individual black criminals to whole races or racial communities of noncriminal blacks. When crime is thus racialized, whole communities or whole categories of phenotypically similar individuals are rendered pre-criminal and morally suspect. In this chapter, I will review and critique the role that these racializing assumptions play in criminological theories.

In its most neutral sense, race refers to a distinct group of people whose members share certain inherited physical characteristics such as skin color and hair texture. A value-free system of racial classification would simply catalogue these superficial physical differences without any effort to imbue them with social meaning. However, these physical markers have long been freighted with tremendous social significance. Even today physical characteristics, classified as racial, continue to be the basis for inferring major (that is, racial) differ-

This article was originally published in *Sociological Forum* 10, no. 4 (Dec. 1995) and is reprinted with permission.

ences in culture, cultural achievements, histories, and behaviors of persons who possess them.

The practice of extending racial typologies to an understanding of cultures, temperaments, motives, responses, and behaviors is called racialization, and it has come in for severe criticism (Webster 1992). Still social scientists in general and criminologists in particular continue to apply racial typologies as though these typologies were non-problematic.

The capacity to type differences in behavior by race has been helped by the longstanding practice in the United States of recording race on birth/death records and in the census. Membership in either the black race or the white race has been most consistently recorded. Asians, Hispanics, and other groups have at varying times been combined and listed as "other." Such records make it possible to apply racial typologies to behaviors based on comparisons between blacks and whites, and less frequently to comparisons between "other" races.

In this chapter, I will consider how racial typologies have been applied to the understanding of differences in crime rates between black and whites; that is, how criminal behavior has been racialized. I will begin by discussing the major sources of data on crime in the United States and briefly address what these crime statistics tell us about race differences (black/white) in offending. In the remaining sections, I will discuss the major criminological theories, which have been used to explain race differences in crime. Interspersed in my discussion will be a critique of these theories, which will focus on the continued use of unproblematized conceptions of race and race differences in theories of crime.

Racialization and Race Records

There have long been several ready sources of data to enable researchers to apply racial typologies to the behaviors of Americans. As Webster (1992) notes, blacks and whites have been classified separately in the census since 1890. This means that it is possible to evaluate longstanding trends in "race" differences in a variety of behaviors. Using census, birth, and/or death records, social scientists have commented on black/white differences in behaviors as diverse as marriage rates, illegitimacy, welfare, and teen pregnancy. They have then theorized about the meaning of those differences.

The same holds true in criminology. Blacks and whites have traditionally been classified separately in the three major sources of data on crime. For example, black and white crime has consistently been counted separately in the Uniform Crime Reports (UCR), the oldest and most quoted source of data on crime. The UCR are based on an actual count of arrests drawn from most police departments around the country. Since 1930, these counts of local arrests have annually been summed and compiled into a national report. Yet even while separate arrest rates have routinely been recorded for blacks and whites, the designation of other minorities (for example, Asians, Hispanics) has either been changed or dropped over the years (Mann 1993). Hence race differences in arrest usually refer to differences between blacks and whites, and these arrest data routinely show that black arrest rates are higher than those for whites.

Unfortunately, there are many problems with trying to count crime using arrest statistics. Among other things, critics have long held that police bias against African Americans may make the police more inclined to arrest them for crimes for which white offenders may be released. Any such biases would, of course, inflate race differences in arrest rates (Mann 1993).

In an effort to avoid these presumed biases, criminologists have long turned to a second source of data on crime, namely self-reports. Self-report data (SRD) are typically based on surveys conducted among samples of high school students. Students are generally asked to report on whether they have committed crimes in the recent past. The early self-report studies showed no race differences in crime, but they were faulted because of their tendency to include too many trivial offenses (for example, underage drinking, use of false identification, and so forth) that never resulted in an arrest (Gould 1969). To many critics, the inclusion of trivial offenses meant arrest data and self-report data were counting two different types of crime; in their view, the absence of race differences in self-reports was no proof that race differences in arrest data were based on police bias.

However, some self-report studies did include serious offenses that would likely end in an arrest, and these studies confirmed the findings of the earlier self-reported studies. In other words, there were no race differences in crime for either serious or trivial offenses. Findings from these studies, then, led to renewed speculation that race differences in arrests reflected police bias (Institute for Social Research 1992; Huizinga and Elliott 1987).

Still many criminologists continued to doubt that the very large black/white differences in arrest rates for violent crimes could be explained by police bias alone. To shore up their arguments, they turned to a third source of crime statistics that would also enable them to count crime while avoiding police bias; that source was the National Crime Victimization Survey (NCVS). The NCVS is an annual survey of a representative sample of 66,000 of the nation's households. It has been conducted continuously since 1972. In this survey, respondents are asked to report on their victimization experiences in the previous year. For certain crimes like robbery, rape, and assault, where victims come into contact with the offender, respondents are asked to describe their assailants. Obviously victims can only identify a minimal number of offender characteristics while they are being victimized, including race, gender, and some crude estimate of the offender's age.

As a number of black households are included among the 66,000 households interviewed, many black respondents—especially black urban respondents—have consistently reported higher victimization rates than whites or Hispanics, and most identify their assailants as black (Bureau of Justice Statistics 1994). Hence, based on victim descriptions of their assailants, data from the victim surveys generally confirm what arrest statistics show. In other words, both surveys show that blacks are more likely to be involved in crime than whites. Therefore findings from the victim surveys suggest that there are race differences in serious street crime even under conditions where the estimates are unlikely to be distorted by race bias.[1]

Because of this agreement between arrest data and victim reports, many criminologists take race differences in crime to be real. Hence, when they theorize about the meaning of these differences they are generally trying to explain why blacks commit so many more crimes than whites.

That black crime rates are higher than those of whites is certainly consistent with some longstanding notions that Americans have about race, and thus criminologists—either wittingly or unwittingly—have long been in the awkward position of (re)producing ideas about the meaning of race and race differences.

1. While many argue that victim surveys are more likely to provide unbiased assessments of black/white differences in crime, there are limits on the accuracy of victim reports. After all, victims may confuse African American offenders with Afro-Caribbean or black Puerto Rican offenders. With white offenders, it may be difficult for victims to discriminate between non-Hispanic whites and Hispanic whites (Mann 1993). Obviously, the magnitude of such errors cannot truly be known, although many criminologists assume that they are rare. Therefore, many see victim reports as a relatively unbiased source for data on race differences in crime.

That criminological ideas about race are being reproduced is evidenced by a perusal of several current introductory criminology textbooks. Most have a section variously titled "race and crime" or "variations in crime rates by race." These sections overwhelmingly address the black/white difference in crime. In addition, a concern with assessing black/white differences in crime is often expressed in requests for grant proposals and in articles in mainstream criminology journals (Young and Sulton 1991). Still, because this is such a sensitive topic, criminologists have, in some years, resisted theorizing about race differences altogether (Hawkins 1983; Mann 1993). This means that while there is a fair amount of theorizing about this difference, the theoretical tradition is somewhat erratic.

The Concept of Race Difference in Race Cultural Theories of Crime

From the outset American criminologists developed theories geared towards explaining variations in crime within the American (white) population. However, crime was not typically understood in terms of white culture or as a uniquely white response to crime. Rather white criminals were generally "unraced," and theorists focused on explaining crime among (white) Americans in terms of variations by class, age, and gender. Hence, a number of theories were geared towards speculating on why low-income individuals or low-income communities would have higher crime rates with no mention of whiteness. Similarly there were efforts to explain why adolescent males would be more inclined to engage in crime than adults, again without mention of whiteness.

As interest increased in race differences in crime, the etiology of crime was racialized. Racial meanings (black cultures, black experiences, black motives, black responses) were ultimately applied to many of the explanations of crime committed by African Americans. The need for a separate explanation of crimes committed by African Americans was justified by the enormous gap between black and white crime rates. Hence, some of these early race-cultural theorists treated black crime as if it were a different and more virulent strain of crime than that found among white criminals. In other words, they extended racial meaning to an understanding of crime that had previously been racially unclassified.

A statement by Wolfgang and Ferracuti (1967) on the subculture of violence represents one early effort to explain the high rates of crime among African Americans in terms of a unique racial (black) subculture. Wolfgang and

Ferracuti argued that a subculture of violence could be identified by finding a community with high rates of homicide and other violent crime. The assumption was that in such communities residents would be quick to resort to violence to defend their status, honor, or reputation. Violence in such subcultures was seen as an appropriate response to threats to a person's honor, and thus assaultive behavior to defend bruised reputations did not generate feelings of guilt. Indeed, failure to respond with violence in the face of threats to honor was cause for embarrassment and even ostracism from the subculture.

While Wolfgang and Ferracuti's "subculture of violence" was certainly used to explain high murder and assault rates in some white communities, they argued that it had particular application to blacks. They suggested that high rates of violent crime among blacks could be explained by their greater tendency to respond with violence in the face of what others might perceive as a trivial affront. For example, blacks might differentially perceive the meaning of being jolted and so might be more likely to retaliate than whites. Members of the black subculture of violence differed from more conventional folks because they valued honor more highly than human life. Further, the authors assert, as members of the subculture they were more likely to be reinforced for their quick defense of honor by their peers than those outside the subculture.

Wolfgang and Ferracuti's analysis was flawed in a number of ways, not least because it failed to specify the origins of the black subculture of violence. In other words, if blacks placed greater value on honor and were more given to violent retaliation in the face of trivial affronts to their honor than whites, how had this come about?

Several theorists did attempt explanation for the seeming race differential in involvement in the subculture of violence. Silberman (1980) argued that the black experience in America has been a particularly violent one relative to that of whites. Blacks, he shows, had been violently uprooted from Africa and transported to America during the Middle Passage. They were then exposed to inordinate amounts of violence during slavery and finally experienced violent repression at the hands of the Ku Klux Klan (KKK) after slavery. Thus because blacks were differentially exposed to violence, Silberman asserts that they reacted by becoming "bad" or more macho as depicted in southern myth. Silverman wrote in the immediate aftermath of a period when black crime rates had mushroomed. He relied upon that fact to conclude that the Civil Rights movement had stirred up a longstanding rage so that more blacks turned to violence (for example, riots) in the aftermath of the movement because they experienced release and liberation through being able to intimidate whites. Unfortunately, in his rush to understand black criminals who victimized whites as involved in a retaliatory response to a uniquely black experience with racist oppression, Silverman ignored the fact that the lion's share of crime that is committed by black offenders is directed against black victims. His theory is, in many ways, ill suited to account for black-on-black crime.

However, Comer (1985) does address the problem of black-on-black crime. He begins in much the same way as Silberman by addressing the black experience with violence in this country during slavery and its aftermath. He argues that this exposure to slavery and violence has resulted in collective feelings of forced dependency and self-hatred. As a result of their history of violent oppression, blacks have identified with their oppressors (slave owners, KKK) and thus assimilated their use of violence. However, their feelings of self-hatred cause them to experience ambivalence and antagonism towards their own group (other blacks), and thus they have turned inward the anger and rage that they feel towards whites and directed them at other blacks.

Comer can be faulted because he ignores similarities in the nature of crimes committed by black and white offenders. Even as he makes much of explaining black-on-black crime rates in terms of a collective response to the black experience, he ignores much crime committed by whites, which is similarly intra-racial (white-on-white). Despite this, no effort is made to account for white-on-white crime in terms of collective feelings of rage and self-hatred among whites. Indeed, "the white experience," "white culture," or "white history" is never invoked to explain white violence. It would seem then that only the motives of black offenders are racialized.

Actually the explanation for black-on-black and white-on-white crime and violence is probably quite simple. It is known that criminals do not travel very far from their residences to commit many of their crimes—particularly their robberies, burglaries, and larcenies (Brantingham and Brantingham 1991; Carter and Hill 1979.) In part, the tendency to commit crimes nearby is based on the desire to minimize visibility and avoid police surveillance. Therefore, because we live in a racially segregated society, black offenders are likely to rob and burglarize their black neighbors while white offenders will similarly victimize their white neighbors.

Also, because many violent crimes such as murder involve victimization of spouses, significant others, friends, relatives, and acquaintances, much violent crime is likewise intra-racial. After all, whites are likely to have white spouses, significant others, and acquaintances, and blacks will similarly be involved with black spouses, significant others, and acquaintances.

The Structural Critique of Race-Cultural Theories

While the explanations of Silberman (1980) and Comer (1985) differ in their understanding of the subculture of violence, both allude to conditions unique to or disproportionately associated with the "black experience" to explain the origins of that subculture (slavery, Middle Passage, oppression after slavery, heightened black rage, and so forth). According to these theories, crime is little more than a racial response (black self-hatred, hatred of other blacks, identification with oppressors, relief from intimidating whites, and so on) to a black-specific legacy of violence and discrimination. While these theories have been challenged on a number of grounds, the most damning critique has come from those who emphasize structure over culture (Calvin 1981; Pope 1979; Walker 1990).

Structural critics (re)assert the importance of class in explaining crime and in so doing suggest that black crime should be assessed in the same way that white crime has been treated historically. In other words, low-income persons—black or white—may be more likely to respond to their limited means for making money by turning to crime. By reasserting the importance of class in explaining crime for all Americans, regardless of race, these theorists deracialize criminological theories. That is, they drop racial motives (increased need of being "bad," macho), racial responses, and racial experiences from the discussion.

Many begin by critiquing the seemingly large "race difference" in crime, such as it is recorded in arrest data and victim reports, as exaggerated. Both the UCR and NCVS compare *all* blacks to *all* whites without any consideration of class differences. However, this is an extremely misleading measure of race differences because blacks are at least three times as likely to be poor as whites (Jennings 1994). Because it has traditionally been expected that crime would be higher in low-income populations, structural theorists argue that the seeming "race difference" in crime may actually be a class difference. Moreover, a larger percentage of the black population is made up of teens and young adults, is unemployed or underemployed, and is urban. These factors are crucial because they have all been shown to bear some relationship to crime, regardless of race (Calvin 1981; Sampson and Wilson 1995; Walker 1990).

The structural theorists seem to be suggesting that cultural theories which explain crime by constructing a racial response to the black experience might better account for crime by looking at noncultural and nonracial factors (social class, age, urban residence, and so forth). Further, because the temptation to explain crime in terms of "race difference" seems to blind some criminologists to across-group similarities in the causes of crime, it might be wise to abandon racial classification when looking at crime and focus on structural factors.[2]

If race categories were no longer included in crime data, many race-cultural theorists would likely be forced to explain crime in terms of youth living in urban poverty. After all, crime levels seem to be elevated in urban neighborhoods where unemployment and underemployment are high. Because black youths are more likely to live in such urban poor neighborhoods than are white youth, their crime rates are probably higher because of these structural conditions rather than because of a uniquely criminogenic black subculture. Obviously, if we shift our focus, high crime rates could no longer be used to tell us something about "blackness"; rather they would point to the structural conditions that disproportionately affect blacks.

Structural Explanations and Underclass Isolation

Clearly the race-cultural theorists can be faulted for theorizing as if the enormous black/white difference in crime indicated by arrest data and victim reports is real. Structural theorists argue that such a comparison of all blacks and

2. In theory, what drives the tendency to explain black crime in terms of racial motives is the high crime rates of blacks relative to whites. However, whites have higher crime rates than Asians and yet whites are not normed on Asians. If anything, this difference is explained, in the converse, by the strengths of Asian culture (for example, greater Asian emphasis on kinship) rather than by the weakness of white culture. The Asian-white difference in crime, then, is not being used to tell us anything about "whiteness." In other words, no effort is made to account for this race difference by pointing to disadvantaged white responses to stressors, white motives, or the white experience. Even more interesting is that whites are almost never normed on blacks for acts of crime and deviance where white rates *exceed* black rates. After all, there is evidence that whites are more likely to be involved in serial killing, patricide/matricide, suicide, illegal drug use, corporate crime, and white-collar crime than blacks. However, explanations for these crimes say nothing about whiteness. Moreover, unlike Asians, blacks are not portrayed as model minorities for their lower rates of crime and deviance in these areas; therefore, there is no need to speculate about any possible strengths of black culture or collective black responses relative to whites.

all whites is misleading. For them, a fairer comparison would be one between matched groups—that is, young, low income, urban white males and young, low-income, urban black males. In fact, when such comparisons are made, race differences in crime are greatly reduced. However, they do not totally disappear, which leads some to argue that some other conditions must be identified to explain residual black/white differences in crime (Harris 1991; Wilson and Herrnstein 1985). This could reopen the door for consideration of black-specific traits that result in high crime rates. However, some have argued that it is difficult if not impossible to make a fair comparison between blacks and whites because blacks live under vastly different structural conditions than do whites.

For example, Calvin (1981) noted that many of those conditions which render a population crime-prone are more likely to appear in conjunction for African American youth than for white youth. In other words, a larger percentage of black youth live in high-unemployment, high-poverty urban communities than is the case for white youth. In fact, white youth are more likely to live in rural poverty (Calvin 1981; Sampson and Wilson 1995). Hence, the structural conditions most associated with crime could be said to be more frequently compounded among African Americans than whites.

Wilson's (1987) thesis regarding blacks living in underclass communities would seem to describe a cluster of structural and demographic characteristics that represent the ultimate admixture of crime-prone conditions. Underclass communities are defined as census tracts with a high proportion (one standard deviation above the national mean) of *all* of the following conditions: (1) high school dropouts, (2) males sixteen years old and over who are not working regularly, (3) welfare recipients, and (4) households headed by women with children (Peterson and Harrell 1992). By Wilson's (1991a) estimate, blacks make up 65 percent of those living in such communities of concentrated poverty.

That the urban underclass is disproportionately African American is no accident. Blacks of all classes were segregated early in urban communities as whites moved to other city neighborhoods and then to the suburbs. As whites moved to the suburbs so too did primary labor market jobs, which required low skills but offered good wages, steady employment, and benefits. Urban blacks were left with secondary labor market jobs and thus lacked the opportunities to be socially mobile afforded their suburban counterparts (Wilson 1987; Peterson and Harrell 1992; Kasarda 1992).

Since the 1970s conditions have worsened for black underclass communities as manufacturing jobs have been steadily eliminated. American corporations have downsized by closing plants in the United States and shifting plants to low-wage economies in other parts of the world. The loss of jobs brought on by disinvestment has worsened conditions for an already devastated black underclass reeling from the suburbanization of jobs (Kasarda 1992).

In addition to long-term joblessness, the black underclass has experienced increasing social isolation. With the enforcement of fair housing laws, middle-class and working-class blacks have been afforded more housing choices and so many have moved out of low-income urban neighborhoods. For Wilson (1987, 1991a), this left an underclass largely composed of (1) the unskilled who were subject to long-term bouts of underemployment or unemployment or were totally out of the labor force, (2) those involved in street crime and other deviance, and (3) families living in long-term poverty or welfare dependency (Wilson 1987, 1991a).

Clearly in his definition of black urban underclass isolation, Wilson defines a host of structural and demographic characteristics that can account for high crime rates among the ghetto poor. Indeed, aggregate-level comparisons of urban neighborhoods indicate that crime rates are highest in crime communities, which could easily qualify as underclass (Taylor and Covington 1988).

Unfortunately, such aggregate-level comparisons merely show that community-level indicators of underclass poverty are associated with high crime. However, "aggregates" do not make decisions about whether to become involved in crime. Hence, it is assumed that some sort of underclass cultural response is required to explain how neighborhood-level structural and demographic risk factors are translated into individual decisions to commit crimes.

Wilson (1987, 1991a) combines structure and culture to address these concerns by speaking to how the isolation of the ghetto poor from middle- and working-class role models has resulted in "self-limiting social dispositions" among the underclass population left behind.

The out-migration of middle- and stable working-class blacks means that the ghetto poor are increasingly isolated from work skills, work values, work etiquette, and the necessary contacts to secure entry-level jobs. Further, as conventional jobs disappear, the illegitimate economy (for example, drug trade) thrives. Hence, the combination of existing role models and a growing illegitimate economy means that the ghetto poor never develop the aspirations, values, and skills that could help them succeed in an increasingly far-off primary labor market. Further, as more and more underclass youth turn to criminal pursuits, a "tipping point" is reached so that illegal behavior becomes the norm (Peterson and Harrell 1992). Thus, the isolation and the "tip" to deviant values cause the underclass to turn in on itself and perpetuate later cohorts with self-limiting social dispositions (Wilson 1991a; Peterson and Harrell 1992).

Certainly the underclass thesis does not suffer from some of the same problems as earlier race-cultural explanations that describe crime as a black reaction to a unique history of racial oppression. Indeed, at some point the underclass thesis makes a race-neutral argument regarding the causes of crime because it assumes that whites exposed to similar structural conditions would likely have high crime rates as well (Sampson and Wilson 1995; Sampson and Laub 1993; Sampson 1987). Still, the fact remains that blacks are disproportionately exposed to underclass conditions and are likely to remain so; therefore the label "underclass" could be seen as little more than a code word for the urban black poor.

Racialization and the Diffusion of Criminal Predispositions

In many ways, however, underclass arguments and the earlier race-cultural explanations share similar flaws. Both can be faulted for encouraging a view that the entire black population or at least the entire black underclass population is high risk for criminal behavior. They accomplish this in slightly different ways.

Race-cultural theorists suggest that high black crime rates can be explained by the black response to a history of racial oppression in which violence was visited upon blacks during and after slavery. Because only blacks were exposed to these conditions, they have developed their own unique racial response by seeking to be "bad" or macho or by experiencing self-hatred and hatred for other blacks. It is this black subcultural response that is presumed to mediate between a very real history of oppression and high black crime rates. In short, phenotypically black offenders have uniquely black motives—the desire to be bad or macho, hatred for other blacks—in deciding to do crime. What has sparked their propensity for criminal acts is a history of racial oppression, and over the years the reaction to that oppression has presumably become ritualized in a black subculture of violence.

With underclass arguments, black criminal propensities turn on self-limiting social dispositions. As an urban population exposed to unprecedented levels of joblessness and living in social isolation from conventional role models and conventional norms, many black underclass persons have tipped towards an embrace of norms more appropriate to surviving in a criminal underground economy. The flaws in both arguments can be revealed if they are applied to a specific example.

Using murder by way of example, there have been approximately 25,000 homicides in the United States per year in the past few years. African Americans make up 12 percent to 15 percent of the population. The individuals responsible for 50 percent of these murders—or approximately 12,500 homicides per year—are classified as African Americans. It is clear from these figures that, in collective race terms, blacks have much higher per capita murder rates than do whites. It is this "race difference" in crime rates that drives both race-cultural and underclass explanations of murder and other crime.

Let us look at these figures from another perspective, however; assuming there are approximately 30 million African Americans, this means that 29,987,500 do not commit a murder in any given year. However, both race-cultural and underclass arguments have the effect of diffusing the propensity for murder and other crime from the 12,500 black killers to the 29million-plus blacks who do not kill in any given year.[3] They accomplish this diffusion in slightly different ways.

A race-cultural theorist might explain high black homicide rates in terms of a black subculture of violence in which the disproportionate use of violence by blacks to settle rival disputes is a reflection of self-hatred, hatred for other blacks, or the need to be "bad" or macho. While these racialized motives would

3. I chose murder for this example because murder has certain advantages over other crimes. In 1992, there were exactly 23,600 murders reported based on arrest statistics and coroners' reports. Only a handful of murders in any year (about 1 percent) involve one offender and multiple victims (for example, serial killers, mass murders). The overwhelming majority of murders (99 percent) involve one offender and one victim, so it is fair to say that 23,600 reported murders suggests that there have been close to 23,600 murderers. However, it is not possible to estimate the number of offenders based on reported crimes for any other offense. For example, in 1992, 672,478 complaints of robbery were made to the police, culminating in 153,456 arrests. Yet, no one would argue that the 153,456 arrests indicted that there were 153,456 different robbers. Moreover, it is unclear how one might go about estimating the number of robbers based only on information about the number of arrests. (Certainly efforts to make such calculations have been attempted.) Hence, I chose murder for this example because it is the one crime where the number of reported offenses closely corresponds to the number of offenders.

distinguish black killers from white killers, they would tie the 12,500 black killers *more closely* to the 29 million-plus blacks who had not killed because black killers and black non-killers share a legacy of slavery and thereby the collective black rage that could manifest itself in either self-hatred, hatred of other blacks, or the need to be "bad." Such racially defined motives then have the effect of diffusing criminal predisposition, and the entire black population is rendered high risk, pre-criminal, and morally suspect.

Underclass theorists are considerably more selective in identifying those segments of the black population with criminal predispositions. In effect, precriminality is located in urban underclass communities. This means that criminal propensities are only diffused across that segment of the black population that lives in underclass communities. Hence, underclass theorists might explain high murder rates in the black underclass in terms of their tipping towards an embrace of underworld values due to their isolation from conventional role models and norms. This isolation is crucial because it means that residents of black underclass communities are not exposed to conventional lifestyles as they are practiced in the labor force or by members of the black working or middle class.

Estimates of the size of the black urban underclass population vary, but if we place it at 3.8 million (see Wilson 1991b; Sampson and Wilson 1995), this type of thinking has the effect of diffusing criminal predispositions to those more than 3.7 million underclass African Americans who are not involved in murder in a given year. That is, they too could be described as high risk for murder and other crimes because they share with black underclass killers those features thought to predispose to murder—isolation from mainstream role models and norms and the consequent self-limiting social dispositions. In short, whole communities are being rendered as high risk for murder not because of the pervasiveness of murderers throughout the black underclass population but because their murder rates are so much higher than those found in white communities.

Racialization and the Uniform Black Response

It should be clear from the foregoing that the sweeping conditions identified to explain black crime or black underclass crime are a bit too inclusive and needlessly assign criminal propensities to many noncriminal blacks. The crudeness of these measures is an artifact of the methods used to define black crime rates as high in the first place. The notion that "black" crime rates are high and thus the desire to theorize about that excess stem solely from a comparison of black and white crime rates. Hence while race-cultural and underclass arguments are used to explain black crime rates, they are really explaining the race differences in crime, that is, black crime as high relative to white crime.

One solution to this tendency to racialize crime lies in pursuing within-race analyses rather than the traditional between-race comparisons. The within-black analysis deracializes because it indicates that there is no single response to a history of racial oppression or underclass social isolation; rather there are many reactions made by blacks. Conversely, between-race analyses, which compare blacks and whites, are able to racialize, in part, because they impose a uniform response on blacks; this means that all blacks are believed to react in like manner (racial response) or to be motivated by similar concerns (racial motives). The assumption of a uniform response shores up the notion that there is such a thing as blackness or a black response—as distinct from the conventional (white) response.

The process of identifying a distinct and uniform black response typically involves a two-stage process. First, black behaviors can be defined as distinct if they are seen as a reaction to racism or more recently as a reaction to living in unprecedented urban underclass social isolation. Obviously, racism and urban underclass isolation distinguish blacks or underclass blacks from whites, and so the association of these conditions with crime can tell us something about "blackness" as distinct from "whiteness." Second, in order to fashion a uniform black response, diverse black reactions to oppression or underclass isolation have to be deemphasized or ignored. This deemphasis encourages a type of analysis in which blacks are allowed to react in only one way to a history of oppression or structural constraints. They are not conceived of as making choices simply because no choices are mentioned. This lack of choices means that a certain selectiveness has to be exercised when deciding on what "best" represents *the* black response to oppression or isolation. The selectiveness required to achieve such racial uniformity can be faulted on four accounts.

First, because an analysis of race differences usually fuels an effort to distinguish the "black" response from the "white" response, a distinct response can only be designated as "black" if black behavior is seen as *solely* a reaction to black-specific conditions like racial injustice or underclass isolation. If this type of analysis is carried too far, it risks making the reaction to racial injustice or underclass isolation *the* defining characteristic for all black (or black underclass) behaviors. In so doing, it does not allow for the possibility that large portions of all black lives are not lived in reaction to racial injustice or race and class isolation.

Second, in the rush to impose a uniform black reaction to racial injustice on an understanding of crime committed by blacks, criminologists have on occasion ignored or distorted actual crime patterns. Hence Silberman (1980) formulated a set of black motivations when he argued that black criminals were motivated by a desire to intimidate and victimize whites. For him, these attacks were experienced as liberating because they were a response to centuries of white oppression. Unfortunately, after making his case, he was unable to explain the bulk of crimes committed by blacks that involve black offenders victimizing other blacks.

Similarly when Comer (1985) argued that black-on-black crime was precipitated by a collective black self-hatred and hatred of other blacks, he had to ignore the fact that many crimes are committed near the offender's home or against acquaintances and significant others. Hence, black-on-black (and white-on-white) crimes are a reflection of the spatial limitations of committing crime in a racially segregated society rather than a reaction to racial oppression.

Using a slightly different approach, some criminologists have argued that black criminals enraged by racial (status and income) inequalities are angry at whites, but frustrated in their attempts to retaliate against whites because their oppressors live in other neighborhoods. Hence, "black rage" is detached from its original source and manifests itself in an anger aimed at anything in its path—mainly other blacks. In these analyses, violent and criminal blacks are characterized as striking out at other blacks in an irrational and meaningless fury. The argument can be made, however, that this characterization is made in order to shore up the notion that black crime and violence are responses to racial injustice (Blau and Blau 1982).

Third, in an effort to identify a distinct and racially uniform response, criminologists can be quite arbitrary in deciding on what makes criminal behavior "black." As it is, it seems acceptable to develop theories of crime that speculate on black motives or black responses when there is sufficient difference between black and white crime rates. However, it is unclear whether racial motives become irrelevant if there is black/white parity in crime rates or racial parity after structural variables are controlled (class, urban residence, and so forth). Further, no rules have been set as to how big the differences have to be before the crime of black criminals requires the identification of some uniquely black phenomenon. In short, criminologists do not clarify when we can safely forego assigning racial motives to criminal behavior and when such motives must be invoked.

Fourth, in the rush to identify uniquely black causes for crime, some criminologists seem to get so carried away with the presumed effects of racial oppression or underclass social isolation that they are blinded to the possibility that *black and white criminals may have more in common with each other* than they do with noncriminal blacks. Purely structural theories certainly take this approach. However, the race-cultural theories, which identify black cultural adaptations to a history of oppression, and the underclass theories, which combine both structural and neighborhood-based cultural adaptations, define an unique black criminal with distinct, racially *localized* criminal propensities.

Yet black criminals and white criminals often behave in remarkably similar ways. Certainly, blacks and whites who burglarize, steal, and rob commit their crimes in like manner, and any seeming racial difference in their selection of victims or crime sites seems to be predicated on a particular neighborhood's ecology rather than on distinct racial motivations (Brantingham and Brantingham 1991; Cornish and Clarke 1986; Carter and Hill 1979). Further, it is hard to discern differences between blacks and whites involved in acts of expressive violence (for instance, spouse abuse, fights in bars over trivial matters, gang turf wars) when comparisons are made across communities, cultures, and historical periods (Katz 1988; Thrasher 1927; Rose 1969). In other words, identifying a uniquely black motive for violence begins to seem unnecessary if all of the crime literature is reviewed and not just the literature on the black underclass.

Conclusion: Racialization, Determinism, and Black Culture

Sociologists of crime have long made use of both structure and culture to explain crime. Many of the early criminogenic cultures, which explained American (white) crime, were based on social class; therefore the gap between criminal and noncriminal behavior was based on the gap between middle-class and lower-class subcultures. Hence, persons born into the lower class were socialized into crime because of class-cultural forces beyond their control. Because criminal propensities were lodged in the lower class, the gap between criminal and noncriminal whites could be bridged with social mobility.

When cultural theories of crime were initially racialized as race-cultural theories, the gap between criminal and noncriminal shifted to that between blacks and whites. These arguments were based upon the notion that because the phenotypically black were the only ones exposed to a criminogenic history of racist oppression and the resulting violent subculture, they were the ones at highest risk for criminal predispositions. In short, these race-based cultures, which predisposed blacks to crime, were adaptations to historical conditions of racist oppression; hence, the racist past had distorted these cultures. It is unclear then how the gap between criminal and noncriminal could have been bridged because the racist past was not subject to change. In short, these theories seemed to permanently impose criminal propensities on all blacks. The fact that black crime rates did go down in some years raised questions about a black culture that was permanently criminogenic by dint of a history of racist oppression (Rose and McClain 1990).

In response to these problems with race-cultural theories, the class structure was reinvoked to explain changes over time in black crime rates. Purely structural theories made no distinctions between lower-class black and lower-class white subcultures in terms of their criminogenic influences. Hence, for both whites and blacks the gap between criminal and noncriminal propensities could be bridged with social mobility.

More recently, structural forces have been used to explain the emergence of a black underclass culture; the black underclass culture has now become the culture at greatest risk for crime. Analyses of this black underclass culture have had the effect of localizing criminal propensities in isolated urban neighborhoods and closing off this urban black lower-class criminal subculture from middle-class black and white noncriminal subcultures and even from lower-class white criminal subcultures. The conditions that mire this black underclass in self-limiting social dispositions are seemingly not so responsive to social mobility.

Stated differently, purely structural theories have allowed for a "softer determinism" in which lower-class noncriminals with criminal propensities might lower their risk with increased opportunities for social mobility.[4] How-

4. The earliest theories of crime were developed by classical theorists who argued that criminal behavior was just like noncriminal behavior, in that both were motivated by the free and rational calculation of costs and benefits. Since the nineteenth century, positivistic criminologists have rejected the notion that criminal behavior is an outgrowth of voluntary calculations based on an individual's free will. For them, crime is *determined* by forces beyond the individual's control, and over the years those forces that have determined criminal predispositions have variously

ever, the global economy and disinvestment in urban ghettos—much touted in underclass theses—raise some realistic and troubling questions about the likelihood of social mobility for the current high-risk black underclass. If their underclass status truly renders them permanently crime-prone, then the gap from criminal to noncriminal may be unbridgeable. Certainly, if underclass juveniles are taken out of these cultures early on and placed in middle-class environments they thrive (Kasarda 1992). However, with some underclass theorists, prolonged exposure to an isolated poor culture seems to lead to self-limiting social dispositions that permanently mire the underclass in proneness to crime and deviance (Jennings 1994).

This is certainly a "harder determinism" than was traditionally encountered with unracialized structural theories. Further, because the self-limiting dispositions of the urban underclass are a reaction to social isolation and social conditions that are more permanent and more devastating than any previously encountered by lower-class whites, the black urban underclass may in fact be more closed off from conventional society than even the white lower class. This borders on a harder determinism than traditional class subcultural theories used to explain lower-class white crime and suggests an even less bridgeable gap between today's black underclass and the rest of society.

While the low probability of change in the social conditions and social isolation that have created underclass culture raises questions about the potential that underclass individuals have for social mobility, more important, for underclass theorists, in explaining the seeming permanence of ghetto poor involvement in crime and deviance is their own peculiar self-limiting dispositions. These dispositions, according to underclass theorists, constitute adaptations to the unique structural conditions faced by the ghetto poor. However, because of these dispositions, they are seen as becoming agents in perpetuating their own criminality and that of their underclass neighbors who live in the selfsame iso-

---

been biological, psychological, and social. Positivists assumed that they had to identify the causes of crime in terms of forces beyond the individual's control because they thought that criminal behavior was different from noncriminal behavior. Positivistic theorists varied in their use of "harder determinism" and "softer determinisms" (Empey 1982). Those theories that relied on a harder determinism made the gap between criminals and noncriminals large and unbridgeable. For example, early biological theorists of crime, who assumed a genetic basis for criminal predispositions, have been associated with the "hardest" determinisms. For them, the gap between criminal and noncriminal was totally unbridged.

lation. From this perspective, structural change may no longer be enough to bring those in prolonged isolation into the mainstream. The urban horror story, as told by some underclass theorists, is one in which we may now be seeing cohorts of deviants who are permanently lost.

If older race-cultural theories and current underclass theories are any evidence, explanations of criminogenic black culture seem to take on a harder determinism than most theories of American (white) crime. For the older race-cultural theorists, black culture was permanently scarred by a history of racist oppression. For some current underclass theorists, structural changes (increased employment) may no longer be enough to bring those transformed by prolonged isolation and cultural disorganization into the mainstream (Jennings 1994).

This type of thinking relies on a caricature of the culture of the ghetto poor. As it is, this culture is represented as one whose sole function has been to adjust to these restrictive conditions. Presumably, the underclass has been totally disadvantaged by these limitations and hence all of its adaptations and all of its cultural creations in the face of these constraints have been pathological. But in order to construct such a culture, defined totally in terms of its many social problems, it has been necessary to select only the most pathological elements (criminals, drug addicts) as representative of the entire culture. An underclass culture is then created by aggregating the acts of the pathological into a single culture (Hawkins 1983). This aggregation means that those in the underclass who have made healthy, or indeed heroic, adjustments must be systematically overlooked or ignored.

Ultimately, this failure to acknowledge nonpathological elements among the ghetto poor hardens the determinism of underclass theories. It means that children growing up in underclass conditions are denied any choice save those that are pathological. They cease to be free agents and become passive pawns as they react in only one way to their negative social conditions. They are reduced to a mass of pathological reactions to poverty; in other words, they become a mere product of horrific social forces.

Certainly, some acknowledge the presence of conventional persons in underclass communities. For example, E. Anderson (1990) describes conventional persons in the underclass as adult "old heads." Unfortunately, for him, age stratification precludes these old heads from having any influence on young underclass criminals, as the latter are disrespectful of their elders and convinced that their own criminal lifestyles are superior to those of the adults. This as-

sumption flies in the face of much traditional evidence that most young criminals—even those disrespectful of their elders—tend to mature out of crime
(Steffensmeier and Allan 1991). Unfortunately, the opportunities to observe
such maturing out are generally foreclosed by the use of ethnographic research
on the underclass, which typically does not follow adolescent criminals over
time. It becomes impossible, then, to observe underclass maturational reform.

Further, by ignoring underclass types—including adolescents—who have
made conventional adjustments, the out-migration of stable working-class and
middle-income blacks can appear to have so isolated those remaining that they
are incapable of leading conventional lives. This type of thinking presumes that
underclass individuals have to be *taught* not to victimize each other *by* persons
in the working and middle class. Apparently, they are incapable of acquiring
such noble moral sentiments on their own.

When underclass citizens are left to themselves, they are assumed, by way
of inbreeding, to develop any number of pathological behaviors. Their social
isolation is used to account for their increases in illegal drug use, teen pregnancy, and single parent households. As the only catalysts identified for underclass cultural development are negative—that is, structural constraints and
social isolations—more "neutral" forces are totally ignored. Hence, social
changes like the sexual revolution, the drug revolution, and increased tolerance
for divorce, which affect the larger society, are never considered as possible influences on the isolated underclass. It is not possible, then, to conceive of increases in underclass drug use, teen pregnancy, and single parent households as
their own particularized appropriation of these society-wide trends (Jencks
1991). However, to conclude that underclass social problems are totally a product of isolated inbreeding, we must ignore underclass contact with the larger
society via consumption of daytime/night-time soap operas, talk shows, and
movies, which have for the past two decades promoted a tolerance for freer sex,
occasional glamorization of illicit drug use, and acceptance of divorce.

Certainly, some criminologists are aware of how race distorts our society's
understanding of crime. Indeed, some have been led to comment on how the
news, which presents itself as fact, often distorts the race-crime relationship by
focusing on black-on-black street crimes while downplaying similar crimes
committed by whites (Kappeler et al. 1993; Surette 1992). This undue media
focus on black criminality has the effect of rendering white criminality invisible. Criminologists have also spoken to the disproportionate media attention

given to crimes involving black offenders and white victims and their potential for encouraging racial divisiveness (Walker 1985). Yet little, if anything, is said about the potential for academic criminology to shore up these media distortions of the race-crime relationship by racializing crime. This chapter has attempted to address that omission.

PART THREE

Immigration and International Perspectives

CHAPTER II

Black Immigrants

The Experience of Invisibility and Inequality, Reintroduced

Roy Simon Bryce-Laporte

Preface: Background on Purpose and Circumstances

The chapter invited for reintroduction in this collection, namely "Black Immigrants: The Experience of Invisibility and Inequality," represents the very first of my several publications and projects on the topic of black voluntary immigration to the continental United States. It was originally published in the *Journal of Black Studies* in the summer of 1973 and emerged in the course of writing a think piece the year before at the Woodrow Wilson International Center for Scholars in Washington, D.C., while on leave from Yale University. At the time I was one of the newest of the very small number of full-time black faculty at Yale College. I was an untenured professor in the Department of Sociology, the field in which I had received my doctorate and in which I had been teaching at other universities prior to coming to New Haven. My principal post at Yale was as the first director of its recently organized Afro-American Studies Program.

The original Yale program (which experienced its advancement to departmental status at the beginning of the year 2000) began with a committed focus

I wish to acknowledge the critical assistance of Marian Holness-Gault, Bruce Hare, and Ellen Kraly in bringing this work to completion. I want to extend special thanks to Mary Keys, Trudy King, and Sally McCarthy of Colgate University for their thoughtful and technical assistance as well as to the professional staff of the Case Library, the Camden County Library, the Schomburg Center, and the Statistics Department of the U.S. Bureau of Records for their support at various points in the production of the manuscript; and to the *Journal of Black Studies* and Sage Publications, Inc. for granting permission to reprint the original article.

on the intellectual examination of deeper and more critical levels of similarities and differences in the histories, experiences, and cultures of black people worldwide. The field of study itself had its early precedence in the works of past generations of scholars such as W. E. B. DuBois and Melville Herskovits. But it truly gathered political force and institutional form within the larger context of the then more recent Civil Rights and later black urban and black student movements of the sixties. Its relatively peaceful emergence at Yale was not without some activist manifestations and intense negotiations pursued by the Yale Black Student Alliance nor without some support among members of the institution's administration and faculty.

Indeed, the Yale program had begun to take its place among higher institutions of learning in the country and elsewhere as a prototype as much for its curriculum, its faculty, and students as for the civil atmosphere and national status provided by its institutional base. Soon after, the City of New Haven experienced its turn at becoming the focal point of massive urban, racial, and antiwar demonstrations. It would become the venue for the trial of Bobby Seale in connection with the alleged execution on his orders of a detractor from the local chapter of the Black Panther Party and as such the focal point for widely projected demonstrations. And thus the scene for the famous May Day protests of the year 1971.

As a consequence, by virtue of my position I was drawn into an increasingly visible and expanded role as the black faculty began to be viewed and to view itself as having to fill a multifaceted vacuum of leadership and guidance created by the crisis. Thus the receipt of an unsolicited invitation for a semester's stay in the following school year at the Woodrow Wilson International Center for Scholars, then located at the Smithsonian's Castle in Washington, D.C., seemed to hold some promise for me for a much-needed moment for temporarily gaining rest and distance from the aftermath of turmoil still gripping the campus and city and keeping me away from my scholarship. I thus viewed the moment as an ideal opportunity to redirect my attention momentarily to other yet unfinished business and still deeply felt areas of scholarly and personal interests. The leave would allow me a respite away from the everyday exposure to the delicate campus politics and administrative demands of program-building particular to African American Studies at that moment in time. It also represented a route to return at least temporarily to attending the intensive scholarly and publication requirements faced by an untenured faculty member, with a growing family, in a competitive and coveted institution such as Yale.

One of the prime areas of my intellectual concern during that period involved the new and changing immigrant patterns that were taking place in the United States at the moment and the particular significance they seemed to hold for blacks, as immigrants, as hosts, and as social science scholars. Moreover, the issue held a special significance for me as a black immigrant myself, who entered the United States in 1959, then primarily to pursue advanced education, always with the idea of reunifying my young family here if appropriate employment or other opportunities arose. Equally important here is the fact that all sides of that family came out of ethnic backgrounds stemming from earlier waves of West Indians that were being recruited since the 1850s to build and maintain the American-funded and administered railroad and later canal-building projects across the Isthmus of Panama. Hence immigration, particularly black Caribbean immigration, was both a long-held personal and professional subject of interest to me. I thus decided for my project to pursue initial research and to share ideas, inquiry, and insights in the form of a provocative article advocating the rekindling of sociological research interests in the study of a new, ongoing massive immigration into the country, noted particularly for its sizeable and numerous but unheralded "black" components.

Moreover, the choice seemed quite timely and legitimate to me. After all, immigration and the lives of new immigrants and ethnics represented primary pillars of concern in the early development of American sociology. But by the 1960s, they seemed increasingly to have become the monopolized preoccupations of historians and political scientists. In the meantime sociologists and demographers seemed oblivious to the emerging new waves of immigrants entering this country. Instead the discipline seemed to have diverted much of its professional interest toward other pressing domestic issues relating more directly to American urban life, race relations, antipoverty movements, and civil rights issues—in all of which blacks necessarily and rightly constituted a major subject of concern and curiosity but not at the expense of ignoring their import to the fuller understanding of new immigration processes taking place in the United States.

The new, nonwhite immigrants were dramatically replacing in rank and exceeding in volume the traditional streams of American immigration, usually from Canada, Western Europe, and Mexico. In combination with native-born or preceding groups of immigrants of similar characteristics or origin, they soon portended significant shifts in the country's racial, ethnic, and cultural configuration and also in its international relationships, especially in the industrial states and metropolitan centers. In general, however, neither these ongoing new voluntary movements of black immigrants nor their relations with either their preceding waves of foreign-born peers or native-born hosts were then a subject of high saliency or centrality in the academic or journalistic writings of the period.

"Black Immigrants: The Experience of Invisibility and Inequality" was an initial attempt to narrate another black experience in the insider's voice of a black person of foreign birth, but also to speak out publicly as well in descriptive, reflective, and analytical terms expected of an engaged academic in those times. More specifically my objective was to call attention not only to the seeming unawareness or insensitivity of the American public but also then to the coexistence of numerous subgroups of diverse origins, subcultures, and orientations within the larger black population of the United States. These subgroups of recent and older black immigrants also suffered pains of discrimination and disregard not only on the basis of race, but additionally on the basis of origin, nationality, ancestry, or identity.

The article was thus intended to debunk on one hand the then widespread, overly simplistic, monolithic stereotype that held sway about all blacks in the United States being one and the same on the basis of their race, provenience, and cultural heritage. On the other hand, it was also intended to demonstrate notwithstanding moments and manners in which both black immigrants and their native-born peers have (1) shared common kinds of inequalities; (2) struggled side by side for survival, success, and attentive justice; and (3) held differences or showed distinctions in behavior, culture, interests, and relations not unlike what took place between previous waves of Old and New Americans. It was to be an invitation to imaginative sociology, a call for projective thinking toward both scholarly research and social action not unlike that which marked the response of the field to the earlier waves of European immigration.

"Black Immigrants: The Experience of Invisibility and Inequality" was also a kindred statement and sequel to a chapter to be named simply "Black Immigrants" that was being prepared at the request of Peter I. Rose, Stanley Rothman, and William J. Wilson for the projected collection *Through Different Eyes—Black and White Perspectives on American Race Relations,* published one year later. Its publication was to be a compendium of essays by a selection of black and white social scientists through which its editors wished to inform and impress their American readership about the scope and variety of views existing on race relations in the wider population of the country at that point in time. Thus, every contributor was held to present the position and perspective of the category assigned within the collection rather than to expand on one's personal political position. This assignment proved to be a task much easier promised than done when one was, or viewed oneself as, an insider of the particular group being presented.

"Black Immigrants: The Experience of Invisibility and Inequality" was also part of a focused collection, in this case as an article in the first special issue of the then relatively new *Journal of Black Studies*. Comparative in its inclination, the journal would be more pointedly race- or ethnic-specific in its objectives than the Rose et al. collection. In addition to my sharing of affiliations and previous collaboration through UCLA with its editors, the policy and language of the journal seemed compatible with my own standards, interests, and orientation: "to sustain a full analytical discussion of issues related to persons of African descent." Their stated preference for innovation, rigor, and thoroughness of research within an interdisciplinary context gave added reasons for my earlier acceptance to become a member of its advisory board and also to propose editing what would turn out to be its first special issue.

The contributors to the issue would comprise a small international, multidisciplinary corps of black social scientists and thus would represent a mix of *insiders,* in contrast to the Rose, Rothman, and Wilson book. In the *Journal's* issue the scholars would project variation not only in academic perspective, but also in personal acquaintance with both the particularities as well as the universalities of racial inequality being presented. Their presentations—which perhaps more aptly could be termed representations—it was hoped would provoke on a whole, as well as individually, comparative sensitivity among readers for the vastness and variety with which blacks faced and felt inequality not only in the United States but across the globe, at that point in time. The idea behind the project was to produce a joint statement giving further visibility to the universality of circumstances and challenges we have encountered over time and space as black people.

Consequently, the title of the special issue was to be "Inequality and the Black Experience: Some International Dimensions." And its editorial introduction would clarify our mission as follows:

> Inequality is a universal aspect of the black experience; our awareness of it as a
> universal aspect of black consciousness; and our commitment to resolve it as a
> universal part of the black movement (however defined) . . . whether the full
> range of that is understood by all is not clear. But as social scientists we believe
> it is our responsibility to make clear a fuller range of meaning and implication
> of inequality.

Some of the contributions to that collection would eventually evolve into larger manuscripts and gain a varying range of celebrity. But to date, "Black Immigrants: The Experience of Invisibility and Inequality" has followed a more modest trajectory and still retains its original state as a chapter or article. Widely read and referred to as a seminal piece in the past, today it continues to be regarded, together with "Black Immigrants" in the Rose, Rothman, Wilson anthology, as among the significant baseline statements in the current study of the "new" post-1960 black immigrations (especially of Caribbean origin) to the United States in the comparative fields of race, immigration, diaspora, and ethnic studies. Over the years, I have authored, edited, and reviewed additional publications and pursued other forms of public dissemination in an effort to fill the once blatant void in the sociological literature on black immigrations and the diaspora.

◆　　◆　　◆

The Negro Immigrant by Ira de Augustine Reid was published in 1939. Until rather recently it was the first and only full-fledged sociological treatise on black immigrants in the United States. It has survived not only an unusually extended test of historicity, but interestingly, only now has it begun to earn the reference and credit it deserved as a classic of its period and genre. In other words, not only had the name of its author and title of his work seem to have fallen out of circulation until recent years, but its very subpopulation had fallen out of the main discourse in public policy or in the social scientific disciplines, except for occasional and light references in works on history of American immigration.

With few exceptions in sociology, voluntary black immigrants were simply subsumed under the umbrella of the larger group of native-born citizens as migrants, or sometimes granted short shrift among those then referred to as the "new" immigrants under the larger studies of foreign-born and ethnic populations of the country. In addition to their sociological treatments in *Beyond the*

Melting Pot, by Moynihan and Glazer, and historical discussion in *Harlem, The Making of a Ghetto,* by Osofsky, references were made to them as "newcomers" by Oscar Handlin and other major scholars of the period within more general or broader treatment of American immigrant groups. The sharpest exceptions to these various practices were to be found in the main among the works of and writings about the Harlem Renaissance, dialogues with or about Marcus Garvey and his mass movement, the collections and commentaries of Arthur Shomburg, and the occasional works and writings of the self-exiled American blacks who in reverse manner reestablished themselves and performed in foreign countries.

It was against such a backdrop of reality and realization, of apprehension and aspiration that the article subtitled "The Experience of Inequality and Invisibility" was written and published in 1973. Its reintroduction here creates an opportunity to share brief preliminary remarks, and by intention to repeat the call and express congratulations for subsequently merited studies about more current characteristics, circumstances, and coverage of the new black immigrant population and its offspring in American society today against the background of observations and opinions made a little over a quarter-century ago.

The Original Article: "Black Immigrants: The Experience of Inequality and Invisibility (1973)

The history of what today is called the United States of America has been from the very beginning characterized by close relations between immigration and inequality. Many of the first European immigrants who came to the colony emerged from situations in which they were struggling to evade political or religious inequality; others were brought here as social, political, and economic unequals to further serve in inequality as bondsman on the plantations. Then came the thousands of Africans, who were brought here by force because they were defined, among other things, as racial unequals. They were contained in a system structured to maintain absolute inequality and condemned to a status of perpetual and hereditary unequals. Ever since, the country has been receiving immigrants, most of whom came in search of equality (at least the opportunity to attain it) and who in the process have suffered temporarily some status and experiences of inequality, if only in the cultural sense, vis-à-vis the newly proclaimed Anglo-American native.

The Subtler Inequalities of Americana

The notoriety and blatancy of inequality suffered by the late immigrants—that is, those who came to the United States after the Civil War from the Mediterranean and Eastern Europe, Ireland, the Orient and Pacific, the American South, Mexico, and even Puerto Rico—have been assimilated into the corpus of intellectual, folk, legal, and historical materials of the country. There are yet, however, some other immigrants who came to this country during that period and, in fact, have continued to do so in large numbers ever since, whose experience with inequality is yet to be fully explored and incorporated into Americana. These are largely blacks in color or perceived origin. Aside from the work done by the black sociologist Ira de Augustine Reid (1939), the black immigrant as a subject has hitherto escaped mainstream social scientists and historians, even those who consider the topic of immigration and ethnic inequality their special fields of interest.[1]

Black immigrants are perhaps the least visible, but most articulate and active of America's black constituencies. On one hand, as blacks, their demands and protests as a constituent group have been responded to with the same disregard shown by the larger society and its leaders towards efforts of native American blacks to reshape the society to meet their particular needs and cultural orientation. On the other hand, while black foreigners (and their progenies) have held a disproportionately high number of leadership positions and have exercised significant influence in black life in this country, their cultural impact as foreigners has generally been ignored or has merely been given lip service in the larger spheres of American life. On the national level, they suffer double invisibility, in fact—as blacks and as black foreigners.[2]

1. Although David Lowenthal's (1967) work is not specifically an analysis of black immigrants, it represents one of the few cases where a white scholar goes beyond the blind or romantic conclusion of the superiority of foreign over native blacks.

2. Professor Constance Sutton wisely points out that the concept of *invisibility* has many meanings in American race relations. These meanings are not necessarily interchangeable. As used in this work, invisibility (disregard) refers to the Ellisonian meaning—that much of black presence and black problems goes unattended in the larger society. In some other usages, it is held that the visibility (difference) of blacks vis-à-vis whites underlies many of the racial problems in the United States. Using the former, black immigrants are said to suffer double "invisibility" as blacks and black immigrants. In the second, black immigrants are "visible" as blacks in the eyes of whites and as foreigners in the eyes of blacks (Fontaine 1983; Hare 1976).

Consider the fact that no place has really been given to black immigrants, and precious little to blacks in that interpretation of American history which describes successive waves of immigrants entering this country in search of new opportunities and contributing by their presence and participation to its cultural richness, its political complexity, its material-technological advance. In fact, it has been suggested that blacks may have been settled in the hemisphere by the time certain early Spanish explorers reached the interior of the American mainland. However, what is important and established is that blacks came to Virginia, Florida, Arizona, New Mexico, and so on "before the Mayflower"—to borrow the phrase of black historian and journalist Lerone Bennett (1961). Technically speaking, then, members of all races now residing in this country (perhaps only with the exception of the Amerindians) were originally immigrants and, accordingly, blacks constitute one of the earliest immigrant groups in the United States or on the larger American continent.[3]

Institutionalized slavery deprived the early African newcomers of making an optimal contribution to the new life of early America. White racism led to the denial and debasement of the Afro-American cultural input and to the historical contributions of blacks as Africans. Until recently, the general reaction of the larger society to most things black was as bad and most things African as dark—meaning by such terms that they were backward, barbarous, brutish, evil, and ugly. It is not surprising therefore that the views and experiences of most recent black immigrants have yet to be regarded as valuable historical or sociological data in their own right. In fact, the behavior and conditions of the black immigrant seem neither to have captured the interest of academicians interested in the exotic as an end in itself any more than they have those who generally pursue studies with clearer policy implications

Thus, we can arrive at one major aspect of American race relations viewed through the prism of the black immigrant—a general disregard of his/her intrinsic cultural worth. Moreover, when his/her feats do win the regard of white

3. My first opportunity to hear this theme developed publicly was by Stokley Carmichael in an address at Syracuse University in 1967. Black author John Killins (1965, 151) explicates the point. Two academicians who have used this point as themes in their writings are Margaret Just Butcher (1965) and, more recently, Sidney Mintz (1970). The notion of blacks as immigrants has been used in other ways by American scholars. Oscar Handlin (1959) and the Taeubers (1964) stressed the difference in experience of the visible and never-enslaved European immigrants (Kerner Commission 1968). The black urban population of the United States is seen by them as "immigrants/migrants" from the South. They have little to say about blacks of foreign ancestry.

society, they are usually presented vis-à-vis the native black American, rather than the larger, foreign-born and native-born populations of the country. And in some cases, no effort is made even to ascertain the origin of such persons or to inquire about its importance in the development of these individuals. There are at least two other forms of inequality suffered by black foreigners on this level. First, America has yet to request a view of itself presented from the black immigrant's perspective along the lines of de Tocqueville, Bryce, Olmsted, or Myrdal. Second, America has yet to encourage a study of black immigrants from within its ranks compared to the works being produced on other minorities, including the mostly American black community.

Immigration Laws and the Black Immigrant

Given the invisibility of the immigrant black, as well as the ambiguities in the definition of the terms "black," "immigrant," and even "foreigner," massive survey statistics and census material on that particular segment of the society are limited, incomplete, and neither precise nor uniformly treated. However, a cursory exploration shows that of the 45,162,638 aliens who entered the United States between 1820 and 1970, about 1,000,000 (2 percent) of them were West Indians and 76,500 (0.1 percent) of them were Africans (U.S. Department of Justice 1970, 1965, 1960). Whether such figures reflect a specific manner or degree of racial differences in the immigration process and related policies cannot be ascertained at the present time. However, it is known that early in the history of the republic, Congress began to institute laws and assign quota and non-quota categories for particular countries or geopolitical areas of the world, which have affected the patterns of foreign immigration into the country. Aside from those for Orientals and Mexicans, most of the laws were phrased to curtail immigration of persons for such explicit reasons as illiteracy, financial insolvency, immorality, or criminal records, insanity, undesirable competitive labor supply, national security, and so on (U.S. Department of Justice 1971). Immigration and consular authorities have also developed much autonomy in deciding on the issuance of visas in particular countries or to particular individuals.

It is not known to what degree these actions may have affected immigration of blacks or persons from predominately black countries. The restriction on Orientals and Mexicans may have affected persons who might ordinarily be perceived as blacks in their country (or even in the United States under other circumstances). The 1924 act that established a non-quota category for immigrants born in independent countries of the Western hemisphere and their spouses and children most likely had a differential effect on black West Indians and sub-Saharan Africans as compared to black Latin Americans, including Haitians and Brazilians. Puerto Ricans and U.S. Virgin Islanders were viewed as American citizens. Other non-Latins were generally still colonial subjects of European metropolitan states and therefore treated within the quota assigned to their respective mother countries.

However, I can recall the charges of many black West Indians that while white Mother England had a high quota that was never approximated by white English individuals coming to America, her black colonies were experiencing an annual excess of applicants over those receiving visas to go to America. It is not clear at this time whether this was a matter of discrimination by British or American authorities, any more than it is clear how other factors such as literacy, health, financial status, political orientation, and police record may have contributed to these differences. Whatever may have been the cause, the opportunity differentiated is believed to explain the large number of East Indian professionals who used to come to the United States ostensibly to "study" but who would find employment under special or surreptitious arrangements. It is also believed to explain the high number of West Indians who used to come to the United States as temporary visitors but then would enter into the labor market illegally, hoping to hold jobs surreptitiously until such time as they were able to obtain permanent status.

However, the Immigration Act of 1965 has had the most significant and direct effect on black immigration to the United States. This act established parity among independent nations in each of the hemispheres. Its impact on the predominantly black sovereign islands of the West Indies is particularly revealing, where, with the exception of Haiti, the islands with "predominantly black population" received their independence only as of 1962. In 1970, there were 5,398 immigrants admitted; 108 (2 percent) were West Indians and 812 (15 percent) Africans (not including the Arabic North and South Africa). The figures show that the number of incoming Haitians in 1965 (3,609) was doubled in 1970 (6,932). In 1965, only 1,837 incoming immigrants from Jamaica were registered. By 1971, 15,033 Jamaicans entered, for the highest number among black countries in that year, an increase of about eight times the 1965 figures. For the same years, 485 and 7,350 immigrants came from Trinidad, respectively, an increase of about thirteen times and thus the highest among the black countries of the West Indies. For the rest of the West Indies (not including the heavily black-populated islands of Cuba, Dominican Republic, and Puerto Rico), the 1965 figure (2,388) was more than doubled (4,949) in 1970 (U.S. Department of Justice 1970; 1965; 1960, 4–6). Of 373,326 immigrants in the year 1970, statistics show a total of 38,380 (10 percent) coming from predominantly black countries (U.S. Department of Justice 1970, 1965, 1960).

Black immigrants constitute a historic, ongoing, and complex segment of the American population. Figures on recent black emigration from this to other countries are not posted, suggesting the numerical infrequency of the phenomenon. Naturalization does not seem to be high among them, either. Even though the difference in fertility between foreigners and natives seems minimal (to the extent that any inferential patterns can be drawn at this time), it can be expected that the number of black immigrants in the country will continue to increase. This anticipated increase can be attributed in part to the expectation that foreigners will therefore contribute, at least, equitably to the general increase of births over deaths in the larger population, thus augmenting the number and generations of black Americans of foreign ancestry in the general population.

Another set of factors to be considered, however, is the increasing population pressures and, therefore, the precarious economic-demographic strain and historical emigration thrust that especially characterize the West Indies. At the turn of the century, according to demographer George Roberts (1957, 133–40), 146,000 Jamaicans left the island for other parts of the continent. Of these, 46,000 left for the United States directly; the others went to Panama, Cuba, and Central America to provide labor for American-owned enterprises. A total of 82,084 emigrants left the West Indies Federation for the United Kingdom from 1958 through 1960 (the period just preceding their independence and also shortly before the 1965 U.S. Immigration Act, discussed previously). The 1960 figure of these emigrants, 46,449, represented 290 percent, or almost three times, the 1958 figure, 15,988, using the total emigration of West Indies to the United Kingdom from 1958 through 1960. Jamaica ranks first, with 54,157 (66 percent); Barbados second, with 7,001 (8 percent); and Trinidad third, with 3,804 (5 percent) (Davidson 1962, 36–46).

One interpretation holds per capita income as the principal determinant. Accordingly, the three countries with largest out-migration flow had the lowest migration pressures as measured by percentage of population acquiring passports. The Windward Islands, which were at the bottom of the national income scale in the federation, had the highest indices of migration pressure. Davidson (1962, 40) concludes with the delicate policy implications that had there been no migration, every year Jamaica would have had 47,000 more people to feed. The migration meant that only 30,000 more people each year have had to find sustenance in the island. In order to keep pace with Britain, even maintaining the existing considerable disparity in living standards, the Jamaican economy would have had to expand several times more quickly than the British economy. And Jamaica's gross national product, which had an increase of 93.8 million dollars between 1955 and 1960, was impressive but in no way adequate to cope with its population explosion.

The realities of demographic pressures versus limited rate of economic development in the islands would suggest increasing migration pressure in the seventies. Given the relative unattractiveness of Africa and Asia as targets of immigration among the masses at this time and also the restrictions of Latin America, Australia, and New Zealand and the reluctance of England, then the thrust of the flow is likely to be directed to the United States and Canada, and possibly the Guineas. If the big North American neighbors choose to be miserly in both economic aid and immigrant admission, the political situation is likely to become acute and unsustainable by the islands, especially since white Americans and Canadians have been buying land indiscriminately in the region, at a time when sentiments of black consciousness and national pride are surging among West Indian islanders and expatriates. It must be recognized that extensive American export and intense American salesmanship of ideas, styles, standards, symbols, products, and processes that local governments and economies can neither produce nor provide for general consumption contribute heavily to the political unrest and illegal demographic out-migration from even the most enlightened of these countries. Such forces thus escalate the levels of dependency between these governments and the United States by heightening from the outside the already existing bridge between the rising levels of expectation of the masses and already weak governments and underdeveloped economies of even the more enlightened countries involved. Thus, if U.S. migration policies do not become more stringent and selective, more of the islanders can be expected to immigrate to this country. However, if the official policies were tightened without a marked improvement in the economic situation of those islands, then it is likely that, in addition to political and economic crises, illegal immigration will take hold as a pattern among non-Spanish-speaking islanders as much as it presumably applies at present to Haitians, Dominicans, and many mainland Latin Americans.

It is not likely that many legal West Indian residents will repatriate voluntarily at this point in time. It is safe to assume that higher proportions of black Africans (except South Africans and perhaps some Biafrans) repatriate than West Indians for at least two other obvious reasons in addition to proximity, cost, and diplomatic facility. Most Africans come as nonimmigrant diplomats, visitors, trainees, or students to begin with, and African countries and individuals in general do not have the land problem that affects the West Indies. Like their North American nationalist counterparts, West Indian nationals have a land question. However, rather than the prospect of nationalism and relative prosperity without nation (land), the islanders face the prospect of nationalism and nation without *enough* land or prosperity. The latter condition not only contributes to emigration, but also to the brain drain of the young, the daring and ambitious, and sometimes the trained and accomplished as well. In fact, the impressive "leadership" and "success" of first-generation West Indian Americans suggest that emigration had a projected loss of human resources built into it for the societies from which they came. Even then, there is no guarantee that in their ancestral homelands they would have been discovered, nurtured, and allowed to excel, given the socioeconomic stagnancy and demographic congestion of those societies.

The advancement of West Indians in the United States speaks perhaps more highly of the immigrants themselves, the fluidity and resources of this society, the untapped potential, and the demographic-economic dilemma of their home societies or region. Many of the English-speaking West Indians (some coming from Latin American countries) represent persons with linguistic and technical skills demanded by the American market. Either many of these jobs are low paying or low status by American standards, or the demand cannot be filled because of under-qualification of the natives, regardless of color. For example, many West Indian nurses and secretaries earn much more in their "professions" here in the States than at home despite the relatively low salary and low status of these jobs in the U.S. job market. In fact, some may not even be aware of the differences in social and economic status of such occupations in American standards. Many of the middle-class black immigrants who are in the country illegally or temporarily may even settle for jobs for which they are not only overly qualified, but ashamed to be associated with, that is, domestic, field, and factory hands. Still, from these jobs, they receive higher salaries than they would receive at home as "professionals."

Racism and Socioeconomic Mobility at Home and in Host Countries

Until the recent post-World War II period, blacks constituted the subordinate segment in most of the countries with large or predominant black populations. Inasmuch as the ruling component in all these societies was white and presumably of European stock, and to the extent that racial membership generally corresponds with stratification and life-chances, it is simply untrue that the average black immigrant has come out of a nonracist situation. American social observers and tourists have been prone to make such a generalization largely because they either (1) misjudge what constitutes the dividing line in the local definition of races; (2) overlook other "visibles" who rather than the blacks may comprise the sociological minority; or (3) above all, fail to recognize the particular nuances of racism in such countries (Hootink 1961, 629–31).

In many of these countries, the white or lighter-skinned elite has capitalized on the myth of no racial problem and has disseminated a false ideology and image of racial egalitarianism to their advantage. Lower- and middle-class citizens of such countries come to accept this myth, which on one hand is ego-inflating and perhaps self-fulfilling, but, on the other, is the basis of a vicious, self-defeating trap that prevents them from responding to subtle racist abuses directly or publicly lest they be considered *racist and unpatriotic.* Sensitive black American visitors often meet rebuff if they inquire about racism and are told they are misguided if they claim such inequities exist in the country they are visiting. Natives hold that they have a "class"-divided society, which may be true in the more homogeneously black countries. But how does one explain in the more heterogeneous countries that most blacks are lower class and, once in a higher class, they may not be conceived of as blacks? The class explanation by itself is obviously insufficient, but even in class terms, they suffer, at least disguised, inequalities.

Black immigrants from such countries often themselves subscribe to the myth once they reach America by denying the existence of color problems at home, often in the pathetic hope that they would escape the stigma and mistreatment directed at native black Americans by the larger society, as well as give the impression that they were not lower class and therefore not conceived as blacks or vice versa back home. Many black immigrants are instructed by persons (white and black) at home and in the United States to emphasize their distinctiveness by use of exotic apparel, display of heavy accents, and avoidance of contact and association with black Americans. Ira de Augustine Reid (1939, 101) observed that the black Latin immigrant would speak Spanish louder in public places than his/her lighter friends to warn the rest of the world that he/she is a Latin American, not a black American, as if in their own country blackness did not bring to them disadvantages relative to their lighter cohorts. One point Reid fails to add to this observation is that this type of Latin ran the risk of being interpreted as loud, rowdy, or noisy, as many Latins and most blacks were stereotyped in the minds of Anglo-Americans. In other words, the black Latin immigrant may have reinforced and broadened two stereotypes rather than have escaped one.

The point is that racism (or at least white ethnocentrism) exists in most of the countries from which black immigrants come to the United States. However, it often differs categorically, manifests itself differently, and may not have the same order of importance or salience as that practiced in the United States. However, if racism is not invisible or deniable in the countries of origin of black immigrants to the United States, it is often not as salient. This lack of salience is because it is less pressing an issue, not a principal mode of organizing, mobilizing, or even perceiving people, and is often obscured by the socioeconomic stagnancy, intertribal or inter-insular rivalries, and internal or neocolonial policies that overwhelm those countries.

In general, the exploitation colonies of the West Indies and West Africa have substantial native black majorities and rather small white, European, administration-entrepreneurial upper classes, so that whatever the form of white racism expressed by the latter, the former had their native communities and culture to draw upon and further were convinced that they could someday dominate the society. Much as is the case of Haiti, Ethiopia, and Liberia, even after independence some forms of extensions of latent racism continue to operate in these predominately black sovereign nations. In the countries of East Africa where the native blacks were in the majority and had anticipated independence, the situation was seriously aggravated by the presence of an entrenched white settler class who insisted on special privileges and engaged in outright practices of white racism. In fact, sociologically South Africa has traditionally been simply a more extreme case of settlement colonialism where an alien white minority has assumed local nationality and dominance over the black indigents and rules them by principles of white racism and colonial exploitation. The Portuguese colonies are the other extreme, more in line with traditional colonialism where the European nationality or "subjecthood" is imposed upon the native, where cultural and ethnic differences continue to be used as power and opportunity differentials. Then there is the American mainland, where blacks range from isolated minorities in countries such as Bolivia, Costa Rica, Mexico, and Uruguay to noticeable minorities in places like the United States, Brazil, Peru, Colombia, Ecuador, and Venezuela and to equal or perhaps larger proportions in places such as Panama, Cuba, and the Dominican Republic, who have no more nor less claims to being natives than the white ruling elements but apparently no realistic expectations of ever gaining dominance in their respective societies. Thus, while almost all black immigrants have come from countries with some racism and colonial practices, the effect on them would differ in relation to the degree of institutionalization or personalization, blatancy or subtlety, permanence or transitoriness that characterized racism in the country (or the section of it) from which they came.

Of equal importance is the matter of how each immigrant would have been perceived and treated within the racial categories of his native land and how he perceived himself in that society and in this one. Most immigrants, black and white, are aware of, even though not personally acquainted with, the severity and blatancy of the race problem in this country relative to their own. Hence, as Mills and others (1950) suggested, it was for this reason that many mixed-race and marginal Puerto Rican blacks hesitated to settle in this country and that many of the other Puerto Ricans who did settle may have tried to pass as non-blacks or even non-Puerto Ricans whenever possible. It is equally true, however, that most immigrants, black or white, are also aware of the wide economic difference between their countries of origin and the United States. And, because of this difference, many foreign blacks have risked the probability of racial conflict or have come prepared to tolerate some manifestations of American racial discrimination in order to make socioeconomic gains.[4] Their deeper objective is to try their luck at improving their life-chances, creating opportunities for their loved ones, or acquiring money, experience, or knowledge to

4. To some extent, this willingness holds true for black Americans as well. Even though complicated by considerations of high risk of physical discomfort, political powerlessness, and family and friendship disruptions, it is largely the fear of relative or absolute economic disadvantages that mitigates against any sizable exodus of American blacks to Africa and Guyana, where there is land and from which invitations have been issued.

return home successfully. Mass media, overseas Americans, inflated correspondence, and impressive remittances or gifts from relatives residing in the States often leave them with both levels of distortion: exaggeratedly negative pictures of the U.S. racial situation and exaggeratedly positive pictures of the economic opportunities.

Thus, in the old push-pull vocabulary of immigration sociology, the black immigrant is pushed more by the adverse socioeconomic conditions of her/his country than by its subtle racism (except perhaps in South Africa). And she/he is pulled by the relatively open socioeconomic opportunity structure of the United States more than she/he is repelled by its severe and institutionalized racial practices. The selection of black persons who immigrate to the United States is largely characterizable as those for whom economic advancement and social mobility have higher positive valence and salience than the negative valence and salience of racism. This selection is not to deny that black persons immigrate to the United States for other reasons, that is, education, family, health, and so on, but perhaps to suggest that some amount of conflict or apprehension arises for those conscious of the race situation and thus relates to the parts of the country where such immigrants are likely to disembark and seek residence. It also suggests that the black immigrants' motives for coming to this country tend to be more specific and instrumental than generalized and expressive.

As a selection of people, black immigrants represent persons who are highly disposed to, and run risks and engage in, sacrificial, persistent, and ingenious activities in order to accomplish their life goals. Before ever dreaming of coming to the United States, they may already have been very mobile people with relatively specified objectives and role models in their own societies. (In the case of the middle class, they may already have achieved serious steps toward their final aspirations.) Their decision to try to enter the United States is often made when they realize they cannot attain their aspirations at home. Coming to the United States often means various preparatory steps, desperate investment measures, and personal involvements in many efforts before passing the consular requirements, that is, obtaining affidavits of support, financial deposit, job permit, literacy and health test, police and tax records, visa and departure permits, money for transit, and so on plus other standards shared by the local people themselves such as new and appropriate clothing, luggage, arrangements for taking care of those left behind, and so on.

For many black immigrants, like their white counterparts, the United States represents a personalized, predefined frontier. Upon arrival, they are desperately eager to, and must necessarily, obtain a job quickly to meet accrued debts as well as to establish independence from their relatives; hence, they have little time or choice. They are not likely to want to underrepresent their noble intentions and feelings of gratitude by loafing or refusing jobs acquired for them by their sponsors. Furthermore, they would have few adequate reference points by which to assess the prestige and profitability of their jobs. They have not been imbued with the distinctively American penchant for conspicuous consumption and symbolic striving, or with predilections for conning their native-born brothers. However, they will have been impressed by mass persuasion of the "opportunities," luxuries, and leisure of American life, and by the expensive and conspicuous American exports that will have become status items in their homelands. They are accustomed to unemployment without welfare, hard work, or underemployment and low pay, and thus to relative deprivation of many of the things black and white Americans consider basic necessities.

The latter may not be true of the black middle-class immigrants, however, who are accustomed to having maids, nurses, gardeners, and perhaps even chauffeurs at a much lower cost than in the United States. The usually agrarian-based status system from which black immigrants come to the United States leads them to want to own land and other immovable properties, to dislike being kept in a perpetual state of debt, and to fear the disgrace that could come from imprisonment, deportation, or rejection. Hence the average black immigrant, even before he arrives in the country, is usually highly disposed to be an ardent practitioner of what Americans call the Protestant Ethic and a true tester of the American Dream. He believes that, within a decade or two, if enterprising and willing to abnegate himself, he will have moved from a low social stratum to reasonable prominence as a professional, local leader, small property owner, small-businessman, or landlord.

The Less Subtle Inequalities of America

Aside from the unusually sophisticated few and those who may have visited the country before, most black immigrants are likely to suffer great shock and anguish upon first reaching the United States. In addition to the distortion upon which they have based their anticipation, most black immigrants are coming from less complex societies and economies, often more personalized and traditional cultures; they are really not prepared to visualize the scale of size, movement, complexity, and anonymity of urban American society (even after reading general literature on the subject). The simplicity to which they tend to reduce the exaggerated messages they have received is not applicable, and the extremes they come to accept are often in areas and magnitude beyond their rustic imagination and alien worldview. However, such immigrants usually do not come to the United States as isolated individuals or recluses; they come to settle with relatives or friends. Even if they come contracted to a white stranger or agency, they tend to locate themselves in areas traversed by a kin network or situated near an ethnic enclave. Within this context, on the first job and as wards of their ethnic elders, family, relatives, and institutions, they undergo the first stage of resocialization. Hence, they get their first lessons in reinterpretation of what America is all about, the black-white problem, and their differences from and *with* black Americans (and even from and with *other* black immigrant subgroups).

America is not just a place of many promises, as they believed, but also one of many prohibitions, one in which "you don't do" many things. Given the population composition of the neighborhoods these newcomers live in, the daily routines they use, and the jobs they take, their fears are directed to the native black and Puerto Rican strangers and stragglers they meet in the passageways, on the sidewalks, and in the subways. Reinforcement of this attitude comes by way of the kinds of newspapers they read, the television programs they watch, the sermons they hear, the admonitions they get from protective relatives and compatriots. Undoubtedly the immigrant family or kin network plays a very important role here, too. The white landlord, the white shopkeeper, and the white boss will also tell them of their moral superiority over the American black and the distinctiveness of their accent, and, if British, the "grammatical correctness" of their English or American, leaving them to believe that they are the recipients of exceptional favor. In many cases, however, the whites who make such pronunciations are immigrants or ethnics themselves, no more prepared in English and Anglo-Saxon orientation or Continental savoir faire than many of the West Indians and Africans they dare to validate and certainly less American than the native blacks they tend to criticize.

It is a general belief that, despite the same kind of discrimination and exploitation, West Indians manage to "make out," perhaps even to "make it," where black Americans flounder and sometimes fail. This statement, while probably true, needs to be explored. The claim is a complex one, because the converse is also true; black Americans also manage to make out where West Indians fail. But each group deals in different realms of activities, with different orientations.

The black immigrant comes from a society that, when compared to the United States, has more limited resources, opportunities, or role components in its organization. Nevertheless, they can often identify with the holders of privileged positions on ethnic or other terms. Frustrated or overwhelmed by the institutionalized immobility of their society and impressed by the wealth and opportunities of America, immigrants come here to fulfill their dreams of obtaining such positions or similar ones in their new country. They soon find either that their assessment of such positions and preparations has been erroneous or that their availability is limited to persons with whom they cannot be identified ethnically. It is also then that many foreigners come to understand that they are perceived and governed by rules created for blacks. They also realize the convergence between institutional racism and socioeconomic political inequality.

As a foreigner, the black immigrant would have come to this country with less inhibitory socialization either in terms of self-pride and self-confidence or previous exposure to de facto or de jure prohibitions about public conduct vis-à-vis whites. Unknowingly, they break barriers and demolish stereotypes by their unrehearsed aggressiveness, naïve open-mindedness, and, thus, apparent easiness in the presence of whites. They force their white adversaries to accept them as an "equal person," which they often do by redefining themselves as exceptional to the extent that is possible and attributing that exceptionality or competence to their foreign background. But, because such logic has its own limitations, by so doing they serve as a broker and vanguard in the actual and symbolic advancement of blacks against white barriers. For, in time, they will have been succeeded or even supplanted by native-born American blacks and thus what may be seen as competition or co-optation on the micro-level may really represent in the larger perspective activities of space-creating and advance probing by foreign blacks to the ultimate benefit of native blacks.

The conflicts and misunderstandings between native and foreign blacks even extend to cultural and political matters. Differences in folk culture, colonial orientation, attributes toward whites, and exposure to metropolitan lifestyles were rather sharp even during the forties (Reid 1939, 93–170). Even though West Indians were represented throughout the entire political and professional leadership stratum of black American politics, great strain and strife pervaded the relations between foreigners and their native-born peers and constituents (Cruse 1967, 115–46). Today there is, for reasons of modernization and the rising consciousness of black culture, less strain among the two subsegments on cultural issues, but aside from a cloaked internal struggle for power and control in local urban politics, there is the subtle ideological difference with respect to what black studies, black politics, or black power meant to these ethnic subgroupings. In a sense, not only are black immigrants pressured by the larger society to be Americans (meaning by this Anglo- and white-oriented), but they also feel pressured to be black Americans and less African, West Indian, or whatever. This latter kind of conformity is expected of them not so much in culture, however, as in their political attitudes toward all those "generalized others" who are conceived as "not-blacks" or as "whites" in North American terms.

This dilemma should not be surprising, however. Did not Sir Arthur Lewis (1969) and the Kerner Commission (1968) conclude that this nation is composed of two societies, one black and one white? Or, to put it more precisely, a black versus a white society? Once conceded as a reality, such a state of relationships approximates a conflict model of plural society (Gordon 1964; Kuper and Smith 1969; Smith 1956). This model holds that ethnic groups organize, compete, and confront each other around their group interests and traditional values. Even in an open society such as the United States, ethnic groups tend to be exclusive and endogenous in their primary level of organization, and to engage in integrated or heterogeneous institutions largely on the secondary or national level (in part to protect such sentiments). Black immigrants operate as blacks and immigrants in the United States under more levels of cross-pressures, multiple affiliations, and inequalities than either native blacks or European immigrants.[5] The additions include: (1) their relatively recent identification and education with colonial officialdom and European culture, and (2) their being treated as blacks and recognized as foreign. This latter fur-

---

5. Clifford Geertz suggested in a discussion of a version of this chapter that another level of assimilative or homogenizing pressure often felt by specific island or tribal groups is perception and treatment of them as monoliths, that is, as West Indians, Africans, or black foreigners. Such generic categorization tends to negate genuine valued differences and even deeply felt animosities among black foreign groups. Milton Gordon (1964, 54–59) speaks to a similar point when he questions the plight of the marginal or nonconforming individualists in a plural society organized around ethnic components and their interests.

ther complicates their case when in addition to individual and socioeconomic differentials, other factors, such as insular or tribal origin and generational affiliations, are included.

Enough is known in sociology about immigrant versus native struggles in colonial societies, about the chances for mobility into interstitial statuses that strangers and marginal people enjoy over local people, and about the dynamics of self-fulfilling prophecies to explain the gains in status and image that black immigrants presumably enjoy relative to black natives and the intra-ethnic conflicts that follow (Blalock 1967, 76–84; Frazier 1957b, 148–51; Lieberson 1961; Smith 1956). Similar observations have been made in East Africa and the West Indies, where Orientals, Middle Easterners, and Jews were imported by white colonizers and then became intermediate ethnic groups between white aliens and black natives; in Central America, black West Indians temporarily enjoyed third-group status vis-à-vis the native populations and white alien superordinates. But more important is the tragedy of any continued divisive tensions and competition among native and foreign-ancestry blacks, in view of their weak collective situation in a society or world nevertheless dominated by white racism. The tragedy is compounded, since such systems cannot fully pursue a policy of differentiation among blacks any more than they can pursue fully a policy of uniform discrimination against all blacks. The first would create so much overlap between some blacks and whites that it would debunk the underlying ideologies of white superiority and racial purity. The second would create such a clean division of the society along ethnic-caste lines that it would destroy the democratic claims of countries like the United States as single, equal, and just societies by minimizing the brokerage, intermediate functions, and linkages that make such societies operate as wholes despite their underlying divisive racist characters. Consequently, continued *divisiveness* among blacks is not only *folly*, but serves to *facilitate their exploitation and subjugation.*

Regardless of their presumed gains and protective caution, which they may have developed concomitantly, it is untrue that black immigrants are not subject to white racist discrimination, not aware of the subjugation, and not prone to sympathize and participate in the domestic struggle for black liberation and community development. The greater truth may be arrived at by raising a few sociologically perplexing questions. When one considers the drive that black foreigners display (not to speak of the previous Anglo-Saxonized conditioning that some underwent in the Indies, the African mainland, and the British and Canadian cities), where would they have been in American social structure and what culture esteem would their tradition have borne if they were not perceived or treated as blacks? Where would they have been permitted to live, work, study, and invest? From this follows all other forms of discrimination, voting, housing, schools, jobs, and the like. Ira de Augustine Reid (1939) illustrated the operation of this principle quite effectively in the case of a Georgia legislature, which redefined the term "persons of color" broadly enough that it would include all persons "having any ascertainable trace of either Negro or African, West Indian or Asiatic Indian blood in their veins," and all descendants of any person having such blood in his or her veins. *Powers do not only divide and conquer; sometimes they aggregate to control.*

Black Immigrants in the Black Movements

The activism and involvement of black "foreigners," not counting those in official esteemed professional leadership positions, can be shown by an extended litany of names just of black immigrants and second- and third-generation individuals who have led protests, labor and civil rights struggles, and who have created or headed local black community institutions, organizations, or projects. They run the entire gamut from conservative to radical, and include both sexes and various age and regional groups. Furthermore, it is not any more possible to use silver "bangles," outmoded clothes, hair styles, or even dance steps and music to identify the second-generation black immigrant. Their identity, loyalty, accent, and traditions have melted rapidly in the *black pots and white pots* of America, leaving only slight residues. Few members of the second or later generations want to be a "minority"; most have been exposed to the same racism as their peers in schools and stores, with the police, the boss, and the "system," and most have been politicized by the same rhetoric and reality as their native peers. If there is action, they want to be in it, as *blacks and as Americans.*

Some of these younger people have returned to the lands of their "roots" only to experience great shock, frustration, and difficulty. They are repelled by the gap in relative prosperity, style of life, comfort, and development between the United States and the old country. They are appalled by the conservatism of the "black" governments of these countries and their dependency on "racist, neo-colonial" assistance. Few remain. Most return with the attitude that the old country is nice to visit, but the action is in the United States. It is only then that most black Americans, whether of native or foreign stock, realize how

American they are. In fact, some are rudely reminded of how "imperialistic, materialistic, mechanical, cold, and arrogant" they can be perceived as by their overseas black brethren, that is, as "ugly" Americans.

Literary sources depict what generally is suggested, that among the young native and foreign blacks, the gaps of difference are inclined to be reduced. Claude Brown (1965, 36–37), in his autobiographical novel *Manchild in the Promised Land,* says, "Mr. Mitchell was a West Indian, and I didn't like him. I didn't like any West Indians. They couldn't talk, they were stingy, and most of them were as mean as could be. I liked Butch, but I didn't believe that he was really a West Indian." Butch could rap, was a regular cat and Claude's buddy in swift spending sprees and street crime—quite a disparity from the image of West Indians held by most Americans. And Paule Marshall, speaking through one of her Barbadian-American teenage characters in *Brown Girl, Brownstones* (1959, 183–84) chides the members of the local Barbadian Association: "You need to strike out that word Barbadian and put Negro. . . . We got to stop just think about just Bajan. We ain't home no more. . . . Our doors got to be open to every colored person that qualify."

It is not that before there were no ties, interaction, or harmony between native Americans and foreign blacks. But much of this took place along lines of what sociologist Milton Gordon (1964, 51–54) called *ethclass.* Mostly, Garvey appealed to the *blacker working class,* foreign and native, and articulated resistance to him came from the *lighter middle class,* foreign and native. In the last two decades of Civil Rights, African and West Indian independence, Black Power, and Power to the People, there has been a kindling and universalization of "black consciousness of kind" that defies even distance, culture, class, or government. There, tunes and themes, rhythms and rhetoric are blending black. As parties walk down 125th Street, Harlem, New York, they can often hear interspersing American soul and spiritual music, Yoruba drumming, Afro-Cuban jazz, Trinidadian calypsos, and Jamaican reggaes. They see black American children dancing to the rhythms and tunes. Were they able to catch the lyrics or note the tunes, they would realize that the themes are not unlike the Afro-American versions. As Afro haircuts and dashikis are exported to Kingston and Port of Spain, West Indian bracelets and cornrow hairstyles take hold of black American youth. As black Americans go to political and cultural conferences, tourist vacations, and religious pilgrimages to the Indies and Africa, Jamaican Rastas are allegedly settling and emerging in New York. Somewhere in England, a Trinidadian protest leader calls himself Michael X, and there is a project in Brownsville, New York, called Garvey Village.

Of course, all this cultural fusion is made more possible by mass media, increased literacy, wealth, and travel among people of color. What impacts the reduction of space and the sharing of soul among those of us of color who constitute the world's majority would have on future race relations still seems at this point an open question. But at least blacks are getting together. This bonding is historically beautiful and politically potent. A legitimate concern can be raised about how restrictive or sympathetic an organization or ideology of "togetherness" can be toward genuine individual, cultural, or even finer ideological variations among blacks. The relevance of the issue cannot be sidestepped. It is a challenge and must always be kept in mind. But it must not be allowed to cripple the movement for strength through solidarity. After all, it will become a real political problem rather than an interesting ethical or academic issue only to the extent that the priorities of black economic and political power and black international unity are attained.

Power and Equality a Universal Challenge

The question is whether black solidarity can be pursued toward an end in complete juxtaposition to that which white solidarity has tried to fulfill. Can it be to the end that no more must people have to dream and die as West Indian-American Malcolm and African American Martin, West Indian Garvey and African American DuBois, West Indian-American Vessey and black Hispanic Melendez, black American Nat Turner, and non-Hispanic white American John Brown did? Will it serve to deter unjust and unequal practices by powerful or privileged black peoples or nations against less powerful or less privileged black peoples or nations? Will it affect the policies of powerful white governments in their relations with less powerful black groups or governments? Hopefully, it will serve to give new humanitarian meaning and use to the notion of collective strength and thus assure positive answers to all these inquiries. The effective and just execution of equality is a universal challenge that blacks in superordinate positions will not be allowed to ignore or avoid, any more than their white counterparts. Power is power, color notwithstanding, and most black immigrants have come to learn this by their experiences "back home."

A Postscript: On Recent Demographics, Migration, Emerging Visibility, and Related Implications in the Study of Black Immigrants

Perhaps here and there small modifications in vocabulary choice were made in the reproduction above to sharpen clarity, grammar, or terminological considerations for keeping up with the changes in use at the current time. For all other matters the work has retained its originality and as such presents some features that are dated compared to the present situation. In that regard the most dated features of the original article were its demographic details. In fact, pertinent statistical data for the years 2000 and 2001 have not become fully available even at the point of completion of this manuscript. Hence, the latest and most detailed extensive profile available on the foreign-born population of the United States is that prepared by its Bureau of Census in 1997.

That profile estimated then 25,800,000 foreign persons in the country or 9.7 percent of its total population, a growth of 6,000,000 or 30 percent from the 1990 figure. Notably this number reflected large and rapid growth of immigration from Latin America and Asia in that year. Immigration from Latin America, which included the Caribbean, accounted for 13,000,000 or 51 percent of the country's foreign-born and signaled the first time that a region other than Europe had accounted for more than half of the total foreign-born in the United States. Of the Latin American subtotal, 2,800,000 were from the Caribbean, 8,800,000 were from Mexico and Central America, and another 1,500,000 were from South America. While the black population from Latin America was claimed to be primarily from the Caribbean, many of the mainland countries share a common Caribbean coastline dotted with offshore islands, and some of them even when having only a Pacific coastline also possess old-black and mixed-black subpopulations in their midst and among their emigrants to the United States. The African foreign-born population in that year was 6,000,000, and Oceania's was 200,000.

Together Africa and the Caribbean accounted for one fifth of the growth of the black population between 1990 and 1997. Of the population of foreign-born from Latin America in 1997, about 15 percent were identified as Black or Black-Hispanic mixed; and from the Caribbean about 50 percent were identified as Blacks or Black-Hispanic mixed. These figures are complicated of course because while in both cases Hispanics constituted the majority, that category itself is viewed as being multiracial or more precisely is defined to embrace people of all races, including Blacks, Black-mixed with others, and Non-Black others. Furthermore, members of any race may be Hispanic in turn. The document further estimates blacks to have constituted 4.7 percent of the native-born population with foreign or mixed parentage, 7.9 percent of the foreign-born population, and 6.2 percent of the population of foreign stock. Foreign blacks represented 5.9 percent of the total black population of the United States; 35 percent of them were citizens; their median length of residence was thirteen years.

Obviously immigration plays a very critical role in the growth and identification of the foreign-born in the total population. The latest available issue of the U.S. Immigration and Naturalization Service *Statistical Yearbook* indicates that in the year 1998, the country received approximately 660,477 legal immigrants (including adjusted cases), among them 75,521 Caribbeans and 40,494 Africans. Among the leading predominantly black-populated source countries of such movements were Haiti and Jamaica from the Caribbean and Nigeria and Ethiopia from Africa. Other countries of the regions with comparable volumes but wider and more mixed range in their racial compositions would include Cuba, Dominican Republic, Trinidad and Tobago, Guyana, and Egypt. Another 30,174,627 foreigners entered the country legally but as non-immigrants with temporary visas rather than residential status. Among them 1,165,286 came from the Caribbean proper and 363,525 from Africa. Of the persons granted refugee or asylum status in that year, 14,915 came from the Caribbean (more precisely from Cuba) and 2,915 came from Africa. In the year 1996 there was estimated a total of 5,000,000 illegal immigrants in the United States. The data indicated that Haiti, Dominican Republic, Bahamas, Trinidad and Tobago, and Jamaica were among the top twenty source countries for persons who either entered the country fraudulently or illegally violated their temporary legal status. Each of the above countries provided 50,000 or more illegal residents to the population of the United States. However, neither the Caribbean nor Africa was represented among the leading countries of destination for emigrants estimated to have left the United States during the 1980s.

Compared to the earlier period in which the original essay was pursued and published, it is obvious that demographically black immigrants or foreign-born peoples (and their descendants) in the United States still constitute a distinguishable presence in keeping with the standard mode of defining race in this country. The picture of their presence includes interesting changes, many of which represent increases and growth relative to their presence and proportions twenty-five years ago when the original article was published. For all purposes, then, all things being equal, if blacks so defined were to continue to immigrate to the United States in comparable number and rate they will affect directly the number, proportion, and composition of the larger black population and also the Hispanic or any other inclusive ethnic category that claims to be composed of all races.

In addition to present tendencies toward some measure and variation of racial intermarriage and racial mixing that would take place among Hispanic or non-Hispanic blacks and non-Hispanic whites, visual communication following the nefarious bombings in New York City suggests the possibility of added breadth and number of people who could be conceived on first encounter as black immigrants or descendants in this country. Reference is being made in this case particularly to some proportion of the people exhibited as Arab or South Asian in the newscasts, who in many ways seem not too distinct from blacks or mixed-blacks of Hispanic or Pacific Islanders categories, and who by their own definition or practice include blacks in their numbers and composition.

At present, perhaps the use of a strict application of Ellison's version of invisibility to designate the plight of the foreign-born or descended blacks in the early essay merits some reconsideration and readjustment. For, as suggested elsewhere, there is ample evidence that black immigrants have gained attention both as blacks and as black immigrants in the society compared to the periods referred to in the past. Such occurrences and observations are indicative of the changes, complexities, differentiation, and dynamics among the immigrants themselves, within the society, and along various levels and kinds of interplay that have been taking place over the years. Of course, they have not always necessarily added to desirable images, experiences, or outcomes, but they testify to the visibility being gained, even though unevenly so, among various black immigrant groups.

Among Haitians, as an example, the attention directed to them by public media in recent times ranges in character from occurrences and patterns of unequal treatment in terms of their relocation and reunification in South Florida compared to whiter Cubans, their deprivation of privilege to donate blood in public health campaigns, their denial of proper assistance in voting and failure to have their full votes counted in the recent presidential elections, to the undeservingly brutal experiences undergone by individual compatriots of theirs at the hands of local thugs or abusive police officers in Brooklyn. Pain, fear, anger, and embarrassment must be brought to every Haitian immigrant upon recall of the treatment of David Aupont and of Abner Louima in Brooklyn. But pride must be evoked among them by the celebrated accomplishments and circulated displays of the works of Jean-Michelle Basquiat in modern art, Edwidge Dandicat in creative writing, Mario Elie in basketball, Wyclef Jean in rap music, Marjorie Vincent as Miss America 1991, and Josephat Celestin as mayor of North Miami. And Panamanian residents of New York City, many of whom share some degree of African or Caribbean ancestry, must have mourned through the weeks of public media description of the injury and passing of members of their community in the massive destruction caused by the bombing of the World Trade Towers. But they must have felt exhilarated by the performance of their compatriot Mariano Rivera as the Yankees won the American League Pennant in the aftermath of the disaster. Whether as activities of reception or exercise, they all aroused deep emotions. Moreover they and the enhanced public attention they derived from the media heightened the visibility of the groups, their neighborhoods, and home cultures. That in turn often would give way to the promotion of continuing expectations and long-lasting stereotypes, as is evidenced by the summer carnival parades that traverse the urban centers of Canada and the United States.

Increasing complexity can be said to operate in much the same way to enhance the visibility of black immigrants among specialized professional groups and disciplines, and through them to pertinent public and policy sectors. Recent academic studies, for instance, by scholars associated with the Russell Sage Foundation, have been suggesting that self-identification, group association, and display of cultural behavior among immigrants or their second-generation peers are not simply based on issues of shared ancestry but may subdivide on the basis of class differences. It has been observed that middle-class students of Caribbean birth or ancestries tend to retain stronger identity, associate with, and emphasize their West Indian roots, images, and cultural traditions while their lower- and working-class peers tend to identify more with African American identities. The obvious suggestion here is first that the black Caribbean community is not monolithic in cultural, economic, sociopsychological, or structural terms, and also that its culture and association patterns via generational studies propose not solely continuities but also changes, changes that seem to relate directly to social class and shifting reference groups.

Another group of professionals associated with the more applied orientation is the locally established Caribbean Women's Health Association. These professionals have been seriously deriving from their research and practice insights into the interplay between immigrant culture, socioeconomics, and effective public health interventions or service for Caribbean and other black immigrant women, especially with regard to early identification, prevention, and early care of widespread chronic and contagious diseases in that population and its residential neighborhoods in Brooklyn. The circulation of findings, pursuit of advocacy, and grassroots counseling—and interfacing with other professional interventional groups as well as with public health and educational services—constitute another mode and level of enhancing the visibility of this group of immigrants.

There is no doubt then that black immigration and corresponding foreign-born or descended populations have become a distinguishably developed interest among various groups of scholars in recent time. Various groups and individuals among them have been expressing their own anxiety and division around issues related to the subject, its study, and its application to various concerns of American society, its interests, and its relation to the larger globe of nations and peoples. Historically and currently the country's leading destination and place of settlement for black immigrants, the foreign-born, and their descendants is New York City and other large metropolitan areas. In keeping with that status New York is also the site of a growing number of academic centers that focus on research of that population. Among its sites are the City University of New York's Caribbean Center at Medgar Evers College in Brooklyn, the Latin American Studies Program at Queens, and the recently inaugurated Center for Latino, Latin American and Caribbean Studies, the Research Center for the Study of Man, the Schomburg Center for the Study of Black Culture of the New York Public Library, New York University's Research Center for Caribbean and Latin American Studies, and the Caribbean Cultural Center. The journal *Wadabagei,* local newsprint such as *Carib News* weekly, and local programs on radio stations such as WBIA or on public television such as "Community Events" both indicate and contribute to public awareness of the black immigrant presence in the city. They compete as expected with less positive images and stigmas that too often are circulated about blacks and other nonwhites, whether foreign or native-born, throughout the country.

With respect to American sociology, immigrants and persons of foreign stock or origin have always played significant roles in the shaping of our discipline both as scholars and as subjects of the study. In tandem with the continu-ing entrance of new immigrants of color and recurring ethnic encounters, we are being confronted with new questions about immigration, racial and ethnic encounters, transnational linkages, and their many levels of implications. But has the politics of our profession arrived at the point where it will boldly, justly, and equally "open the golden doors" of research and resources to us all—immi-grant and host, foreign-born and native, majority and minority colleagues—and to the inclusion of our issues and our works to the fuller avenue of discourse, debate, and dissemination?

Those of us who have been long at the study of racial or ethnic "minori-ties" and more so of new immigrants among them are neither immune to nor ignorant of the relationship between the politicization of issues and the gaining of visibility and relevance for certain problems, certain segments of the popula-tion, or certain studies of the issues to which either relates.

◆　　◆　　◆

The day for Ira Reid's classic, *The Negro Immigrant,* seems finally to have come. A legacy even seems to be in formation around his pioneering attempt within the discipline. At last, there is now noticeable appreciation and centrality being given to his work, and to the subject and subpopulations that he treated in his pages. And the cadre of present-day authors specializing in the study of black immigrants includes a growing number of young blacks and other scholars of native as well as of immigrant birth or background, and others yet of foreign status and with residence abroad.

Here, then, being signaled is yet another level in which black immigrants as scholars or subjects have gained visibility. Hopefully, it marks the beginning of a century where our profession will proceed decidedly toward greater inclusion and collaboration, and one in which our students will be taught more earnestly the value not only in looking around and between, but also in looking forward and back. In that sense, "Black Immigration: The Experience of Inequality and Invisibility" (and its counterpart "Black Immigrants") stands ready for closer rereading and evaluation in the context of then and now. It might be curious and insightful to see how many of its points and preoccupations have or will have gained relevance and recognition since its first publication—if only as a matter of making more visible the history and sociology of the study of black immigrants (and immigrations) in the United States.

CHAPTER 12

Sociology of "Primitive Societies," Evolutionism, and Africa

S. N. Sangmpam

Sociology of "primitive societies" has revised its earlier views about "kinship," lineage, or lineage mode of production. It now shows that lineage did not pervade African precolonial societies and that other relations, such as capitalist and class relations, were also present. This chapter seeks to reestablish, contrary to the revisionist view, the centrality of lineage in African precolonial societies to allow for a paradigmatic shift that repudiates evolutionism and brings precolonial societies back to the center of African debate. Because in such a reoriented debate Africa ceases to be marginalized and on the fringes of other historical experiences, the shift allows, paradoxically, the integration of scholarship on Africa into universal social theory.

Introduction

Today's academic debate about marginalized groups in multiethnic and multiracial Western societies and about formerly colonized territories of Africa, Asia, and South America is about redefining them vis-à-vis the "dominant" groups and former colonial powers. The "multicultural" debate is, wrongly or rightly, an aspect of this broad debate. African Americans, as "racial" groups, and Africa, as a formerly colonized entity, are two categories in the debate. Each maintains its particularities but shares common traits with the other. One of the crucial differences is that American racialized society, of which African Americans are an integral part, is at the same time a highly developed capitalist

This article was originally published in *Sociological Forum* 10, no. 4 (Dec. 1995) and is reprinted with permission.

society; their relationship with the "dominant" group is not only closer than that prevailing between Africa and foreign powers but is shaped by a highly dynamic capitalist society. And although racial considerations apply in both instances, they are more directly felt in the United States in the relationship between African Americans and the "dominant white" group. This relationship explains, perhaps, the curious phenomenon that American scholars of European descent are more interested in developing expertise in African studies than they are in African American studies.

Yet, as categories in the current debate, the analysis of African American and that of Africa share common traits. Among these, two are particularly worth mentioning because they constitute themes of this chapter. The first is that data related to African Americans and Africa, whether these are collected by scholars of African or European descent, are hardly used as raw materials to be processed for general or universal scholarship in sociology or other social sciences. That is, they scarcely become integrated into the basic concept and theory building. Often, if not always, they are relegated to "arena studies," "black studies," or "ethnic studies" for policy recommendations. A corollary is the expertise syndrome, according to which African Americans and Africans are automatically designated "experts" or can be experts only in "African studies" or "Black studies." The second common trait is that the need felt by sociology and other fields to isolate African and African American data from universal scholarship is translated into an insidious way of framing the issues in both instances. "Race relations" (read: race differences) in the case of African Americans and "primitive societies" or "traditional societies" in the case of Africa are so rigidified in order to justify this marginalization and to conceal its real causes. Although I do not subscribe to the view that the marginalization of African American data and scholars results necessarily from the conscious racism of scholars of European descent, it is certainly a structural effect of historically constructed "race differences" maintained and strengthened by these scholars under the euphemistic notion of "race relations." In the case of Africa, on the other hand, the concepts hide and protect pervasive evolutionism in African studies. In this chapter, I address this last issue.

Much of the "sociological imagination" about noncapitalist and non-Western societies is referred to as "primitive societies" by anthropology. Because of this focus and its traditional sisterhood with sociology, anthropology can appropriately be called "sociology of primitive societies." Students of African affairs owe a debt to the insights provided by the latter discipline. Yet reliance on anthropology carries with it a heavy toll. Evolutionary thought, which pervades anthropology, is transmitted to the sociology of development and too much of the scholarship about today's Africa, which has several implications for social prescriptions. One of the main causes and effects of evolutionism is the paradoxical marginalization of the much-discussed yet silenced lineage in the contemporary African debate. This chapter desires to reestablish, contrary to traditional and revisionist sociology of "primitive societies," the centrality of lineage in African precolonial societies to allow for a paradigmatic shift that repudiates evolutionism and brings the specificity of precolonial societies back to the center of the African debate. This reestablishment is done by arguing against the unfounded claims that class relations coexisted with or prevailed over lineage relations. I conclude that, paradoxically, only serious attention to this specificity helps one avoid the marginalization and "nationalization" of scholarship about Africa and allows its integration into universal social theory.

Evolutionism and Paradigms of Society in Africa

Society in Africa, like capitalist society in the West, comprises ethnic, religious, racial, cultural, and other non-economic dimensions. However, its specificity is perhaps best defined by socioeconomic traits: the non-central position of capitalist core relations built around the capitalist and the worker; the non-commodification of much peasant agriculture by the capitalist sector; the marginal position of indigenous capitalist and non-capitalist enclaves; the persistence of pre-capitalist relations; the oscillation of social groups and classes between capitalist and non-capitalist relations; and (as a consequence) lack of integration in the economy from geographical, sectoral, and input-out points of view; extreme dependence on the world market and the West, hence, unequal exchange; and the smallness of the internal market. The ramifications of these traits are low per capita gross national product, generalized economic deprivation, social despair, political authoritarianism, bureaucratic ineptness, and strife, which constitute the African crisis.

These traits and attempts to eradicate them dominate the African debate. Yet the latter is vitalized by evolutionism. Although most theoretical paradigms recognize that these traits—which I have called "pseudocapitalism" elsewhere (Sangmpam 1994)—result from the contact between capitalism/imperialism and precolonial societies, and that precolonial relations had some impact on capitalism, they fail to explain them by not going further than this obvious and uncontroversial recognition. Regardless of their ideological differences, both Marxists and non-Marxists explain African society today by what "almighty" capitalism and imperialism did or did not do. In imperialism-inspired theories (dependency, world-system, imperialism) (Amin 1976; Amin 1989, 118–23; Chinchilla 1983, 159–69; Wallerstein 1976, 1980, 1984; Frank 1969, 221–30; Frank 1981; Bagchi 1982, 13; Johnson 1983, 238; Laclau 1982, 37–38; Leys 1975, 171–74; for a full critique, see Sangmpam 1994, chap. 2), precolonial societies are reduced to lifeless and breakable entities, whereas in dualism and modernization theory their influence is equated with "stagnation" that retards capitalist "progress" (Weaver and Berger 1984, 59; Boeke 1953; Lewis 1954; Bauer 1972, 1981; Bauer and Yamey 1978, 102, 104; Agarwal 1983; Higgins 1984; Hyden 1983; for a full critique, see Sangmpam 1994, chap. 2).

Evolutionary thought has two aspects: "the idea that a common form becomes differentiated, and that a simple form becomes more complex" (Cheater 1986, 2). This definition applies to both dualism/modernization and imperialism-inspired theories. In both, capitalism is posited in theological terms as the "more complex form" or the yardstick for progress. In an evolutionary fashion, it is construed as the natural/inevitable ending stage of development to be reached by stagnant precolonial societies that are both the "common" and "simple" forms in the evolutionary chain. Precolonial societies thus are passive, lifeless, and "transient" entities waiting for their "differentiation" and metamorphosis into the "superior" and complex form, capitalism, which is given unlimited and exclusive power to make and break them. Neither type of theory contemplates the possibility of precolonial societies as active (as opposed to stagnant) formidable forces of resistance because of their differential developmental path in precolonial times. The repudiation and nonrecognition of the dynamism of precolonial societies perpetuate the "myth of Western civilization" and "Eurocentrism" that some of the proponents of these paradigms ironically combat (Amin 1989).

Because they are crucial in explaining today's African society, how does one incorporate precolonial societies in the explanation? Society cannot be defined in a vacuum—that is, outside material production and its attendant network of social relationships. This view is not (exclusively) Marxist as often wrongly claimed; it was recognized by almost every well-known thinker before

Marx, including Plato, Aristotle, and Cicero.[1] African "culture" is not an exception to this social rule. Even where appearance suggests to some anthropologists the sheer need to "accumulate subjects in order to rule" as the determinant factor of politics (Fairley 1987, 91–100), in reality, for Africans not even governing is independent; governing, whatever its local flavor, reflects the core relations that structure the challenges of material production. Accumulation of and control over subjects is very consistent with this reality. Government, as the people of the Kongo kingdom learned well before Marx, is not something established to govern a territory in the abstract but to represent the power of those whose lineage controls the land (MacGaffey 1970, 263). Hence, to define the impact of precolonial societies on today's Africa, the leading question ought to be: what relations structured the African response to the challenges of material production and subsistence around which other aspects of the culture revolved in precolonial times?

The answer is simple: lineage relations were the ordering relations, which does not imply that they have always existed since human beings appeared in Africa (Vansina 1990, 101–10). ("Lineage" is used here as a generic term to refer to descent reckoning as opposed to kinship reckoning; that is, it refers to a corporate group reckoned by steps of filiation to a real or fictitious common ancestor, a group whose rights and obligations are deeper and more constraining than those of a kinship group found in Western societies (Fortes 1963, 276–310).

Yet being itself evolutionary and by distorting and contesting the primacy of lineage, sociology of primitive societies lends its evolutionary lenses to the interpretation of today's Africa. Africanist anthropologists and historians have revised their views about "kinship," lineage, or lineage mode of production. They attempt now to show that lineage did not pervade African societies and that other relations, such as capitalist and class relations, only were present (Vansina 1980; Harms 1987; Kopytoff 1987, 3–78). The revisionists seek to assert Africans' "individualism" and "initiative," as if Africans were deprived of individualism and initiative within the lineage structure. In addition to the in-

---

1. Plato admits that society occurred so that humans could distribute and combine the product of their industry (Newman 1973, 36). Aristotle subordinates the ability to rule to property ownership (*Politics*). And in Cicero's words, "Men founded states and cities primarily on the principle that private property may be retained" (*De Officiis*).

herent theoretical defects of the earlier models on "kinship" and lineage mode of production, there are three reasons for the revisionism. The first is academic faddism that allows "models" to supercede each other on the basis of their ephemeral "popularity." An example of this faddism is the claim that the concept of (lineage) mode of production was "invented" by French Marxist anthropologists and should be abandoned because they failed. The truth is that mode of production is a universal concept and not a "French" concept (Sangmpam 1994, ix–xii). At any rate, proponents of the concept of lineage mode of production failed not because of the concept but because of their evolutionism and delectation with "primitive societies" and Marxist exegesis, which had nothing to do with explaining contemporary Africa (Rey 1971; Terray 1972, 1975; Meillassoux 1960; Jewsiewicki 1981, 101–3; Jewsiewicki 1985, 1989; Kitching 1985, 117–18). The second reason is paternalism associated with the "canons of the same," which has forced Africanists to think of African societies as "being just like us," leading to the claim about the existence of class and capitalism in precolonial Africa. This second reason of revisionism is directly linked to, and indeed embedded in, the third reason, which is evolutionary thinking shared by both African and non-African scholars; according to this thinking, Africa is at an earlier stage of Western societies, which requires that historically specific subconcepts (as opposed to universal concepts) characteristic of the West, such as class or capitalism, be found at any cost in their nascent state in Africa. The view that the existence of class relations is a *sine qua non* for "civilization" or for the policies of change (Coquery-Vidrovitch 1976) has led to the unfortunate conclusion that a discussion of African precolonial societies is not valid unless one attempts to find class relations even where they cannot be found; a discussion about lineage relations becomes an anathema whereas "class" is fetishized. For this reason, the presence of slavery and tribute paying in precolonial Africa are confused with "class society." Attempts to deprive precolonial lineage relations of their centrality has led to the strange elevation of Islam as core relations in these societies just because it infiltrated them as early as the seventh century and is "strongly implanted" there.[2] In reality, neither "class" nor capitalism is the *sine qua non* for every society's historical development; nor should a mere reference to them be a substitute for hard-sought explanations.

2. Ali Mazrui's views on Islam in Africa come close to this position; see *The Africans: The Triple Heritage (1986)*. For a reply, see the debate between him and Wole Soyinka in Transition *(1991)*. It is important to note that Mazrui is not the only one to express this view; it pervades African historiography.

Goran Hyden (whose effort needs to be reacknowledged here, although, by faddish academic standards, the work is "outdated") attempted to go beyond Marxist exegesis and to explain contemporary Africa with the concept of lineage mode of production, which he terms "peasant mode of production." Hyden is correct on six points. First, he subordinates his analysis to African material production, the "determining human progress" that "sets the historical stage for other activities (Hyden 1983, xiv). Second, Africa does not have a feudal tradition despite persistent claims to the contrary (P. Anderson 1979, 1980). Third, excessive emphasis on the role of imperialism vitiates the analysis of African societies. Fourth, Africa's development process is not similar to Europe's or North America's earlier industrial development, although he wrongly claims that Africa cannot be compared to Asia and Latin America (for a refutation of this view, see Sangmpam 1993). Fifth, Africa's specificity, embodied in the lineage ("peasant") mode of production, has consequences for contemporary Africa. Sixth, there is need for socioeconomic change in Africa.

Unfortunately, Hyden's theoretical matrix and policy recommendations, developed around Africa's specificity, rest on evolutionary and dualist assumptions discussed above and do not distinguish him from modernization theory and its pioneers, Max Weber and Talcott Parsons. The "economy of affection" (the underlying economy of the peasant mode of production) rests on four elements: (1) It is based on a rudimentary division of labor and lacks cost-benefit considerations; (2) the needs for humans prevail over the development of the means of production; (3) there is limited surplus, and family solidarity is placed above personal economic achievement; and (4) the principles of reciprocity embedded in customary rules prevail over universal and abstract laws. More generally, the economy of affection is prescientific, organic, locale-specific, less differentiated, and generates clan politics and inept and personalized bureaucracy and state (Hyden 1983, 6; Hyden 1980, 14, 161).

Quite apart from the fact that no economy can meet the needs of humans without cost-benefit considerations and some changes in the means of production, one recognizes easily here the Parsonian dichotomic variables of modernization: modern achievement versus family/clan ascription, modern universalism versus traditional particularism, modern specificity versus traditional diffuseness, and modern competent and impersonal bureaucracy versus traditional patrimonial and incompetent bureaucracy. Because evolutionism rests on the idea of traditional "stagnating," it has severe analytical consequences for Hyden. First, the economy of affection is a given; there is no attempt to explain why it exists or functions the way it does, except by linking it to a network of blood and clan ties. Second, Hyden maintains that the peasantry is "uncaptured" because of the economy of affection while, contradictorily, claiming that this economy has been and can be destroyed by capitalism (Hyden 1980, 4; 1983, 7). Obviously, what cannot be "captured" cannot be destroyed. Third, given the evolutionary assumption of the inevitability of capitalism, the economy of affection retards capitalist development and explains African society today. And the contemporary African crisis in institutions, elites' political behavior, and policy is also a direct outcome of the economy of affection (Hyden 1983, 7–8). Fourth, Hyden's solution is inescapably evolutionary as he seeks to replace the "stagnant economy of affection" and its related "soft state" with capitalism and the bourgeois-led strong state.

The weakness in Hyden's work exemplifies analyses and prescriptions based on good intentions but that are tributary to an evolutionary interpretation of lineage. To counter these evolutionary views, the first step is to reestablish the primacy of lineage by showing that the class argument proposed by Africanists is unfounded. For space reasons, the discussion is limited to societies in eastern Africa (Kikuyu, Lou, Baluyia, and marginally, other groups), southern Africa (Nguni-Zulu, Xhosa, Swazi, Ndebele-Tsonga, Sotho, and Khoisan), and central Africa (Ambuun, Bading, Basongo, Ngombe, Luba, Kuba, and Kongo). Space considerations also preclude a detailed account of each of these societies; the focus is instead on their general traits.[3]

Precolonial Societies in Africa

Lineage constituted the backbone of social relations in these societies. It included roughly the same major units: the nuclear family, the extended family, the subclan, and the clan. In all of them, the nuclear family, although independent in some aspects, remained subordinate to the requirements and needs of the whole lineage. The mode of descent reckoning was based on patrilineage (for example, Kikuyu, Baluyia, Zulu, Xhosa, Ngombe, Luba) and matrilineage (for example, Ambuun, Kongo, and Kuba).

The clan was the highest lineage unit in all these societies. Like the subclan, it comprised individuals tracing patrilineal or matrilineal unilateral descent

---

3. The discussion about precolonial societies in Central Africa and Zaire is based on Sangmpam (1994).

from a common ancestor and included both the living and the dead. The clan has two quite contradictory roles. On the one hand, it differentiates its members from other members of the larger society ("tribe" or "subtribe"). On the other hand, it lacks the cohesion characteristic of the subclan and the nuclear family. Although clans in most of these societies were totemic and exogamous, there is some evidence that some of them were not. Thus, the Luba clan does not seem ever to have been totemic, and the rule of exogamy did not always apply, for example, to ritual marriage between a political leader and a women of his clan in the Kongo (Peires 1981, 6; Cagnolo 1933, 22; Muriuki 1974, 35–36; Schapera 1956, 29–33; Sangmpam, 1994).

Politically and administratively, all these societies were originally noncentralized (which is different from "stateless"); some of them became centralized. Although centralized societies maintained some specificity, in general all the societies shared roughly the same basic political and administrative structure. The lineage, the village (homestead in the Kenyan societies), and, in many cases, the chieftainship constituted the pillars of such a structure. The lineage, in addition to its own internal organization, politically and administratively structured the village/homesteads and chieftainships through its internal subdivisions. Among some of the societies, the basic politico-administrative authority was supplied by the autonomous extended family subclans (for example, Kikuyu, Ambuun, and Kongo). In some cases, such as the Basongo, the clan itself played a much more centralizing role administratively and politically for its members. In many of the Kenyan and southern African societies, the clan, depending on the circumstances, played a more active administrative and political role in conjunction with or in lieu of the localized, autonomous lineage unit through village councils or other assemblies (Muriuki 1974, 35–36; Kenyatta 1965, 186–87).

Each of the lineage units was led by a lineage head. Although in most cases the normal succession was determined by seniority, other circumstances (for example, breakaway, heroism, choice of dying lineage head) allowed a nonimmediate claimant to head the group. The head of the lineage organization fulfilled several functions, including that of referee, legal representative, youth educator, marriage counselor, migration judge, ambassador for other lineage groups, and guarantor of the group's property.

The village/homestead was the politico-administrative coordinating center. In some cases (for example, Sotho and Ngombe), it was a one-lineage village that coincided with the local lineage organization. In most cases, it comprised several subclans of different clans that did not claim common ancestry. Among the Luo, as elsewhere, "every village was associated with the lineage of some clan on which its cohesion and individuality [was] based" (Ocholla-Ayayo 1980, 55). That is, because the lineage structured the village, the latter was headed by a chief who, as a rule, represented the senior or dominant lineage. In many cases, the senior lineage owned the land on which the village stood. The village chief was assisted by a council of elders representing different lineages and performed, with their assistance, a variety of administrative tasks. Some of these councils (for example, in Kikuyuland) were the focus of the Nguni groups; the village chief organized ancestral rituals as lineage head and representative of the ancestors. In most cases, chiefs were granted high marks of deference and, in some instances, tribute by their subjects (Schapera 1956, 40–>60; Ocholla-Ayayo 1980, 52–58; Kenyatta 1965; Sangmpam 1994).

In highly centralized societies (for example, the Kongo kingdom), a founding king's lineage imposed a highly hierarchical structure on the top of the state apparatus. In most societies, however, especially noncentralized ones, the highest politico-administrative structure that displayed direct connections with both the lineage and the village was the chieftainship. Weak and almost nonexistent among the Kikuyu, the chieftainship existed in various forms in other eastern, southern, and central African societies where it played an instrumental role.

As a "grand chief" (to distinguish him from the king), the head of the chieftainship was assisted by a council of elders dominated by (but not exclusively composed of) his own lineage, an executive council, and a local administrative body. As a representative of the senior lineage, the grand chief had lineage bonds with deceased chiefs, which endowed him with supernatural powers. Known under various names in different societies, the grand chief performed generally the same tasks as the local lineage heads and village chiefs but on a grander scale. He appointed the councilmen, received tribute, distributed goods, presided in court, offered rituals to the ancestors, made rain, and required labor service from his subjects. He also distributed land and decided about seasonal hunting and fishing (Kenyatta 1965, chap. 9; Muriuki 1974, 35 ff; Schapera 1956, chap. 3–5; Sangmpam 1994).

Although centralized societies maintained an economic advantage over noncentralized societies with regard to economic accumulation, production forces in both types of societies were roughly similar. All of them practiced hunting, fishing, and gathering, agriculture, handicrafts, and manufacturing as main economic activities by means of various forms of labor cooperation. In manufacturing, ironwork helped the production of spears, swords, hoes, machetes, knives, bracelets, and so forth. Animal husbandry, generally less developed in central African societies, was more developed in eastern and southern African societies. In the east and south, goats and cattle were so central that "he who controlled the cattle also controlled the men who depended on them" (Peires 1981, 128). In most of the societies, the major economic activities and the overall process of production took place under the aegis of the lineage. This explains the association of the ancestors in the production process and in ironwork and in the elaborate rituals performed by the lineage elders as the opening of the farming season or to obtain fertility and good harvest. Slavery caused by war, crime, sale debt, famine, and rejection by one's lineage provided part of the productive forces. Slaves were used to transport goods for agricultural and other work, as payments for a debt, and as wives. Above all, they were used to increase the size of one's lineage. As a general rule, centralized societies had more elaborate networks of trade than noncentralized societies. Because of their tribute requirements and expansionism, Ndebele, Zulu, Luba, Kongo, and to an extent Kuba kingdoms developed intense trade activities. To these two general reasons one needs to add local reasons. For instance, the need to extract tribute from subject societies caused the Zulu kings to encourage trade in Maputoland (Mozambique); the peacemaking role played by the Luba empire before 1700 allowed trade to flourish; and Kongo's early exposure to European trade roads and Atlantic slavery also encouraged trade activities. While barter was practiced in many of the societies, in many others, shell, raffia cloth or square, and other items were used as means of exchange/money (Cagnolo 1933, 43; Kenyatta 1965, 22–94; Ballard 1981, 1002 ff; Schapera 1956, 6, 34, 99–100).

Because these were societies based in socially, geographically, and environmentally different spaces, they displayed some differences in their relations of production. For instance, among the Kikuyu, unlike in similar noncentralized societies in Central Africa, an individual could sell a piece of the lineage-owned land for a short period provided that sooner or later the land was recovered by the whole lineage organization. Moreover, the extraction of surplus by the head of the chieftainship does not seem to have been as important as in other societies. In eastern and southern African societies, the importance of cattle in social relations of production differed from those prevailing in Central Africa. And in centralized societies, especially southern Africa, the state played a more interventionist role in the extraction of the surplus.

Despite these differences, all these societies displayed striking similarities. Social relations of production were dominated by the lineage. The whole society ("tribe") and the chieftainship exercised the negative right to exclude foreigners from using their land. Their positive rights, however, differed. The chieftainship held the positive right to allocate plots of land to its members in some societies (Basongo, Luba, and the Nguni group) but not in others (Ambuum, Kikuyu, Ngombe, and Kongo). The tribe, in most cases, did not have the positive right to allocate land except in one sense; in centralized societies, the king, as the representative of the whole society, had the ideological and political right to do so but through the local lineage chiefs. For all these reasons, the relations of production functioned best at the clan and subclan levels.

At these levels, the lineage head stood at the center of a network of relationships involving the ownership of the means of production and the extraction and distribution of the surplus product. Land was inalienable because it was ultimately the property of the ancestors; living members were simply guardians, and the lineage head, by virtue of his ancestor-derived powers, was its guarantor and manager. Although lineage members chose land to till, the tacit or explicit approval of the lineage head was important in most societies. Lineage members owned their instruments of labor, houses, livestock, their fields, and the product of their work on the fields. Because individual ownership was not synonymous with strict private property, instruments of labor were easily shared among lineage members. The lineage head indirectly controlled the labor process and could extend or withhold his blessing, in the name of the ancestors, for productive activities. Relations of production also meant extraction of the surplus product in the form of a trust fund for the lineage (including the bride wealth received by the lineage) and labor services and goods owed the eldest members by their juniors. In almost all of the societies, the justification for the extraction was the intermediary role played by the lineage chief and elders with the ancestors. A portion of the surplus was given to the ancestors to harmonize the homestead. In patrilineal societies, the father played a major role in the extraction of the surplus. The right of the patrilineage head to sell, kill, or enslave his sons was the equivalent of the authority of the matrilineage head to do the same to his nephews or nieces that he "owned." In most cases, both goods put in trust and those extracted were redistributed in many ways among the members of the lineage (Kenyatta 1965, 22–94; Cagnolo 1933, 22, 29–31, 50, 105–10, 140–41; Schapera 1956, chap. 1, 102, 115; Coray 1978, 190–93; Guy 1981, 30–35, 129; Sangmpam 1994).

The pivotal role played by the lineage, the ancestors, the elders, and the chiefs in all the societies was accompanied by an abundance of rituals. In the 1930s, an Italian Catholic priest, C. Cagnolo, counted seventy-seven instances in which the Kikuyu performed what he termed "superstitious" rituals (Cagnolo 1933, 175–87). All other societies discussed here did the same. In almost all of them, the cult of the ancestors went arm in arm with the code of seniority. The attachment to the ancestors stemmed from the concept of the lineage as a continuum whose ends were its deceased members in the other world and its living members. The ancestors owned the lineage property and were the source of happiness, success, and health for the living members. To maintain their presence among the living, their burial ground was surrounded by their belongings. To obtain happiness and success, the living members had to invoke the ancestors (even when they worshiped God) properly with offerings such as food and beer. By virtue of their age, the lineage elders were junior to the ancestors yet were close to them within the lineage continuum. This closeness qualified the elders to represent the ancestors among the living members of the lineage. Attachment to the ancestors enhanced the status of the elders. In return, lineage elders enjoyed a vast degree of deference shown to them by their juniors. The prominent role played by the lineage elders was reflected in the political arena, where, as mentioned, chiefs or grand chiefs were credited with supernatural powers to provide prosperity to their subjects, and in the economic field, where lineage elders controlled the relations of production. The unbreakable link between the happiness and misfortune of the living members, on the one hand, and the will of the ancestors on the other, explains the proliferation of divination and sorcery practices (Cagnolo 1933, 2, 8–83; 1975, 189; Kenyatta 1965, 96–103, 193, 206, 252, 230, 256; Cavicchi 1953, 16–17; Ocholla-Ayalo 1980, 32–35; Were 1977, 1–3; Schapera 1956, 125; Sangmpam 1994).

Although all the societies shared the above social and political features, they differ in one important aspect. Centralized societies distinguished themselves by their territorial expansion and the existence of centralizing state apparatuses and kings. But, such centralized state apparatuses did not lead to uniformity; some states were more or less federated (for example, Luba, Kuba, Xhosa), and others were sharply centralized (for example, Kongo, Shaka's Zulu, Ndebele,

Swazi). In general, their political and administrative structure included the village, the district, or province, and the central administration dominated by the royal court. The village administration was dominated by the lineage heads, as in noncentralized societies. An extensive network of officials represented and performed tasks for the king at the district and provincial levels. They were appointed, in some cases, by the king himself or by his representatives who, usually, were members of the royal lineage or allied lineages. In the capital city, the king was assisted by a royal council comprising aristocratic lineages and some client lineages, by a well-regimented military presence, especially in the Swazi, Zulu, and Ndebele kingdoms, and by various state officials in charge of taxes, the kings' fields, foreign affairs, justice, wars, social welfare, rituals, and so forth.

In all the centralized societies, the state apparatus revolved around the king, who was an imposing figure. Known by different titles that expressed his preeminence, the king was venerated and quasi-divine. He "owned" the land and his people. He was the kingdom and provided rain and fertility to his subjects and was the source of prosperity for the territory, the herdsman of his people. This role placed him at the center of elaborate rituals, taboos, and obligations that isolated him, mystically protected him, and caused people to express respect and fear towards him (Balandier 1968, 176, 191–98). Like his Kongo and Luba counterparts, the southern African king

> Organized religious ceremonies upon the due performance of which his tribe's security and prosperity are held to depend. His dead ancestors . . . provide supernatural protection and help to the people they had once ruled, and therefore he visits their graves to pray and sacrifice to them on behalf of the tribe. . . . In all groups, he also has horns or other vessels containing "medicines" compounded of many different ingredients including very often portions of a human being specially killed for the purpose; and he may further have brass rings (Zulo and Tsonga), drums (Venda and Northern Sotho), or other sacred objects . . . to which the skin, nails, hair, etc. . . . of his predecessors are added as they die. (Schapera 1956, 73)

Because the king derived his supernatural power from the ancestors, his investiture and succession rituals resembled those of the lineage head and the "grand chief"; they differed only in their magnitude and more solemn character. Rules of succession to the royal throne reflected also, in general, those at the local level. The eldest son of the first "great" wife or the king's brother succeeded the dead king in patrilineal societies, whereas the king's brother or sister's son succeeded him in matrilineal societies.

The tremendous power of the king explained his authority over the various policy issues attended to by the central, regional, and local officials. A king's power was not unlimited, however, even in such "despotic" states as Shaka's Zulu. Counterbalancing influences were provided by the king's lineage, the royal council, and the popular threat of secession by alien or client lineages or by the king's own kin. The threat of secession was an effective deterrent to abuse of power because of the strong dependence of the state on tribute that was paid in cattle, salt, iron, raffia cloth, food items, luxury products, and so forth. Tribute was redistributed in the form of social welfare benefits and payment to state officials and allied lineage heads. The distributive functions of the king made him "the wife of the tribe" among the Tswana and the "breast of the nation" among the Zulu (Schapera 1956, chap. 1–3; Guy 1981, 33, 59–60; Cobbing 1981, 160–65; Sangmpam 1994).

Thus, the central position of the lineage organization in social, political, and economic activities of all these precolonial societies is undeniable. To be sure, local and historical factors caused variations in the actual development and functioning of lineage—for example, passage from matrilineage to patrilineage and vice versa. Also, to assert the lineage primacy is not to suggest that everything was reducible to lineage. As in any society, there were activities, subgroups, and organizations that displayed relative autonomy vis-à-vis lineage: religious societies, age-grading systems, gender associations, and socioeconomic activities that displayed individualism and initiative. The central position of lineage can be appreciated only in comparative terms. Indeed, as religious and other groups in capitalist societies do not operate outside the limits imposed by capitalism, so, too, autonomous groups in lineage societies scarcely avoided the lineage's influence. The central position of lineage went hand in hand with the pervasiveness of the rituals accompanying most of the social activities influenced by it—the Italian priest's "superstitions" referred to in the anthropological literature as myths, witchcraft, religion, belief system, and so forth.

Why was there the primacy of lineage in the African precolonial societies discussed? I shall now show that, contrary to persistent claims, an absence of class relations explained the primacy.

Precolonial Societies and the Unfounded Class Argument

To refute the claim about class relations in African precolonial societies in support of my argument, a definition of class is not enough. A close reading of some of the writings is in order. Proponents of the class argument propose a four-set class relations explanation about the societies discussed and African precolonial societies in general: (1) slaves versus their owners (Thornton 1983, 17, 32; Schapera 1956, 64–65, 128–29; Guy 1981, 30), (2) nobles versus commoners (Thornton 1983; Vansina 1978, 165; Schapera 1956, 56; Guy 1981, 39; Davidson 1992, 67), (3) kings/chiefs versus commoners (Davidson 1992, 95; Schapera 1956, 4, 14, 130 ff; Vansina 1978; Thornton 1983; Peires 1981, 125–35), and (4) the king and his aura versus everyone else (Schapera 1956, 105–10; Vansina 1978, 165; Thornton 1983; Packard 1981, 28).

African slavery has been amply debated (Miers and Kopytoff 1975; Meillassoux 1991). Despite the various reasons that caused it, it cannot be confused with a class situation resembling Roman slavery, let alone plantation slavery. It is true that in many cases slaves were sold to aristocratic lineages. As captives of war, they also generally served these lineages, which were established in towns, for instance in the Kongo kingdom. Nevertheless, important reasons refute the application of the class concept. First, in the Kongo kingdom most town-bound slaves served the Catholic Church and not the "town nobles." Second, and more importantly, in all the societies discussed, the central position of the lineage neutralized class exploitation; slaves controlled their own labor process and fed themselves thanks to the organization of lineage as a whole. Even proponents of the class argument recognize this integration of slaves within the lineage (Guy 1981, 30; Schapera 1956, 132). Some of them speak of "slaves only in name" (Thornton 1983, 22). And lineage being what it is, one's integration into it scarcely makes one a class exploitation object. That slaves married in the same way as their "owners" and that some of them became powerful chiefs within the lineage and a counterbalancing force at the royal court amply confirms the point. Even the pain they felt as slaves was caused by their acute awareness of losing their lineage and not by class exploitation, which further confirms the centrality of the lineage. The claim that war slaves were an exploited class because they were captive does not stand in the face of any historical evidence; any war captive suffers the consequences of war without being a class object. *Vae victis* (too bad for the vanquished!), said the Romans long ago. In any case, in precolonial Africa, war captives were not turned into an exploited class. One needs only to read Achebe's *Things Fall Apart* (1958) to be convinced of these points.

The class nomenclature built around "nobles versus commoners" is weak as well. Consider the following claim about southern African societies: "In most Bantu tribes there are usually at least two well-defined social classes, often distinguished by name, which we may term nobles and commoners respectively. The former includes all people held to be of the same origin by descent as the chief. The remainder are commoners" (Schapera 1956, 56). The notion of class relations in this quote is used regardless of the implications of the fact that nobles were "of the same origin by descent [lineage] as the chief." Regardless of one's understanding of class relations, a social class cannot revolve around a lineage, which has its own specific relations of production. The two, by definition, are contradictory. But, more importantly, according to the quote, one becomes part of the "noble class" simply by belonging to the chief's lineage; apparently, no class exploitation is necessary. And what is referred to as class practice/exploitation is nothing more than practices normally associated with the seniority of the chief/king's lineage: "[Among the Venda], the chief and his clan are something apart from the rest of the tribe; unlike commoners they have their own burial groves where they perform sacrificial rites that are unique to them; and their children receive a special training at the chief's village, where they learn many things that the vhalanda, the ordinary folk, never get to know about" (Schapera 1956, 112). The truth is that these are not class practices but the secret rituals consistent with the aura of the chief/king discussed earlier. One needs to explain these rituals. As for the "class of the commoners," called "serfs," it comprises war captives, who, in light of my previous comments, obviously disqualify as a social class.

In addition to these claims, the nobles versus commoners class argument is supported by the facts that (1) in some precolonial societies, town nobles did not operate on the basis of lineage but on the right of conquest and the specificity of their households; and (2) the size and organization of noble households were different from those of the commoners/villagers. These claims rest on shaky ground. While denying the influence of lineage on town nobles, proponents of the class argument recognize that nobles and commoners shared the same type of economic production (Thornton 1983, 28, 57; Guy 1981, 39). Despite protests to the contrary, a social class cannot be defined outside production. And given that commoners and nobles shared the same type of economic production dominated by lineage, it is inconceivable that the nobles would operate as a class outside the lineage production sphere. Town nobles, like the commoners, were profoundly governed by the lineage ethics and lineage-based production. The size and organization of the houses of some individuals or the aristocratic lineages are no proof of class relations either. They simply denote social inequalities that African precolonial societies shared with every society on earth. Such inequalities were made even more pronounced around the apparatus of the centralized state because of the distribution of tribute in the form of income. Even in the Zulu kingdom, where an individual who was isolated for some reason from his original lineage became a client to another individual or lineage, the noble-serf relation never developed. Through the *ukusisa* practice, he was afforded the opportunity to use his patron's cattle (which he herded) to collect buttermilk, which he exchanged for goats and later exchanged for cows, which helped him acquire wives and develop a lineage segment of his own.

Whereas in the nobles versus commoners class set, all those belonging to the chief's lineage are the noble class, in the "king/chief versus commoners" nexus, chiefs and kings comprise a special social class. A common theme among anthropologists and historians is "territorial ties," according to which most precolonial rulers acquire their power without lineage involvement. Through individual ambitions or wars of conquest, leaders emerged and assumed political power. Because the "right of conquest" by the king and "territorial ties" are posited as the very foundation of kingship, they become the embodiment of a network of class relations and not of lineage ties. The relation between chiefs/kings and commoners is thus likened to that which prevailed between lords and serfs in Europe (Peires 1981, 130). Unfortunately, this argument does not fare any better. Whenever invoked, the territorial ties thesis fails to prove that lineage was not involved in the acquisition of territorial ties by the conquering leader. The previous description has amply shown how precolonial political power could not escape the constraints of lineage. Territorial ties were always accompanied or preceded by lineage-based arrangements between a local lineage head/organization and the invading forces or would-be ruler. The claim about the class position of the chiefs is further supported by the fact that the class conflict between them and the commoners is played out "in the framework of customary procedures relating to tribute and judicial fines" (Peires 1981, 136–37). One wonders how state officials who impose fines on tax delinquents can be involved in a class conflict between themselves and the delinquent taxpayers. The relation between state officials and the commoners in itself is not (in any type of state) a class relation. Attempts to turn chiefs/kings from lineage heads into a class easily lead to contradictory statements; for instance, the Xhosa king is compared to the feudal lord while his ownership of land is attributed to his ancestors/clan; the chiefs are said to form a class front against the commoners while "the primary loyalty of the homestead head was to his clan-section head and not to the chief himself"; and the ideology of the chiefs is deprived of the lineage import while at the same time the chiefs are said to perform "the necessary functions of the old clan heads" (Peires 1981, 130, 131, 135–36).

The confusion about class relations has repercussions on the explanation of the king's aura and quasi-divine nature. Because the centrality of lineage is avoided, this nature is also explained by the territorial ties argument and other related factors, such as the king's wealth, his archsorcery, his ability to invoke the myth of conquest, his investiture, and the intrinsic qualities of kingship. These explanations are highly questionable because none of these factors can escape the impact of lineage. That political power was based on lineage is supported by the charter myth and dynastic line it sought to legitimize; the heavy involvement of matrilineages or patrilineages in the selection and support of the chiefs/kings; the whole system of interlocking political alliances between ruling lineages and founding clans; and the king's invocation of his predecessors' conquest, and hence, of his descent reckoning. Even in cases where many aliens had become part of the state, lineage was still determinant because it defined who controlled power and how. The omnipotent and divine role of the king did not derive from his investiture, contrary to persistent claims by anthropologists. Rather, it derives from his position within the lineage organization and the overall lineage ideology. Investiture only formalized his power. The simplest way of understanding this point is to recall that the king was a lineage elder who, like a simple lineage head, was expected to mediate between the homestead/the living and nature/ancestors. Both played this mediating role because of their position in the lineage organization and not because of the investiture. The king's investiture was more elaborate than that of the simple lineage head simply because he was the king and the other was not.

Thus, the primacy of lineage over class relations is unquestionable. Because they could not free themselves from the lineage's influence, even relatively autonomous groups never succeeded in creating class relations. To take the example of the age-grading system that has been referred to as "age class system" (Bernardi 1985), among the Kongo, its dependence on lineage was revealed by

254 | S. N. Sangmpam

the fact that one of its aspects, the initiation, aimed precisely at reinforcing one's link to a lineage by despising those who lacked lineage ties. In other societies, the rights and obligations of each age grade did not reflect class domination and exploitation but political/public and lineage obligations. An example is the Masai in Kenya, whose four age groups corresponded to military activity (first grade), family and economic activity (second grade), decision-making power (third grade), and religious and ritual power (fourth grade). Although the promotion from one grade to another involved inequality, it did not constitute class exploitation and domination. On the contrary, the age-grading system "ensure[d] the distribution and diffusion of status and power to all male members of society" (Bernardi 1985, 54).

Social classes can be analyzed only through the relations they involve; these, in turn, are indissociable from production. Therefore, class relations involve the exploitation that production relations generate. More specifically, one class appropriates a part of the surplus product that is produced by another class and also controls the conditions under which the exploited class works. The control involves four elements: (1) the exploiting class controls the means of production; (2) it determines what portion of the production generated by the exploited class goes where and for what purpose; (3) it can lower or raise at will the portion of the product allocated to producers/exploited class; and (4) except under capitalism (where workers, as individuals, can sever their relation with individual capitalists and not with the capitalist class as a whole), the exploited class has no way of "withdrawing" from the exploited class because they cannot subsist unless the exploiting class ("lord/master") allows them access to land (Marx 1904, vol. 1; Kitching 1980, 443–44).

Lineage was a deterrent to this type of class control. The collective ownership of the major means of production—land—despite the dominant position of the lineage head, the dual control over the labor process whereby lineage and the producer *qua* lineage member owned different categories of the means of production, and the loophole that allowed lineage members to own property, was incongruous with class exploitation as defined here. Among the Zulu, for example, laws prohibited the head of the homestead from transferring property from one segment of the homestead to another; among the Kikuyu, the transfer could take place only after consultation with other members of the homestead. In theory and in practice, lineage juniors could rebel against their seniors, which constituted a "withdrawal" from the dominant relations. Not only could they withdraw, but withdrawal did not "cut off" the juniors' means of subsistence, because they still had access to land. (Seniors, of course, imposed sanctions, such as curses, but they differed from class sanctions.) Undoubtedly, some lineage leaders extracted a high level of surplus product. What distinguished this relation of extraction from a class one, however, was the modality of the distribution of the surplus product. And, although I argue that social groups associated with the state in precolonial societies were not classes, I do not suggest that social classes cannot be associated with the state. Nor do I suggest that the state apparatus cannot reproduce social classes. The state can and does help reproduce social classes. Feudal and capitalist states are cases in point. The state does so, however, only where the society is dominated by class relations, which is not true for the societies under discussion.

These are more important reasons why class relations did not obtain in precolonial lineage societies than those often proposed in the "blood ties" argument. After all, a lineage did not always include people linked by blood. It is irrelevant whether the absence of class ties or lineage came first. (On attempts to reconstruct the origin of lineage, see Vansina 1990.) The crucial fact is that structural conditions, which fought off and stifled class relations, asserted the primacy of lineage relations.

Conclusion

The foregoing discussion has implications for both scholarship about and social prescriptions for Africa. First, reestablishing Africa's specificity through the reaffirmation of the primacy of lineage is not to argue for *sui generis* Africa requiring that Africa be studied as an idiosyncratic phenomenon; nor does it suggest, as falsely claimed by some, that only Africans are qualified to study Africa. It is not a plea for cultural relativism either. On the contrary, the paradox is the evolutionism *"sui generises"* Africa and breeds these dangers, whereas reestablishing Africa's specificity does much to avoid them by integrating Africa into universal scholarship. Consider, for instance, Hyden's previously mentioned concept of "economy of affection," through which he attempts to explain today's African society. This "economy of affection" is nothing more than the primacy of lineage relations and their elaborate network of rituals and requirements. It is the outcome, as I argued here and elsewhere (Sangmpam 1994, 1995), of classless societies attempting to offset the nonuse of economic and political/physical coercion associated with class societies. As such, it does not have any *direct* link to the characteristic features of African postcolonial politics.

The link is indirect, that is, structural. This structure—pseudocapitalism—needs to be explained first. Yet, by not taking into account this explanation and by viewing the economy of affection as a sign of the "simple form" of African primitive societies in the evolutionary chain, Hyden offers an erroneous explanation of clan politics and of inept and personalized bureaucracy in Africa; these are explained by this unexplained economy of affection, leaving unanswered the question of why Africa shares both clan politics and personalized and inept bureaucracy with Asia and South Africa, which presumably are not characterized by an economy of affection. Thus, because it reduces crucial historical specificities, Africa is made *sui generis* instead; the explanation of its problems is dangerously reduced to what the ideological "African man" does.

Second, because it subordinates all historical experiences to the inevitable transition to the "complex form" in the evolutionary chain, evolutionary sociology easily displays a tendency for false omniscience and omnipotence. In so doing, it provokes revolts among those who are part of these experiences. It subverts the drive toward universal social theory by creating conditions for dissent scholarship by Africans or people of African descent who (understandably) claim to have the monopoly of counter-truth about Africa. Whatever one's opinion about Afrocentricity may be, it is hard not to view it as an example of such dissent. Sociology of primitive societies is responsible for the fractionalization of scholarship. Serious investigations of precolonial lineage societies, not automatic class assumptions about them, would do much to respond to the Afrocentric legitimate concern that Africans be studied as subjects of historical experiences rather than as objects on the fringes of Europe.

Third, evolutionary sociology, by design or implication, is contemptuous. Because it cannot logically separate African scholars from the African "simple form" in the evolutionary chain, it is no surprise that in many instances these scholars are automatically assigned the task of exclusively analyzing Africa since it is the only world they can know, and they cannot, presumably, develop expertise in matters related to the Euro-American world, which is part of the complex form. The rejection of evolutionism would yield beneficial effects in this respect. For instance, by positing lineage and class as social relations tied to historical particularities, "class" ceases to be a universal concept; it and lineage become subconcepts reflecting these particularities and are in need of integration into broader, universal concepts (for example, "mode of production"). Because it deprives "class" of its undeserved aura and superiority in the evolutionary chain, the focus on universal concepts deprives evolutionary scholarship of its superiority complex as well; indeed, it becomes clear that knowledge depends not on who is part of the simple or complex form in the evolutionary chain, but on how universal concepts and methods are used to shed light on historical particularities and their attendant subconcepts.

With respect to social prescriptions sociology's assumptions and analyses inevitably lead to solutions that celebrate the "complex form," that is, the Euro-American world at the expense of a real appreciation of constraints and possibilities for policy in Africa. Solutions such as the "market," "good governance," "strong institutions," and others derive from analyses that shy away from serious investigations into the structural implications of the primacy of lineage for postcolonial Africa. Effective prescriptions for action in Africa are possible only by integrating its scholarship into universal social theory.[4] Such an objective is attainable only by not viewing Africa as *sui generis,* which requires, paradoxically, that its historical specificity be taken seriously.

4. I attempt such a theory in Sangmpam 1995.

CHAPTER 13

Globalization and the African Experience

Pade Badru

As the global economy slips into a recession, the fate of the forgotten half of the world becomes even more desperate. Globalization, as not so recent a phenomenon, has connected remote orbits of the modern world into one network of a global empire. This chapter assesses the impact of globalization on the society and economy in Africa. It argues that recent globalization has produced new forms of dependence in peripheral states in Africa with consequences not anticipated even by the most optimistic of liberal economists. It further argues that globalization, like colonialism, has led to the strengthening of the links of dependence in the underdeveloped section of the global economy, producing, in the process, unimaginable misery and poverty especially in formations that are already at the point of total economic collapse.

Introduction

The later part of the twentieth century saw a rapid increase in technological innovation, especially in the areas of information sciences. The invention of the Internet and the development of more sophisticated computer networks meant that information could be delivered simultaneously to the entire global economy at speeds previously unimaginable. While this speed has helped improve commerce by removing impediments to global trade, it has also aided the process of recolonization of weak and least competitive economies in the least developed part of the world, with dire consequences. The emergence of international institutions, such as the World Bank (WB) and International Monetary Fund (IMF), has speeded up the legitimization of international trade, with these institutions serving as capitalist brokers within the world system. The end result of this process of globalization is the reshaping of political systems, world-

wide, in accordance with the new global economy in which the former impe-
rial states continue to sustain their previously held hegemony. With the demise
of the old Soviet Union, opposition to capitalist globalization and its inherent
banalities is becoming an exercise in futility.

This chapter will be argued in three parts. The first part will survey the old debate of global development to examine how old ideologies are being passed along
into the new age of globalization. The second part will look at the role of new and
old institutions of capitalist developers such as the IMF, the World Bank (WB),
and the United Nations, with the goal of evaluating their roles in facilitating
global underdevelopment of the poorest section of the world economy. Finally,
the third part will evaluate the experience of the African economies in this new
age of globalization.

Development Debates Revisited

In his most celebrated work, Immanuel Wallerstein (1974) speculated the future direction of the world capitalist system in which he sees a movement toward increasing concentration of economic wealth in metropolitan capitalist
countries. Unlike the optimism expressed by the modernization scholars
(Rowstow, Eisenstadt, Lewis), Wallerstein perceived globalization as a threat to
global equality and peace. In a similar vein, other radical theorists have warned
of the intrusiveness of the capitalist mode of production into backward
economies because such penetration could either lead to a dependence or to a
deformed type of capitalist development that is incapable of solving problems
of poverty in the periphery. Indeed, most economic policies advocated for the
developing world by these international agencies are still rooted on old economic theories developed during the Cold War.

Modernization School and African Development

The most dominant perspective in the study of social change is the modernization school of thought. Many modernization theorists see the problems of
transformations as intricately linked to the rigidity of the traditional social
structure of the developing societies (Eisenstadt 1966, 1973; Hokowitz 1988).
Eisenstadt argues that internal obstacles imposed by the rigidity of traditional
structure contribute to the lack of transformation in many traditional societies.
In Eisenstadt's work, political modernization is often seen as a prelude to the

process of economic development, and by inference, the historical path taken by Western societies is similarly proposed as the necessary path toward the evolution of structures that would allow for social and economic transformation (Moore 1998). As Horton (1993) argues, political modernization must, above all, entail intellectual transformation, since traditional systems of thoughts are not compatible with the requirement of a modern economy (Horton 1967, 1993). This tradition/modernity approach has its roots both in Western metaphysics and in Weberian analysis of the transition to Western industrialism. Modernity, of the transition to industrialism, is characterized by the rationalization of the economic, politic, and cultural structures of a given society. This transformation is necessary in order to achieve the type of efficiency upon which modern industrialism can be built (Abrams 1982, 73–107). Using these structures as indices for measuring development, modernization scholars see the European historical trajectory as a gauge for defining development.

Theoretically, the traditional perspective may contain some useful points only if one is looking at the system of international economic development or global social change in a vacuum. This metaphysical viewpoint summarizes clearly what is wrong with Western interpretation of realities in the developing world. In short, it calls into question whether Western social sciences, such as sociology and economics, have really understood the meaning of development. By defining social change in terms of the European historical trajectory, scholars like Eisenstadt and Horowitz not only foreclose the possibility of a different path of historical transition, but also deny the specificity of conditions in all human societies. The tradition/modernity perspective did not begin with Eisenstadt but represents the culmination of a long line of platitudinous analyses that continue to characterize post-World War II economic analyses of developing societies. The neoclassical Rostowrian perspective, which provided the intellectual and ideological basis for the postwar capitalist development model for developing societies, has confused our understanding of development in non-Western societies.

The inability of many sociologists and development specialists to recognize the fact that Western imperialism has complicated, and continues to complicate, Third World development experience calls into question the utility of this traditional approach in sociology. Eisenstadt's analysis has further contributed to the lack of theoretical clarity in development discourse. This discourse is often predicated upon some ontological notions of human nature and history.

In Rostow's work (1960), there was a more coherent modernization theory that relies exclusively on positivistic and metaphysical interpretation of development. In the Rostowrian model, development is like a copycat game in which the developing world simply adopts fiscal policies that have enabled the Western societies to develop. In this neoclassical schema, development is measured as a percentage or ratio of investible savings to consumption. In the end, growth is defined purely in quantitative terms, especially by the gross national product (GNP). The modernization idea of development, as exemplified by Rostow, erroneously assumed equity and progress in the growth of the capitalist economy and, as result, ignores the painful realities of income distribution, the monopoly of resources by dominant classes, and the export-oriented nature of production that limits economic growth in most developing societies.

By believing in the metaphysics of the free-market economy, the modernization school of thought calls for international capital's participation in Third World development. According to Rostow, countries that are lacking in development resources could open their doors to multinational corporations, the so-called agents of change, and with the right political climate, such countries could be on the road to a self-sustaining development. Available evidence suggests the opposite (cf. Susan George 1992). Indeed, the current IMF proposal for economic recovery in most of the developing world is based on these neoclassical ideas. In fact, the past decade has witnessed many desperate African nations executing structural adjustment programs (SAP) that promised quick economic fixes.

In his seminal paper, Horowitz (1988) introduces new absurdities to the modernization debate, classifying societies in terms of how closely they resemble the Western model of development. In his latest article, "Three Worlds Plus One," Horowitz is at odds with himself in stressing that despite the modernization dreams of progress in the periphery of the world economy, the global economy is still basically divided between the rich North and the poor South. The industrialized countries of the North, according to Horowitz, continue to prosper and enjoy breakthroughs in science and technology, while the nations of the South sink deeper into poverty. But Horowitz is unable to explain the dynamics that are responsible for the persistence of this dichotomy within the world system. Like Horton's, Horowitz's metaphysics clearly demonstrates the type of arrogance that often characterizes Western scholars' analysis of the problems of

African development experience. The ahistorical nature of Horowitz's reasoning brings up the question of whether modernization theorists have an agenda separate from their scholarly pursuits.

After fifty years of faithful commitment to the modernization paradigm, economic conditions in most developing nations, including those in the communist block, have deteriorated sharply. But, despite the glaring failure of the neoclassical model, the developed industrial countries continue to promote this model in the developing world. The question then must be which economic interest benefits from the continuing advocacy of this paradigm in Third World development? Indeed, many developing nations are yet to see tangible results of years of participation in the global economy. Which brings us, further, to the question of dependency in the world system.

Globalization and Dependency

The failure of the modernization model in analyzing class relations in the Third World led to the development of an alternative paradigm often dubbed as the radical or conflict perspective in development circles. This paradigm ranges from the simplistic dependency model to the more sophisticated world system theory. Unfortunately, this radical approach within sociology and political economy has ended up with the same problems that marred the modernization theories of development. Essentially, by sharing the same basic metaphysical belief in the possibility of a late capitalist development in the periphery of the world economy, the radical school went the same road as their modernization counterpart. This is not to suggest that what the radical school has to say has no explanatory value.

The radical scholars reminded us of the ahistorical character of the modernization theory. They sought explanation of underdevelopment in the very logic of capitalist development. Andre Gunder Frank (1966, 1970), one of the early popularizers of the dependency theory, blamed capitalist development in the metropolis for causing underdevelopment in the periphery. True enough, but how? Frank's main argument rests mainly on the role that colonialism played in the early development of European capitalism. Colonialism, the argument goes, provided the initial accumulation for capitalist development, which at the same time created the very conditions for Third World underdevelopment. These conditions include among others (1) the drainage of potential investible resources from the periphery to the European metropolis through unequal exchange; (2) the creation of a particular form of world division of labor that assigns subordinate and dependent roles to former European colonies (the periphery of the world economy); and (3) the dominance of development ideology that locks bureaucrats in the developing world into believing in the fairness of the current global political and economic arrangements (Amin 1974, 1976; Wallerstein 1986; Stavenhagen 1973).

Thus, for dependency scholars, peripheral formations can achieve sustained and autonomous economic growth only by breaking away from the suffocating world economic order. Breaking away from the international economic order, according to the dependency school, would require a socialist revolution. But Frank and the other radical scholars were hardly able to prescribe how this would be achieved given the current reality that the international economic order represents. In Frank's work, as in Rostow, Lerner, and Eisenstadt, we have a new ideology, or religion of development, one that pays very little attention to the internal contradictions and capabilities of the developing societies. In fact, these radical development theories have very little vision of economic development that would be qualitatively different from the Western European experience. In a sense, we are made to believe that the answer to the developing world's problems can come from this sort of analysis that does not take into consideration the realities or the perspectives of the poor men and women in the poorest section of the global economy.

Immanuel Wallerstein (1974) transformed dependency into a more coherent thesis in which the capitalist world system incorporates both the developed and developing world with shared characteristics of development and underdevelopment. Unlike the dependency theory, underdevelopment, in this world system paradigm, is not a function of the capitalist development process but is instead an essential aspect of global capitalist accumulation, incorporating specific forms of division of labor that distinguish the center from the periphery.

In its broader argument, the world system theory sees development as a temporary advantage. It argues that, within the global capitalist system, the developed Western metropolis has a temporary advantage, and with the possibility of a shift, the developed section of the world economy may occupy the subordinate position that is currently being occupied by the peripheral nations. What a relief! This dynamic equilibrium model draws its theoretical strength from the thesis of permanent revolution (McIntyre 1992). However, it should be pointed out that the world system theory differs significantly from the dependency theory in its dogmatic belief in world revolution that would shift the balance of power from the center to the periphery.

The political climate of the 1960s may have given inspiration to the ideas of a global revolution. However, there was hardly any clear indication that the system of capitalist expropriation was under any threat from internal social classes in the metropolis. Except for challenges that were posed by decolonization and the Civil Rights movement in the United States, increasing poverty in the periphery was accompanied by increased accumulation in the metropolitan centers of global capitalist production. Indeed, there was never a material basis for global working-class unity that could generate the type of revolution envisaged by the dependency and world system theorists.

Paul Barren's (1956) critique of the neoclassical perspective inspired several radical researchers in the late 1960s and 1970s. In particular, younger economists at the Economic Commission for Latin America (ECLA), like Cardoso (1979), Furtado (1970), and Dos Santos (1973), began to apply the political economy and dependency models to the understanding of the structures of underdevelopment in the Third World. Unlike the modernization theorists, these scholars saw underdevelopment not as a stage in the process of economic development, but as a peculiar condition brought about by capitalism's incursion into Third World economics. They emphasized the overdependency of Third World economics on the Western metropolis, which continues to dictate the internal dynamics of the former. Colonialism, these authors argue, was a precursor to this peculiar situation of development (Frank 1969).

Emmanuel Arghiri (1972) identified the problem as one of unequal exchange between the periphery of the world economy and the Western metropolis. He argues that unequal exchange between the underdeveloped countries and the Western nations arose out of "the maintenance of depressed wage rates and the use of monopoly power by industrial nations to turn the terms of trade against the Third World" (Eicher 1990, 11). Emmanuel suggests that the developing nations could unite in creating their own cartels as a means of confronting the traditional hegemony of the industrial nations within the world system. In an unusually defensive article, William Arthur Lewis (1978) disagrees with the thesis of unequal exchange. Lewis argues that unequal exchange in the global economy arose not because of the persistence of colonial dependence and monopolistic practices by the West, but because of the failure of Third World countries to invest adequately in their internal production (Lewis 1978). Perhaps, in his desperate attempt to defend the market theory of agricultural development in the developing world, Lewis ignores the fact that potential investible resources in most developing countries are largely under the control of international capital. Lewis also ignores the fact that the pattern of investment in many developing societies by transnational corporations is largely determined or dictated by profit motives and not by any social or moral concern, which is outside of the realm of capitalist economic calculation. Whatever the strengths of their argument, the inability of dependency and world system theorists to transcend the positivism of the modernization school renders their models inappropriate or limited when it comes to understanding the persistence of economic backwardness in the Third World. Consequently, what was proposed as a science ultimately ended up as a new metaphysics in development study.

Modes of Production in the Periphery

While the dependency and the world system theories failed to provide a more coherent explanation of Third World underdevelopment, a new school, the mode of production school, turned attention to the modes of production specific to the Third World. This school recognizes (1) that the dependency theory represents a valid, if not coherent, critique of the neoclassical modernization school of thought; and (2) that the dependency theory remains essentially within the modernization problematic. John Taylor (1979), in particular, contends that the inability of the center–periphery paradigm to transform the positivism and teleology that structured the modernization perspective renders this paradigm inadequate in understanding economic crisis in the Third World. The mode of production school addresses the question of the various forms of articulation within the global capitalist mode of production and within the non-capitalist sectors. The goal of these scholars is to understand how these articulations shape the pattern of capitalist development on the global scale (Taylor 1979; Amin 1974).

According to the mode of production scholars, it is essential to understand how capital expands by maintaining non-capitalist sectors within the global system of production (Taylor 1979). In other words, by retaining the pre-capitalist modes in their original forms (preserving their ideological purity), the mode of production school argues that the dominant capitalist mode of production is able to exploit these modes to meet the conditions of its own reproduction. This idea of "reproductive needs" of capital later led to the development of the dualism theory. This theory conceptualizes economies of developing societies as being divided into two separate sectors: (1) the enclave of advanced capitalist sector and (2) the backward rural sector that continues to generate resources for metropolitan capitalist development. The lack of articulation (linkage) between the two sectors necessarily creates a more rigorous account of how dualism creates underdevelopment, and it was soon to be challenged by other radical scholars.

In his contribution to the debate, the Argentinean sociologist Ernesto Laclau points to the confusion that often arose in the understanding of the processes of economic development in the Third World. For instance, he points to the readiness of Western-trained economists and sociologists to confuse separate levels of analysis. By confusing economic systems with modes of production, Laclau contends that sociologists often gloss over an important component that may render their analyses and conclusions invalid (Laclau 1977). For Laclau, an economic system comprises different modes of production and their interconnections. The mode of production, he argues, defines a specific articulation between the relations of production (mode of surplus appropriation) and forces of production (mode of expropriation of nature) (Laclau 1971, 37–38).

Laclau further argues that the dependency and the world system theorists have confused contradictions that are essentially at the level of the mode of production with contradictions generated at the level of the economic system. As a result Laclau contends that the link of dependence between the advanced capitalist West and the Third World is seen, by these analysts, as the primary cause of Third World underdevelopment. Instead, Laclau sees these contradictions as the manifestation of the effects of articulation of the global capitalist mode of production with the different non-capitalist modes in the periphery. This articulation, Laclau insists, is the generation of wealth in the metropolis of the global economy and the generation of poverty and misery in the underdeveloped world.

The World Bank, IMF, and Economic Deprivation in Africa

By the early eighties, modernization policy had produced economic disaster in most of the developing world. In black Africa, the policy had resulted in a total collapse of many economies. Debts to international banking institutions had reached levels unknown before. Most infrastructures were certainly at the point of collapse in many African states. Export-related activities were reaching levels incapable of supporting state activities, while food production had come to a halt as a result of shifting land to export crops. It was this desperation that led the International Monetary Fund (IMF) to intervene. This intervention came in the form of the structural adjustment program (SAP), which I will discuss below. However, I must emphasize that prior interventions of the World Bank had failed in stabilizing economic production in sub-Saharan Africa (cf. Badru 1998). The introduction of the structural adjustment policy, as we shall see below, simply complicated matters more for most of the sub-Saharan African states.

Structural Adjustment Program (SAP)

The IMF began to implement its structural adjustment program in Africa in the mid-eighties. The introduction of SAP was intended to stem the tide of sharp economic decline. The structural adjustment program included nine policies, or what the bank officials chose to call "conditionalities." The execution of all of the conditions specified in the program, according to the IMF, will qualify a country for a new round of lending. These conditions are briefly summarized below:

Devaluation of the national currency and the abolition of foreign exchange control;

Fiscal anti-inflationary policies that call for removal of subsidies on essential items including leading export goods;

Reduction of state spending on social services such as health and education;

Trade liberalization, maintaining an open door to investment and importation of foreign goods;

Privatization of public enterprises (parastatals) and sale of government shares in private companies;

Open-door policy for multinational corporations including free repatriation of accumulated profits;

Monetary anti-inflationary policies, including, but not limited to, control of bank lending and higher interest rates;

Control and reduction of wages paid to labor;

Anti-inflationary dismantling of price controls and minimum wages.

When fully implemented, the program, according to the IMF officials, is expected to generate positive results in the economy. The implementation of these policies will generate the following outcomes:

Raise the rate of utilization of existing installed capacity in agriculture and industry;

Accelerate food production and rural development and encourage the use of local raw and intermediate materials;

Gear fiscal and economic policy toward growth through tax incentives and growth-oriented commercial policy and, by reorganizing the tariff, make it less restrictive and more competitive;

Reform the public service, making it more efficient and through privatization and commercialization of government enterprises, where appropriate, reduce the scope of government intervention;

Promote job security by widening employment opportunities;

Keep external debt-service to a limit of 30 percent of export earnings (Okigbo 1989, 176).

The overall effect of these bizarre policy recommendations was in the opposite direction from their anticipated goals. In most cases, these policy recommendations have in fact reduced capacity building in countries that have implemented them. In addition, structural adjustment had certainly produced disastrous consequences for dependent economies. For instance, in Nigeria, the implementation of SAP had led to quadrupling of workers' retrenchment, devaluation of the national currency, and collapse of the educational sector. Most African countries that adopted the policy have also seen a catastrophic fall in the standard of living of their citizens, while state policy continues to enhance the economic advantage of the elite and, of course, international capital (Adepoju 1993).

Indeed, available evidence suggests that wherever SAPs have been executed in the Third World, there has rarely been a successful restructuring of their national economies (Hutchful 1987). It has been shown that adjustment policies have complicated efforts toward sustained economic development in the developing societies of the South. At the same time, IMF-imposed structural adjustment policy has resulted in the consolidation of economic advantage of international capital (Onimode 1988; Hutchful 1987). In Ghana, Nigeria, and Sierra Leone, the adoption of SAP has also led to stiff rises in the price of basic consumer goods, which in some cases has risen more than 100 percent. To make matters worse, wages paid to workers remain at pre-SAP levels, and, coupled with the currency devaluation, the purchasing power in most of these countries has declined more than tenfold. In fact, the devaluation of the national currency, which in some cases amounts to 500 percent of the pre-SAP value, made foreign exchange unaffordable to local importers, thereby exacerbating the commodity scarcity problems and capacity building for many local industries.

The low exchange value of national currency to major international currencies, particularly the U.S. dollar, meant that agricultural exports were recording downward trends in revenue. Contrary to the IMF's optimistic views, the overall impact of the adjustment program was to make farming less and less attractive to local farmers. In the end, food prices went up, and with rising unemployment in the industrial sector due to lower capacity, the economy in most of these countries had gone to a state of permanent recession. This is what globalization brought to the people of Africa.

The Debt Burden

The impact of globalization on African economies can be seen more poignantly in the increasing indebtedness of African states to international banking. Since the implementation of the structural adjustment program, African debts to international finance institutions have gone up by more than 500 percent. This increase is not only because of new lending but also because of the compounding of interest payments. Today, sub-Saharan Africa's total debts stand at around $231 million U.S. dollars, with debt service amounting to $15.2 billion. This debt service amount is roughly 39 percent higher than it was in 1990, then only $10.0 billion (cf. IMF debt data and the Jubilee 2000 Coalition Report [Owusu et al. 2000]). In most cases, debt service payments represent more than 33 percent of GNP, and what this means for development is that there is very little money left to pursue crucial social and economic programs. The three tables below illustrate the current level of debts owed to various banking institutions.

In desperation, these countries then go back to the IMF for additional loans to finance pending programs. According to the Jubilee 2000 Coalition Report, African countries have paid to the IMF more than $1.2 billion more than they received from the bank. Most of these countries, such as Nigeria, are also the most indebted countries in sub-Saharan Africa. Nigeria, for example, with its petroleum wealth, owed a total of $30.3 billion dollars to lending institutions globally in 1998 (see table 13.2 below). While Africa has only 5 percent of the Third World income, its debts represent 9 percent of the total Third World debts.

Table 13.1

Total Fund Credit and Loans Outstanding
(Billions of SDRs [Short-term drawing reverse])
End of October, 2000

Region	SDRs
World	46.0
Africa	6.5
Asia	18.6
Europe	14.7
Middle East	.06
Western Hemisphere	5.4

Source: IMF Fact Sheet 2000

Table 13.2

Debts Burden for Nigeria, 1980–98
(in millions of U.S. dollars)

	1980	1985	1990	1994	1996	1997	1998
Total Debt	8,921	19,950	33,440	33,092	31,407	28,455	30,315
GNP	61,079	78,040	25,585	21,310	33,068	37,620	38,481
Debt to exports (%)				250	240	164	184
Debt service paid	1,151	4,502	3,336	1,872	2,509	1,416	1,320
Grants	3	4	125	43	24	27	33

Source: Owusu 2000

Table 13.3

Debts Burden for South Africa, 1980–98 (in millions of U.S. dollars)

	1980	1985	1990	1994	1996	1997	1998
Total Debt				21,671	26,050	25,221	24,712
GNP				133,397	139,920	144,406	130,444
Debt to exports (%)				70	72	67	4,378
Debt service paid				2,902	4,236	6,542	4,378
Grants				146	143	200	246

Source: Owusu 2000

State Instability

The debt crisis in Africa has resulted in state instability, with most nations in Africa resorting to one form of dictatorship or the other. In most cases, military rule has been the norm with dire consequences for the civil society. Increasing economic difficulties have sparked old conflicts left behind by the colonial masters, and competition for scarce resources has led to ethnic conflicts in Rwanda-Burundi, Somalia, the Congo, and Nigeria, where millions of Africans have lost their lives. The African states in most cases are faced with the difficult choice of responding to the needs of their people or implementing economic policies that further marginalize the masses. In the first place, the state must provide a stable economic climate where international businesses can operate, and failure to do so will automatically result in sanctions from the World Bank and the International Monetary Fund. A glaring example of this requirement is the recent decision of the government in Yugoslavia to arrest its former leader, Slobodan Milosevic, as a condition for the country to receive a $1,000 million standby loan from the IMF. President Bush made it very clear that if the government in Belgrade failed to arrest the former president, then the IMF would not release the funds.

The West, faced with the idea of maintaining human rights globally, has been forced to promote some sort of limited democracy in Africa and other parts of the Third World. However, the type of democracy that is being promoted is not the sort that guarantees free elections. Most elections in Africa are staged, managed to produce candidates that are acceptable to the West, particularly the United States. Examples of these are not farfetched. In Ghana, the former military dictator, Gerry Rawlings, was advised to retire from the army as a show of his commitment to democratization. He later contested in a dubious election that was sanctioned by international lenders, and whose outcome was already well known. Rawlings, as it turned out, was able to stabilize Ghana by getting rid of opponents who stood in his way, and by impoverishing large segments of the Ghanaian society. Toward the end of his dictatorial rule, Ghana was presented to the rest of Africa, by the West, as a model of an IMF success story. In real terms, Ghana under Rawlings went into an economic decline from which it has yet to recover. All civil associations, except those personally approved by Rawlings, were proscribed, while leaders of radical opposition parties were forced either to seek refuge abroad or be exterminated.

In Nigeria, the West was able to implement a bogus transition agenda that brought to power a former military dictator, Olusegun Obasanjo, whose disdain for democracy can hardly be hidden. As a former military dictator, Obasanjo presided over the most corrupt government in Nigeria's history. In spite of the irregularities surrounding the election that brought the general to power, the United States wasted no time in embracing the new president. As of now, the Nigerian economy continues to slip desperately into recession, with national currency worth 500 percent less than it was a decade or two ago. Today, Nigeria's debts stand at over $30 billion, and with its riches in crude oil (seventh largest producer in the world), Nigeria is classified amongst the poorest countries in the world. The political situation is hardly different from other African countries like the Republic of Congo, Rwanda, Burundi, Uganda, or even the newly constituted multiracial "democracy" in South Africa, where white power and apartheid continue to rule. One can go on and on citing cases of state instability in the continent. But one common factor is that this instability is not unrelated to the sort of economic programs that the IMF has forced on these nations.

Conclusion

While it is difficult to say what the future holds for many countries in Africa, it is clear that rapid globalization will continue to impoverish large sections of this humanity. Already, the digital divide between the developed and the developing world is a clear indication that this trend will continue possibly into the next millennium. The gradual collapse of civil authority in most of these states, and the marginalization of Africa in international circles, mean that Africa will have to come up with a solution to deal with the new situation. Many liberals and progressive-minded individuals in the West have called on the World Bank and the IMF to write off the debts owed by these countries, but these calls have fallen on deaf ears. While this is a very commendable and ambitious call on the part of these liberals, it most certainly will not resolve the problems faced by many African states.

What is needed is a reorganization of the world economy system in a direction that will bring justice and fairness to all actors involved. New structures must be built that will enforce sanctions on multinational corporations for the manner in which they do business with the developing world. Beyond this, the international institutions must also be restructured in a way that increases

African representation and effectiveness. Currently at the UN Security Council, there is no African presence in terms of veto power. So what good is it for Africa if their voices were never taken seriously? Finally, the World Bank and the IMF must reverse their economic strategies for Africa by backing away from further implementation of the structural adjustment program. Recently, the World Bank admitted its two decades of errors and promised to revise its economic policies toward the developing world. In its 1996 report *Participation Source Book,* the bank admitted to the failure of its agricultural development projects in Africa and elsewhere in the developing world. As I write this chapter, very little has changed in terms of the bank's policy recommendation toward the developing world. It is thus accurate to conclude that current movement within the world system represents very clearly a new pattern of re-colonization of the poorest segments of the global economy. Africa, once again, is at a crossroad of a new Euro-America partition.

PART FOUR

Future Directions

CHAPTER 14

Dominant and Subdominant People of Power

A New Way of Conceptualizing Minority and Majority Populations

Charles Vert Willie

This chapter is based on the Robin M. Williams Jr. Lecture presented at the Philadelphia annual meeting of the Eastern Sociological Society in 1995. In his important book *American Society,* published in 1960, Williams stated that the increased public attention and recognition of the social sciences demand "careful self-criticism" and "continuous revision" based on "penetrating research and theoretical reflections" (Williams 1960, vii). Martin Luther King, Jr. stated that "one of the sure signs of maturity is the ability to rise to the point of self-criticism" (King 1958, 199). As sociology approaches maturity as a discipline, it is appropriate to reflect upon the concepts that we use.

This discussion may be classified as fragments of theoretical reflection on some contemporary social issues such as affirmative action and school desegregation and the relevance of sociology to their solution. The goal of the discussion is to show how our diagnosis of social problems and prescriptions for their solution are related, in part, to the analytical concepts we use.

It is fair to say that some of the remedies for segregated education and the dual, inequitable school systems that the Supreme Court declared illegal and unconstitutional were faulty because they did not take into consideration some of the theoretical principles and concepts in sociology articulated by Williams as early as 1954.

A study that Williams conducted with Margaret Ryan about community experiences in school desegregation included facts and theories that could have assisted the Supreme Court in wisely formulating the *Brown II* decision in 1955. This decision provided guidelines for redressing the illegal practices of segregation and discrimination in public education mentioned in *Brown I* (1954). In *Schools in Transition* (Williams and Ryan 1954), Williams and Ryan discovered that (1) "public school desegregation or integration is only loosely correlated with the attitudes of prejudices of population" (240–41); (2) "successful public school desegregation has been carried out in places where other institutions continued to be segregated" (241); (3) "long drawn-out efforts and fluctuating policies appear to have maximized confusion and resistance" (242); (4) "a clear cut policy, administered with understanding but also with resolution, seems to have been most effective in accomplishing desegregation with a minimum of difficulty" (242); and (5) "a clear definition of law and policy by legitimate social authorities may reinforce willingness to conform to the requirements of new [desegregated] situations" (247). In a summary statement of these findings, Williams and Ryan said, "the great importance of clarity and decisiveness in early policy and practice in the desegregation process cannot be overemphasized" (Williams and Ryan 154, 247).

The *Brown II* decision of 1955 assigned primary responsibility for solving the problem of segregation and discrimination in public education and for performing judicial review of the implementation process, respectively, to the local school authorities and to U.S. district courts. The Supreme Court followed this course of action because of the proximity of local school authorities and district courts to local conditions. These local establishments, the Supreme Court reasoned, could take into account public and private considerations such as the revision of local regulations that may be necessary in solving the problem of segregated education or granting additional time, if necessary and in the public interest, to carry out the order of the Court in an effective way. The Court reminded local school authorities and district courts that the basic issue at stake is the admission of racial minorities to public schools on a nondiscriminatory basis as soon as practicable. Then, the Court relented and said that defendant school boards that have been found guilty may be credited with understanding good-faith efforts if they proceed "with all deliberate speed" to redress the grievances of the racial minority plaintiffs rather than addressing them immediately.

If the findings of Williams and Ryan had been used in fashioning the remedy, the Supreme Court would have realized that the law to integrate schools could have been implemented even though some local regulations continued to support segregation in other areas, since "public school desegregation . . . is only loosely correlated with attitudes of prejudice of the population" (Williams and Ryan 1954, 240–41). If the findings of Williams and Ryan had been consulted, the Supreme Court would have realized that the phrase "with all deliberate speed" opened the door to stalling and evasive tactics in implementing school desegregation and that a clear-cut policy administered with resolutions and decisiveness would have been more effective. The requirement that local school authorities make only "a prompt and reasonable start toward full compliance" with the law meant that delay of the opportunity to attend integrated schools actually denied justice to many racial minority students for up to a decade after the *Brown* decision.

Desegregation did not appear in full swing until after the Civil Rights Act of 1964 was passed. The language of this act was more in keeping with the 1954 findings of Williams and Ryan and did not encourage dilatory and evasive tactics. All of this is to say that sociology in particular and social sciences in general have important roles to play in the forming and fashioning of public policy. Robin Williams was on the cutting edge of providing sound and useful information that, regretfully, was not used by the Supreme Court and local school boards. If the 1954 findings of Williams and Ryan had been used by the Supreme Court in fashioning a remedy for the school desegregation cases that were combined in the *Brown* decision, equity in public education and peaceful school desegregation might have been achieved more quickly.

There is evidence that some sociologists have neglected to consult their own peers for the purpose of diagnosing the nature of social problems and prescribing appropriate remedies. In his 1963 presidential address delivered at the annual meetings of the American Sociological Association in Los Angeles, Everett Hughes asked what he characterized as a deep question concerning sociology and social life. His question was this: "Why did social scientists . . . and sociologists in particular—not foresee the explosion of collective action of [African] Americans toward immediate full integration into American society?" (Hughes 1963, 879). It is an interesting coincidence that the annual meeting of the American Sociological Association on the West Coast occurred at the same time that the historic March on Washington was in progress in the District of Columbia on the East Coast. This coincidence enhanced the significance of Hughes's question. To answer this question fully, the professional practitioners of sociology and other social sciences must engage in careful self-criticism and theoretical reflections recommended by Williams.

It is my contention that sociologists failed to predict the Civil Rights revolution because the knowledge they were willing to accept as valid and reliable was too limited. This criticism has been lodged against several important books on the way of black people in America such as *An American Dilemma* by Gunnar Myrdal (1975 [1944]).

Although sociologists and other social scientists tend to fixate on studying social problems, they tend to study them from the perspective of dominant people of power. This is an error and, in part, may account for their misprediction of the Civil Rights movement.

What follows are two examples that indicate our preference to read the signs of the times from reports and interpretations provided by dominant people of power. Back in 1941, Saunders Redding, a black intellectual and a gifted writer, prepared a revealing book, a powerful personal document entitled *On Being Negro in America*. It was a book, said the publisher, "which takes you inside the [African American] world as no other book ever has before!" Writer William Shirer said the book was "eloquent" and provided "great insight" on what life is like for a black person in the United States. Redding said his goal was "to externalize the struggle for human dignity" (Redding 1964, 114). Notwithstanding this broad thrust and these glowing comments, *On Being Black in America* never received the attention it deserved.

Instead, John Howard Griffin's book *Black Like Me*, published in 1961, was more widely read. It won an award from *The Saturday Review* and the *Ainsfield-Wolf Award in Race Relations*. Griffin was a white liberal with an abiding interest in justice who experimented with chemicals that darkened his skin temporarily without any permanent side effects. With a darkened complexion, Griffin traveled throughout the South as if he were African American. The publisher stated that Griffin's book tells us what it is really like to be black in the United States. Griffin's book was widely acclaimed and read as if it provided a more authentic report than earlier works such as Redding's book. The *Atlanta Journal Constitution* called Griffin's story one of the most penetrating documents yet written on the racial question. Could it be that Redding's book was not read as frequently by whites because of the author's racial minority status? Was Griffin's account of being black in America more believable because of his status as a member of the white majority? It would appear that whites are more inclined to believe what it is like to be black in America if the report is made by a member of their own race. Do whites believe such a report is more truthful than a report on the black experience offered by a person who is black? Based on information and evidence, the answer is yes.

Black and brown scholars are treated more or less as invisible persons. Their works are seldom quoted even in publications on race relations. Yet their version of truth may indeed be different from the version of truth reported by white scholars, not because black scholars are more insightful than others, but because they may ask different questions than whites and, consequently, obtain different answers.

The race of the scholar who is believed more or less by blacks, browns, and whites is a problem in the sociology of knowledge. As stated by Robert Merton, "what it takes as 'data' and what as 'problematical' are significant in scientific analysis" (Merton 1949, 221). Michael Polanyi observed that "each person can know directly very little truth and must trust others for the rest" (quoted in Merton 1972, 10). Thus, if white sociologists are more trusting of other whites than of black and brown scholars to advance their knowledge about the racial minority experience in this nation, there will likely be great gaps in their knowledge. Knowledge of the impending Civil Rights movement of the 1950s, 1960s, and 1970s was one such gap.

Recently, Robert Kuttner, a syndicated columnist, discussed the tendency in the mass communication media to depend on their own kind for information about an unlike kind. Kevin Costner's *Dances with Wolves* was acclaimed as a story about the Sioux from the point of view of American Indians. Kuttner noted, however, that the story was told through the eyes of a white Civil War officer who ends up living among Native Americans (Willie 1991, A48). Apparently, information about Native Americans is more believable if it is relayed to our society at large by a white medium.

The retention of Gunnar Myrdal by the Carnegie Corporation to do a thorough ongoing study of blacks in the United States is another illustration of our tendency to believe people who are similar to us even when the subject discussed is of people who are dissimilar from us. Merton claimed that Myrdal, a white Swedish economist, was selected to study blacks in the United States because he was an outsider (Merton 1972). Using the nation/state as a frame of reference, Myrdal was an outsider; but using the white majority race in the United States as a frame of reference, Myrdal was an insider. And white sociologist Robert Lynd called this racial insider's study of race relations in America "the most penetrating and important book on our contemporary American civilization" (Myrdal 1975 [1944]). This evaluation ignored the scholarly works of black social scientists such as W. E. B. DuBois, E. Franklin Frazier, Charles S.

Johnson, Ira de Augustine Reid, Kenneth Clark, Ralph Bunche, John Hope Franklin, and Abram Harris, to name a few who published during this era.

Thus we sociologists missed predicting the Civil Rights movement because we paid too much attention to scholars who were designated as "mainstream." Although a very enlightened scholar, Myrdal fitted this category very well. Moreover, his principal assistants were mainstream and white scholars, Richard Sterner and Arnold Rose.

With the advice and assistance of mainstream social scientists, Myrdal described American blacks as occupying caste-like status in this nation. Caste-like arrangements are permanent, fixed, and unchangeable. Moreover, according to anthropologists Eliot Chapple and Charles Coon, lower caste members tend to respond in "set events" toward ruling caste members because caste membership is sanctioned by economic, political, and religious institutions (Chapple and Coon 1942, 435–37).

While Myrdal understood race and caste as concepts and described concepts as social constructions that have no other form of reality than our own usage, he violated his own understanding of concepts like caste and race by imputing to them tradition and permanency (Myrdal 1975 [1944], 667, 669, 675), thus making caste and race ascribed rather than constructed realities. Beyond attributing to caste and race a reality other than that of a social construction, Myrdal placed the responsibility for the continuation of the so-called racial caste system upon whites and portrayed blacks as passive adapters to the system. He described the "caste order" as fundamentally a system of disabilities forced by whites upon blacks (Myrdal 1975 [1944], 669). In other words, "the Negro problem," according to Myrdal, "is primarily a white man's problem" (Myrdal 1975 [1944], 669). Describing the population group with less power as passive and totally dependent on the group with more power was a major error in Myrdal's formulation because it did not factor in the veto power of subdominants and their capacity to disrupt the orderly ways of society.

In *A New Look at Black Families,* I disagreed with Myrdal's formulation and stated that: "It is doubtful . . . any group can fully dominate the social life of another. All ghettoized populations everywhere have maintained their folk beliefs and values despite external pressure to conform to the dominant group . . . The spirituals, for example, emerged out of a common experience of black folk that no dominant group could suppress" (Willie 1988, 26).

All of this is to say that the concepts of race and caste as used by Myrdal did not fully explain interracial activities in the United States because many blacks never believed their own values and customs were unworthy. Also, they never accepted their oppressed status as fixed and permanent. Finally, their religious and other cultural institutions did not sanction the arrangements of oppression under which blacks lived.

In *The Philadelphia Negro* (1967 [1899]), DuBois tells us that a major purpose of the church among blacks was to teach its members ways of restoring their race to the dignity it had lost (DuBois 1967, 198) by continuously discussing the race problem in all its phases (DuBois 1967, 207). DuBois further said that blacks seemed to be particularly adept in comprehending the political aspects of social organization (DuBois 1967, 207).

To comprehend the way of life of black people in America, it is important to understand how reform tendencies and conservative tendencies within this group coexist and are complementary. By consulting mainstream sociologists as the principal bearers of valid and reliable information about the African American experience in the United States, subtle nuances in this cultural group could be missed.

The University of Pennsylvania understood this a century ago when it solicited funds for "a study of obstacles . . . encountered by the colored people in their endeavor to be self-supporting" (DuBois 1967, viii). A leader of the College Settlement House in Philadelphia, with whom the university cooperated in launching the study eventually published as *The Philadelphia Negro* in 1899, believed that it would be best if the information about obstacles and opportunities "comes . . . through the colored people themselves" (DuBois 1967, ix). He did not suggest in any way that the research by blacks about blacks is crude. However, he did suggest that the research of scholars with black and brown cultural backgrounds sometimes asks different questions, uses different methods, collects different data, and draws different inferences from the data analyzed than the research of scholars with white cultural backgrounds.

Although Myrdal claims that he predicted fundamental changes would come to pass in American race relations, my reading of *An American Dilemma* is that Myrdal described race relations in the United States as fixed in a more or less permanent racial caste-like structure. Myrdal mentioned the need for "social engineering" and said it will be increasingly demanded. But he devoted only a few pages at the end of his book to a discussion of social change. Even this brief analysis focused on what dominant people of power should do through their planning and practical actions in the federal government.

If Hughes and other sociologists were relying on the data and the interpretation of data provided by Myrdal and scholars like him, then one may understand how they failed to predict the Civil Rights movement. Hughes, for example, assumed that African Americans "want to disappear as a group . . . to become invisible as a group . . . [to] be judged as if [being African American] did not matter" (Hughes 1963, 883) Hughes really believed the goal of blacks will have been gained "when Negroid characteristics and African descent matter no more and no less than other physical traits and quirks of ancestry" (Hughes 1963, 883), although he acknowledged that not all African Americans might be content "to wipe out their collective past and all features of [African] American culture" (Hughes 1963, 883). Despite his liberal orientation and his desire for equality, Hughes assumed that the way of life of the dominant people of power would prevail. The ultimate goal, according to his understanding, was to integrate minorities into the majority way of life in an equitable way.

Hughes's idea did not take into consideration DuBois's assertion in *The Souls of Black Folks* (1965) that blacks wished to give up neither their African nor their American heritage. Hughes's solution was based on the Myrdal idea that whites must solve the problem of social oppression experienced by blacks and did not take seriously King's assessment that "the Negro has now been driven to reevaluate himself. He has come to feel that he is somebody" (King 1958, 167). Then King admonished blacks that if first-class citizenship is to become a reality, "[they] must assume the primary responsibility for making it so" (King 1958, 187). These are not the words of a passive assimilationist.

Although Hughes's attitudes about race relations and other forms of intergroup relations were conventional as measured by today's knowledge, he nevertheless was a change agent who admonished sociologists to "break the bonds of ordinary thought and moral inhibition so as to conceive a great variety of human situations, even the most outrageous" (Hughes 1963, 89). Since a generation has passed since Hughes published his paper "Race Relations and the Sociological Imagination" (Hughes 1963), I declare that now is the time to "break the bonds of ordinary thought" so as to conceive of women, African Americans, Latinos, Native Americans, Asians, gays and lesbians, physically challenged people, French-speaking Canadians, and other subdominant populations as not wishing to be made over in the image of men, whites, straight people, the able-bodied, and English-speaking people. These populations wish to offer their cultural adaptations as unique contributions, and in some instances, as corrections to the community at large, knowing that without their contributions the whole society is impoverished.

To understand why we should take seriously Hughes's admonition and how it may help us understand society better, we need to modify and possibly develop some new concepts in the lexicon of our sociological language.

The metaphor *mainstream* that is so frequently used to refer to normative activities needs to be redefined. We tend to refer to groups such as the underclass or racial and ethnic minority groups such as blacks and Latinos as outside the mainstream. Other groups such as the middle class, upper class, or whites are characterized as in the mainstream.

The sociological synonym for mainstream is macrosocial, a collectivity with member groups that exhibit a large range of variation. This definition suggests that particular groups in a society such as the underclass, the middle class, as well as the upper class are all microsocial units; they participate in the macrosocial structure of society in an additive way. Alone, none of these groups is a macrosocial collectivity or the mainstream because none of these groups alone is self-sufficient. In physical terms, this redefinition means that the river is the mainstream and that all tributaries contribute to the river. The river or mainstream is dependent on its tributaries to continue to ripple and flow, and the tributaries are dependent on the river to prevent backup, overflow, and flooding. If the underclass is a microunit of society, then all social classes are microunits. Thus, the underclass is part of the mainstream as is the middle class, upper class, and any other social class. From a macrosocial perspective, all classes are interdependent; they both give to and take from the society at large—the mainstream, the macrosocial unit. It is inappropriate and even harmful to refer to the normative customs of middle-class people, upper-class people, or any other social class as the mainstream and the normative customs of poor people or the underclass as outside the mainstream.

The microsocial world and the macrosocial world are interconnected even as "the microscopic world . . . . [is] inextricably connected to the macroscopic world" (Lee 1988, 28). In the physical system, the macrounit is dependent on the microunit; but in the social system, the macrounit is dependent on the macrounit. The relationship in the social system between microunits and the macrounit is the reverse of that which exists in the physical system. The microunit is basic in the physical system but the macrounit is basic in the social system. This means that microsocial units should never be classified as deviant or outside the mainstream. They are what they are because of the main-stream—the macrosocial unit in whose image the microsocial units are fashioned. As stated by W. J. Watkins, "the social whole determines matters for the individual that one cannot avoid" (quoted by Knorr-Cetina and Cicourel 1981, 8).

This discussion on interdependence between microsocial and macrosocial units of society points toward the theory of complementarity, which helps us go beyond linear or logical thinking in the social sciences to a more complex form of analysis. The principle of complementarity specifies the ways in which racial, socioeconomic, gender, and other social structures or processes are interdependent, how one group does for another what the other cannot do for itself.

An idea from the nineteenth century that still dominates the minds of knowledgeable people, according to E. F. Schumacher, is the idea of evolution. It asserts that higher forms continually develop out of lower forms in a kind of natural and linear way. Based on this idea, that which is higher is always better than that which is lower, and that which is stronger is always better than that which is weaker. This idea does not work when applied to mental and social phenomena. History has demonstrated that the brightest are not always the wisest.

Physicist George Seielstad states that continuity demands diversity (Seielstad 1989, 132). And where there is diversity in society, there are likely to be groups that oppose each other. Economist Schumacher claims that the real problem in society is that of reconciling opposites (Schumacher 1973, 98–99). Harmonizing disparate interest groups is one of the chief and most challenging functions of effective public administrators.

My comparative studies of black and white families by social class demonstrate the value of diversity in social organization. Among poor whites, for example, I discovered that they had a good understanding of the value of contributive justice, the responsibility of the individual for the group, while poor blacks had a good understanding of distributive justice, the responsibility of the group for the individual.

When U.S. President John F. Kennedy told the citizens of this nation "to ask not what America can do for them, but what they could do for America," he set before the nation an idea that had been cultivated and well-developed among poor whites. They understand very well the responsibility of the individual for his or her family group. The individual in a poor white family will make great sacrifices for his relatives largely because the family is one group that will not give up on the individual; the family is one group that cares for each of its members when others do not. In asking not what the family can do for the individual but, instead, what the individual can do for the family, poor whites practice an exemplary form of contributive justice.

When Benjamin Elijah Mayes, former president of Morehouse College, told his black students "there is only one way for the human family to survive and that is for one generation to give life to the next" (Mayes 1969, 85), he shared with them wisdom derived from the everyday experiences of poor black people. In my comparative studies of family life, I discovered that this family group makes great sacrifices for individuals, especially relatives. They will not hold back on group resources if an individual is in need. As a result, when any family member is saved and ultimately succeeds, the whole kinship clan basks in the reflected glory. By giving all for an individual in need even if it jeopardizes the welfare of the group, poor black families exhibit an excellent example of distributive justice, the responsibility of the group for the individual.

A good society achieves its effectiveness by way of both contributive and distributive justice. The gift of poor white families to the society at large is a working model of contributive justice and the gift of the poor black families to the society at large is a working model of distributive justice. Thus, each microsocial unit has something unique and significant to give to the macrosocial structure. The macrosocial structure is both enriched and self-corrected by the interaction of diverse and even disparate microsocial groups, all of which are part of the mainstream. A social organization cannot rightfully say that it has no need of constituent groups that differ from the prevailing group. Each group has something of value to contribute to the whole, according to the theory of complementarity.

A final statement on complementarity and the reconstruction of opposites has to do with individuals and groups. They, too, must be harmonized. We sociologists have not served the society well in the affirmative action debate. We have not helped the society to understand that both individuals and groups are essential in social organizations. Syndicated columnist Richard Cohen declared in the *Boston Globe* that "affirmative action is doomed." He explained that "it violates that American creed that we must be judged as individuals, not on the basis of race or sex—a group" (Cohen 1995, 15).

The fact is that both groups and individuals are essential in social organizations: one without the other is incomplete. All effective individuals are connected with groups and all effective groups consist of individuals. It is inappropriate to argue the premise that individual interest should take precedence over group concern and vice versa. The individual and group complement each other. According to the theory of complementarity, they are opposites that must be reconciled if both are to prosper.

Cohen's declaration—"the Civil Rights era is over. The civil liberties era must begin"—is both premature and wrong (Cohen 1995, 15). Cohen's formulation represents linear thinking, that an era focusing on group opportunities is necessarily succeeded by one focusing on individual freedoms. Actually, individual freedom and the constraints of group opportunity complement each other. Each controls the excesses of its opposite.

The truth is that any society including the United States that attempted to pay exclusive attention to individuals at the expense of groups will eventually bring harm on itself and so will any society such as the Union of Soviet Socialist Republics that attempted to pay exclusive attention to groups at the expense of the individual. A good society will do the right thing for individuals and groups and will do it for both simultaneously; it will enhance the person while advancing the community and vice versa. Actually, self and society exist in a dualistic relationship with each dependent on but not fully controlled by the other.

Here we are dealing with morality and ethics. The two go well together. Morality is a property of the individual and ethics has to do with relationships and is a property of the group. To be moral, one should not have to be unethical toward others; and to be ethical toward others should not require that one violate personal morality. The problematic issue in the discussion is this: How does one negotiate a solution to a social problem that is both moral and ethical? What compromises are inevitably necessary? This is what affirmative action is about. It does not embrace the ideology of individualism or collectivism. It is about the combining of these toward a compromise that is fair to all, which is a wonderful problem for sociologists to help solve.

Thus, we see that morality and ethics complement each other. To understand this better, we need to reconceptualize morality and ethics, not as synonyms as they frequently are used in conventional speech, but as different and distinct actions that facilitate each other because they are different, although interdependent.

John Gardner (1968, 145–46) describes identity as the assurance that comes from knowing and being known. And he calls the loss of identity failure in relationships between the individual and society. Gardner further states that "those who suffer from a sense of anonymity [a loss of identity] would feel better if they could believe that their society needed them" (Gardner 1968, 148). The search for identity, a signature of individuality, seems to be a search for security and acceptance and a need to be needed by others in a group. In the end, therefore, full identity depends on the individual's action and action of groups. Identity, therefore, is a result of affirmation and confirmation, knowing and being known, needing and being needed. To claim that identity involves personal action and group reaction is another way of saying that both moral and ethical components are involved in individuality. And obviously, both moral and ethical components are involved in social organization.

I discovered in my school desegregation research the principle of simultaneity mentioned above. Actions that appeared as failures when implemented singly or sequentially actually were successful when implemented simultaneously. Some activities require a multifarious process, according to naturalist Adrian Forsyth (1993, 140). While a goal of science is parsimony of explanation, "one cannot choose among factors in a multifarious process. Instead, one must build a model that incorporates them all" (Forsyth 1993, 140). Some outcomes, therefore, cannot be explained by a single law but require a model that explores the operation and conflict of several forces and influences (Forsyth 1993, 140).

This is precisely what happened in school desegregation. Integrated schools that did not result in improved education were unsatisfactory to many parents in the plaintiff group that fought for school desegregation. Magnet schools that improved education but accommodated only about one-third of the student body of a school system and frequently less were unfair to students who wanted to but did not relieve the educational distress of most students who could not afford the cost of long-distance commuting to schools. Moreover, state financial allocations per student in such choice plans were subtracted from the sending district (usually a central city school system) and added to the receiving district (usually a suburban school system). This arrangement was the Robin Hood story in reverse. It took from the poor and gave to the rich. It failed to fulfill the twofold goal of education—individual enhancement and community advancement; the sending school system was harmed, not helped.

School districts throughout the United States have implemented the programs and student assignment methods mentioned above singly and sequentially. When one program or method did not work another was tried; it too usually was unsatisfactory. I discovered that none of these programs or methods was unworthy, although none yielded a satisfactory outcome. The problem is that these programs or methods were implemented sequentially when they should have been implemented simultaneously.

Michael Alves and I developed a student assignment method called Controlled Choice (Alves and Willie 1987) that has been effective because it accomplishes several goals simultaneously. It desegregates all schools when school assignments are made in accordance with racial fairness guidelines; it provides for enrollment in a school of choice from amongst several schools that make up a large zone of students who are racially, socioeconomically, ethnically heterogeneous; and it contributes to school improvement, since school systems are obligated to help least chosen schools become more attractive learning environments. When school desegregation, school improvement, and choice occur simultaneously, there is a good outcome for all. Ninety percent of the students in the Boston Controlled Choice program receive their first-choice or second-choice school and all elementary and middle schools are desegregated. Our program's failure in the community, especially in education and in other forms of human relations, may be not so much because of the merits or demerits of programs but because they are serially rather than simultaneously implemented.

In light of the discussion above, I believe we need to abandon the essentialist tradition of conceptualizing racial and ethnic groups as fixed in caste-like relationships. We need to reconceptualize these as flexible power groups that may change according to requirements of situations.

Power is to the social system what energy is to the physical system. Without power, nothing happens. Some of the social components of power are numbers, valued attributes, and efficient and effective social organizations. Groups that have more than others in any two of these components usually prevail in human society. Yet it should be recognized that all groups have power. Those that cannot implement social norms without help from others, nevertheless, can disrupt social organization. This disruption is veto power that subdominant as well as dominant groups possess.

If racial and ethnic groups are reconceptualized as community power groups, further explanation is necessary regarding why some groups have more and others have less power and regarding the consequences that flow from one's position as dominant or subdominant in the power structure.

In this connection, I divide the community power structure into two complementary groups that are labeled dominant and subdominant rather than superior and subordinate. The new language overcomes the connotations of the past that the weaker power group called the subordinate group is inferior, lower, and secondary, and that the stronger power group called the superior group is preferred, higher, and primary. Dominance has to do with that which prevails. While the dominant characteristic is manifested, we know that it may be masking a contrasting characteristic that is present but recessive or subdominant.

Thus, dominance connotes who and what is in control and not who and what is superior. Under different circumstances, that which is dominant may become recessive and that which is recessive may become dominant. Another example of the coexistence of dominance and subdominance comes from music. The fifth tone of a diatonic scale is dominant and the tone next below is subdominant. Both dominant and subdominant tones have intrinsic value as do both a major and minor chord; each is a different chord. There is no connotation of better and worse or superior and inferior in the concepts dominant and subdominant. Moreover, these concepts clearly indicate that controlling characteristics in one situation may not be controlling in other situations. This understanding protects our discourse from the essentialism that has crept into meanings when racial and ethnic groups are discussed as superior and subordinate groups.

I have discovered that dominant and subdominant power groups complement each other in some very important ways so that one without the other is incomplete. Dominant power groups tend to be more concerned with stability and the past. Subdominant power groups tend to be more concerned with change and the future. There is no intrinsic value either in the past and stability or in change and the future. One should not be more valued than the other. We should change what in social organization harms any individual and stabilize what in social organization helps all. Dominant and subdominant power groups and their different inclinations enable a society to perpetuate its helpful traditions and correct its harmful customs.

Affirmative action emerged in our society as one way of guaranteeing the presence of diversity, since dominant and subdominant power groups tend to perform different but necessary functions that complement each other. Sociologists have not forthrightly explained the essential function of diversity in human society because they have tended to discuss racial and ethnic groups as occupying fixed positions and have analyzed these groups in terms of their cultural functions and not so much in terms of their existing and changing power relationships.

Scholars like Martin Luther King, Jr., whose undergraduate degree concentration was sociology, understood the different functions of dominant and subdominant power groups very well. He explained in *Stride toward Freedom*, his account of the Montgomery bus boycott, that:

> Integration is not some lavish dish that the federal government or the white liberal will pass out on a silver platter while the Negro merely furnishes the appetite. One of the most damaging effects of past segregation on the personality of the Negro may well be that he has been victimized with the delusion that others should be more concerned than himself about his citizenship rights.
>
> [the] Negro must come to see that there is much he himself can do about his plight. . . . The Negro can take direct action against injustice without waiting for the government to act or a majority to agree with him or a court to rule in his favor. (King 1958, 188)

King suggested that the most appropriate action for a subordinate population of people to take is nonviolent resistance. He explained that "like the synthesis in Hegalian philosophy, the principle of nonviolent resistance seeks to reconcile the truths of two opposites—acquiescence and violence—while avoiding the extremes and immoralities of both" (King 1958, 190). King identified a militant, nonviolent, mass movement led by African Americans as the most appropriate organizational structure to secure justice in the United States (King 1958, 191). It is interesting to note that King identified the militant, the nonviolent, and the mass component of the movement as three actions that had to exist simultaneously (King 1958, 191).

King's diagnosis of social problems and prescriptions for changes are much different from those offered by Myrdal. Myrdal did not comprehend and predict the dynamic possibilities of race relations in the United States in which blacks would emerge as a self-determining population. In the introduction of *An American Dilemma*, Myrdal offered these propositions: (a) that "the Negro problem is predominately a white man's problem," (b) that a realistic understanding of power in the United States is that "the Negro people succeed . . . in acquiring . . . power in society with the help of interested white groups," and (c) that "the Negro problem exists and changes because of conditions and forces operating in the larger society." Thus, "in all parts of [his] inquiry,

Myrdal's attention is given over to the characteristics of the American Society at large in which, in his words, the Negro becomes a problem" (Myrdal 1975 [1944], xxvi-xxvii). Myrdal gave little, if any, attention to self-initiated behavior by blacks.

For reasons mentioned above, sociologists in particular and social scientists in general failed to predict the Civil Rights movement. They paid little attention to what was happening among the subdominant people of power. Unfortunately, some contemporary sociologists continue in the Myrdal tradition. William Wilson, for example, used the Myrdal frame of reference when he described the system of Jim Crow segregation in the South as a function of the "collapse" of what he called "a paternalistic bond between blacks and the southern [white] business elite" (Wilson 1978, 147). Here, Wilson is describing blacks as dependent on whites, as Myrdal so described them. Moreover, Wilson imputed a caste-like characteristic to the underclass among blacks by calling their circumstances intractable (Wilson 1987, 57–58, 113). Finally, Wilson asserted that the problems of the "truly disadvantaged" can be effectively attacked only by way of programs that focus on the society at large. Specifically, he said, "the hidden agenda is to improve the life chances of groups such as the ghetto underclass by emphasizing programs in which the more advantaged groups of all races can positively relate" (Wilson 1987, 120). Wilson does not explain how programs that focus on the society at large will help the ghetto underclass "the most" (Wilson 1987, 121). And neither does Myrdal clarify how focusing on the society at large will remedy what he called "the Negro problem."

Myrdal did not understand the benefit of empowering blacks and other subdominants to identify their own self-interests and to negotiate with their adversaries for mutual fulfillment. According to Myrdal, any power that blacks obtain is conferred upon them by way of the goodwill of whites. Self-determined efforts by subdominants were seen by Myrdal and Wilson as self-defeating. Wilson, who followed the Myrdal tradition in his research, discounted black political control of the central city as of little importance in providing economic and social mobility. Rather, he states, it will merely heighten racial antagonism (Wilson 1978, 120).

Historian Meyer Weinberg said that "the single most important factor in the lives of African Americans [since 1940] has been the rise of the civil rights movement." "In the main," Weinberg explained, "it was a movement of black people led by black people and has been deeply responsive to the historic goals and aspirations of black people" (Weinberg 1991, 3).

The theory of complementarity discussed allows for flexibility unlike the historical determinism into which racial and ethnic groups have been frozen by some social scientists. The Civil Rights movement could have been predicted if the concepts of analysis that we used had provided for spontaneous transformation and continuous reform in human society rather than a fixed relationship

CHAPTER 15

The Historical Black Freedom Struggle

The Legacy and Challenges of Contemporary Inequality

Aldon D. Morris

It is important for African Americans, as well as all Americans, to take a look backward and forward as we enter a new century, indeed a new millennium. When a panoramic view of the entire history of African Americans is taken into account, it becomes crystal clear that African American social protest has been critical to black liberation. In fact, African American protest has been critical to the freedom struggles of people of color around the globe and to progressive people throughout the world.

The purpose of this chapter is (1) to revisit the profound changes that the modern Black Freedom Struggle has achieved in terms of American race relations; (2) to assess how this movement has affected the rise of other liberation movements both nationally and internationally; (3) to focus on how this movement has transformed how scholars think about social movements; (4) to discuss the lessons that can be learned from this groundbreaking movement pertaining to future African American struggles for freedom in the new century; and (5) to contrast a recent instance of race-based insurgency with similar protest in the Civil Rights period in order to illuminate how contemporary insurgency may differ from that of the past.

It is hard to imagine how pervasive black inequality would be today in America if it had not been constantly challenged by black protests throughout each century since the beginning of slavery. The historical record is clear that slave resistance and slave rebellions and protest in the context of the abolitionist movement were crucial to the overthrow of the powerful slave regime.

The establishment of Jim Crow was one of the great tragedies of the late nineteenth and early twentieth centuries. The overthrow of slavery represented one of those rare historical moments where a nation had the opportunity to embrace a democratic future or to do business as usual by reinstalling undemocratic practices. In terms of African Americans, the white North and South chose to embark along undemocratic lines.

For African Americans, the emergence of the Jim Crow regime was one of the greatest betrayals that could be visited upon a people who had hungered for freedom so long; what made it even worse for them is that the betrayal emerged from the bosom of a nation declaring to all the world that it was the beacon of democracy.

The triumph of Jim Crow ensured that African Americans would live in a modern form of slavery that would endure well into the second half of the twentieth century. The nature and consequences of the Jim Crow system are well known. It was successful in politically disenfranchising the black population and in creating economic relationships that ensured black economic subordination. Work on wealth by sociologists Melvin Oliver and Thomas Shapiro (1995), as well as Dalton Conley (1999), is making it clear that wealth inequality is the most drastic form of inequality between blacks and whites. It was the slave and Jim Crow regimes that prevented blacks from acquiring wealth that could have been passed down to succeeding generations. Finally, the Jim Crow regime consisted of a comprehensive set of laws that stamped a badge of inferiority on black people and denied them basic citizenship rights.

The iron fist of southern state power, the United States Supreme Court, and white terrorist organizations backed the Jim Crow regime. Jim Crow was also held in place by white racist attitudes. As Larry Bobo has pointed out, "the available survey data suggests that anti-black attitudes associated with Jim Crow were once widely accepted . . . [such attitudes were] expressly premised on the notion that blacks were the innate intellectual, cultural, and temperamental inferior to whites" (Bobo 1997, 35). Thus, as the twentieth century opened, African Americans were confronted with a powerful social order designed to keep them subordinate. As long as the Jim Crow order remained intact, the black masses could breathe neither freely nor safely. Thus, nothing less than the overthrow of a social order was the daunting task that faced African Americans during the early decades of the twentieth century.

The voluminous research on the modern Civil Rights movement has reached a consensus: That movement was the central force that toppled the Jim Crow regime. To be sure, there were other factors that assisted in the overthrow including the advent of the television age, the competition of northern black voters between two major parties, the Cold War, and the independence movements in Third World countries that sought to overthrow European domination. Yet, it was the Civil Rights movement itself that targeted the Jim Crow regime and generated the great mass mobilizations that would bring it down.

What was the genius of the Civil Rights movement that made it so effective in fighting a powerful and vicious opposition? The genius of the Civil Rights movement was that its leaders and participants recognized that change could occur if they were able to generate massive crises within the Jim Crow order—crises of such magnitude that the authorities of oppression would be forced to yield to the demands of the movement to restore social order. Max Weber defined power as the ability to realize one's will despite resistance. Mass disruption generated power. That was the strategy of nonviolent direct action. By utilizing tactics of disruption, implemented by thousands of disciplined demonstrators who had been mobilized through their churches, schools, and voluntary associations, the Civil Rights movement was able to generate the necessary power to overcome the Jim Crow regime. The famous crises created in places like Birmingham and Selma, Alabama, coupled with the important less visible crises that mushroomed throughout the nation, caused social breakdown in southern business and commerce; created unpredictability in all spheres of social life; and strained the resources and credibility of southern state governments while forcing white terrorist groups to act on a visible stage where the whole world could watch. At the national level, the demonstrations and the repressive measures used against them generated foreign policy nightmares because foreign media in Europe, the Soviet Union, Asia, and Africa covered them. Therefore, what gave the mass-based sit-ins, boycotts, marches, and jailings their power was their ability to generate disorder.

As a result, within ten years (1955 to 1965) the Civil Rights movement had toppled the Jim Crow order. The 1964 Civil Rights Bill and the 1965 Voting Rights Act brought the regime of formal Jim Crow to a close.

The Civil Rights movement unleashed an important social product. It taught that a mass-based grassroots social movement that is sufficiently organized, sustained, and disruptive is capable of generating fundamental social change. In other words, it showed that human agency could flow from a relatively powerless and marginalized group that was thought to be backward and incapable of producing great leaders.

Other oppressed groups in America and around the world took notice. They reasoned that if American blacks could generate such agency they should be able to do likewise. Thus, the Civil Rights movement exposed a source of agency available to oppressed groups. By agency, I refer to the empowering beliefs and actions of individuals and groups that enable them to make a difference in their own lives and in the social structures in which they are embedded.

Because such agency was made visible by the Civil Rights movement, disadvantaged groups in America sought to discover and interject their agency into their own movements for social change—movements as diverse as the student movement, the women's movement, the farm workers movement, the Native American movement, the gay and lesbian movement, the environmental movement, and the disability rights movement. From that movement, other groups discovered how to organize; how to build social movement organizations; how to mobilize large numbers of people; how to devise appropriate tactics and strategies; how to infuse their movement activities with cultural creativity; how to confront and defeat authorities; and how to unleash the kind of agency that generates social change.

For similar reasons, the Black Freedom Struggle was able to affect freedom struggles internationally. For example, nonviolent direct action has inspired oppressed groups as diverse as black South Africans, Arabs of the Middle East, and pro-democracy demonstrators in China to engage in collective actions. The sit-in tactic made famous by the Civil Rights movement has been used in liberation movements throughout the Third World, in Europe, and in many other foreign countries. The Civil Rights movement's national anthem, "We Shall Overcome," has been interjected into hundreds of liberation movements both nationally and internationally. Because the Civil Rights movement has been so important to international struggles, activists from around the world have invited Civil Rights participants to travel abroad. Thus, early in Poland's Solidarity movement, Bayard Rustin was summoned to Poland by its protest leaders. As he taught the lessons of the Civil Rights movement, he explained that "I am struck by the complete attentiveness of the predominately young audience, which sits patiently, awaiting the translation of my words" (Rustin, undated).

Therefore, as we seek to understand the importance of the Black Freedom Struggle, we must conclude the following: The Black Freedom Struggle has provided a model and impetus for social movements that have exploded on the American and international landscape. This impact has been especially pronounced in the second half of the twentieth century.

What is less obvious is the tremendous impact that the Black Freedom Struggle has had on the scholarly study of social movements. Indeed, the Black

Freedom Struggle has helped trigger a shift in the study of social movements and collective action. The black movement has provided scholars with profound empirical and theoretical puzzles, because it has been so rich organizationally and tactically, and because it has generated unprecedented levels of mobilization. Moreover, this movement has been characterized by a complex leadership base and diverse gender roles, and it has revealed the tremendous amount of human agency that usually lies dormant within oppressed groups. These empirical realities of the Civil Rights movement did not square with the theories used by scholars to explain social movements prior to the 1960s.

Previous theories did not focus on the organized nature of social movements, the social movement organizations that mobilized them, the tactical and strategic choices that make them effective, nor the rationally planned action of leaders and participants who guide them. In the final analysis, theories of social movements lacked a theory that incorporated human agency at the core of their conceptual apparatuses. Those theories conceptualized social movements as spontaneous, largely unstructured, and discontinuous with institutional and organizational behavior. Movement participants were viewed as reacting to various forms of strain and doing so in a nonrational manner. In these frameworks, human agency was conceptualized as reactive, created by uprooted individuals seeking to reestablish a modicum of personal social stability. In short, social movement theories prior to the Civil Rights movement operated with a vague, weak vision of agency to explain phenomena that are driven by human action.

The predictions and analytical focus of social movement theories prior to the 1970s stood in sharp contrast to the kind of theories that would be needed to capture the basic dynamics that drove the Civil Rights movement. It became apparent to social movement scholars that if they were to understand the Civil Rights movement and the multiple movements it spun, the existing theoretical landscape would have to undergo a radical process of reconceptualization.

As a result, the field of social movements has been reconceptualized and will affect research well into the new millennium. To be credible in the current period, any theory of social movements must grapple conceptually with the role of rational planning and strategic action; the role of movement leadership; and the nature of the mobilization process. How movements are gendered, how movement dynamics are bathed in cultural creativity, and how the interactions between movements and their opposition determine movement outcomes are important questions. At the center of this entire matrix of actors must be an analysis of the central role that human agency plays in social movements and the generation of social change.

Thanks, in large part, to the Black Freedom Struggle, theories of social movements that grapple with real dynamics in concrete social movements are being elaborated. Intellectual work in the next century will determine how successful scholars will be in unraveling the new empirical and theoretical puzzles thrust forth by the Black Freedom movement. Although it was not their goal, black demonstrators of the Civil Rights movement changed an academic field.

A remaining question is: Will black protest continue to be vigorous in the twenty-first century, capable of pushing forward the Black Freedom agenda? It is not obvious that black protest will be as sustainable and as paramount as it has been in previous centuries. To address this issue we need to examine the factors important to past protest and examine how they are situated in the current context.

Social movements are more effective when they can identify a clear-cut enemy. Who or what is the clear-cut enemy of African Americans of the twenty-first century? Is it racism and if so, who embodies it? Is it capitalism, and if so, how is this enemy to be loosened from its abstract perch and concretized. In fact, we do not currently have a robust concept that grasps the modern form of domination that blacks currently face. Because the modern enemy has become opaque, slippery, illusive, and covert, the launching of black protest has become more difficult because of conceptual fuzziness.

Second, during the closing decades of the twentieth century the black class structure has become more highly differentiated, and it is no longer firmly anchored in the black community. There is some danger, therefore, that the cross-fertilization between different strata within the black class structure so important to previous protest movements may have become eroded to the extent that it is no longer fully capable of launching and sustaining future black protest movements.

Third, will the black community of the twenty-first century possess the institutional strength required for sustaining black protest? Black colleges have been weakened because of the racial integration of previously all-white institutions of higher learning and because many black colleges are being forced to integrate. The degree of institutional strength of the church has eroded because some of them have migrated to the suburbs in an attempt to attract affluent blacks. In other instances, the black church has been unable to attract young people of the inner city who find more affinity with gangs and the underground economy. Moreover, a great potential power of the black church is not being realized because its male clergy refuse to empower black women as preachers and pastors. The key question is whether the black church remains as close to the black masses—especially to poor and working classes—as it once was. That closeness determines its strength to facilitate black protest.

In short, research has shown conclusively that the black church, black colleges, and other black community organizations were critical vehicles through which social protest was organized, mobilized, and sustained. A truncated class structure was also instrumental to black protest. It is unclear whether during the twenty-first century these vehicles will continue to be effective tools of black protest or whether new forces capable of generating protest will step into the vacuum. In this context it is unclear how far-reaching technological changes will affect black protest. In particular, it is not clear how the Internet and associated forms of electronic communications will affect protest movements.

I foresee no reason why black protest should play a lesser role for black people in the twenty-first century. Social inequality between the races will continue and may even worsen, especially for poorer segments of the black communities. Racism will continue to affect the lives of all people of color. If future changes are to materialize, protest will be required. In 1898, as DuBois glanced toward the dawn of the twentieth century, he declared that in order for blacks to achieve freedom, they would have to protest continuously and energetically. This will become increasingly true for the twenty-first century. The question is whether organizationally, institutionally, and intellectually the black community will have the wherewithal to engage in the kind of widespread and effective social protest that African Americans have utilized so magnificently. If previous centuries are our guide, then major surprises on the protest front should be expected early in the millennium.

Social protest has continued to occur since the Civil Rights movement, but in a more limited and localized fashion. It is instructive to examine such protest because it contains the seeds that germinate into a widespread and coherent social movement. During the Civil Rights movement racial equality was sought throughout the larger society. At that time, the majority of institutions discriminated against African Americans, including professional social science organizations. These prestigious learned societies were not able to escape social protest aimed at achieving racial equality. The American Sociological Association (ASA) was one such organization that became the target of protest by black sociologists in the late 1960s and early 1970s. The protest that they launched resulted in significant racial change. It enabled blacks to become participants in many aspects of the ASA that had been closed to them previously. Nevertheless, by the late 1990s, blacks had not gained equal access to many important positions in the ASA. Once again, some black sociologists, along with their supporters, found it necessary to protest such practices as early generations had done during the Civil Rights movement. Below, I will contrast these two instances of social protest in order to discern how contemporary black insurgency may differ from that of the past.

Three analytic points guide my analysis of racial inequality in the American Sociological Association (ASA). First, national social science organizations matter, despite the relative lack of scholarly attention they have received. Second, in their structure and behavior, national social science organizations tend to mirror and reproduce the social stratification system of the larger society. Thus, in the American context such organizations mirror and reproduce the class, race, and gender hierarchies of America. These outcomes should be anticipated despite the expectations that such organizations should be enlightened in matters of social inequality and embrace values of social justice. To the contrary, the material and symbolic interests of social scientists of the dominant group often override values of social justice in the absence of strong change forces. Third, social science organizations are likely to embrace values of social equality and undergo significant change when pressured to do so by formidable social protest. In the absence of such pressure they are likely to pull back on the throttles of change. They may even revert to exclusionary values and practices commonplace prior to the changes generated by social protest. This reversion is especially true if additional changes being sought appear to threaten the fundamental structure of the privileges enjoyed by social scientists of the dominant group.

This analysis of the ASA focuses on racial equality although it is relevant to gender and class equality as well. Indeed, Pamela Roby (1992) found that widespread discrimination against women in the ASA was pronounced until women engaged in protest during the late 1960s that resulted in significant gender change. I will begin this analysis with an assessment of the importance of a national organization of sociologists. The arguments that social science organizations reproduce structures of social inequalities and change only when challenged by social protest will be demonstrated through the use of relevant historical and contemporaneous data.

Importance of ASA

The ASA matters to the academic discipline of sociology. It currently has over 13,000 members and its annual budget runs into millions of dollars. The founding of this national organization in 1905 signaled to the larger society and the scientific community that sociology exists as a discipline, and that sociology had come of age. Principal goals of the ASA have been to promote and defend sociology as a discipline. Moreover, the ASA has played an important role in the production of sociological knowledge by providing outlets for sociologists to present scholarly papers and to disseminate their findings at its professional meetings and through publication in its journals. The ASA has played an important role in the production and maintenance of a status hierarchy among sociologists to visible positions in the scientific community. From such platforms elite sociologists have been able to enhance their abilities to secure research funds, to address governmental bodies, and to play prominent roles in their local academic settings.

The annual meetings of the ASA enable thousands of sociologists to interact and discuss their intellectual work. In fact, such gatherings function much like a vast four-day seminar housed in hotels and restaurants. In these spaces new ideas are born and old ones are refined and recycled. The ASA meetings also provide opportunities for sociologists to meet publishers and secure book contracts. The annual meetings cement social relationships and help sociologists develop a sense of community and shared identity. Thus, the ASA is an important tool for sociologists because it houses important material and symbolic resources. Given this reality, the issue of whether this organization serves its dues-paying constituency free of racial bias becomes significant indeed.

Racial Hierarchy inside the ASA: Jim Crow

Social science organizations tend to mirror and reproduce the social stratification system of the larger society. The structure and functioning of the ASA throughout America's Jim Crow period are fully consistent with this postulate. Indeed, it is accurate to conclude that the ASA mirrored the Jim Crow order from its founding in 1905 until the early 1970s. The power structure of the ASA is comprised of inseparable administrative and intellectual components. They include the organization's executive office, its board of directors known as the Council, and its offices of president, vice president, and secretary. The central ASA mechanisms through which sociologists achieve visibility and recognition are its journals, annual meetings, and academic awards. For the ASA to mirror and reproduce the Jim Crow racial order, blacks would have to be largely excluded from its overall power structure during the Jim Crow era.

The relevant data confirm this contention. For this analysis data were obtained from ASA's national office, from Lawrence Rhoades's (1981) history of the ASA, and from secondary sources, especially the volume *Black Sociologists* (1974), edited by James Blackwell and Morris Janowitz. Data were also gathered from a variety of articles published in the spring 1992 volume of *The American Sociologist*.

The data reveal a pattern of black exclusion during ASA's sixty-four years of existence during the Jim Crow order. Thus, out of the 61 ASA presidents only 1 was black; out of the 109 vice presidents only 2 were black; out of the 15 ASA secretaries, none was black; out of the 5 executive officers none was black; during these sixty-four years only 4 blacks served on ASA's Council. Additionally, during the Jim Crow era ASA produced eight journals with no blacks serving as editors.

During the same period ASA established two major awards for academic work—the MacIver Award and the Sorokin Award. Out of fourteen recipients only one was black. During the sixty-four-year Jim Crow period, black participation in ASA's annual meetings was nearly invisible. Blackwell found that "toward the end of the 1960s, in the period between 1965 and 1968, the ASA had 23 constitutional, standing and ad hoc committees. Of the 203 total members in each of those years, no more than 3 blacks ever served in any year" (1992, 12). Moreover, Blackwell revealed that "in 1968, only one black sociologist appeared on the program (12). In the Jim Crow period the sociological discourse of the ASA was conducted in a white voice.

These data clearly documented that for sixty-four years, the ASA walked in lockstep with America's Jim Crow order. Blacks were largely excluded from its decision-making bodies, from editorships of its journals, from its executive offices, from its scholarly prizes, from managerial positions, and from participation in its annual meetings. The exclusion from annual meetings was especially painful, for as Blackwell stated, "blacks felt victimized by deliberate acts of exclusion from intellectual discourse" (1992, 12).

Thus, for sixty-four years, the ASA was a de facto Jim Crow organization fully congruent with the racial status quo of the times. Nevertheless, by the

1960s winds of social change roared through the larger society, and it was only a matter of time before they struck the American Sociological Association.

Social Protest and Social Change in the ASA

In 1971, major racial changes occurred in the ASA. Those changes included establishing a committee on the status of racial and ethnic minorities; an ad hoc committee on the relationship of black sociologists to the ASA; a committee to develop a graduate fellowship program for minority students and to secure the necessary funds; the DuBois-Johnson-Frazier Award to honor exemplary research in minority communities. Other changes occurring during this pivotal year included the appointment of a full-time staff sociologist in the executive office to deal with fundamental issues regarding the professional development of racial minorities and women. For that year's annual meeting fifteen minority scholars chaired scholarly sessions. Finally, in 1971, ASA President William Sewell appointed a black sociologist to that year's all-white Council.

Clearly, in 1971, a limited but significant racial transformation occurred in the ASA. Summing up these changes, Sewell (1992) wrote that "no meeting since has had this high a proportion of its sessions planned and chaired by minority members" (62). Why was this so? This was no internal revolution, for in the last of the 1960s the leaders of the ASA had no proposals on the drawing board to address the Jim Crow practices of the organization.

Change occurred in the ASA because some of its black members revolted and attacked ASA's racism. The Civil Rights and Black Power movements that were exploding around them during the late 1960s inspired these sociologists. This embryonic social movement of black sociologists formed during the 1968 annual meeting in which only one black was on the program.

During the association's 1968 business meeting these insurgent black sociologists presented six resolutions that would eventually change ASA's racial regime. These resolutions called for black representation in ASA; for blacks to become members and chairpersons of ASA's committees; for blacks to become chairpersons of sections; for blacks to become presenters of papers and serve as discussants at annual meetings; that black people be allowed to have equal access to ASA's journals; and that blacks become readers and referees of papers in ASA's journals. In addition, at the 1969 annual meeting those black sociologists made an additional demand: That ASA establish a fellowship program for black students interested in becoming professional sociologists.

At this time a caucus of black sociologists formed to carry forth the challenge. As a result, ASA's Council approved the pending resolutions. However, ASA responded like most dominant groups when challenged by the oppressed; it approved the resolutions, but failed to implement real change. By 1970, the social movement of black sociologists confronted the ASA by organizing themselves into a caucus of black sociologists and demanding change. As Blackwell (1992) put it, "tensions mounted and the demand for inclusion escalated . . . the session was bitter, acrimonious, contentious and occasionally uncivil" (13).

The protest was successful, in part, because ASA's president, William Sewell, embraced the challenge and used the power of his office to push through many of the changes advocated by the black caucus.

The social protest of that period is largely responsible for the significant level of minority inclusion in the current ASA. For example, at its annual 2000 meeting, minority sociologists were visible throughout the program. At that meeting, one of the members of the original protest group, Charlie U. Smith, was awarded the DuBois-Johnson-Frazier award. The Minority Fellowship Program has become a highly successful enterprise enabling significant numbers of minorities to obtain their doctorate in sociology. An African American woman is currently serving as secretary of the association. Minorities are currently serving on the ASA Council and currently the vice president-elect is an African American male. *The American Sociological Review* for the first time in its history has a black co-editor.

Clearly, a minor revolution of racial inclusion has occurred in the ASA. But the record is clear: protest triggered that revolution. Reflecting on the significance of that social protest movement, former ASA president Sewell (1992) wrote that it "demonstrated that organized and vigorous protest is the most effective means of bringing about change" (57). Protest during the same period was responsible for the revolution in women's participation in the ASA. Explaining this change, Pamela Roby (1992) wrote that it occurred because "within sociology, we organized, organized, organized" (25). Yet that "revolution" proved limited and unfinished. I turn now to that unfinished business and one particular response to it.

The Unfinished Revolution

Black exclusion as editors of ASA's academic journals has remained intact since its Jim Crow period. The journals are one of the major intellectual lifelines of the association and the larger discipline of sociology. Yet blacks remain largely excluded from that lifeline. Shortly, I will deal with this form of exclusion in depth because of its consequences and the revolt it recently triggered. At this juncture, it is instructive to point out that other forms of racially based academic apartheid continue to exist in the ASA.

Conferring academic awards is an important function of learning societies. Such awards help determine which kinds of scholarship are deemed worthy of honor. They also play a significant role in facilitating the upward mobility of the scholars chosen to be honored. It is rare for African Americans to win major academic awards from ASA. For example, no blacks have ever won the prestigious "Career of Distinguished Scholarship Award." The DuBois-Johnson-Frazier Award appears to have become the "Career of Black Distinguished Scholarship Award" for African Americans. While the establishment of this award represents a measure of progress, legitimate questions can be raised as to whether it has had the unintended consequences of leaving white privilege intact.

The program committee of ASA is important because it has the responsibility of planning the annual meeting and establishing its intellectual tone. A new program committee of approximately a dozen members is appointed each year to carry out this function. A trend of academic tokenism has developed regarding black participation on this committee, given that during eighteen annual meetings since the Jim Crow period, only one black person at a time has ever served on the program committee. Five of the past Jim Crow committees have had no African Americans. Finally, the day-to-day administration of the ASA is the responsibility of an executive director. Even though the ASA has existed for nearly a century, no black person has ever served in this capacity. I return now to the issue of ASA journals and their editorships.

Black participation in the editorship of ASA journals has remained largely unchanged since the Jim Crow era. Since that period, ASA has had thirteen journals and ninety-eight editors. Of the ninety-eight editors, only two have been black; Jacquelyn Jackson edited the *Journal of Health and Social Behavior* from 1973 to 1975; Franklin D. Wilson currently serves as co-editor of the *American Sociological Review* (ASR). Wilson was appointed to a three-year term that ends in 2002. Thus, although the ASR was founded in 1936, it would take two thirds of a century for a black person to become one of its editors. Unlike the overwhelming majority of his predecessors, Wilson served as a co-editor and is accompanied in that capacity by a white colleague.

The ASR is the flagship journal of the American Sociological Association. Articles published in the ASR generate visibility, prestige, and upward mobility for their authors. By publishing in the ASR one has a chance to influence important scholarly debates and shape future research. Because of its status as ASA's premier journal, the ASR is a valuable resource that should operate in a nondiscriminatory manner. The journal's editor and its editorial board members are the key actors who determine which articles to publish, how intellectually diverse the journal will be, and whether the ASR will be free of ascriptive biases including racial discrimination.

Over the last decade, the ASR has come under scrutiny by some members of the ASA who argue that the journal is intellectually narrow and has a history of excluding people of color from its editorship and as editorial board members. Internal studies have been conducted by concerned ASA members (for example, Feagin Memorandum of Council 1995) and elected officers of the ASA. One fact was clear as the twentieth century closed. No black person or other persons of color had ever served as editor of ASR. It was also argued that few people of color published in the ASR because previous editors and editorial teams did not value the kind of scholarship produced by scholars of color. They were very serious and public charges of exclusion that ASA could not ignore.

In 1995, the ASA Council responded to charges pertaining to the lack of diversity in the ASA generally and with respect to its journals in particular. The Council passed a number of resolutions to increase diversity overall in the ASA and to implement measures that would produce diversity in its journals. The Council informed editors of its journals to "take aggressive action to increase the representation of women and people of color" (ASA *Footnotes,* March 1996). The publication committee, an elected body of the ASA, was given the charge to solicit proposals from potential editors of ASA journals. This committee is crucial to the diversification of the journals because historically the Council prior to 1999 had never overruled its recommendation as to who should become ASR's editor. In the late 1990s, the Council directed the publication committee to take action to make sure ASA's flagship journal, the ASR, would become diversified.

In 1999, the publication committee made a historic recommendation to the Council. It recommended that Walter Allen, a distinguished sociologist at the University of California, be named ASR's first black editor. Moreover, Allen's proposed editorial team consisted of six members, four of whom were distinguished minority scholars who held academic posts at major universities. This was a bold recommendation that would have brought instant diversity to ASR's editorial positions. These sociologists were embedded in diverse networks that would enable them to solicit manuscripts from dissatisfied members of the ASA as well as from the typical submitters. The ASR appeared to be on the brink of change given that the Council had always accepted the recommendation of the publication committee.

When the recommendation reached the Council, some of its members were dissatisfied with the choice advanced by the publication committee. Those members organized themselves in opposition to the Allen recommendation, arguing that Allen was not qualified to edit the ASR. Originally, the publication committee advanced Allen as their first choice and another white candidate as their second choice. All of the other applicants' proposals were deemed to be less meritorious and were not recommended to the Council. In an unprecedented action, those opposed to Allen and his proposed editorial team asked to review a proposal that was not advanced by the publication committee. A black and a white colleague at the University of Wisconsin who sought to co-edit the ASR had developed that proposal. Following heated debates, the Council narrowly decided to appoint the interracial team as co-editors of the ASR. Never before had the Council rejected the recommendation of the publication committee or appointed an editor whose proposal that committee deemed insufficiently meritorious. The deliberations of the Council were supposed to be confidential. Those Council members who voted to reject the Allen candidacy were confident that their unprecedented actions would not be disclosed to ASA's general membership.

The Revolt

The secret could not be contained. The contents of the deliberation were "leaked" by insiders who were startled by the highly unusual action. The actions of the Council became widely known when a prominent member of the publication committee resigned and placed his resignation letter on the Internet so those interested could be informed of his reason for resigning. In that letter, Burawoy wrote: "I was elected to the Publications Committee to reflect a variety of perspectives current in our discipline, and to speak for the diverse interests of its membership. In our deliberations, we were following the directives of the Council itself, which several years ago urged the publication committee to insure the openness of the American Sociological Review as our flagship journal. Yet, as soon as we recommended distinguished editors with new visions that we believe would enrich our discipline, we are arbitrarily over-ruled without consultation, discussion or dialogue" (Buroway 1999). Buroway referred to the Council's actions as a "flagrant transgression of substantive democracy." Within days of Buroway's letter, sociologists had begun a vigorous debate over this issue. Much of that debate occurred electronically and in the pages of *Footnotes,* the official organ of the ASA.

Discontent over the decision was conveyed largely through e-mails and electronic attachments. Those opposed charged that the decision was racially motivated and that the Council violated its own procedures. One group of sociologists charged that Allen and his mostly minority editorial team were rejected because they were considered "too black" and "too political." They concluded, "for us . . . the claim that Allen and his team are not 'qualified' smacks of elitism which is indistinguishable from white racial privilege" (*Footnotes,* November 1999).

Those Council members who supported the decision maintained that the best candidates were chosen and that constitutionally the Council had the power to make the final decision. Sharp battle lines were drawn between the summer of 1999 and the August 1999 annual meeting. During this time, the conflict was conveyed mostly through the electronic media. It was agreed that the insurgent sociologists would protest the decision at the annual 1999 business meeting. That was to be the first face-to-face meeting of the protesters. Up until that time, discontent had been mobilized electronically.

At a 7:00 A.M. business meeting on August 22, over 300 sociologists confronted the leadership of ASA. These scholars expressed their anger and opposition over the decision and demanded change. In particular, they presented and passed a resolution that called for the Council to postpone its earlier decision so that a search and a decision on an editor could be implemented. In the end, the Council tabled this resolution and stood by their earlier decision. They maintained that "the new editors were appointed based on their merit and according to current procedure and the transition of the new office has already occurred" (quoted in American Sociological Association, Section on Racial and Ethnic Minorities 1999). The protest group was appalled by the action of the Council and vowed to continue the struggle.

Following the Council's action to stand by its decision, the insurgent sociologists escalated their tactics. They drew up a petition that stated that "the current editors' term will end in the year 2001 reducing their term from three to two years. Walter Allen will be appointed editor of ASR for a three-year term beginning at the end of their term, with the transition beginning in the summer of 2001" (ASA Members Resolution 1999). Additionally, they called for a boycott of the ASR by ASA members, stating that, "in addition to signing the petition please discontinue subscription to ASR until there is a satisfactory solution to this controversy" (ibid.). With this action, the conflict had sharpened and could not be reconciled between the two groups through polite and civil negotiations.

The petition needed 500 signatures of ASA members in order for this effort to be successful. That number of signatures would have empowered the protesters to demand that a general vote of the membership be taken to determine the legitimate editor of the ASR. The petition drive was mobilized through the electronic media. The petition was sent to sociology departments and ASA members by way of an e-mail attachment. In the end, the protest movement was unable to generate the number of signatures required for the general vote of the membership. As a result, the action of the Council prevailed and their two choices became the co-editors of the ASR. The Council did concede to demands to change the procedures through which journal editors were appointed, and it established a task force to explore ways by which the ASR could become more diverse. In the final analysis, ASA's power structure emerged victorious over the protest movement.

Two Struggles Compared

It is instructive to explore why the protests of the late 1960s and early 1970s were more effective than the one to diversify the ASR three decades later. Two differences between these struggles are apparent. That is, over the decades the social environment in which the two struggles occurred had changed significantly and so had the mobilization process. These two factors affected the final outcomes. The earlier protest occurred during the heyday of ASA's de facto Jim Crow regime. As pointed out earlier, during that period blacks were excluded from meaningful participation at all levels of the association. This reality could not be disguised or hidden. The transparent nature of the racial discrimination afforded the protesters a clear-cut enemy that could be attacked and a moral high ground that legitimized and energized the protest movement. Additionally, the earlier struggle emerged during the period of a larger social movement where blatant Jim Crow practices were being overthrown, especially in the South. In this environment, a learned society could lose legitimacy if it were unwilling to change practices not drastically different from those which southern segregationists were being forced to abandon. In the late 1960s, black sociologists were able to effectively attack a Jim Crow regime that was losing its grip nationwide.

The insurgents who led the challenge during the ASR controversy faced a drastically different environment. The formal Jim Crow regime as well as its de facto counterpart in the ASA no longer existed. The opposition to the movement could maintain that their actions were based on meritorious grounds rather than racism. The presence of a number of black and other minority sociologists in visible positions in the ASA provided a measure of credence to this view. The earlier protestors operated in an environment where racial segregationist ideologies were being openly espoused. The latter protesters confronted an environment where ideologies of reverse discrimination and color blindness were seeking dominance. No clear-cut enemy reared its head during the ASR controversy.

The opposition gained the upper hand in the controversy when they chose a black sociologist to become co-editor despite the fact that the proposal of him and his white colleague did not clear the publication committee on meritorious grounds. The view that racism played no role in the Council's decision was buttressed by the fact that their action resulted in the first black becoming an editor of the ASR. Leaders of the protest movement responded that this view "ignores that in post-civil rights America racial issues are no longer just about having 'symbolic representation . . . this challenge should not be undermined by attempting to handpick the minority candidates that the Council believes to be most qualified" (Section on Racial and Ethnic Minorities, *Footnotes*, November 1999). Nevertheless, the decision of the Council to appoint a black person was a formidable barrier for the protestors to overcome. Whites who might have supported the petition decided otherwise because they worried that such support could be construed as racism against the black co-editor. The division also cut into the support of some black and minority sociologists because they were not prepared to argue that the black co-editor was an "Uncle Tom" unworthy of being an ASR editor. They were outraged over the decision to reject Allen and his team rather than by the candidacy of the black co-editor.

When the dust cleared the petition failed in part because the opposition succeeded in appearing to be above racism and the presence of a black person on their slate eroded crucial support needed for the movement to triumph. The social environment in which they struggled had shifted significantly so that the "enemy" was able to clothe itself in an opaque garb that enabled it to appear to some as a friend rather than foe.

This changed environment allowed members of the power structure to vigorously attack the movement. In the earlier protest, the president of the ASA embraced the goals of the challengers and used his office to make changes. This is not to argue that those earlier insurgents operated in a benign environment. Indeed, Blackwell (1992) informs us that back in 1970, "those who presented the resolutions and argued for their approval were labeled 'house niggers, careerists, militant opportunists'. In fact, a few prominent sociologists either resigned or threatened to resign from ASA membership because of the positive response to most of the resolutions" (13). Nonetheless, such reactions did not prevent ASA's president from supporting the movement. By the late 1990s that environment had changed such that the president of the ASA castigated the movement rather than embrace its goals. Indeed, Portes advised sociologists "to put a halt to this destructive process." He went on to argue that "together we must vigorously resist attempts by mobilized activist groups to impose their will on the majority, disregarding democratic principles and properly conducted elections" (Portes 1999). Protest movements for racial justice in the post-Civil Rights period confront an environment far less hospitable and clear-cut than was the case during the dark days of the Jim Crow era.

It was impossible to mobilize protests through an electronic media during the Civil Rights movement. The technological superhighway was not available to insurgents during that era. The original ASA protest was planned and mobilized through face-to-face contact. In those gatherings, members of the aggrieved population were able to build social solidarity and to pledge to each other that they would perform the tasks required, producing effective collective action. Their discontent and mobilization were crystallized and politicized through interpersonal networks and friendship bonds.

In contrast, the ASR rebellion was mobilized largely through electronic media consisting of e-mails, attachments, and the Internet. This approach to mobilization raises the fundamental question of whether collective discontent can be effectively forged through electronic media. It is not clear that these media are effective in generating and directing the anger required for people to engage in risky collective action. It is true that electronic media can provide inexpensive modes of communication that enable members of protest groups to receive vital information swiftly. However, instant communication does not automatically translate into commitment and the concrete actions crucial for a challenge to succeed. Once the electronic buttons have been pushed, activists run the risk of relaxing, thinking they have laid the groundwork for mobilization to occur. In the end, such communication may produce a "virtual movement" but fall short of the commitment and disciplined work needed to generate social change through collective action.

It is not possible to determine definitively if the petition drive during the ASA controversy would have been successful if face-to-face organizing had been the dominant mode of mobilization. However, anecdotal information suggests that few potential supporters of the movement were contacted directly and asked to sign the petition. It is reasonable to assume that the 300 people who attended the 7:00 A.M. business meeting and supported the resolution would have signed the petition. If this were true, the movement would only have had to garner another 200 signatures from the remaining 13,000 members of the ASA. Initially, the leaders of the petition drive were confident that they would easily surpass the number of required signatures. Yet they had few firm commitments and failed to engage in the hands-on organizing that would have enabled them to make realistic projections and to engage in the work needed to overcome the shortfall. In the end, it appeared that movement participants placed far too much confidence in "virtual mobilization" rather than in the kind of hands-on mobilization that occurred in black communities, churches, colleges, and homes during the Civil Rights movement (Morris 1984; Payne 1995). While the technological revolution can function as an asset to protest movements, it may also contain hidden liabilities that dilute the effectiveness of protest. It is quite possible that this informational revolution played a role in slowing the progress to diversify the ASR while giving the appearance that the movement was headed toward victory at a supersonic pace.

In summary, the Civil Rights movement ushered in profound changes on the racial front and set the stage for other types of protest movements to emerge and transform the nation. The original ASA protest belongs to that era and played a crucial role in toppling many of the Jim Crow practices of the American Sociological Association. Referring to the protest of the late 1960s and early 1970s, ASA's 1971 president, William Sewell, stated, "I find it puzzling that organized protest took so long to develop and become effective in the

American Sociological Association." He summed it up this way: "I must say that I do not think the recent increase in the participation of women and minority sociologists would have come about, if it had not been for those who played important roles in the caucuses. They are the ones who forced us to recognize the validity of their pleas for equal opportunity in the affairs of the association. They are the ones who will have democratized the American Sociological Association" (1992, 62).

The challenges faced by contemporary movements for racial justice and democracy include undressing and exposing the modern barriers that stand in the path of progress and directing new technologies to serve the interests of social change rather than the beneficiaries of an unequal status quo. The insurgents of the Civil Rights movement revealed that durable mobilizing and organizing efforts, along with creativity, commitment, and courage, were the cornerstones of change. In the modern era these same qualities, coupled with a grasp of how new technological innovations can speed up the change process, will prove crucial to effective social protest movements.

CHAPTER 16

The Social Situation of the Black Executive

Black and White Identities in the Corporate World

Elijah Anderson

Blacks in corporate executive-level positions in the United States today must deal with extremely complex social dynamics. Although as blacks they are identified first and foremost as members of a historically stigmatized group, as executives they are also identified as members of an elite and powerful class of today's corporate world. A case study of their problems, and the manner in which they have been resolved or left unresolved, will yield insights into the situation of minorities generally.

In preparing to "enter the field," I requested complete access to the people of one work setting within a company, a major financial service corporation in Center City Philadelphia. Such access would have afforded me the opportunity to follow and observe the subjects of the study in their daily activities and to question them all. My intent was to engage in an intensive participant-observation, an ideal situation for generating "slice of life" portrayals of the work setting and for gleaning important insights into the corporate culture generally and the social situation of minority employees of the company more particularly. The company declined this plan. Instead, I was permitted to roam the premises and interview persons referred to me by the vice president for employee relations, who is himself black.

The representation here is therefore based both on observation of the social setting and on intensive ethnographic interviews with a small sample of executive-level "minority" employees including blacks, Jews, and women. Accord-

I would like to take this opportunity to thank Victor Lidz, James Kurth, Kenneth Shopshire, John Skrentny, Harold Bershady, Acel Moore, Nancy Anderson, and Christine Szczepanoski for helpful comments on this work.

ingly, the resulting observations are not meant to be representative but rather suggestive of the quality of experience within the company. Over the course of six months, the interviews were conducted on the work premises or at area restaurants during the workday, and they frequently extended to ninety minutes. (In order to build on this primary research experience, I informally interviewed a variety of black and white, male and female executives of organizations throughout the Philadelphia area over a ten-year period.) The company was generous in providing office space as well as time for employees to be interviewed, and the interviewees were most helpful and quite candid in their discussion of questions put to them by me. The interviews were open-ended and informal in an attempt to elicit information and insights into the personal lives of employees and their situation within the organization.

Historical Basis of Affirmative Action

An adequate assessment of the present-day situation of executives in this company, and in the American corporate world in general, requires some historical perspective on black mobility. Such a viewpoint is important since social change within this corporate environment is related to important changes in other major institutions of American society. Over the past half-century, American society has changed profoundly in the area of race relations (Myrdal 1944; Drake and Clayton 1962; Cox 1948; Hacker 1995; Wilson 1980, 1987, 1996). Largely as a consequence of affirmative action programs, black Americans, long segregated in ghettos and treated as second-class citizens, have recently begun to participate in the wider society in ways previously restricted to privileged members of the white majority group. This process of racial incorporation signaled the beginning of the still very slow decline of the American caste-like system of race relations, and it may be traced to certain general socio-historical developments. The most dramatic changes were spurred by the Civil Rights movement, the subsequent major civil disorders, and the social and political responses to these new and provocative developments (Kerner 1968).

Major policy responses included the Civil Rights legislation of 1964, 1965, and 1968. Perhaps most important for the subject of this essay was the executive order issued and signed by President John F. Kennedy in 1961 and later revised by President Lyndon Johnson in 1964 prescribing "affirmative action" as an important remedy for racial discrimination, social injustice, and the resulting inequality. At the time, public support for these remedial measures was widespread and overwhelming but by no means unanimous. Some critics have argued that because of the overarching concern of government, business, and academia for social peace, these policies were simply desperate measures to "cool out" the "long hot summers," in particular, and to mollify alienated black Americans and their white allies, more generally.

I believe that while there was concern on the part of policymakers to prevent further outbursts of violence and disorder in American cities, there also appeared to be a genuine national consensus to make the socioeconomic system more equitable, particularly to members of the national black community. But also important was the provocative international specter of black Americans being whipped and beaten daily in their efforts to obtain the basic civil rights to vote in the "world's leading democracy." This image was simply too much of a contradiction for many Americans, including policymakers, to bear, particularly with emergence of so many newly independent "colored" nations of Africa and other parts of the Third World, which were in the process of trying to decide whether to follow in the orbit of the Soviet Union or the West in the midst of the Cold War.

Whatever the reasoning or intentions of policymakers, American social life has moved toward equality for blacks since that time. Moreover, to a significant degree, the events that provided increased mobility for blacks also did so for other minority groups. Blacks, women, and members of other minority groups, including newly arrived immigrants, have become the beneficiaries of significant Civil Rights legislation, including affirmative action, which has been strictly enforced by successive federal administrations, with the exception of those of Reagan and Bush. As a result, members of these groups, most notably white women, are now participating in the American occupational structure at levels inconceivable a few decades ago.

Consistent with these trends, the black middle class has expanded in both size and outlook and appears to be in the process of transforming from a class of small-business operators and professionals serving the black community almost exclusively, to one that is increasingly economically independent of that community (Frazier 1957a; Wilson 1980; Landry 1987; Collins 1997). With such developments, members of this group appear increasingly involved in the corporate and business sectors of society at large. Even to the casual observer, black Americans appear to be considerably more fully included in American life than ever before. Largely shut out from becoming bankers, stockbrokers, corporate executives, and responsible government agents before the social upheaval brought on by the Civil Rights movement (Stryker 1953), blacks have become increasingly visible in such occupations, although very few move beyond the middle levels to areas of major influence.

Beginning in the 1960s, as part of the general movement toward greater black incorporation, an impressive number of African Americans began attending predominantly white colleges and universities from which they were previously excluded, at times by law, and the number of black professors, particularly those teaching at predominately white institutions, also increased. This general process of incorporation did not bypass the corporations, some of which gladly recruited blacks; others, though, needed to be pressured into establishing affirmative action programs to remedy past under-representation and discriminatory behavior.

However, as African Americans have become ostensible beneficiaries of affirmative action, leading to a growing presence of middle-class blacks in major social positions, especially in corporate life, growing numbers of white Americans began to feel highly threatened. In an era of de-industrialization and corporate downsizing and the resulting insecurities of the American workforce, policies that were once indulged became viewed negatively as so many "race preferences" for blacks. In these circumstances, efforts to include blacks worked to create a growing backlash and resentment among a number of those whites, and some blacks. Those who opposed this desegregation have gone so far as to mount legal and ideological challenges to affirmative action programs, arguing "reverse discrimination" (Glazer 1987, 1997; *Regents of the State of California vs. Bakke* 1978; Skrentny 1996; Bearak 1997). All this has culminated in a growing nationwide movement to legally dismantle affirmative action programs through state initiatives. Proposition 209 has outlawed affirmative action in California, foreshadowing what could happen throughout the United States.

Ironically, along with the apparent growth of black representation and participation in various areas of American life, but particularly in the workplace, fewer citizens see a need for affirmative action. With such visible black participation, as well as growth of the presence of other minorities in the workplace, including white women, it becomes increasingly difficult to make the argument that racism is the sole factor denying opportunities to blacks and that the system itself is racially exclusionary. In these circumstances, race is prematurely degraded as a powerful explanation of inequality. In essence, the power of the concept has been weakened by the proliferation of symbolic elements that contribute to the appearance of inclusiveness—particularly successful blacks—in the corporate workplace; by their presence and high visibility, they strongly imply that the occupational structure is now open and egalitarian, if not entirely meritocratic.

Nevertheless, black executives often express their doubts. While it is clear that social conditions have improved considerably for many middle-class blacks, and that the resulting progress toward attaining social parity with middle-class whites has given many hope, it must be pointed out that racial inequality continues to be endemic to American society, and that tremendous numbers of blacks as well as other people of color remain segregated in ghettos, are poor, and continue to be treated as second-class citizens (Massey and Denton 1993; Feagin and Sikes 1994; Cose 1993). In fact, as improvements in the condition of the black middle class become more pronounced, a social and economic split between members of the black middle class and the black lower class becomes more discernible.

The initiatives and policies mentioned above had their most direct and immediate effect on blacks that were well-prepared and poised to take advantage of any opportunity that arose in the occupational system. In this scenario, the lower class was largely ignored at a time when the jobs on which this class depended started to be lost due to automation, de-industrialization, and the rise of global economy (Wilson 1980, 1987, 1996; E. Anderson 1990; Rifkin 1995). This historical context is important for understanding aspects of the social life of the company on which this report is based.

After President Johnson issued his executive order prescribing affirmative action, the company I studied instituted its programs to recruit and train blacks. Without such pressure and the initiatives that followed, the number of blacks working and being promoted within the company would have been significantly smaller. A few blacks have indeed been highly successful, occasionally reaching upper-level management positions. But many others are frustrated, feeling strongly that they have been detained and kept from rising because of an invisible "job ceiling" for blacks; they believe there are certain jobs that blacks will never obtain and others into which blacks are being channeled. Moreover, it is difficult for them to feel and act as if they are accepted as full participants in the organization (Cose 1993).

Since skin color, particularly its social and political significance, appears to be such a problematic issue for the personnel of the organization, it would be conceptually useful, following Goffman (1963), to consider its relationship to the concept of stigma, or "spoiled identity." Goffman distinguishes three cate-gories: "the own," the wise," and "the normal." The own represents the stigma-tized group in society. This group consists of a collection of individuals with a similar "negative" difference. Within the group, there is a discrepancy between each person's "virtual" and "actual" social identities, which can be seen as the difference between his or her "good," "virtuous," and "positive" qualities and "negative" attributes. Stigma thus is a matter of degree and perhaps best viewed as a product of social interaction; in effect, it is a transaction between those who are stigmatized and those who assign stigma (Becker 1963). For Goffman, those who assign stigma include the normals (those members of the organization who feel essentially that corporate life is fair to them and others and have few complaints) and the wise ("normal" people who have the capacity for empathy toward outsiders and who tend to extend themselves to the "own" to assist them and make them feel welcome within the organization) as well as mem-bers of the own themselves.

However, it is important to keep in mind that much has happened in the politics of difference since Goffman advanced his position. Today, Goffman's view of stigma appears rather absolutist insofar as he has a generally clear con-ception of what does and does not constitute stigma. In his view, the person in our society without stigma is the young, married, white, urban, northern, het-erosexual Protestant father, college educated, fully employed, of good com-plexion, weight, and height, and a recent record in sports (Goffman 1963, 128). All others, we are to presume, are in some way compromised and would really rather be "normal"; they would be more than ready to trade in their sta-tus and identity as "stigmatized" if that were possible.

With respect to the "tribal" stigma of race, such an analysis is weakened by the fact that, since the beginning of the Civil Rights and Black (cultural) Na-tionalist movements that have culminated in today's Afrocentric movement, many black people, but not all, appear increasingly black and proud and would cringe at the thought of giving up their blackness for promises of racial inclu-sion or assimilation. Such positions have their parallels among feminists, gays, and various ethnic groups. In fact, in present-day America, there seems to be an emerging concern with valuing one's differences, playing up one's particularity, be it ethnic, racial, or sexual, and attempting to compete effectively for place and position among so many others who make up our pluralistic society (Rose 1990; Schlesinger 1992; Feagin and Sikes 1994; Glazer 1997). Nevertheless,

Goffman's typology, taken as conventional commentary on race and difference, provides us with a conceptually useful, if ideologically conservative, benchmark from which to approach the social situation of the black executive.

The Own

Within the organization I studied, the own may be characterized as a loosely knit collection of black employees. Such people may at first glance appear, especially to outsiders, to be a monolithic, tightly knit, "self-interested" group. The actual situation, however, is more complicated than that. Membership in the own is usually involuntary and, because it is determined by skin color, persistent, although in reality its members at times may "fade" in and out of the association. To a certain degree, this is a matter of perception, and putative members become more or less closely affiliated with the own depending upon the issue at hand and the attendant social circumstances. Moreover, individuals with observable phenotypical features identifiable by all Americans but especially by blacks as "black" or black African origin are automatically made eligible for membership in the own. During social interaction and instances of sociability, fellow blacks in effect claim them, and whites readily associate them with the own.

Among some blacks in the organization, the sense of affiliation with the own can be situational, while for others it can be a full-time preoccupation. At the same time, however, the frustrations of black employees resulting from an awareness of the job ceiling and other indications of negative differential treatment, mixed with hurt but often hidden feelings, may work to set them apart from others in the company, including other minorities. Many feel strongly that their experiences in the American occupational structure are unique and that other minorities—women, Asians, Jews, and Hispanics—do not confront the same personal and social problems. They come to see their skin color and the social significance it has acquired over the centuries as their chief and lingering problem, not just in the workplace but in society in general (Cose 1993). Hence, for a large number of blacks in the organization, skin color is *the* persistent issue, a conspicuous and observable characteristic that often makes them subject a priori to negative consideration and treatment. But they tend to keep such views to themselves or to share them mainly with fellow blacks who they think are trustworthy or, rarely, with whites who have earned their confidence.

At the same time, many of those blacks who are doing well in the organization have found it necessary to distance themselves from the own and to present themselves as individuals who have struggled despite great odds and have made it. Indeed, for them, it is generally considered bad form to define oneself as publicly preoccupied with race, as a "race man" or "race woman" or as one who promotes "the race" over others (Drake and Cayton 1962; Goffman 1963; E. Anderson 1997). In this context, at times with deep ambivalence, some feel it prudent to tone down their enthusiasm for company policies that appear to favor "the race" (Steel 1990); Carter 1991; Kennedy 1997). For instance, such people may feel they must publicly distance themselves from the concept of affirmative action, even though without this policy and the accompanying governmental pressure, many of them probably would not hold the positions they do, because many white executives engaging in business as usual would simply have overlooked the many talented blacks they now count, occasionally with displays of pride, among their number.

Accordingly, it is not uncommon to hear some of these blacks voice complaints about the wisdom of affirmative action programs and quotas. These complaints often stem from a complex psychological need to identify publicly with a corporate culture that at times denies them full participation. In working to resolve this dilemma, many have internalized conceptions of the organization as a virtual meritocracy, while others are left embittered by what they see as a sham of equal opportunity.

Generally in their daily behavior at work, however, most find themselves enacting their versions of the corporate orientation, a clear commitment to organizational rules and values that their white counterparts and superiors readily sanction. To enact such a role effectively strongly implies that the individual himself or herself is included as a standing member of that system. But in terms of feeling fully included, most are left with reservations. It may be that at least some of this acceptance of the corporate orientation has to do with the felt need to present oneself as a "team player," or they may hope to benefit—or at least to cover themselves—by "going along to get along," while offering up the classic caveat about not selling out and "remembering where you come from."

It is conceptually useful to divide the black executives into two groups: the core own and the peripheral own. The core own may be identified as those blacks who have recently emerged from traditional, segregated black communities or who maintain a strongly expressed or a racially particularistic sense of identity, while the peripheral own are often the products of less racially isolated backgrounds and tend to be more universalistic in outlook (E. Anderson 1990, 40–42). Generally speaking, the core own tends to be organized around the belief that American society is irredeemably racist and that relationships with whites are to be entered into with a certain amount of suspicion, if at all, and such relationships are best understood as being primarily of an instrumental nature. Hence, those of this position tend to interact with whites only on a formal level; their friendships are mainly with other blacks who are "black enough," meaning those with an orientation that places race first and emphasizes solidarity with the African American community.

The peripheral own, on the other hand, tend toward a more cosmopolitan orientation, while regarding the problem of American race relations as difficult but hopeful. In deference to norms of racial caste, they tend to engage other blacks for close relationships, but are open to friendships with whites and others. Imbued with values of social tolerance, such blacks tend to be comfortable in relationships with various kinds of people, and tend to see them as individuals first and people of a certain race second. As a result of these differential identifications, the core and the peripheral own tend to have different corporate experiences.

Complicating the picture, however, is the fact that certain coworkers, black and white alike, will lump all blacks together into something of a single group. For such people, the member's skin color and physical attributes help define the person's special relationship with the company. Members of the own, who are generally expected to acknowledge, befriend, and support one another on the basis of skin color, thus assume a common social and cultural history with respect to the white American norms of racial prejudice and discrimination toward blacks (Hughes 1945; Blumer 1958; Wellman 1977; Pettigrew 1980; Feagin and Sikes 1994; Hacker 1995). These assumptions serve as an important organizing principle for the own.

When brought to the organization, the core own's identity and its related values become sharpened by the distinctions they draw between themselves, the peripheral own, and other coworkers, who tend to be white and of middle-class background. Therefore, a core own member whose sense of identity is threatened by the everyday vicissitudes of life within the organization, particularly by the extent to which he or she is required to interact closely with whites, often gravitates to others who are black and have similar social attitudes and values. These individuals then find racial solidarity particularly valuable as a defense because of what they view as a generalized pattern of bad treatment at the hands of whites and, by extension, because of white oppression of black communities.

In these circumstances, many of the black employees are reminded of the strong adversity their people traditionally experienced in their everyday dealings with whites; when the experience is not personally remembered, it may be socially reconstructed by members of the own. Collectively, the own, particularly those in the core, tend to subtly define the present situation as a hostile one, thus making it ever more difficult for them to trust white coworkers and easier to trust fellow blacks. This oversimplified view further encourages association on the basis of color and as a result contributes to the reification of a racial division of labor, while working to undermine comity and good will among blacks and whites in the workplace.

Among themselves, functionally "backstage," members of the own commune and commiserate with one another. Here they may "talk black," both articulating the frustrations they experience in working among insensitive whites and identifying the work-related issues they believe are racially based. They may greet one another as "sister" and "brother," invoking feelings of familial solidarity. On these occasions, members of the own appear relatively relaxed, but often they may not fully be so. For many feel they must be alert and aware of those who might turn on them, selling them out to those in authority.

Highly motivated to succeed, they feel competitive not only with their white coworkers, but at times with their black colleagues as well. As the issue becomes survival, they learn to watch and protect their backs, at times from one another. Yet, as they meet and talk, and to a degree collude, they learn to trust and find themselves socializing, often on the basis of race unity. Here, not only do they make small talk, perhaps discussing what was on television last night, they also discuss public issues of the day, particularly issues that impact on the lives of blacks in corporate life. They pass around relevant news clippings and through sociability gain perspective on the corporate world. But equally important, it is in these gatherings that members of the own compare notes on experiences with their white colleagues, at times collectively distinguishing between "enemies" and "friends," or the "wise" in the general organization, and discussing issues pertinent to their jobs. It is here also that some might complain about problematic supervisors or about an errant white secretary who shows too little respect for blacks, or might even single out peripheral own members who have shown themselves to be outside the fold or have blatantly violated the rules of the own.

As a group, the peripheral own tend to have a more cosmopolitan orientation and in general are better educated than their core own counterparts. They thus tend to occupy a higher status in the organization. For such blacks, there is a strongly felt need to believe they are present in the organization not solely because of the color of their skin, but because of their own excellence in the general business world. Furthermore, in cases where racial particularism among blacks might be invoked to favor a black or other minority individual, and for some of the complicated reasons mentioned above, those blacks who occupy positions of authority might hesitate to offer such endorsements. Rather, they sometimes bend over backward to judge an individual not on the basis of color, but with regard to the issue at hand and on their own perceptions of that person's merit.

A major reason for this hesitancy and the attempt to neutralize racial particularism in public has much to do with the standing power relationships within the organization, as well as feelings of insecurity experienced by members of this group. As indicated above, one way of dealing with such feelings is through acts of overcompensation by strongly embracing the corporate culture, including the meritocratic norms of the organization, and by demonstrating their team loyalty and worthiness at every opportunity. Such norms may be strongly affirmed through close attention to presentational rituals in the areas of dress, speech, and manners. But if such behavior promises the approval of corporate higher-ups, such rituals may put off members of the core own, sharpening the division between the two groups.

Compared with others in the company, both whites and blacks, the members of the peripheral own appear utterly "polished." The men usually dress in stylish fashions, wearing expensive "corporate" outfits tending toward dark pinstriped suits; their appearance seems carefully chosen to conform to some handbook on dressing for success. The black women often appear glamorous, not limiting themselves to the dark and subdued colors worn by the white women of their corporate status. In general, those of the peripheral own tend to be "impressive looking" to their white coworkers, particularly for persons of their color-caste. Moreover, their use of language suggests that they have been well educated; over the phone they are at times mistaken for educated whites.

As indicated above, not only do they seem to feel at ease in the company of whites, but also their demeanor in the presence of whites seems almost casual and certainly confident. During such interactions, they leave no doubt that they are the social and intellectual equals of their white coworkers. Moreover, they give the impression of having had personally satisfying interactions and positive experiences with whites, and they are mostly willing to blame whatever bad experiences they may have had on errant individuals, not on whites generally.

In managing the various and sundry issues of the corporate world, members of the periphery like to appear to be colorblind, indicating that race plays a limited role in their understanding of the social world, but they display some ambivalence in this regard, particularly as the conservative political establishment effectively assaults the very basis of their existence: by actively questioning affirmative action and other policies they feel have provided blacks with opportunities in the corporate world. It is such reservations, and the dynamic tensions they create, that allow race to continue to play an important role in their work and personal lives. But it may well be just such ambivalence that encourages some of these individuals to simply defer to the powers that be, at times playing along with what they think their white colleagues would like to think.

It is in just such sets of circumstances that such individuals experience most acutely the racial "twoness" of which DuBois spoke about a century ago (DuBois 1995). Some others, to be sure less ambivalent, but well-schooled by the dominant system and its ideology of egalitarianism, individualism, and merit, embrace the corporate culture more fully. It is with these ambivalences and reservations that, on a social basis, the peripheral own tend to fraternize with both blacks and whites, often believing they are making little distinction on the basis of skin color, yet doing so all the while.

Within this context, this benchmark, they project a kind of cosmopolitan ideal. Yet, as indicated above, in reality, when it comes to most issues affecting them personally, they do make distinctions based on color. Moreover, because of their class position and sense of privilege flowing therefrom, the activities the peripheral own pursue during time out are likely to be those the core own most often associates with whites: such activities as golf and tennis as well as occasional evenings at the symphony, the opera, or the theater, at times in the company of white coworkers and friends. During backstage sessions, the core own sometimes jokingly accuses them of selling out or being co-opted by the system. While these barbs may seem humorous, they sometimes hit home. According to one black senior vice president with whom I discussed my analysis:

> In terms of their lifestyle, some do the opera thing and the art museum thing. But all black executives will also do the jazz. They also do the house party. You would have some where you would do some socializing and you would bring a few whites into it. But the ones that were really serious parties were kind of isolated. You would have two different sets of agendas: one where you

would want to create some cohesion with some of the whites so they could
see how nice you could socialize, but where you would really want to let
yourself go and get down and talk about issues, then it would be blacks only.
The core would never do that [invite whites to a party].

And they play golf, play tennis. About ten, twelve years ago, my wife bought
me some golf clubs for Christmas. I never thought about playing golf before
that. She said, you need these to be part of the team. So I took up golf. I bought
her golf clubs the following Christmas. And I play several times a year. Before
that, whenever we would go on a company retreat, there was always some free
time, and there would be some golf and some tennis and some volleyball. And
I would be in the volleyball game because I did not have the skills to play tennis—I was not too good at that—and I never touched a golf club. And those
folks are into a different group. I think that whole thing is gonna change twenty
years from now because of Tiger Woods. We will still have exclusive clubs because of the money but it will be less so. So it will not be as prestigious because
everybody is out there doing it.

To members of the peripheral own, such experiences support their values
of openness to new social experiences and to social relationships more general
than those bounded by color and race. Bent on upward mobility, they usually
have some plan for realizing success, and to a degree most have already experienced it within the firm. However, because of their ambivalent relationship
with the own, they run a distinct risk of becoming for some whites the subject
of ambiguity. This question of their place in the structure becomes especially
acute when members of this group are seen by whites congregating or frater-
nizing closely with other blacks. *There are* times when outsiders might interpret
such close associations as a violation of organizational etiquette regarding ambivalence with respect to the own as they are haunted by the concern that associating closely with the own may seriously impair their own chances of
advancing in the organization. Yet, for reasons noted above, they feel some obligation to engage in such associations.

As indicated above, when blacks rise in the company, they tend to move
away from the core own to the more loosely knit peripheral own. A person
whose status changes may easily be accused of disavowing membership in the
own, for his or her behavior, including styles of interacting with white associates, can suggest a certain distancing from more ordinary black employees. As
this distancing occurs, depending on his or her status and behavior, the indi-

vidual may be subject to sanctions by the loosely knit group of the own; to deal with such an individual, members of the own may come together. Their sanctions may amount to expressions of hostility—including angry looks and gossip—and the threat of ostracism from the own. It must be remembered, however, that because of the professional nature of business occupations, these sanctions are usually of a mild and somewhat indefinite kind. Their real impact is negated by the possibility that the person being sanctioned at one moment may be needed for *support* at a later point in time.

Instead of forcing issues, some people simply "stew" and gossip when they observe one of the own violating group norms. When stewing does occur, it may take the form of pouting, and it usually goes on behind a person's back, not to his or her face. Thus, the complaints often remain subtle and only marginally effective. In general, the own becomes and remains something of a shadow group, emerging when it or one of its members is being or is feeling threatened; seldom, if ever, does it strike out as a major force.

The basis of the club of the own has to do primarily with the insecurities of its members about their standing in the wider group. This standing is thought to be strongly affected by their blackness and its meaning within a predominately white firm. The members of the own believe skin color has a direct impact upon the way they are regarded within the firm. Many have the recurring feeling of being persecuted or "on" when in the presence of whites, a sense that someone is always watching and "just waiting to get something on me." There is also a general belief that although individuals may be unsure of themselves, the members of the own may be able collectively to do something about their situation. There is a sense that they are strangers in hostile territory and that the formation of an informal club is partly a matter of self-defense. Hence, "unity" becomes an important social value, if not a major principle of social organization.

Yet some of the own, particularly those on the periphery, are not sure how much legitimacy the group deserves. Accordingly, those seriously attempting to negotiate the organizational ladder tend to be careful about the racial and political implications of their public associations, particularly when on the job. They are cognizant of the fact that they have to avoid compromising themselves in the eyes of the powerful members of the organization. It is this set of issues that operates to confuse and somewhat frustrate certain members of the own, thus contributing to their worries about appearing "too black" in one set of circumstances and "too white" in another. Whites are inclined to see these ambivalent blacks one way and fellow blacks are inclined to see them in another. Many of the whites may become disturbed by what appears to be insincerity on the part of a trusted black friend and colleague. But often this "insincerity" is an outgrowth of the black person's attempts to successfully manage the various and sometimes conflicting demands placed on him or her by color and by its social meanings within the organization. The own and the larger white group are deeply implicated in the black executive's mode of operation.

The members of the own appear to understand and to be somewhat tolerant of the black executive's excesses, appreciating this member's need to deal with his or her white colleagues. In the words of one executive, it is acceptable to be "white"—but only to a degree. To venture beyond the acceptable degree of association—and thus of perceived identification—is to risk the already discussed sanctions of the own. It is important here to understand that such limits on behavior are in reality a matter of social negotiation and, depending on the executive's social resources in the situation, he or she may thus be able to get away with more or fewer transgressions in the face of the own. The executive's behavior may be interpreted simply as competence on the job and not as a conscious attempt (without good reason) to approximate "white" ways.

On the other hand when the person negotiates effectively with the own group, he or she runs the distinct risk of alienating white coworkers and superiors. Given the political realities of this situation, the black executive often resolves the conflict by risking his or her relationships with other members of the own, assuming those other members lack real power and influence in comparison with supervisors and other higher-ups, who tend to be white. From this perspective, fellow blacks are relatively politically expendable, whereas the upper-level whites are not. The understanding of this reality creates tolerance in members of the own for the "deviance" of their members. In the words of the senior vice president referred to earlier:

> The [peripheral] own was like a support group. At the same time, I went to great lengths to keep a good relationship with the core group. I could not do everything that they would do because some things I did not think were correct or politically savvy in terms of progressing. One of the issues is [as a member of the peripheral own] you can go along with the core and do everything they do, but the end result is you have no influence with the company. So by doing that, you hurt the core. So, even though the more astute ones will say

what he is doing is OK, some of the core folks say that if you do not act the way I act, you have sold out. But some of them give the peripherals slack, because they understand you have to do that to stay in the good graces and have some kind of minimal power, marginalized power, whatever it is. So they do not call it acting white necessarily, it varies by the individual.

Some folks who were black executives whom I saw in that vein, whom I saw identifying a lot less than I did with blacks—at the bottom line, I also found out that they were doing things, low-key things, that would improve the plight of the black employees, but they just were not raising the banner about it. They were keeping a low profile. I think it is a rare black executive who has no consciousness about reaching back and doing something for his people. Some will go out of their way to relate, mentor, and coach, etc. Others will keep a distance. But even with that distance they will do things as the opportunity arises. And the thing is that the further you stay away from the core, the more power you have to make things happen. You might meet with the core privately, but some of these folks did not meet with the core at all, did not want to be seen with them.

I could see those things being played out. For the most part, I got very positive feedback [from the core], but I am not sure there were some folks saying, "he sold out. He is not one of the brothers." So even with myself I think it was a negative reaction at times, but those folks who got an even more negative reaction were the very same folks who had the ability to make change. Those people would never socialize with the core [although] they would say hi. They would take the company position on issues. They would not assume that everything was racist. They [the peripheral own] would ask questions as if they were objective arbitrators versus somebody who is going to defend their race to the end. So they would do things that would come across as being conservative or not understanding. And, I think they were going through the process of trying to appear to be superobjective even to the point of being overly so, and making you prove your case. I think in their heart, in small settings among the club, you would hear what was really happening. But they would behave as if the structure was correct. And that would give them coin [leverage] with the power structure.

I had a lot of positive feedback but just reading it as a possibility that there were folks who thought I sold out was painful. [But] in your heart you know you are doing good things and you are trying to do the right thing and you are doing what you need to do to now assimilate but at least have people not be concerned about you in terms of wanting to cut you out of any kind of power, decision-making process. In terms of who is going to be downsized, you need to act in a certain civil manner so they will say this guy, he is part of the group. You are never really part of the group, but you are close enough that you can sit in the group. And the thing is that once you get on that management track, either you change right away and you start wearing different suits and different clothing or you never rise any higher. They are never going to envision you as being a white male, but if you can dress the same and look a certain way, and drive a conservative car and whatever else, they will say, this guy has a similar attitude, similar values. He is a team player. If you do not dress with the uniform, obviously you are on the wrong team. I have talked to young guys who are becoming managers about the dress, the style, and why it is important. The way I would always put it to them would be, it is a choice. You do not have to do what they do, but let me tell you what you are giving up. You dress like this [in a flamboyant, stereotypically black way], you are not part of the team. It should not be important, but these are the rules. And, so they can make conscious choices.

People [the normals] will not reach out to you if you do not at least look like you are trying to act like them. Because they are afraid of people who are looking like that [flamboyant]. I can be in a suit and tie and still be a threat, but a guy like that is really a threat. He might remind them of a drug dealer or somebody. He might pull out his knife if he does not like you. So the peripheral own dress in the conservative style, Brooks Brothers.

At the same time, for the larger organization, the members of the peripheral own often serve (although sometimes their role is unacknowledged) as cultural brokers of a sort, working to bridge the social gap between members of the minority community and management (Collins 1997); and in fact, such peripheral blacks often informally see themselves as communication links between people of their own racial background and the predominately white firm. In informal conversations, they sometime attempt to edify and sensitize their white colleagues about black life. They are sometimes successful in this regard and thus are often highly valued by those of the enlightened management group who increasingly must come to terms with minority issues. But, because of this communication function and because blacks are so poorly represented at the higher reaches of the organization, the black executive runs the further, and often debilitating, risk of becoming all-consumed by this role.

Sensitive to the risks involved, many black executives strongly resist this feature of their positions, at least formally. They would much rather see and identify themselves as persons with more general roles (or with roles they view as more central to the mission of the organization) than that of managing the minority community. When they feel themselves being used simply as communication links and representatives of blacks, many feel themselves seriously compromised and complain that they are unable to do the work for which they have been trained. They worry that they may be seen as tokens, and they often begin to question the roles they play in the organization. For some, this perception leads to demoralization, cynicism, or deeper questions concerning their real value to the organization. This role can also create difficulties for them within the own. Although whites may view their role as mainly helping expand the horizons and influence of blacks within the company and as leaders and role models, members may enact it somewhat grudgingly.

In general, however, the members of the peripheral own tend to display a positive attitude about life in the company and may become spokespersons for the company. This outlook is enhanced by their perception of the individual as master of his or her own destiny. If they have complaints, they take them to those in authority, as individuals, not as members of their own, thereby creating fewer tensions with white leadership. Also, with their presentation of self, including their dress and demeanor and general social outlook, they are the ones who seem most able to seek and to gain effective relationships with white mentors or with white political allies in the company.

For members of the general organization, however, the distinctions between the core own and the peripheral own are often invisible. Rather, "the blacks" signify a reference group, although whites and blacks see the significance and meaning of the group quite differently (Shibutani 1961; Merton 1957). When whites think of blacks, they may find it conceptually convenient to consider the individual as part of the black group. Although some whites may pride themselves on seeing and treating blacks as individuals, blacks often remain unconvinced of their ability to do so.

The Wise

This brings us to "the wise." The wise are people in the organization who are privileged in some respect (usually upper middle class) but who, because of their upbringing, education, or general life experiences, have developed a deeply sympathetic or empathetic orientation toward people they define as unfortunate victims of social injustice. The members of the wise have an appreci-

ation of the special background of their own and so bring a unique brand of social awareness to the corporate setting. This awareness, mixed with their own
intelligence and their understanding of the corporate world, generates in them
a rare ability to appreciate the contributions of minorities to the corporation
and to society in general. Combining this sense of appreciation with a real sensitivity to life within their own caste and its relation to the minority caste, such
persons have developed a certain wisdom mixed with a sense of tolerance in the
area of human relations. Compared with others in the organization, the executives in the wise are particularly strong in the field of human affairs.

The wise are often made up of Jews, women, successful blacks (members of
the peripheral own), and other minority members who occupy high-status positions within the firm. Significantly, liberal Jews tend to be overrepresented in
this category. Because of the Jews' long history as victims of prejudice and discrimination at the hands of the majority group, such people are often in a position to observe and to appreciate the plight of blacks in American society in
general and in the corporation in particular. Because of their own group and
personal experience with prejudice and discrimination or because they have
simply taken a liking to the member of the own with whom they work, the
wise are often able to empathize with the dilemmas of the black executive, particularly if he or she is young and located low on the corporate ladder.

Occupying positions of authority and influence, as well as having certain
independence, these executives have a chance to do something to alleviate the
problems they see. They often go on record to demonstrate their empathy for
the plight of blacks and other minorities in the organization. Among the own,
such persons may be identified and spoken of as allies. With an understanding
of the ways of both whites and blacks, the wise are able to express their special
identity in ways that other whites might not notice but that are unambiguous
to many blacks. They may demonstrate this quality by assisting a black employee during a difficult period or by associating closely with blacks at certain
corporate functions, by showing a real and sincere interest in issues important
to minorities, by displaying a tolerant manner toward minorities, or by appreciating contributions of the own and other minorities in the company. Of all
the whites of the organization, in the minds of members of the own, the wise
are viewed as the most likable and trustworthy. Because of these abilities, the
wise more readily appreciate contributions of the own and other minorities to
the company.

While members of the wise are usually privileged and white, they may be located almost any place within the organization. In addition, blacks on the corporate ladder sometimes report how they have been befriended by a black janitor or doorman; in their encounters with such individuals, they discover how much more they have to discuss with them than with white peers or superiors who are not members of the wise. At times, a lower-level white person may serve a similar purpose. The main quality all such persons have in common with the member of the own is their perception of him or her as "alone," as needing social support, or simply as "approachable." Key features of members of the wise are their ability to understand the situation and their general receptivity to members of the own.

Because of their openness, the well-connected members of the wise often provide valuable connections for the upwardly mobile members of the own, particularly people who tend to make up the peripheral own. By developing this connection into a social relationship, the own member can gain even more mobility as well as a rare and useful perspective on the hierarchy of the organization and on how it may or may not be negotiated. Opportunity for protégé-mentor relationship often grows out of such connections. One male black executive had such an experience.

My first mentor in the corporate world was a Jewish man, and he helped me quite a bit. This man helped me, and after he left our company, he still stayed in contact; when my brother lost his job, I reached out to him and he hired my brother. My brother was desperate. But he had the power to bring people in. If he said it would happen, it would happen. So he said to my brother, based on my knowledge of your brother, I know you must have some of the same qualities, so you are hired.

Normally, you do not have that kind of leverage, that kind of ability to reach out and say, hey, would you mind so-and-so, and have somebody help. He could really shut the door, but I had nurtured this relationship with him over several years at one company. Then when he left, he was there to help. And again, this was a Jewish man. I would not call him racially sensitive, where he was on top of all the issues, but he was a fair-minded man.

The relationship [between us] started when I was having a problem. I was, I guess pretty much full of myself and I knew I was good at what I did. If I was at a meeting and somebody wanted to do something that was bureaucratic or would slow me down or whatever, I would say that. And this person would not raise an issue at the meeting, but they would go behind my back and undermine what I was doing behind the scenes. So this Jewish guy came to me and told me what was happening: You need to learn how to not wear your emotions on your sleeve. It was the first time I thought about that, but he was right. He plays cards quite a bit. He was talking about, it like playing poker and you are gonna gain and everybody else is holding their cards and you can not see what they are, but your cards are lying face up on the table. And I was used to being straight out and honest—this is how I feel. A lot of people would not come out with it, but if they had some agenda, they would go about taking care of it. And I learned that. He explained it to me, how you need to mellow out and not be face to face in terms of how you address issues and how you deal with people. I guess the expression he used was that you have enough enemies in the corporate world, without creating new ones. And it may not even be obvious that they are going after you, they are gunning for you. But, he said, if you put somebody down, say something ugly at a meeting, and the person has the opportunity to hurt you, they will. My attitude at the time was, because I am good at what I do and I know what I am doing, I could say just what I felt like saying. But, that was not really the case at all.

So, we would socialize. I played golf with him. We played racquetball together several times. He had my wife and me over to his house. I had risen to middle management just acting a certain way. So since that carried me that far, why change? He explained to me why change, because it would hinder you as you went forward. And, I used that same logic in terms of choosing my battles with my children, family, friends, other employees, whatever. I explained to them, that I had the wisdom that I picked up and used and now I was passing it on to them.

At the same time, the member of the own has a chance to mentor the wise and even sometimes the "normal" person. Michelle is a case in point. A black manager, who considers herself a member of the peripheral own, she in fact transcends all three categories while maintaining links to all of them. She has used her considerable understanding to get on in the corporation and in the process has herself become wise in its ways. She has become a strategic actor (Goffman 1961) who can in turn edify and assist members of the various categories with their problems in the organization. As such, she reverses the model by mentoring normals in the ways of the own and in their sensitivities to race issues. In return, she can wield a certain amount of power by helping them perform better for the organization. Unlike the male executive quoted earlier,

Michelle is not ambivalent about her intermediate position between the core own and the normals; she is not concerned about being seen by the core as selling out because she is convinced that her style of behavior benefits all blacks:

First of all, when I joined the department, I was basically the only black professional. There was one other black person who was, as far as they were concerned, the typical ghetto Negro, because she came from there. She lived in North Philadelphia, made no bones about it, she looked as the stereotype, and she behaved as the stereotype. And I wanted to create my own positive image, not just as a black person, but as a person who is committed to professionalism but who happened to be black. So that my blackness would not be the only thing that they were concerned about.

I would always deal with people in a way that respected who they were so that I would get the respect that I was demanding by my behavior. I also reported to someone who was a bright, young, Catholic male, who went to a Jesuit school and recognized that we have something in common in that he was Catholic and I was Catholic. He was young. He came to the position of course because of his father. And he certainly recognized that, so he took pains to always tell me how hard he worked and how he worked from the mail room up to where he is, which was not true—he spent maybe two minutes in the mail room of his entire career. And he was made in charge of the department very young, probably at the age of thirty something. And he was not in a sense filled with all the old traditional tapes of people who would think about black people in a certain way. To him, it was something that you looked at sort of funny or joking or whatever, but he was not punitive. If he did it, it would not be what I considered malicious. He would have done it based on what I think most white people have a problem with, and that it is not by commission or omission, by not realizing what it means. If confronted with it, which I constantly did, he was always, oh, I did not realize it, oh, I am sorry.

There was another manager who was there who was also Italian, that he tried to be buddy-buddy with, but this Italian person had been with me for a long time so he knew me. So, he would also share with me what they shared in the bathroom that he did not tell me. He told me, Michelle, a lot of decisions are made in the bathroom. So he would tell me, so I had this other relationship with this other person that sort of helped me deal with the boss.

My boss let me hire one other professional person [a black man] and he also put me in charge of the word processing pool, and I made sure that I hired people of color. So I changed the complexion of the pool.

Even today, I will tell you something else; when our jobs [hers and the Italian manager's] were downsized, I went and interviewed for a job at Merrill Lynch and it was clear to me they did not want a woman because how could a woman know anything about financial stuff? So, he had a job he did not like. So I called him and said, why don't you go and apply for the job? He got the job and eventually became a vice-president. Now he is still at Merrill Lynch and I call him frequently, and he still calls me for advice. And every once in a while, I have lunch with him and I make him pay for it and I say, you still owe me.

In my organization, I must say that there were a number of white people who were friends; when I say "friends," I mean work friends. The white women were not hostile to the other blacks, or me as long as they did their work, as long as they felt they were competent. A lot of the white women came to me for advice about how to deal with their boss and how to deal with situations, because they saw how I handled things.

Ironically, members of the core group, because of different styles of communication that are compounded by the social distance that normally exists between the core own and whites, have relatively little opportunity to make positive impressions on members of the wise. Members of the core group, more sensitive to race than the colorblind peripheral own, are likely to perceive such a wise person as white first, making him or her ineligible for trust. In an important sense, the members of the core own appear handicapped by their inability to make distinctions among whites, to trust whites, or to conceive of a white person being able to go out of his or her way for a black person. For the core own, all relationships with whites tend to be instrumental, whereas the peripheral own are able to establish and sustain expressive friendships and associations with white people.

The Normals

The last group, "the normals," are people who make up and identify with the majority in the corporate culture. Handicapped by their close identification with the majority, they are generally oblivious to the special situation and plight of blacks and other minorities in the company. Even when they understand the special problems minorities encounter, many tend to be unsympathetic to them; they often feel the workplace has done enough for minorities. They may feel this way in part because they have been conditioned to perceive the minority person as a threat to their own interests; many such people emerge from a situation without advantages, and they are inclined to look upon a black person or another minority group member as a competitor within the organization, even when there is no basis for such thinking. Furthermore, many are of the opinion that the company has already done enough or too much. These people often believe that blacks and other minorities, assisted as they are by the government programs to remedy past prejudice and discrimination, do not deserve to be employed by the company, particularly when there are so many well-qualified normals around.

This outlook is at times shared, perhaps to an increasing degree, by some of the minority employees of the corporation themselves, including a number of the blacks. Such beliefs reflect an ethos that emphasizes homogeneity in a culture where white skin color and male gender predominate. There exists a need for all members of the corporation to present themselves and to pass as normals. Blacks, women, Jews, and other minorities with conspicuous and observable differences find passing difficult. Those who more readily approximate the dominant standards and values, including language, dress, and style of self-presentation, may find it easier to pass. This group includes white minorities, particularly when their members are almost indistinguishable from the white majority.

In such an environment, certain minorities in pursuit of status within the organization may assume the supposed posture of the majority, including a degree of indifference to the special needs of minorities within the company. Some minority individuals may consciously sever all connections with their respective groups. And given what has become an increasingly competitive context, striving minorities may find some reward—psychological or otherwise—in ignoring or deemphasizing the importance of the special concerns of blacks and others.

Because of a certain dissonance that results from being caught between the poles of fully accepting this position and identifying as members of the own, blacks are more sensitive to the shortcomings of this outlook. Thus, most blacks find themselves working to reshape the corporate ideology and culture to allow their own incorporation. Such actions ultimately place them outside of the normal group. Those minority group members who are white may not suffer the same dissonance and, because of their own group's divergent interests within the corporation, they may find it difficult to display a tolerance of blacks and others who may be viewed as outsiders within the corporation.

In their efforts to embrace the normal identity, such people may show their annoyance with the black presence by actively discrediting blacks wherever possible. They seldom facilitate the hiring of blacks in their immediate surroundings and may be heard telling sad tales of the last one who failed to work out, stories that the wise and the other must often suffer through. In their conversations on the subject, they like to emphasize "standards." Members of the own, being aware of such implicit charges against their competence and integrity, are then encouraged, if not required, to be more formal, distant, and guarded with whites in general. Such experiences, and the responses to them, help solidify the own's generally negative working conception of life in the company. The prevalence of such experiences encourages an ambivalent stance by the members of the peripheral own as they try to negotiate the organizational ladder of the company.

Conclusion

A major result of this country's Civil Rights movement of the 1960s was the incorporation of large numbers of blacks into the American occupational structure. Since then, through antidiscrimination legislation, including affirmative action, the black middle class has grown; it presently amounts to roughly a third of the black population. In addition, with the arrival of "fair housing" legislation, it has gravitated away from the inner-city black communities. Over the years, in effect, middle-class black people have begun to participate in the broader society in ways that would have astounded their predecessors.

However, a primary instrument of this incorporation process, affirmative action, is now being seriously challenged, becoming increasingly untenable ideologically and politically. Strikingly, the process, at least in part, is being undermined by its seeming success: the apparent proliferation of blacks, and other minorities of color, in the professions, academia, business, and government, at a time when the workplace is becoming increasingly competitive. In effect, the advent of "diversity" seems to have been the political price required by affirmative action to survive. In addition, the appearance of such diversity serves as impressive evidence that the system is open, fair, and egalitarian, while restrictions of race become obscured. With such ostensible success, the former participants and their allies (the wise) in the Civil Rights movement recede, feeling they have little left to fight for, especially when preferences are severely criticized as "racially based," in the current social and political context. Moreover, de-industrialization, corporate downsizing, and increased immigration have led to a highly competitive workplace in which established but insecure workers tend to be much less generous in their support of social programs of almost any kind, but particularly those viewed as favoring one race over another. In these circumstances, many former liberals question their earlier support for remedial measures like affirmative action as a tool for achieving equal opportunity.

In this context, they simultaneously degrade racism as an explanation for a black person's inability to succeed, a position strongly held by powerful and well-organized conservatives. Moreover, conservative activists have been successful in challenging and outlawing affirmative action policies in California, and are presently waging similar campaigns in other states. Their goal is to ideologically redefine affirmative action as a beatable menace that is inimical to the interests of whites and others who view their rights as threatened, if not abrogated, by such policies. If successful, such campaigns will have important implications and consequences not just for colleges and universities throughout the land, but for the American workplace as well. As black presence in such settings seriously declines, the struggle for black equality is set back, further alienating many black people.

In the organization I studied, before affirmative action was initiated, there were almost no black people present. In the average firm of thirty years ago, when present at all, blacks were most often found in the lowliest positions, including those of janitor, night watchman, doorman, elevator operator, secretary (at times required to work out of sight), or an occasional assistant director of personnel. With the arrival of affirmative action policies, the situation began to change, as the workplace became more inclusive. Accordingly, top executives and supervisors began to actively recruit blacks, providing them with a new kind of racial coin. This development enabled blacks to negotiate not only with their talents, including education and "people skills," but also with their skin color. Thus, one of the important effects, if not a goal, of affirmative action was to place a premium on black skin color, negating its historical demerit.

Traditionally, the racial system has provided preferences to those with white skin color, but now the tables would be somewhat turned. For many corporate, political, and civic leaders, the social "good" or racial incorporation, at least for a time, outweighed the ambiguous, if sometimes arbitrary, invocations of "meritocratic" standards. During the tensions of the Civil Rights movement, and later the civil disorders occurring in many cities, business and government leaders encouraged racial peace and social progress, creating incentives that strongly motivated their organizations to absorb and use black workers. Strikingly, many who were now being recruited as corporate employees had once been involved or sympathized with the college student and "black power" movements of their day. Now they were upwardly mobile, residing outside the ghetto, driving "nice" cars, sporting expensive dress, lunching in upscale restaurants with white colleagues, and at times discussing business strategy with high corporate officials.

In time, these direct beneficiaries of affirmative action, particularly members of the peripheral own described in this chapter, gravitated from group concerns long associated with liberating subjugated blacks to more individualistic concerns associated with personal economic well-being. In general, theirs was often a socially tense passage through a kind of nether world, fraught with risks, including taunts and criticisms of being an "Oreo," a "sellout," or an "Uncle Tom." Most dealt with their dilemmas with ambivalence, either by forging a strong relationship with the own or by actively distancing themselves from it. Regardless, such tensions and choices took their toll on black unity.

Here, as suggested throughout this chapter, many executives occupied an ambiguous position, which was at times resolved superficially by "code switching." Depending on the issue and the audience at hand, they might behave in a racially particularistic manner in private, while embracing more mainstream behavior in public (DuBois 1995). Most had the strong desire to be included as full participants in the organization and to effectively meet the standards that "everyone else" was expected to meet. Yet, on their jobs, many have experienced all manner of reaction to their presence in the organization—from effective mentoring and acceptance with "open arms" to "cold stares" and "hostile" receptions and persistent racial discrimination.

Presently, with increasingly effective assaults on affirmative action policies, many black executives become disillusioned and insecure. Over time, alienation takes a toll, and people become more isolated in the workplace, gravitating to what I call the "core own." Here, in response to perceptions of an unreceptive work environment, they may keep to themselves, looking inward, while becoming racially energized to collaborate in the outright racial polarization that infuses so many work settings today (Cose 1995).

But, by such behavior, a social cost is sometimes exacted that works to compound the initial problems at work. In the corporate setting, blacks who become so isolated often remain a group apart, inhabiting a social ghetto on the lower rungs of the corporate ladder. From this perspective, frankly, when the occasional black person achieves success, the promotion may be met by cynicism among certain black peers rather than unqualified praise; ambiguity often rules. Among those strongly associated with the own, depending on how he/she wears success, epithets like "token" or "sellout" may be whispered behind their backs. Although government pressures and policies have enabled many blacks to land executive positions in major corporations—and most perform their duties with real competence—many have been unable to attain the corresponding informal social power, along with relative feelings of security, taken for granted and enjoyed by many of their white counterparts in the workplace.

Moreover, in the changing economy and the increasingly competitive workplace, uncertainty often prevails, negating feelings of generosity and empathy with those that are most often marginalized and excluded. Therefore, accomplishing the unfinished business of equal opportunity and the full incorporation of blacks promises to be extremely difficult. The task at hand cannot be fully achieved without the support and active engagement of the wise—enlightening normals with the strong capacity of empathy with outsiders—who willingly go about the sometimes daunting social task of reaching out to blacks in the firm, recruiting, welcoming, befriending, and carefully mentoring them. In actively supporting the prevailing levels of black presence in the workplace, such socially liberal people were at times actively engaged as though they were on some kind of mission, and many were: their collective if unstated goal was to move our society forward by creating black access to meaningful positions in the workplace, furthering the process of incorporation and racial equality. Ironically, in the present socially and politically competitive context, enacting such roles may seem inappropriate, even quaint, a throwback to the "do-gooder" era of not so long ago. Such people who once reached out to blacks are much less visible in today's workplace.

Hence, for the laudable goal of equal opportunity, the real challenge is that of somehow edifying, encouraging, cultivating—in essence, growing—the wise, including blacks who have risen in the firm. All this, at a time when many feel the economic pie to be shrinking, when often ambiguous notions and tests of "merit" are invoked, and when blacks are at times portrayed as unworthy and undeserving of close mentoring or a "hand up." Without the full engagement of such allies in the struggle for racial justice, blacks and other minorities will remain marginalized, creating even more tension in the workplace. Thus, a major task is that of growing the wise and bringing them together with the own, in spite of unrelenting social forces that are hard at work to create fewer of their collective number.

CHAPTER 17

The United States

A Study in Political-Class Racism

Joseph W. Scott

The English-American Solution to the "Negro Problem"

"The arrival of black slaves in mid-seventeenth-century Virginia confronted English settlers with problems for which there were no obvious Old World solutions," write historians T. H. Breen and Stephen Innes (1980, 4). At that time, England was neither a slave-user nor a slave-dependent society. Notwithstanding this fact, the historical record indicates that the founding fathers quickly forged a racial estate system solution. Within just a few decades after the first African slaves came to the colony of Virginia, they fashioned a series of judicial decisions and legislated statutes that intentionally divided this society into hereditary racial orders (Hening 1809–23).

Did they let the market system determine the social orders of market winners and market losers? They did not. Through decidedly *political* measures, they intentionally institutionalized racial stratification and ascribed to so-called "whites" a station above so-called "blacks." Historian William Wiecek (1977), in "The Statutory Law of Slavery and Race in the Thirteen Mainland Colonies of British America," corroborates this conclusion: "When the statutes, by the mid-eighteenth century, had defined these four basic elements of slavery—lifetime status, partus sequitur ventrem, racial identification, and slave-as-chattel—slavery as a legal institution was fully-fledged" (264).

Policies, Law, and "Race" Relations

"Race" relations in the United States are not market relations. They are political relations. "Law is power. Law is politics. Law is politics in the sense that it is the persons who have political power who determine which persons or bodies create law, how the validity of law is to be assessed, and how the legal order is to operate," writes professor of law Alan Watson (1989). The legal order of "race" relations is in its essence a matter of law, power, and politics.

Sociological and historical records of U.S. "race" relations clearly document that the colonial and postcolonial leaders conceived of, defined, and codified in law an arbitrary "race" classification (Rose 1976; Furer 1972; Wiecek 1977; Watson 1989; Stephenson 1970; Ballagh 1968; Scott 1977). Historian Gilbert T. Stephenson described the process this way:

> If race distinctions are to be recognized in the law, it is essential that the races be clearly distinguished from one another. If a statute provides that Negroes shall ride in separate coaches and attend separate schools, it is necessary to decide first who are included under the term "Negro." It would seem that physical indicia would be sufficient, and, in most instances, this true. It is never difficult to distinguish the full-blooded Negro, Indian, or Mongolian one from the other or from the Caucasian. But the difficulty arises in the blurring of the color line by amalgamation . . . It is this gradual sloping off from one race into another which has made it necessary for the law to *set artificial lines*. (1970, 12–14, italics mine)

Using legislative acts and judicial decisions, the leaders of the colony of Virginia "set artificial lines" of who was "black" and who was "white," then assigned unequal powers, privileges, and economic opportunities to these "artificial" classifications, and made them hereditary. As arbitrary and artificial as this hierarchy of so-called "races" was, it still relegated "blacks" to a social order designated as human beings and chattel property at the same time.

From that moment on, "black-white" relations became derivations of statutory racial inequalities. Over the course of the next two centuries, the founders multiplied the "race-conscious" laws designed to bar "blacks" from learning and practicing certain trades, from carrying weapons even for self-defense, from enjoying the freedoms of speech and worship, from enjoying the freedoms of the press and the vote, from migrating freely from one locale to an-

other, and from owning land, assembling peacefully, petitioning the government, testifying in court, and holding elective offices (Russell 1969; Berry
1971). The founders fortified these restrictions with additional laws extending
all the way to beating, torturing, mutilating, maiming, branding, choking,
scalding, and killing those "blacks" who ran away or openly rebelled against this
totalitarian racism (Hening 1809–23; Watson 1989, 63–83; Scott 1976).

Egon Bergel, a leading scholar of global social stratification, studied the
United States and came to the same conclusion I did. He wrote:

> There is one feature, however, that under most conditions cannot be recon-
> ciled with a class system: slavery. Since freedom as well as slavery was heredi-
> tary and status was shared by the entire family, we have at least in this respect
> an indisputable estate system based on legally established differences between
> kinship units. This system may have been simpler than its European counter-
> part but elements of it existed in varying degree in most parts of what was to
> become the United States. (Bergel 1962, 151)

In summary, historical documents (Rose 1976; Bergman and Bergman
1969) prove the following: The contemporary U.S. racial hierarchy is grounded
in "race-conscious" laws; the laws are perpetuated by public and private
"race-conscious" politics; and the intent of such politics is to impose a set of
self-perpetuating disadvantages on "blacks" for all time. Discrimination—economic, educational, political, and other kinds—is perpetuated to maintain
"white supremacy." Thus, contemporarily, the social and economic life-
chances of "blacks" are tied to the racial politics of corporate bureaucracies and
their functionaries rather than pure market processes.

A Theory of Estate Systems

The simplest estate system usually has three strata: one of nobility, one of commoners, and one of slaves. Within each stratum, there are usually economic dif-
ferentiations; that is to say, there are economic classes. Statutory slavery, as
erected in the United States, was a simplified estate system. That system has
separate strata of free persons, indentured servants, and chattel slaves who were
rank ordered from highest to lowest.

William Goodell (1969), the author of *American Slave Code,* described the
rights and obligations of how the highest and lowest social orders were related:

"A slave is one who is in the power of a master to whom he belongs. The master may sell him, dispose of his person, his industry and his labor. He can do nothing, possess nothing or acquire anything, but what must belong to his master (Louisiana)" (Goodell 1969, 23). Clearly then, such statutory stratification is not market stratification. It is political stratification—a derivation of polity. Market dynamics create economic differentiation and economic hierarchization, and political dynamics create estate differentiation and estate hierarchization (Lenski 1966, 75–79).

Social scientists Egon Bergel (Bergel 1962) and Max Weber (Gerth and Mills 1946) reasoned that any society with statutory social orders of free persons, bond persons, and slaves does not have market classes. The derivation and function of the orders makes them a species apart. The politically assigned economic, educational, and civic inequalities among them make them a species apart. The statutory ceiling on achievements from individual hard work, self-denial, thrift, and sobriety makes them a species apart.

Estate Mobility

Estate legislation makes social mobility of all types virtually impossible. Individuals cannot change orders except by a legislative act or a court decision. Statutory stations are designed to preclude individual and collective mobility. The rights of the individual are embedded in the rights of the group. What rights and obligations the group has, the individual has also. Owner-masters who might be swayed by personal sympathy or religious morality to manumit or not manumit bond persons can do so only by an act of a legislature. Bond persons who might want to change their individual or their collective station in life can do so by changing the constitutional laws of estate stratification.

Bond persons cannot exercise the option of self purchase and self manumission without enabling legislation, and master-owners cannot exercise the option of freeing their own enslaved offspring without enabling legislation. The estate-establishing and estate-maintaining legislation and judicial decisions are designed to prevent members of the various orders from changing places. They are also designed to prevent the orders from changing places as well.

Conflicts of interest are inherent in the laws and are hereditary. Thus, estate conflicts of interest periodically ignite political contests for state power and influence. The polity of necessity becomes *the* pivotal battleground. As Goodell's analysis above points out, the conflicts of interest of the masters and the slaves

348 Joseph W. Scott

are actually structured in opposition as in a zero-sum equation model: the gains of "haves" are proportionate to the losses of the "have nots." The confiscatory rights of the "haves" are directly proportionate to the surrendering obligations of the "have nots." The categorically high incomes and education of the "haves" follow from ascription and not from market competition. Thus, they are both unearned and undeserved.

It follows, therefore, that the stratum of bond persons has to stop the stratum of free persons from buying, selling, and working them, and from confiscating the fruits of their production. In a word, they have to abolish the estate codes. But, such abolitionists cannot just eliminate the hereditary hierarchy by self-betterment programs of working harder, denying themselves, and saving money. These efforts do create economic differentiation *within* each stratum, but do not eliminate the political inequalities between these strata. The statutory advantages and disadvantages inherent in the estate system remain until the laws and customs themselves are abolished.

For that reason, the lowest stratum within an estate system has to engage in corporate-class struggles until it abolishes the system of ascription. It can open up the system for upward and downward mobility only by abolishing the inequality of opportunities prescribed by statutes and customs.

The Chain of Being Idea and Estate Racism

From where did the Anglo-Americans get their ideas of a hierarchy of human order? The history of ideas indicates that the ideology of racism precedes the ideology of capitalism in time. Thus the idea of a hierarchy of "races" does not depend on capitalism for its emergence, maintenance, or change. The ideology of racism has its own independent origins and has its own independent causes for its maintenance and change. For example, "white supremacists" pursue "white supremacy" mostly for reasons of bio-racial domination, not for financial profit. The Chain of Being idea (Lovejoy 1936, 59, 197, 247–48) is one of the origins of estatism, racism, and Social Darwinism. The ideology of estatism came as much from this course as anywhere.

The "Chain of Being" (sometimes called the "Scale of Being") is an idea that Plato introduced that asserts that the multiplicity of species of creation exists in a continuous hierarchy. That is to say, there exists an infinite number of separately created species linked together continuously in hierarchical order from the lowest entities to the highest possible creatures.

Within the "Chain of Being" idea, there are two underlying assumptions: "plentitude" and "continuity." First, the "plentitude principle." God created the world full and complete once and for all, and in this world He included angels, men, beasts, birds, fish, and insects. Second, the "continuity principle." All of these creatures are arranged in an unbroken continuous ascending hierarchy.

Within the "Chain of Being" or the "Scale of Being" idea, all humankind has a purposive place in the universal hierarchical moral order, and it also follows logically that each of the "races" of mankind has a "place" in the human hierarchical moral order.

"The result," according the leading authority on the subject, Arthur O. Lovejoy (1936, 59), "was the conception of the plan and structure of the world which, through the Middle Ages and down to the late eighteenth century, many philosophers, most men of science, and indeed, most educated men, were to accept without question—the conception of the universe as a 'Great Chain of Being.' "

The Chain of Being idea both motivated and justified European expansionism and Social Darwinism. Europeans used the Chain of Being idea to rationalize conquering and colonizing people of color from one end of the earth to the other. Long before capitalism was invented as a social idea, Europeans believed that Africans were just a step up from the anthropoid apes. So, when the British came to North America, they were imbued with the Chain of Being idea and Social Darwinism (Mason 1971, 31–36).

According to Mason:

> The preoccupation with the question of man's relation to the anthropoids gave an especial "philosophical" interest to the rather numerous descriptions of the Hottentots by late seventeenth- and early eighteenth-century voyagers. They were probably the "lowest" savage races thus far known; and more than one writer of the period saw in them a connecting link between the anthropoids and homo sapiens. (234)

To show that the early Anglo-American settlers also held the "Chain of Being" idea in their religious and secular belief system, we need only look at one court decision that occurred in 1630, scarcely a decade after the first "blacks" arrived at Jamestown, Virginia. On September 17, a "white" man was punished for consorting with a black woman. The transcript below reveals how the "Chain of Being" idea permeates their religious beliefs and secular decisions: "Hugh Davis, to be soundly whipped, before an assembly of Negros and others for abusing himself to the dishonor of God and shame of Christians, by defiling his body in lying with a Negro" (Hening 1809–23, 1, 146).

The "Chain of Being" idea is still being espoused in contemporary religious and secular belief systems. The World Church of the Creator (W.C.O.T.C.) is one of the groups promoting this idea. Their publication entitled, *FACTS That the Government and the Media Don't Want You to Know*, states the following:

> The frontal lobe of the black forebrain is less developed than that of white. Thus, their ability in the performance of thinking, planning, communication, and behavior is more limited than in whites. Professor Coon also found that this area of the black brain is thinner and less grooved on the outer surface than in that of a white person, and that the development of this part of the brain ceases at an earlier age in the black, thus, limiting further intellectual advancement. (Hale n.d., 22)

This same publication says: "Raw brainpower is not the only mental difference between whites and blacks." Blacks are more excitable, more violent, less sexually restrained, more impulsive, more prone to crime, less altruistic, less inclined to follow rules, and less cooperative" (Hale, 23). Further it says: "It should also be noted that those of mixed blood score higher than those of pure black ancestry, but lower than those of pure white ancestry. This explains why light-skinned blacks are almost always more intelligent than dark-skinned" (Hale, 22).

This version of the "Chain of Being" idea as espoused by the W.C.O.T.C. still motivates "white supremacists" to kill "people of color" or people like Jews they assign to that category. The *USA Today* (Tuesday, July 6, 1999, 3A) reported that a self-confessed follower of the W.C.O.T.C. ideology shot and killed two people—one black and one Korean—and wounded at least seven others, mostly Jews, during a shooting spree. The alleged killer had been a devoted member of the W.C.O.T.C.—a "white supremacist" group, showing that the idea is alive and well in the United States.

The Anglo-American Culture of Colonialization

An Anglo-American culture of colonization has evolved out of the "Chain of Being" idea. Of all the Europeans coming to these shores, the Anglo-

Americans have been most adamant about using this idea to shape the political and social culture of the United States (Jordan 1968). Ironically, even in the midst of codifying the high ideals of revolution, freedom, liberty, equality, and justice for all in their Constitution, they institutionalized the "Chain of Being" idea in the form of statutory slavery, based on "race." They embarked on a course of enslaving American Indians and Africans and then justified it by declaring their hierarchy of "races" the natural moral order. The Anglo-Americans declared themselves "civilized" and "superior" and declared the American Indian and Africans "uncivilized" and "inferior" in a state of "pupilage" of the "white race" for their own benefit.

Chief Justice Roger B. Taney of the United States Supreme Court asserted as much in the Dred Scott decision (*Dred Scott v. Stanford* (60 US [19 How.] [1857]). He said that the Constitution did not mean to include "blacks" as "citizens" of the United States of America. Moreover, he maintained that "blacks" were a "subordinate and inferior class of beings" to be kept forever separate and unequal.

In the now infamous passage, Chief Justice Taney, speaking of "blacks," wrote: "They had for more than a century before been regarded as beings of an inferior order, and although unfit to associate with the white race either in social or political relations; and so far inferior that they had no right which the white man was bound to respect; and that the Negro might justly and lawfully be reduced to slavery for his benefit" (60 U.S. at 40).

The political, economic, educational, and biological ideologies above are negations of the ideals of freedom, liberty, equality, and justice for all. But the Anglo-American colonists and framers of the U.S. Constitution developed a social and political culture *a culture of colonialization*.

"A culture of colonialization" is a set of cognitive, affective, and behavioral orientations conceived and used systematically to support and rationalize the subjugation and exploitation of racial and ethnic minorities. "A culture of colonialization" refers to thought-ways, feeling-ways, and action-ways of racism.

The Anglo-American culture of colonialization is really an offshoot of the European culture of colonialization. Anglo-Americans came to this continent with "race" and "color" prejudice. They also came with the "Chain of Being" idea. They elaborated this cultural mind-set over three centuries in the New World, and achieved a shining record of racial and ethnic subjugation of all people who were not members of the "white race." No other society before this one perfected chattel slavery like this society did, and no other society ever expended so much of its financial resources to kidnap, transport, and hold in slavery so many African people.

From the beginning, Anglo-Americans embarked on a course of procuring and exploiting cheap labor and cheap natural resources. They first introduced a system of indentured servitude. Next, they introduced Indian slavery in the early 1600s. When the Indians did not work out, they soon switched to the enslavement of Africans. With westward and eastward expansion, they conquered the Mexicans in the Southwest and the Puerto Ricans in the island of Puerto Rico and introduced a system of wage peonage.

Africans, Mexicans, and Puerto Ricans were forcefully "Americanized" and forcibly incorporated into this society as second-class "citizens." They were not asked (as Chinese, Japanese, Filipinos, Cubans, and Asian Indians were) if they wanted to come here and be enculturated. At the beginning, Africans, Mexicans, and Puerto Ricans were not voluntary immigrants. They were not asked if they wanted to be incorporated. They came under the political jurisdiction of the United States government as colonized subjects, and for that reason, in the aggregate, each has had a collective social and economic status significantly lower than that of the Europeans, Asian Indians, Chinese, Filipino, Japanese, and Cuban citizens. In contrast to these advantaged minorities just mentioned, Africans, Mexicans, and Puerto Ricans have been categorically subordinated to "white" people by social and political design. As colonized "citizens," they have not only been displaced, they have also been dispossessed of their political, economic, cultural, and land rights. Colonization accounts in large part for their relatively lower socioeconomic achievements in U.S. society compared to uncolonized minorities mentioned above.

The "Black," "Red," and "Bronze" Cultures of Liberation

Cultures of liberation were inevitable in a society with a culture of colonialization. The social and political thought-ways, feeling-ways, and action-ways to counter racism are perhaps most developed among African Americans in America. Mexican American, Puerto Rican American, and Native American cultural nationalists are actively resurrecting ancient cultural patterns and generating new ones in efforts to develop counter-strategies to the Anglo-American culture of colonialization. These groups in the vanguard are about not only the business of resurrecting culture and building culture, but also they are about the business of indoctrinating their youth with the culture of liberation.

The rallying ideology of each movement is cultural nationalism. Cultural nationalism resurrects and promotes cultural patterns that heretofore had been lost, stolen, or hidden from mainstream America by the educational and communications media. The ethnic studies, cultural studies, and comparative cultural programs are evidence of the rise of oppositional paradigms.

The so-called "black, brown, and red" people of this country have all experienced statutory discrimination, which in design reduced them to second-class "citizens." These oppositional cultures are a direct reaction to the politics of categorical exclusion and subordination that they have all experienced.

The most influential liberation movements in the United States to date are the ethnic power movements: the Black Power movement, the Bronze Power movement, the Puerto Rican Power movement, and the American Indian Power movement. Politically, these movements represent most of the minority peoples of color in the United States.

Their key goals are self-determination, self-legitimization, and self-promotion. Like all cultures, they are purposive and utilitarian: They aim to counter the racist social, economic, political, and psychological ideas that presently dominate the public discourse in this country. They aim to raise in sharp relief the invalidity of W.C.O.T.C. ideologies, sentiments, and values, which on one hand degrade people of color and on the other promote "white superiority" in the minds of the "white" majority.

These ethnic nationalists have socially constructed alternatives to the standards of beauty, behavioral styles, and political and economic agendas of the Anglo-American culture of colonialization. The nationalists have promoted arts and entertainment in the form of films, television shows, and radio programs that the mainstream networks are airing and selling to the general public, and they have motivated the formation of ethnic voting blocs that are now targets of co-optation by both the Democrat and Republican parties. What is new is that the Democrat and Republican parties are not asking them to become Anglo-conformists in brown and black skins. These parties are willing to co-opt "black, red, bronze" cultural nationalists just as they come. This may mean that the racial estate system, long a feature of American society, may be abolished from within the polity by "black, red, and bronze" participation in it.

"Black-White" Conflict

Anglo-America's "black-white" relations have been and continue to be estate relations. They are not market relations. They are politically shaped relations. They do not conform to pure capitalistic relations where impersonal market processes like unrestrained economic competition determine the economic hierarchy. The hierarchy is prescribed by customary practices and statutory rules.

It follows, therefore that "black-white" conflicts are not economic class conflicts (Waskow 1967). They are conflicts between racial orders within a statutory racialized estate system. And estate theory predicts that there will be political-class struggles that pit the "black" stratum against the "white" stratum until the system is abolished.

The U.S. Constitution is a pro-slavery document (American Anti-Slavery Society 1970). Chief Justice Taney proclaimed as much in the *Dred Scott v. Sandford* decision (1857). He proclaimed that within the meaning of the U.S. Constitution, "blacks" were "beings of an inferior order"; they were not "citizens" of the federal government and as such had no rights that "whites" had to respect.

So, how do human beings of a so-called "inferior order" rise out of such statutory degradation? The answer lies in changing the constitutional norms of society. Racial equality in the economy, in the polity, and in the academy cannot be achieved in the aggregate without such change. Personal values, family values, and individual efforts count for little in a statutory-class system that allows the highest achievable positions only to those classified as "whites" and limits the lowest achievable positions only to those artificially classified as "blacks."

It is understandable then that "blacks" and "whites" continue to be locked in statutory class conflict after almost four centuries, and that each racial order is a power-seeking and a power-keeping group. Each is striving to acquire enough influence and control over the machinery of government and its functionaries to write or rewrite the legal rules regulating economic, educational, and political achievement (Geranios 1997).

Just within the 1990s, we have seen the removal of jobs from the inner cities; the removal of affirmative action requirements from the law books; the removal of majority black voting districts from the political landscape (Barrett 1996); the removal of public funds from the racially integrated public schools and the giving of it to racially segregated "charter" schools; the changing of "race" classification to include so-called "bi-racials" (Holmes 1997; Jones 1994); and changing the definition of what is a "minority-owned" business (Thomas 1999).

Historically, government and corporate procurement have required at least 51 percent minority ownership. A few years ago some major corporations changed the definition of "minority-owned" to companies with at least 10 percent minority holding as long as the firms had minority management. The National Minority Supplier Development Council is considering approval of the new definition (Thomas 1999). In the aggregate, the consequences cannot be positive for "blacks" as a whole.

From the above, it can be seen that the dominant "race" order continues to use estate-like decision-making. It continues to block the "black" stratum from achieving full educational, economic, or political parity with them. The program to restore "blacks" to their rightful place in this society gets diluted into oblivion.

Clearly then, political-class discrimination is alive in America. To eliminate the contemporary collective disadvantages, "blacks" must strive to gain more power and influence so they can get restitution and compensation for damages they have suffered and continue to suffer.

The problem is that the dominant "race" order still controls a monopoly of the political power needed to pass the legislation or to render the judicial decisions giving "blacks" restitution and compensation. The dominant order is in the enviable position of being able to unilaterally decide whether or not to voluntarily give up any racial powers or privileges. They have to be forced to change.

Race Mobility

Racial mobility and economic mobility are not the same things. Racial equality and economic equality are not the same. So, how does the lowest order within a racialized estate system enjoy the rights, privileges, and opportunities of the highest order? To be sure, they cannot achieve it by individual effort alone since their rights, privileges, and opportunities are group prescribed and proscribed.

Historical records (Aptheker 1968, 5–9) indicate that "blacks" revolted violently hundreds of times by various means before the Civil War. In addition to the strategy of destruction, they also used nonviolent direct action and flight to disrupt the system of slavery. But their most effective attack on the estate system then and during the twentieth century was with litigation and legislation.

"Black" abolition and "black" Civil Rights movements have been effective, potent weapons (Quarles 1969; Berry 1971; Meier, Rudwick, and Broderick 1965). Through "race-conscious" corporate-class movements such as antislavery, civil rights, and desegregation campaigns, "blacks" have incrementally eliminated most of the racial distinctions in the laws and customs of this society (Russell 1969, 43–87; Watson 1989, 75; Bracey, Meier, and Rudwick 1971; King 1958). Manumission, desegregation, fair employment opportunities, and voting rights all required legislative changes before they could be enjoyed. Slavery, segregation, and discrimination had to be eliminated by legislation and litigation before the freedoms above could be enjoyed. No "black" could enjoy these freedoms individually: all "blacks" had to be enabled to enjoy them or none could enjoy them. Such was and still is the way of estate systems.

The creation of an organization like the National Association for the Advancement of Colored People (NAACP) was inevitable in an estate system. The logic of the estate system forced "blacks" to conceive of an organizational weapon that would focus on litigation and legislation. And "blacks" did conceive of and develop this kind of organization wherever statutory and customary codes placed an artificial ceiling on the aspirations and achievements of upwardly mobile "blacks." It is not surprising therefore that for all of the twentieth century, the NAACP used the weapons of litigation and legislation to incrementally dismantle the customary and statutory foundation of the "white-over-black" estate system.

Other "statutory minorities"—specifically women, Native Americans, Hispanics, and Asians—currently enjoy more political, economic, and educational opportunities relative to "whites" because of the corporate-class movements and corporate-class victories of "blacks." Immigrants of color are coming to the United States from all over the world and are laying claim to the same jobs, the same loans, the same government set-aside contracts, and the same scholarships as native-born African American descendants of slaves without having to spend one day on the cross (*Wall Street Journal* 1997; *USA Today* 1997). Affirmative action was originally predicated on the premises of restitution and reparations. The concept has been diluted to include the deserving and undeserving, with negative consequences for the original "protected" groups.

According to the U.S. Commission on Civil Rights Clearinghouse Publication 91 (1988):

> With respect to affirmative action policy, protected groups including the following racial and ethnic groups: blacks, Hispanics, Asian Americans, and Native Americans. The category of Asian American has changed over time. Originally called "Orientals" this category included persons of Japanese, Chinese, Korean, and Filipino descent. In 1976, Asian Indians who had been classified as white or Caucasian, lobbied to be included in Affirmative Action programs.

Set-aside programs constitute a third type of policy aimed at helping socially or economically disadvantaged minorities. In general, these programs "set aside" or funnel government contracts to minority-owned businesses. Until 1980 set-aside programs excluded Asian Americans; they were confined to helping businesses with black, Hispanic, or Native American ownership. However, other groups could petition for designation as socially disadvantaged. Japanese and Chinese Americans gained this status in 1980. They were followed by Asian Indians in 1982. This list of racial and ethnic groups that are considered to be socially disadvantaged under the current Small Business Administration guidelines includes blacks, Hispanics, Native Americans, and Asian and Pacific Islanders (U.S. Commission on Civil Rights 1988, 8A, 16). The newly included groups are doing so well so quickly that they are wondering why "blacks" have been complaining all of these years.

Why "Blacks" Campaign Differently

Koreans, Asian Indians, and Cubans in particular, and Chinese and Japanese immigrants, after World War II, have not been forced to use the kind and number of political strategies to advance themselves as "blacks" have. By law, Japanese citizens were locked up in concentration camps for three to four years during World War II, and then and only then did they have to resort to litigation and legislation to free themselves and to get reparations (Takaki 1987). The Chinese Americans were not locked up at all during World War II (Tung 1974). In point of fact, during World War II, Chinese Americans served in military units designated for "whites." Moreover, during the years of Jim Crow segregation in the South, Chinese Americans went by law and custom from the status of "blacks" to the status of "whites" in two generations (Loewen 1988). Asian Indian, Cuban, and Korean immigrants have not had to do very much to integrate themselves into the institutions of this society by having themselves classified as "disadvantaged." By and large they were welcomed by the "whites" with openness and generosity. So they had the best of both racial statuses.

But, "blacks" have not had it so easy. Thus, they have had to act differently (Cohen and Murphy 1966). In contrast to how the Koreans, Cubans, and Asian Indians have been treated, the racial estate system of the United States was purposively crafted to deny "blacks" participation in the mainstream institutions. Specifically, this system was instituted to keep "blacks" from achieving any sort of equality with "whites." The laws and customs categorically limited the economic, educational, social, and political advancement of the "black" masses in an effort to stifle their progress (Scott 1979).

If the "white" social order had not shackled "blacks" with statutory and customary restrictions, they could have been spending most of their time, money, and energy using economic strategies to advance themselves, as new Asian immigrants and Cubans have done. But the dominant "race" structured the statutory and customary discrimination against "blacks" in such ways as to preclude any collective advancement of "blacks" (Grimshaw 1969). So "blacks" have had to act differently. Until the ceiling on "black" progress can be removed, full educational, social, economic, and political enfranchisement of the black masses cannot happen. The "blacks" have taken almost four centuries to bring down this statutory and customary system, and they still have not completed the task.

The historical facts as presented above refute the popular analyses by certain social scientists such as Nathan Glazer (1987), who claim that "blacks" have been just another immigrant group going through the usual immigrant trials to raise themselves up economically, but failing due to their own ineptitude. A closer reading and understanding of the logic of the system of "race" relations in the United States indicates just the opposite (Takaki 1987).

A closer reading indicates that the dominant "race" order used not only statutory economic measures, but also statutory political measures to block inclusion of "blacks" in the mainstream of this society. They did not use such measures against the Asian Indians, Koreans, and Cubans who are time and time again compared to "blacks." In point of fact, since 1965, the Asian Indians, Koreans, and Cubans have been able to walk right in and take advantage of the opportunities created by "blacks" and despise "blacks" in the process (U.S. Commission on Civil Rights 1995, 15–16).

Asian Indians are an interesting case in point. They had themselves legally reclassified from "Caucasians" to "minority" so as to qualify for the government entitlement programs for those classified as "protected minorities" and "disadvantaged minorities." The other immigrants mentioned above also discovered that they did not have to have a history of discrimination in this country to have themselves classified as "minorities" or "disadvantaged" before they could take advantage of the special entitlements. These immigrants learned quickly that the United States was a society of political classifications and that how they were classified affected their economic opportunities. They also learned very quickly before and after they came that the dominant "race" order was racially biased and selectively inclusive, and they learned very quickly that the dominant "race" order favored them to "blacks" in every situation from store clerking to intermarriage. So, they are coming, they are reclassifying themselves, and they are succeeding with the assistance of the dominant "race" order that recruited them for insertion into the middle levels of economic and political positions ahead of "blacks."

Estatism, Capitalism, and Racism

Pure capitalism presumes free labor, free capital, and free markets of free producer-sellers and free consumers. Pure estatism assumes the opposite. Slavery was not a capitalistic system; neither was the Jim Crow system. From its inception to now, political stratification has reigned in this society. Even a slave auction was not pure capitalism.

Political-class hierarchies and economic-class hierarchies appear to be the same because racism and capitalism are "class" systems and have been made conformable to each other. Both are hierarchical systems based on usurpation; both are systems that allocate unearned profits and privileges to the dominant group; both are systems wherein the dominant order can confiscate the surplus value of the laborers' work; and finally, both are capable of mutually confirming and reinforcing each other. Appearances aside, racism and capitalism are not the same things in origin or in functioning. Getting rid of capitalism does not get rid of racism and vice versa (Scott 1986).

Scholars of social stratification like Bergel (1962) and Weber (Gerth and Mills 1946) noted long ago that economic differentiation exists within estate systems. It is not surprising, then, that there has been and is now economic differentiation among both the "whites" and the "blacks." Despite this economic differentiation, this society is still segregated into dominant and subordinate racial orders, and it is getting more segregated as busing for school integration, affirmative action, and minority voting districts are abandoned.

Now, at the beginning of the twenty-first century, the pivotal social problem of this society is still the problem of the racial divide—the color line. The public laws governing the racial estate have been repealed, but the estate mentality and customary practices are still alive and thriving among those of the dominant "race" order. The public governance of "race" relations has given way to the private governance of "race" relations (Scott 1985), and the "Chain of Being" ideal remains the basic organizing principle of private corporations. In the aggregate, private economic corporations are nearly as segregated now as they were at the end of slavery. They have nearly the same "race"-gender representation at the top now as then. The ideological rationale for this organizing disparity is the same now as it was then: There is a hierarchy of "races" on the basis of intelligence. And since "whites" presume themselves to be the most intelligent, they feel they are in their rightful place, which is at the top of the corporate hierarchy. The estate principle has been reproduced and reinstitutionalized within the corporate bureaucracies of America.

Given the logic of how estate systems maintain themselves and are changed, "blacks" will have to get busy once again and take their struggle against racism to the next level. This time, they have a history of how to change estate systems that tells them exactly what they must do to open this system more.

Private Governance of Relations: 2000 and Beyond

I believe it is irrefutable that compared to "whites" and most Asian and Latino groups, "blacks" have been relegated to the most subordinate and separate social stratum in the society. In term of citizenship status, servitude status, and honor status (Stone 1997), "blacks" have been singled out for ascription to the lowest social order in society.

The Republicans and the white supremacists would have us believe that "race-conscious" policies and affirmative action programs for "blacks," even for remedial purposes and even for designated time duration, are neither needed nor justified. They call restitution for "blacks" reverse discrimination. They have not called restitution and reparations for Japanese Americans, Native Americans, and Jewish Americans reverse discrimination.

Nathan Glazer, in his book *Affirmative Discrimination* (1978), is one of those who offers the conclusion that racial claims such as those in the affirmative action plans constitute a new and unneeded course for America. About affirmative action programs, he said:

> We have created two racial and ethnic classes in this country to replace this disgraceful pattern of the past in which some groups are subjected to an official and open discrimination. The two classes are those groups that are entitled to statistical parity in certain key areas on the basis of race, color, and national origin, and those groups that are not. (Glazer 1978, 197)

This new course threatens the abandonment of our concern for individual claims to consider on the basis of justice and equity, now to be replaced with a concern for rights for publicly determined and delimited racial and ethnic groups (Glazer 1978, 197). Continuing, he says:

> Was it true that the only way the great national effort to overcome discrimination against groups could be carried out was by recording, fixing, and acting upon the group affiliation of every person in the country? Whether this was or was not the only way, it is the way we have taken. (Glazer 1978, 32).

In the aggregate at the end of the twentieth century, "black" male workers still achieve less financially and occupationally than their "white" male counterparts with equal schooling. In the aggregate, "white" male workers of even lower education and training than "black" workers still achieve even higher incomes than those "black" males of higher skills, education, and training.

A Congressional Budget Office (CBO) study of unemployment patterns among nonwhite Americans found: "There appears to be agreement that discrimination plays a major role in explaining a significant part of the unemployment rate differential" (Mundel 1976, 22). The CBO report calls it "statistical discrimination" and explains it as follows:

> At the most blatant level employers may make observations about nonwhites as a group, relative to whites, and then on the basis hesitate to hire individual

nonwhites. At a more subtle level employment tests may contain sections that are not precisely relevant to the job for which the applicant is applying and the scores on these tests may reflect socioeconomic or racial background rather than potential job performance. (Mundel 1976, 22)

Without a doubt, "statistical discrimination," or "racial profiling," accounts for much of the job hiring discrepancies at every occupational level. At every occupational level, black workers are clustered in the lower-paying job classifications. This holds true whether controlling for either age or years of schooling completed.

For all that has been written about legal-rational bureaucracy and the universalism connoted by testing, certification, and technical expertise, Weber warned us that *in reality,* "Bureaucracy as such is a precision instrument which can put itself at the disposal of quite varied interests—purely political as well as purely economic, or any other sort of interests in domination" (Gerth and Mills 1946, 231). Legal-rational bureaucracy can be an efficient instrument of racial, ethnic, and gender domination and often is. According to Weber: "Bureaucratic administration is deliberately connected with the formation of *estates,* or is entangled with them by the force of the existing groupings of social power. The expressed reservation of offices for certain status groups is very frequent, and actual reservations are even more frequent" (Gerth and Mills 1946, 231).

So, we come full circle. Racial and ethnic distinctions can be made functional to and can be made conformable to bureaucratic structure and administration, and vice versa. Contrary to the belief that bureaucratic administration is universalistic in performance, bureaucracy administration can be and often is an instrumentality for the creation and maintenance of certain status inequalities for "blacks" and females in particular. Racial, ethnic, and gender segregation and subordination, far from being precluded within legal-rational bureaucratic administration as we know it today, may even be facilitated by it.

Glazer is patently incorrect and self-contradictory about the claim that racial and ethnic justice and equity and individual claims rather than group claims have been the American political tradition. He is equally incorrect when he says that legislative grants and programs for "publicly determined and delimited racial and ethnic groups" represent a new course for America. Glazer forgot about Indian removal, slavery, Alien Land Law, and the Naturalization Act of 1790, which restricted naturalization to only immigrants of the "white race" (Takaki 1987, 26–37).

If discrimination at any time in American history had been simply a matter of personal prerogatives or personal tastes, Glazer might be on firmer ground about the nature of contemporary discrimination and the remedies for it. But, even today as I speak, racial discrimination is reportedly occurring as matters of policies and practices of public agencies and private corporations. The most blatant and virulent discrimination today is the kind perpetrated by private corporations like Texaco and Boeing (*Wall Street Journal,* Nov. 18, 1996; *Wall Street Journal,* Dec. 18, 1996). Glazer's perception of America as a society based on individual and equal rights for all bears no resemblance to the historical acts for the people of color of the United States. His perception ignores the private governance of "race" relations by private corporations that are the functional equivalents of private governments.

Private corporations for the longest time have lobbied local, state, and federal governments for sufficient autonomy to regulate themselves in intra- and inter-corporate matters. Private business corporations, in the main, do regulate their own product decisions, marketing decisions, quality decisions, quantity decisions, finance decisions, and personnel decisions. Because so many such decisions are left to the discretion of private business corporations, the net result is that they reach into every neighborhood, rural district, and household and influence, if not actually govern, "race" relations.

Virtually every power structure constructed thus far has been dominated by representatives of business and financial corporations. They are the elite of the local, state, and national power structures. They govern everything else in society, and "race" relations are no exception. The regulation of "race" relations falls within their spheres of decisions.

For example, employment decisions are left almost completely to the discretion of private businesses; for the most part, they have a free hand in choosing which prospective employees they will employ. This autonomy allows them to fit their hiring and job allocation practices to the local communities and local prejudices wherein they are located.

Labor utilization decisions are largely left to private corporate governance, we are told, because of "business necessity." Of course, those familiar with command economies such as the Chinese economy know that job assignment decisions and job allocation decisions are made by public, not private, authorities. What this juxtaposition of styles of governance suggests is that private corporations, in the aggregate, have in America garnered mostly unto themselves the power of determining who works and who does not and at what level of remuneration regardless of the skills, knowledge, and performance capabilities that potential workers bring to the marketplace.

Wage and salary differentials based on rank, seniority, "race," ethnicity, sex, and other considerations are determined largely by the bureaucratic rules and procedures of these private governments and their associated unions. The selection devices they use, such as aptitude tests and personal interviews, frequently go beyond "business necessity" all the way to blatant racial, ethnic, and gender discrimination (Jurgensen 1996).

The screening devices of inclusion are also screening devices of exclusion. By design, these instruments serve both functions, and private corporations have been left with the prerogatives of including and excluding people from their work forces.

Eells (1962, 267), in his studies of private governance in corporations, found that they intentionally limit employment and advancement of minority employees. Within the past two years, both Texaco and Boeing have agreed to pay for damages that resulted from what appears to be discriminatory corporate practices. For the "black" and other minority employees, they also agreed to change their corporate practices and procedures that have negative racial, ethnic, and gender consequences.

Conclusion

I have studied the organization and operation of United States "race" relations, and I have uncovered how that system emerged, how it maintained itself, and how it changed. I am convinced that historical records show that "black-white" relations are not, at base, economic relations. "Black-white" relations are at their roots political relations. The American "race" relations system is rooted in political stratification wherein individual achievements continue to be predetermined by racial politics inside both public and private corporations. Moreover, the "Chain of Being" ideology has been and still remains the governing ideology of corporate America today and for the foreseeable future.

The moguls of mass media recently claimed that they do not have any "blacks" in leading roles on television during prime time because the market will not allow it (*USA Today* 1999). What do you think would happen if all the prime-time shows had "blacks" in leading roles? To be sure, Americans would not turn off their TV sets and go to the movies. And so, in corporate America, the "Chain of Being" ideal goes on under the guise of economic decision-making.

BIBLIOGRAPHY

INDEX

Bibliography

Abbott, Andrew. 1997. "Of Time and Space: The Contemporary Relevance of the Chicago School." *Social Forces* 75: 1149–82.

Abrams, Philip. 1982. *Historical Sociology.* Ithaca: Cornell Univ. Press.

Achebe, C. 1958. *Things Fall Apart.* London: Heinemann.

Adepoju, Aderanti, ed. 1993. The Impact of Structural Adjustment on the Population of Africa: the Implications for Education, Health, and Employment. London: James Curry; Portsmouth, N.H.: Heinemann.

Agarwal, N. 1983. *The Development of a Dual Economy.* Calcutta, India: K. P. Bagchi and Company.

Agger, Ben. 1989. *Socio(Onto)logy.* Chicago: Univ. of Illinois Press.

Alexander, Jeffrey. 1987. *Twenty Lectures.* New York: Columbia Univ. Press.

Allen, Walter R. 1978a. "The Search for Applicable Theories of Black Family Life." *Journal of Marriage and the Family* 40 (Feb.): 117–29.

————. 1978b. "Black Family Research in the United States: A Review, Assessment and Extension." *Journal of Comparative Family Studies* 9: 167–89.

————. 1979. "Family Roles, Occupational Status, and Achievement among Black Women in the United States." *Journal of Women in Culture and Society* 4: 670–86.

————, and Joseph O. Jewell. 1995. "African American Education since *An American Dilemma.*" *Daedalus* 124 (winter): 77–100.

————, Edgar G. Epps, and Nesha Z. Haniff, eds. 1991. *College in Black and White: African American Students in Predominately White and in Historically Black Public Universities.* Albany: State Univ. of New York Press.

————, R. English, and J. Hall, eds. 1986. *Black American Families, 1965–1984: A Classified, Selectively Annotated Bibliography.* Westport, Conn.: Greenwood Press.

————, Margaret B. Spencer, and Geraldine K. Brookins. 1985. "Synthesis: Black Children Keep on Growing." In *Beginnings: The Social and Affective Development of Black Children,* edited by M. B. Spencer, G. K. Brookins, and W. R. Allen. Hillside, N.J.: Lawrence Erlbaum Associates.

Alves, Michael J., and Charles V. Willie. 1987. "Controlled Choice—An Approach to Effective School Desegregation." *The Urban Review* 19 (Nov.): 67–88.

American Anti-Slavery Society. 1970. *The Constitution: A Pro-Slavery Compact.* New York: The New American Library.

American Sociological Association, Section on Racial and Ethnic Minorities. 1999. "Institutional Racism, ASA Council, and the ASR Editorship." *Footnotes, American Sociological Association,* November.

Amin, Samir. 1974. *Imperialism and Unequal Development.* New York: Monthly Review Press.

———. 1976. *Unequal Development.* New York: Monthly Review Press.

———. 1989. *Eurocentrism.* New York: Monthly Review Press.

Anderson, Elijah. 1990. *Streetwise: Race, Class and Change in an Urban Community.* Chicago: Univ. of Chicago Press.

———. 1997. "The Precarious Balance: Race Man or Sellout?" In *The Darden Dilemma: 12 Black Writers on Justice, Race and Conflicting Loyalties,* edited by Ellis Cose. New York: Harper Collins.

Anderson, James D. 1988. *The Education of Blacks in the South, 1860–1935.* Chapel Hill: Univ. of North Carolina Press.

Anderson, Margaret L. 1993. *Thinking about Women: Sociological Perspectives on Sex and Gender.* 3d ed. New York: Macmillan.

Anderson, Margaret, and Patricia Hill-Collins. 1995. *Race, Class and Gender.* New York: Wadsworth.

Anderson, P. 1979. *Lineages of the Absolutist States.* London: Verso.

———. 1980. *Passages from Antiquity to Feudalism.* London: Verso.

Ansell, Amy Elizabeth. 1997. *New Right, New Racism: Race and Reaction in the United States and Brittain.* New York: NYU Press.

Aptheker, Herbert. 1968. *American Negro Slave Revolts.* New York: International Publishers.

Arghiri, Emmanuel. 1972. *Unequal Exchange and the Imperialism of Trade.* New York: Monthly Review Press.

Asante, Molefi K. 1988. *Afrocentricity.* Trenton, N.J.: Africa World Press.

Astone, Nan Marie, and Sara S. McLanahan. 1994. "Family Structure, Residential Mobility, and School Dropout: A Research Note." *Demography* 31: 575–84.

Austin, J. L. 1962. *How to Do Things with Words.* New York: Oxford Univ. Press.

Badru, P. 1998. *International Banking and Rural Development: The World Bank in Sub-Saharan Africa.* Aldershot, England: Ashgate Publishing Company.

Bagchi, A. K. 1982. *The Political Economy of Underdevelopment.* Cambridge: Cambridge Univ. Press.

Balandier, G. 1968. *Daily Life in the Kingdom of the Kongo.* New York: Pantheon Books.

Ballagh, James C. 1968. *A History of Slavery in Virginia.* 1902. Reprint. Baltimore, Md.: Johns Hopkins Univ. Press.

Ballard, C. 1981. "Trade, Tribute and Migrant Labour: Zulu and Colonial Exploitation of the Delagoa Bay Hinterland, 1818–1879." In *Before and After Shaka,* edited by J. B. Peieres, 100–124. Grahamstown, South Africa: Institute of Social and Economic Research, Rhodes Univ.

Banks, William M. 1996. *Black Intellectuals: Race and Responsibility in American Life.* New York: W. W. Norton.

Barrett, Paul M. 1996. "Minority Voting Districts Struck Down by High Court for Lack of Compactness." *Wall Street Journal,* June 14, A3.

Battistich, Victor, Daniel Solomon, Doug-II Kim, Marilyn Watson, and Eric Schaps. 1995. "Schools as Communities, Poverty Levels of Student Populations, and Students' Attitudes, Motives, and Performance: A Multilevel Analysis." *American Educational Research Journal* 32: 627–58.

Bauer, P. 1972. *Dissent on Development.* Cambridge, Mass.: Harvard Univ. Press.

———. 1981. *Equality, the Third World, and Economic Delusion.* Cambridge, Mass.: Harvard Univ. Press.

———, and B. Yamey. 1978. "The Third World and the West: An Economic Perspective." In *The Third World: Premises of U.S. Policy,* edited by S. Thompson, 99–121. San Francisco: Institute for Contemporary Studies.

Bearak, Barry. 1997. "Between Black and White. *New York Times,* July 27, sec. 1, p. 1.

Becker, Howard S. 1963. *Outsiders: Studies in the Sociology of Deviance.* Glencoe, Ill.: Free Press.

Bennett, L. 1961. *Before the Mayflower: A History of the Negro in America.* Chicago: Johnson.

Bergel, Egon E. 1962. *Social Stratification.* New York: McGraw-Hill.

Berger, Peter L., and Thomas Luckmann. 1966. *The Social Construction of Reality.* Garden City, N.Y.: Doubleday.

Bergman, Peter M., and Mort N. Bergman. 1969. *The Chronological History of the Negro in America.* New York: The New American Library.

Bernard, Jessie. 1966. *Marriage and the Family among Negros.* Englewood Cliffs, N.J.: Prentice-Hall.

Bernardi, B. 1985. *Age Class Systems.* Cambridge: Cambridge Univ. Press.

Bernstein, Richard J. 1972. "Critique of Gouldner's *The Coming Crisis of Western Sociology.*" *Sociology Inquiry* 42: 65–76.

Berry, Mary F. 1971. *Black Resistance/White Law.* New York: Appleton-Century-Crofts.

Billingsley, Andrew. 1968. *Black Families in White America.* Englewood Cliffs, N.J.: Prentice-Hall.

———. *Climbing Jacob's Ladder: The Enduring Legacy of African American Families.* New York: Simon and Schuster.

Blackwell, James E. 1986. *Mainstreaming Outsiders: The Production of Black Professionals.* 2d ed. Bayside, N.Y.: General Hall.

———. 1992. "Minorities in the Liberation of the ASA?" *The American Sociologist* spring: 11–17.

———, and Morris Janowitz. 1974. *Black Sociologists—Historical and Contemporary Perspectives.* Chicago, Ill.: Univ. of Chicago Press.

Blalock, H. M., Jr. 1967. *Toward a Theory of Minority-Group Relations.* New York: John Wiley.

Blau, Peter. 1977. *Inequality and Heterogeneity: A Primitive Theory of Social Structure.* New York: Free Press.

Blau, J., and P. Blau. 1982. "The Cost of Inequality: Metropolitan Structure and Violent Crime." *American Sociological Review* 47: 114–29.

Blauner, Robert. 1969. "Internal Colonialism and Ghetto Revolt." *Social Problems* 16: 393–406.

———. 1972. *Racial Oppression in America.* New York: Harper and Row.

Blumer, Herbert. 1958. "Race Prejudice as a Sense of Group Position." *Pacific Sociological Review* 1: 3–7.

Bobo, L. 1997. "The Color Line, the Dilemma, and the Dream: Race Relations in America at the Close of the Twentieth Century." In *Civil Rights and Social Wrongs: Black-White Relations since World War II,* edited by J. Higham, 31–55. University Park: Pennsylvania State Univ. Press.

Boeke, J. H. 1953. *Economics and Economic Policy of Dual Societies.* New York: Institute of Pacific Relations.

Bonacich, Edna. 1972. "A Theory of Ethnic Antagonism: The Split Labor Market." *American Sociological Review* 37: 547–59.

Bosserman, Phillip. 1968. *Dialectical Sociology: An Analysis of the Sociology of Georges Gurvitch.* Boston, Mass.: P. Sargent.

Bouchard, Thomas J., Jr., et al. 1990. "Sources of Human Psychological Differences: The Minnesota Study of Twins Reared Apart." *Science* 250 (Oct. 12): 223–28.

Bowen, William G., and Derek Bok. 1998. *The Shape of the River: Long-Term Consequences in Considering Race in College and University Admissions.* Princeton, N.J.: Princeton Univ. Press.

Bowles, Samuel, and Herbert Gintis. 1976. Schooling in Capitalist America. New York: Basic Books.

Boykin, A. Wade, Andrew J. Franklin, and J. Frank Yates, eds. *Research Directions of Black Psychologists.* New York: Russell Sage Foundation, 1985.

Bracey, John. 1991. *The Black Sociologists: First Half of the 20th Century.* Belmont, Calif.: Wadsworth Publishing.

————. 1994. Interview by Donald Cunnigen. Association of Black Sociologists, Los Angeles, Calif.

————, August Meier, and Elliott Rudwick. 1971. *Blacks in the Abolitionist Movement.* Belmont, Calif.: Wadsworth Publishing.

Braddock, Jomills H., and Marvin P. Dawkins. 1993. "Ability, Grouping, Aspirations, and Attainment: Evidence from the National Longitudinal Study of 1988." *Journal of Negro Education* 62: 1–13.

Brantingham, P., and P. Brantingham, eds. 1991. *Environmental Criminology.* Prospect Heights, Ill.: Waveland Press.

Breen, T. H., and Stephen Ines. 1980. *Myne Owne Ground.* New York: Oxford Univ. Press.

Bronfenbrenner, Urie. 1979. *The Ecology of Human Development: Experiments by Nature and Design.* Cambridge, Mass.: Harvard Univ. Press.

Brown vs. Board of Education. 1954. Topeka, Kans. 347 US 483.

Brown, C. 1965. *Manchild in the Promised Land.* New York: Macmillan.

Brown, Richard. 1987. *Society as Text.* Chicago: Univ. of Chicago Press.

Bulmer, Martin. 1992. "The Growth of Applied Sociology after 1945: The Prewar Establishment of the Postwar Infrastructure." In *Sociology and Its Publics—The Forms and Fates of Disciplinary Organization,* edited by Terrence C. Halliday and Morris Janowitz. Chicago: Univ. of Chicago Press.

Bunche, Ralph J. 1940a. To Butler A. Jones, May 27. Ralph Bunche Papers, Box 36, Folders 7, 8, New York Public Library, Schomburg Center for Research in Black Culture, New York.

————. 1940b. To Butler A. Jones, May 7. Ralph Bunche Papers, Box 36, Folders 7, 8, New York Public Library, Schomburg Center for Research in Black Culture, New York.

————. 1940c. To Butler A. Jones, Mar. 19. Ralph Bunche Papers, Box 36, Folders 7, 8, New York Public Library, Schomburg Center for Research in Black Culture, New York.

————. 1940d. To Butler A. Jones, Feb. 20. Ralph Bunche Papers, Box 36, Folders 7, 8, New York Public Library, Schomburg Center for Research in Black Culture, New York.

————. 1940e. To Butler A. Jones, Jan. 27. Ralph Bunche Papers, Box 36, Folders 7, 8, New York Public Library, Schomburg Center for Research in Black Culture, New York.

————. 1940f. To Butler A. Jones, Jan. 17. Ralph Bunche Papers, Box 36, Folders 7, 8, New York Public Library, Schomburg Center for Research in Black Culture, New York.

———. 1973. *The Political Status of the Negro in the Age of FDR.* Edited by Dewey W. Grantham. Chicago: Univ. of Chicago Press.

Bureau of Justice Statistics. 1994. *Criminal Victimization in the U.S.* Washington, D.C.: BJS.

Buroway, Michael. 1999. "Letter to Aljandro Portes." *Footnotes, American Sociological Association,* July/August.

Butcher, M. J. 1965. *The Negro in American Culture.* New York: Alfred A. Knopf.

Butler, Judith. 1991. "Imitation and Gender Insubordination." In *Inside/Out: Lesbian Theories, Gay Theories,* edited by Diana Fuss. New York: Routledge.

Cagnolo, C. 1933. *The Akikuyu: Their Customs, Traditions and Folklore.* Nyeri, Kenya: Mission Printing School.

Calhoun, Craig. 1995. *Critical Social Theory* Cambridge, Mass.: Blackwell.

Calvin, A. 1981. "Unemployment among Black Youths, Demographics and Crime." *Crime and Delinquency* 27: 234–44.

Cardoso, Fernando Henrique. 1979. *Dependency and Development in Latin America.* Berkeley: Univ. of California Press.

Carter, Ronald L., and Kim Q. Hill. 1979. *The Criminal's Image of the City.* New York: Pergamon.

Carter, Robert T., and A. Lin Goodwin. 1994. "Racial Identity and Education." *Review of Research in Education* 20: 291–336.

Carter, Stephen L. 1991. *Rejections of an Affirmative Action Baby.* New York: Basic Books.

Castenell, Louis A. 1983. "Achievement Motivation: An Investigation of Adolescent Achievement Patterns." *American Educational Research Journal* 20: 503–10.

Catania, Joseph, et al. 1995. "Risk Factors for HIV and Other Sexually Transmitted Diseases and Prevention Practices among U.S. Heterosexual Adults: Changes from 1990 to 1992." *American Journal of Public Health* 85 (November): 1492–1549.

Cavicchi, E. 1953. *Problems of Change in Kikuyu Tribal Society.* Bologna, Italy: EMI.

Chapple, Eliot D., and Charleston S. Coon. 1942. *Principles of Anthropology.* New York: Henry Holt.

Cheater, A. 1986. *Social Anthropology: An Alternative Introduction.* Gweru, Zimbabwe: Mambo Press.

Chinchilla, N. S. 1983. "Interpreting Social Change in Guatemala: Modernization, Dependency, and Articulation of Modes of Production." In *Theories of Development,* edited by R. Chilcote and D. Johnson, 139–78. Beverly Hills, Calif.: Sage Publications.

Chipuer, H. M., M. J. Rovine, and R. Plomin. 1990. "LISREL Modeling: Genetic and Environmental Influences on IQ Revisited." *Intelligence* 14: 11–29.

Cicourel, Aaron, and John Kitsuse. 1963. *The Educational Decision Makers.* Indianapolis, Ind.: Bobbs-Merrill.

Clark, Kenneth B. 1965. *Dark Ghetto.* New York: Harper and Row.

Clark, Reginald M. 1983. *Family Life and School Achievement.* Chicago: Univ. of Chicago Press.

Cobbing, J. 1981. "The Ndebele State." In *Before and After Shaka,* edited by J. B. Peires, 160–70. Grahamstown, South Africa: Institute of Social and Economic Research, Rhodes Univ.

Cohen, Jerry, and William S. Murphy. 1967. *Burn Baby Burn.* New York: Dutton.

Cohen, Richard. 1995. "Yes, Antidiscrimination Policy Discriminates." *Boston Globe,* Feb. 23, p. 15.

Coleman, James. 1990. *Foundations of Social Theory.* Cambridge, Mass.: Harvard Univ. Press.

College Board. 1999. *College Bound Seniors 1999: A Profile of SAT Program Test Takers.* New York: The College Board.

Collins, Patricia Hill. 1998. *Fighting Words: Black Women and the Search for Justice* Minneapolis: Univ. of Minnesota Press.

Collins, Sharon M. 1997. *Black Corporate Executives.* Philadelphia, Pa.: Temple Univ. Press.

Comer, James. 1985. "Black Violence and Public Policy." In *American Violence and Public Policy,* edited by Lynn Curtis. New Haven, Conn.: Yale Univ. Press.

Conley, Dalton. 1999. *Being Black, Living in the Red: Race, Wealth, and Social Policy in America.* Berkeley: Univ. of California Press.

Conyers, James E. 1968. "Who's Who among Black Doctorates in Sociology." *Sociological Focus* 19: 77–93.

Cooper, Anna Julia. 1892. *A Voice from the South; By a Black Woman of the South.* Xenia, Ohio: Aldine Printing House.

Coquery-Vidrovitch, C. 1976. "The Political Economy of the African Peasantry and Modes of Production." In *The Political Economy of Contemporary Africa,* edited by P. C. W. Gutkind and I. Wallerstein, 90–111. Beverly Hills, Calif.: Sage Publications.

Coray, M. 1978. "The Kenya Land Commission and the Kikuyu of Kiambu." *Agricultural History* 52: 179–93.

Cornish, D., and R. Clarke. 1986. *The Reasoning Criminal.* New York: Springer-Verlag.

Cose, Ellis. 1995. *The Rage of a Privileged Class: Why Are Middle Class Blacks Angry?* New York: Harper-Collins.

Cox, Oliver. 1948. *Caste, Class and Race.* New York: Doubleday.

Crouse, James, and Dale Trusheim. 1988. *The Case Against the SAT.* Chicago: Univ. of Chicago Press.

Cruse, H. 1967. *The Crisis of the Negro Intellectual.* New York: William Morrow.

Cummings, Scott. 1977. "Family Socialization and Fatalism among Black Adolescents." *Journal of Negro Education* 46: 62–75.

Davidson, B. 1992. *The Black Man's Burden*. New York: Times Books.

Davidson, Douglas. 1977. "Black Sociologists: A Critical Analysis." *Contributions to Black Studies* 1: 44–51.

Davidson, R. B. 1962. *West Indian Migrants*. London: Oxford Univ. Press.

Davis, Allison, and John Dollard. 1940. *Children of Bondage: The Personality Development of Urban Youth in the Urban South*. New York: Harper and Row.

Davis, F. James. 1991. *Who is Black? One Nation's Definition*. University Park: Pennsylvania State Univ. Press.

Davis, James Earl, and Will J. Jordan. 1994. "The Effects of School Context, Structure, and Experiences on African American Males and High School." *Journal of Negro Education* 63: 570–87.

Derrida, Jacques. 1984. *Grammatology*. Baltimore, Md.: Johns Hopkins Univ. Press.

Dos Santos, T. 1973. "The Crisis of Development Theory and the Problem of Dependence in Latin America." In *Underdevelopment and Development: The Third World Today: Selected Readings*. Hammondsworth: Penguin.

Dowd, Jerome. 1926. *The Negro in American Life*. New York: Century.

Doyle, Bertram W. 1933. "Sociology in Negro Schools and Colleges, 1924–1933." *The Quarterly Review of Higher Education among Negroes* 1: 7–14.

Drake, J. G. St. Clair, and Allison Davis. 1940. "The Negro Churches and Associations in Chicago." Unpublished memorandum prepared for the Carnegie-Myrdal study.

———, and Horace Cayton. 1962. *Black Metropolis: A Study of Negro Life in a Northern City*. 1948. Reprint. New York: Harper and Row.

Dred Scott vs. Sandford. 1857. 60 US (19 How.) 393.

———. 1967. *The Philadelphia Negro—A Social Study*. 1899. Reprint. New York: Schocken Books.

———. 1995. *The Souls of Black Folk*. 1903. Reprint. New York: Dutton.

Duncan, Greg J. 1994. "Families and Neighbors as Sources of Disadvantage in the Schooling Decisions of White and Black Adolescents." *American Journal of Education* 103: 20–53.

Durkheim, Émile. 1964. *The Division of Labor in Society*. Translated by George Simpson. 1933. Reprint, New York: Free Press of Glencoe.

Economic Commission for Africa. 1990. *Economic Report on Africa, 1990. United Nations Economic Commission for Africa*. Ethiopia: Addis Abba.

Edwards, G. Franklin. 1980. "E. Franklin Frazier—Race, Education and Community." In *Sociological Traditions from Generation to Generation—Glimpses of the American Experience,* edited by Robert K. Merton and Matilda White Riley. Norwood, N.J.: Ablex Publishing Corporation.

Eells, Richard S. 1962. *The Government of Corporations*. New York: Free Press.

Eicher, Carl K., and John M. Staatz. 1990. *Agricultural Development in the Third World*. Baltimore: Johns Hopkins Univ. Press.

Eisenstadt, Shmuel Noah. 1966. *Modernization: Protest and Change*. Englewood Cliffs, N.J.: Prentice-Hall.

———. 1973. *Tradition, Change, and Modernity*. New York: Wiley.

Empey, L. 1982. *American Delinquency*. Homewood, Ill.: Dorsey.

Entwisle, Doris E., and Kari L. Alexander. 1992. "Summer Setback: Race, Poverty, School Composition, and Mathematics Achievement in the First Two Years of School." *American Sociological Review* 57: 72–84.

Epps, Edgar G. 1969. "Correlates of Academic Achievement among Northern and Southern Negro Students." *Journal of Social Issues* 24: 55–70.

———, and Patricia Gurin. 1975. *Black Consciousness, Identity, and Achievement: A Study of Students in Historically Black Colleges*. New York: Wiley.

———, and Sylvia F. Smith. 1984. "School and Children: The Middle Childhood Years." In *Development during Middle Childhood: The Years from Six to Twelve*, edited by W. Andrew Collins, 283–334. Washington, D.C.: National Academy Press.

———, and Kenneth W. Jackson. 1988. "The Educational Attainment Process among Black Youth." In *Desegregating America's Colleges and Universities*, edited by John W. Williams III, 137–58. New York: Teachers College Press.

———, and John J. Lane, eds. 1992. *Restructuring the Schools: Problems and Prospects*. Berkeley, Calif.: McCutchan.

Epstein, Joyce L. 1995. "School, Family, Community Partnerships: Caring for the Children We Share." *Phi Delta Kappan* 76: 701–12.

Fairley, N. 1987. "Ideology and State Formation: The Ekie of Southern Zaire." In *The African Frontier: The Reproduction of Traditional African Societies*, edited by I. Kopytoff, 91–100. Bloomington: Indiana Univ. Press.

Farley, W. Reynolds, and Walter R. Allen. 1989. *The Colorline and the Quality of Life in America*. New York: Oxford Univ. Press.

Feagin, Joe. 1995. Memorandum to American Sociological Association Council, Jan. 7.

Feagin, Joe R., and Melvin P. Sikes. 1994. *Living with Racism: The Black Middle Class Experience*. Boston: Beacon.

Fontaine, Pierre-Michel. 1983. "Haitian Immigrants in Boston: A Commentary." In *Caribbean Immigration to the United States*, edited by Roy S. Bryce-Laporte and Delores M. Mortimer, 111–29. Washington, D.C.: Research Institute on Immigration and Ethnic Studies Occasional Papers, no. 1.

Fordham, Signithia. 1993. " 'Those Loud Black Girls': (Black) Women, Silence, and Gender 'Passing' in the Academy." *Anthropology and Education Quarterly* 24, no. 1: 3–32.

Forsyth, Adrian. 1993. *A Natural History of Sex*. Shelburne, Vt.: Chapters Publishing.

Fortes, M. 1963. *Kinship and Social Order*. Chicago: Aldine.

Foucault, Michel. 1970. *Economic Development of Latin America*. Cambridge: Cambridge Univ. Press.

———. 1973. "The Concept of External Dependence in the Study of Underdevelopment." In *The Political Economy of Development and Underdevelopment*, edited by C. K. Wilber. New York: Random House.

Frank, Andre G. 1966. "The Development of Underdevelopment in Latin America." Monthly Review, no. 4: 18.

———. 1970. *Latin America: Underdevelopment or Revolution*. New York: Monthly Review Press.

Frankenberg, Ruth. 1993. *White Women, Race Matters: The Social Construction of Whiteness*. Minneapolis: Univ. of Minnesota Press.

Franklin, V. P. 1984. *Black Self-Determination: A Cultural History of the Faith of the Fathers*. Westport, Conn.: Lawrence Hill and Company.

Frazier, E. Franklin. 1932. *The Negro Family in Chicago*. Chicago: Univ. of Chicago Press.

———. *1939. The Negro Family in the United States*. Chicago: Univ. of Chicago Press.

———. 1957a. *The Black Bourgeoisie*. New York: Free Press.

———. 1957b. *Race and Culture Contacts in the Modern World*. Boston: Beacon.

———. 1966. *The Negro Family in the United States*. 1939. Reprint. Chicago: Univ. of Chicago Press.

Furer, Howard B. 1972. *The British in America, 1578–1970*. Dobbs Ferry, N.Y.: Oceana Publications.

Furtado, Celso. 1970. *Economic Development of Latin America; a Survey from Colonial Times to the Cuban Revolution*. Cambridge: Cambridge Univ. Press.

Gallagher, Charles. 1998. "White Reconstruction in the University." In *The Social Construction of Race and Ethnicity in the United States*, edited by Joan Ferrante and Price Brown, Jr. New York: Longman.

Gardner, John W. 1968. *No Easy Victories*. New York: Harper and Row.

Gardner, Howard. 1993. *Frames of Mind: The Theory of Multiple Intelligences*. New York: Basic Books.

———. 1998. "A Multiplicity of Intelligences." *Scientific American Presents* 9 (winter): 19–23.

George, Susan. 1992. *The Debt Boomerang: How Third World Debt Harms Us All*. Boulder, Colo.: Westview Press.

Geranios, Nicholas K. 1997. "Black Veteran to Get Medal of Honor for WWII Service." *Seattle Times*, Jan. 12, p. A5.

Gerth, Hans H., and C. Wright Mills. 1946. *From Max Weber: Essay on Sociology.* New York: Oxford Univ. Press.

Giddings, Franklin H. 1921. *The Principles of Sociology.* New York: Macmillan.

Gilroy, Paul. 1993. *The Black Atlantic: Modernity and Double Consciousness.* Cambridge, Mass.: Harvard Univ. Press.

Glazer, Nathan. 1966. Foreword to *The Negro Family in the United States,* by E. Franklin Frazier. 1939. Reprint. Chicago: Phoenix Books.

———. 1983. *Ethnic Dilemmas.* Cambridge, Mass.: Harvard Univ. Press.

———. 1987. *Affirmative Discrimination: Ethnic Inequality and Public Policy.* New York: Basic Books, 1975. Reprint, Cambridge, Mass.: Harvard Univ. Press.

———. 1997. *We Are All Multiculturalists Now.* Cambridge, Mass.: Harvard Univ. Press.

Goldberger, Arthur S. 1979. "Heritability." *Econometrica* 46 (Nov.): 327–47.

Goodell, William. 1969. *American Slave Code.* New York: Negro Universities Press.

Goffman, Erving. 1959. *The Presentation of Self in Everyday Life.* New York: Doubleday.

———. 1961. *Strategic Interaction.* Indianapolis, Ind.: Bobbs-Merrill.

———. 1963. *Stigma: Notes on the Management of Spoiled Identity.* Englewood Cliffs, N.J.: Prentice-Hall.

Gordon, Edmund T., Edmund W. Gordon, and Jessica G. G. Nembard. 1994. "Social Science Literature, Concerning African American Men." *Journal of Negro Education* 63: 608–31.

Gordon, M. 1964. *Assimilation in American Life.* New York: Oxford Univ. Press.

Gossett, Thomas. 1963. *Race: The History of an Idea in America.* Dallas: Southern Methodist Univ. Press.

———. 1965. *Race: The History of an Idea in America.* New York: Schocken.

Gottfredson, L. 1998. "The G-Theory." *Intelligence* 22 (June): 1–30.

Gould, L. 1969. "Who Defines Delinquency." *Social Problems* 16: 325–36.

Gouldner, Alvin W. 1970. *The Coming Crisis of Western Sociology.* New York: Equinox Books.

Grant, Linda. 1985. "Race-Gender Status, Classroom Interaction, and Children's Socialization in Elementary School." In *Gender Influences in Classroom Interactions,* edited by Louise Cherry Wilkinson and Cora B. Marrett, 57–77. Orlando, Fla.: Academic Press.

Greene, Harry Washington. 1946. *Holders of Doctorates among American Negroes, 1876–1943.* Boston, Mass.: Meador Publishing Company.

Greene, Maxine. 1994. "Epistemology and Educational Research: The Influence of Recent Approaches to Knowledge." *Review of Research in Education* 20: 423–84.

Grier, William, and Price M. Cobbs. 1968. *Black Rage.* New York: Bantam Books.

Griffin, John H. 1961. *Black Like Me.* New York: New American Library, Signet.

Grimshaw, Allen D., ed. 1969. *Racial Violence in the United States.* Chicago: Aldine.

Guilford, J. P. 1968. "The Structure of Intelligence." In *Handbook of Measurement and Assessment in the Behavioral Sciences,* edited by D. K. Whitla. Boston: Addison-Wesley.

Gurin, Patricia, and Edgar G. Epps. 1975. *Black Consciousness, Identity and Achievement: A Study of Students in Historically Black Colleges.* New York: John Wiley.

Gurvitch, Georges. 1971. *The Social Frameworks of Knowledge.* Translated by Margaret A. Thompson and Kenneth A. Thompson. Oxford: Blackwell.

Gutman, Herbert G. 1976. *The Black Family in Slavery and Freedom, 1750–1925.* New York: Vintage Books.

Guy, J. J. 1981. "Production and Exchange in the Zulu Kingdom during the Reign of Cetshwayo." In *Before and After Shaka,* edited by J. B. Peires, 33–73. Grahamstown, South Africa: Institute of Social and Economic Research, Rhodes Univ.

Habermas, Jürgen. 1971. *Knowledge and Human Interests.* Translated by Jeremy J. Shapiro. Boston: Beacon.

———. 1984. *The Theory of Communicative Action.* Vol. 1. Boston: Beacon Press.

———. 1989. *The Theory of Communicative Action.* Vol. 2. Boston: Beacon Press.

Hacker, Andrew. 1995. *Two Nations: Black and White, Separate, Hostile, and Unequal.* New York: Charles Scribner's Sons.

Hale, Matt. N.d. *Facts that the Government and the Media Don't Want You To Know.* East Peoria, Ill.: World Church of the Creator.

Hall, Stuart. 1992. "New Ethnicities." In *'Race', Culture and Difference,* edited by James Donald and Ali Rattansi. London: Sage Publications in association with the Open University.

Hallinan, Maureen T. 1988. "Equality of Educational Opportunity." *Annual Review of Sociology* 14: 249–68.

Handlin, O. 1959. *The Newcomers.* New York: Doubleday.

Hare, Bruce R. 1977. "Black and White Children Self-Esteem in Social Science: An Overview." *Journal of Negro Education* 46: 141–56.

———. 1980. "Self-Perception and Academic Achievement Variations in a Desegregated Setting." *American Journal of Psychiatry* 137: 683–89.

———. 1984. "Development and Change among Desegregated Adolescents: A Longitudinal Study of Self-Perception and Achievement." In *Advances in Motivation and Achievement,* vol. 1. Greenwich, Conn.: JAI Press.

———. 1985. "Stability and Change in Self-Perception and Achievement among Black Adolescents: A Longitudinal Study." *Journal of Black Psychology* 11: 29–42.

———, and Louis Castenell. 1985. "No Place to Run, No Place to Hide: Comparative Status and Future Prospects of Black Boys." In *Beginnings: The Social and Affec-*

tive Development of Black Children, edited by Margaret Beale Spencer, Geraldine K. Brookins, and Walter R. Allen. Hillsdale, N.J.: Erlbaum.

Hare, Nathan. 1976. "What Black Intellectuals Misunderstand about the Black Family." *Black World* Mar.: 4–14.

Harman, Harry H. 1960. *Modern Factor Analysis.* Chicago: Univ. of Chicago Press.

Harms. R. 1987. *Games Against Nature.* Cambridge: Cambridge Univ. Press.

Harris, A. 1991. "Race, Class and Crime." In *Criminology,* edited by J. Sheley. Belmont, Calif.. Wadsworth.

Harris, Robert L. 1987. "The Flowering Afro-American History." *The American Historical Review* 92: 1150–61.

Hawkins, D. 1983. "Black and White Homicide Differentials: Alternatives to an Inadequate Theory." *Criminal Justice and Behavior* 10: 407–40.

Hawley, Amos H. 1950. *Human Ecology: A Theory of Community Structure.* New York: Ronald Press.

———. 1971. *Urban Society: An Ecological Approach.* New York: Ronald Press.

Hening, William W. 1809–23. *The Status at Large Being a Collection of All Laws of Virginia from the First Session of the Legislature in the Year 1619.* Richmond, Va.

Henry, Charles P. 1990. "Civil Rights and National Security: The Case of Ralph Bunche." In *Ralph Bunche—The Man and His Times,* edited by Benjamin Rivlin. New York: Holmes and Meier.

———. 1999. *Ralph Bunch—Model Negro or American Other?* New York: New York Univ. Press.

Herrnstein, Richard J. 1971. "I.Q." *Atlantic Monthly* 288 (Nov.): 43–64.

———. 1973. *I.Q. in the Meritocracy* Boston: Little, Brown.

———, and Charles Murray. 1994. *The Bell Curve: Intelligence and Class Structure in American Life.* New York: Free Press.

Heyns, Barbara. 1978. *Summer Learning and the Effects of Schooling.* New York: Academic Press.

Higgins, B. 1984. "The Dualistic Theory of Underdeveloped Areas: Economic Development and Cultural Change." In *Leading Issues in Development Economics,* edited by G. M. Meier. New York: Oxford Univ. Press.

Hill, Robert B., et al. 1993. *Research on the African American Family: A Holistic Perspective.* Westport, Conn.: Auburn House.

Himes, Joseph Sandy. 1949. "Development and Status of Sociology in Negro Colleges." *Journal of Educational Sociology* 23: 17–32.

Hines, Ralph H. 1967. The Negro Scholar's Contribution to Pure and Applied Sociology." *Journal of Social and Behavioral Sciences* 8: 30–35.

Holmes, Steven A. 1997. "Panel Balks at Multiracial Census Category." *New York Times,* July 9, A8.

Hootink, H. 1961. "Colonial Psychology and Race." *Journal of Economic History* 21 (Dec.): 629–40.

Horowitz, Irving L. 1993. *The Decomposition of Sociology.* New York: Oxford Univ. Press.

Horton, R. 1967. "African Traditional Thought and Western Science." In *Africa.* Vol. 37.

———. 1993. *Patterns of Thought in Africa and the West: Essays on Magic, Religion, and Science.* Cambridge and New York: Cambridge Univ. Press.

Hughes, Everett C. 1945. "Dilemmas and Contradictions of Status." *American Journal of Sociology* 40: 353–59.

———. 1963. "Race Relations and the Sociological Imagination." *American Sociological Review* 28 (Dec.): 879–90.

———. 1984. *The Sociological Eye: Selected Papers.* 1971. Reprint. New Brunswick, N.J.: Transaction Books.

Huizinga, D., and D. Elliott. 1987. "Juvenile Offenders: Prevalence, Offender Incidence, and Arrest Rates by Race." *Crime and Delinquency* 33: 206–23.

Hutchful, Eboe, ed. 1987. *The IMF and Ghana: the Confidential Record.* London: The Institute for African Alternatives; New Jersey: Zed Books.

Hyden, G. 1980. *Beyond Ujamaa in Tanzania: Underdevelopment and Uncaptured Peasantry.* Berkeley: Univ. of California Press.

———. 1983. *No Shortcuts to Progress: African Development in Perspective.* Berkeley: Univ. of California Press.

IMF Fact Sheet 2000. Washington, D.C.: International Monetary Fund.

Institute for Social Research. 1992. *Monitoring the Future.* Ann Arbor, Mich.: ISR.

Irving, Jacqueline Jordan, and Darlene Eleanor York. 1993. "Teacher Perspective: Why Do African American, Hispanic, and Vietnamese Students Fail?" In *Handbook of Schooling in Urban America,* edited by Stanley W. Rothstein, 161–93. Westport, Conn.: Greenwood Press.

Jackson, Daisy W. 1939. To Butler A. Jones, Nov. 14. Ralph Bunche Papers, Box 36, Folders 7, 8, New York Public Library, Schomburg Center for Research in Black Culture, New York.

Jackson, Jacquelyne Johnson. 1974. "Black Female Sociologists." In *Black Sociologists—Historical and Contemporary Perspectives,* edited by James Blackwell and Morris Janowitz. Chicago, Ill.: Univ. of Chicago Press.

Jackson, Walter A. 1990. *Gunnar Myrdal and America's Conscience—Social Engineering and Racial Liberalism, 1939–1987.* Chapel Hill: Univ. of North Carolina Press.

James, C. L. R. 1939. *Preliminary Notes on the Negro Question.* African Studies Association, Internal bulletin no. 9, 2–18.

Jaynes, Gerald, and Robin Williams, Jr., eds. 1989. *A Common Destiny: Blacks and American Society.* Washington, D.C.: National Academy Press.

Jencks, Christopher. 1991. "Is the American Underclass Growing?" In *The Urban Underclass,* edited by Christopher Jencks and Paul E. Peterson. Washington, D.C.: Brookings Institute.

————, and Meredith Phillips, eds. 1998. *The Black-White Test Score Gap.* Washington D.C.: Brookings Institution Press.

Jennings, J. 1994. *Understanding the Nature of Poverty in Urban America.* Westport, Conn.: Praeger.

Jensen, Arthur R. 1980. *Bias in Mental Testing.* New York: Free Press.

Jewsiewicki, B. 1981. "Lineage Mode of Production: Social Inequalities in Equatorial Central Africa." In *Modes of Production in Africa: The Precolonial Era,* edited by D. Crummey and C. C. Stewart, 93–113. Beverly Hills, Calif.: Sage Publications.

————, ed. 1985. *Mode of Production: The Challenge of Africa.* Ste-Foy, Canada: Safi Press.

————. 1989. "African Historical Studies: Academic Knowledge as 'Usable Past' and Radical Scholarship." *African Studies Review* 32: 1–76.

Johnson, Charles S. 1934. *Shadow of the Plantation.* Chicago: Univ. of Chicago Press.

————. 1941. *Growing Up in the Black Belt: Negro Youth in the Rural South.* Washington, D.C.: American Council on Education.

Johnson, D. 1983. "Class Analysis and Dependency." In *Theories of Development,* edited by R. Chilcote and D. Johnson, 231–53. Beverly Hills, Calif.: Sage Publications.

Jones, Butler A. 1939. To Ralph Bunche, Nov. 11. Ralph Bunch Papers, Box 36, Folders 7, 8, New York Public Library, Schomburg Center for Research in Black Culture, New York.

————. 1940a. "The Political Status of the Negro." Unpublished research memorandum prepared for Carnegie-Myrdal Study. Ralph Bunche Papers, New York Public Library, Schomburg Center for Research in Black Culture, New York.

————. 1940b. To Ralph Bunche, May 15. Ralph Bunche Papers, Box 36, Folders 7, 8, New York Public Library, Schomburg Center for Research in Black Culture, New York.

————. 1940c. To Ralph J. Bunche, Feb. 25. Ralph Bunche Papers, Box 36, Folders 7, 8, New York Public Library, Schomburg Center for Research in Black Culture, New York.

————. 1940d. To Ralph J. Bunche, Jan. 22. Ralph Bunche Papers, Box 36, Folders 7, 8, New York Public Library, Schomburg Center for Research in Black Culture, New York.

————. 1940e. To Ralph J. Bunche, Jan. 17. Ralph Bunch Papers, Box 36, Folders 7,

8, New York Public Library, Schomburg Center for Research in Black Culture, New York.

———. 1940f. To Ralph J. Bunch, Jan. 14. Ralph Bunch Papers, Box 36, Folders 7, 8, New York Public Library, Schomburg Center for Research in Black Culture, New York.

———. 1974. "The Tradition of Sociology Teaching in Black Colleges: The Unheralded Professionals." In *Black Sociologists—Historical and Contemporary Perspectives,* edited by James Blackell and Morris Janowitz. Chicago, Ill.: Univ. of Chicago Press.

Jones, Rhett S. 1992. "Beginning in An-Other Place: Oppugnancy and the Formation of Black Sociology." *The Griot* 1: 15–26.

———. 1993. Interview by Donald Cunnigen. American Sociological Association meetings, Pittsburgh, Pa.

———. 1994. "The End of Africanity: The Biracial Assault on Blackness." *Western Journal of Black Studies* 18, no. 4: 201–10.

Jordan, Winthrop D. 1968. *White over Black.* Baltimore, Md.: Pelican Books.

Joreskog, Karl G., and Dag Sorbom. 1993. *LISREL 8: A Guide to the Programs and Applications.* 3d ed. Chicago: SPSS Inc.

Jurgensen, Karen. 1996. "Texaco Tapes Show Bias in Workplace Far from Gone." *USA Today,* Nov. 14, 14A.

Kamin, Leon J. 1974. *The Science and Politics of I.Q.* Potomac, Md.: Erlbaum Associates.

Kappeler, V., M. Blumberg, and G. Potter. 1993. *The Mythology of Crime and Justice.* Prospect Heights, Ill.: Waveland.

Kardiner, Abram, and Lionel Ovesey. 1951. *The Mark of Oppression.* New York: Norton.

Kasarda, J. 1992. "The Severely Distressed in Economically Transforming Cities." In *Drugs, Crime and Social Isolation,* edited by A. Harrell and G. Peterson. Washington, D.C.: Urban Institute Press.

Katz, Irwin. 1967. "The Socialization of Academic Motivation in Minority Group Children." In *Nebraska Symposium on Motivation,* edited by D. Levine. Lincoln: Univ. of Nebraska Press.

Katz, J. 1988. *Seductions of Crime.* New York: Basic Books.

Kelley, Robin D. G. 1990. *Hammer and Hoe—Alabama Communists during the Great Depression.* Chapel Hill: Univ. of North Carolina Press.

Kennedy, Randall. 1997. "My Race Problem, and Ours." *Atlantic,* May, 55–66.

Kenyatta, J. 1965. *Facing Mt. Kenya.* New York: Vintage Books.

Kerner Commission. 1968. *Report of the National Advisory Commission on Civil Disorders.* New York: Bantam.

Key, R. Charles. 1975. "A Critical Analysis of Racism and Socialization in the Sociological Enterprise: The Sociology of Black Sociologists." Ph.D. diss., Univ. of Mis-
souri, Columbia.

————. 1978. "Society and Sociology: The Dynamics of Black Sociological Nega-
tion." *Phylon* 39.

Killian, Lewis M. 1994. *Black and White: Reflections of a White Southern Sociologist.* Dix
Hills, N.Y.: General Hall.

Killins, J. O. 1965. *Black Man's Burden.* New York: Trident.

King, Martin Luther, Jr. 1958. *Stride toward Freedom.* New York: Harper.

Kitching, G. 1980. *Class and Economic Change in Kenya.* New Haven, Conn.: Yale Univ.
Press.

————. 1985. "Suggestions for a Fresh Start on an Exhausted Debate." In *Mode of Production: The Challenge of Africa,* edited by B. Jewsiewski. Ste-Foy, Canada: Safi Press.

Knorr-Cetina, K., and A. V. Cicourel, eds. 1981. *Advances in Social Theory and Methodology,* Boston, Mass.: Routledge and Kegan Paul.

Kopytoff, L. 1987. Introduction to *The African Frontier,* edited by I. Kopytoff. Bloomington: Indiana Univ. Press.

Kotlowitz, Alex. 1991. *There are No Children Here: The Story of Two Boys Growing Up in
the Other America.* New York: Doubleday.

Kozol, Jonathan. 1991. *Savage Inequalities.* New York: Crown Publishers.

Kuper, L., and M. G. Smith. 1969. *Pluralism in Africa.* Berkeley: Univ. of California
Press.

Laclau, Ernesto. 1971. "Feudalism and Capitalism in Latin America," New Left Review, 67: 19–38.

————. 1977. *Politics and Ideology in Marxist Theory: Capitalism, Fascism, Populism.* London: New Left Books.

————. 1982. *Politics and Ideology in Marxist Theory.* London: Verso.

Ladner, Joyce. 1971. *Tomorrow's Tomorrow: The Black Woman.* Garden City, N.Y.: Doubleday.

————. 1973. *The Death of White Sociology.* New York: Vintage Books.

Landry, Bart. 1987. *The New Black Middle Class.* Berkeley: Univ. of California Press.

Lavin, David. 1963. *The Predictions of Academic Performance.* New York: Russell Sage
Foundation.

Leake, Donald O., and Brenda L. Leake. 1992. "Island of Hope: Milwaukee's African
American Immersion Schools." *Journal of Negro Education* 61: 24–29.

Lee, T. D. 1988. *Symmetries, Asymmetries and the World of Particles.* Seattle: Univ. of Washington Press.

Lee, Valerie E., and Robert G. Croninger. 1994. "The Relative Importance of Home and School in the Development of Literacy Skills for Middle-grade Students." *American Journal of Education* 102: 286–329.

Lemann, Nicholas. 1991. *The Promised Land: The Great Black Migration: How It Changed America*. New York: A. A. Knopf.

———. 1999. *The Big Test: The Secret History of the American Meritocracy*. New York: Farrar, Straus.

Lemert, Charles. 1979. *Sociology and the Twilight of Man*. Carbondale: Southern Illinois Univ. Press.

Lenski, Gerhard. 1966. *Power and Privilege*. New York: McGraw-Hill.

Levi-Strauss, Claude. 1963. *Structural Anthropology*. New York: Basic Books.

Lewis, A. 1954. "Economic Development with Unlimited Supplies of Labour." Manchester, England: Manchester School.

Lewis, Diane. 1975. "The Black Family: Socialization and Sex Roles." *Phylon* 36: 221–37.

Lewis, Hylan. 1955. *Blackways of Kent*. Chapel Hill: Univ. of North Carolina Press.

Lewis, William Arthur. 1978. *The Evolution of the International Economic Order*. Princeton: Princeton Univ. Press.

Leys, C. 1975. *Underdevelopment in Kenya: The Political Economy of Neo-Colonialism*. Berkeley: Univ. of California Press.

Lieberson, Stanley. 1961. "A Societal Theory of Race and Ethnic Relations." *American Sociological Review* 2: 902–10.

Logan, Rayford W. 1956. *The Negro in the United States: A Brief History*. Princeton, N.J.: Van Nostrand.

Loewen, J. W. 1988. *The Mississippi Chinese: Between Black and White*. Prospect Heights, Ill.: Waveland.

Loews, John. 1987. "Intellectual History after the Linguistic Turn." *American Historical Review* 92: 879–907.

Loubser, Jan. J., et al. 1976. *Explorations in General Theory in Social Science: Essays in Honor of Talcott Parsons*. New York: Free Press.

Lovejoy, Arthur O. 1936. *The Great Chain of Being: A Study of the History of an Idea*. New York: Harper and Brothers.

Lowenthal, D. 1967. *Race and Color in the West Indies*. Daedalus (spring): 580–625.

MacGaffey, W. 1970. *Custom and Government in the Lower Congo*. Berkeley: Univ. of California Press.

Macleod, Jay. 1995. *Ain't No Makin' It: Leveled Aspirations in a Low-Income Neighborhood*. 1987. Reprint. Boulder, Colo.: Westview Press.

Maehr, Martin, and A. Lysy. 1979. "Motivating Students of Diverse Sociocultural Backgrounds to Achieve." *International Journal of Intercultural Relations* 2: 38–70.

Mann, C. R. 1993. *Unequal Justice.* Bloomington: Indiana Univ. Press.

Manning, Winton H., and Rex Jackson. 1984. "College Entrance Examinations." In *Perspectives on Bias in Mental Testing,* edited by by C. R. Reynolds and R. T. Brown. New York: Plenum.

Marshall, P. 1959. *Brown Girl, Brownstones.* New York: Random House Avon.

Marx, K. 1904. *A Contribution to the Critique of Political Economy.* Chicago: Charles H. Kerr.

Mason, Phillip Mason. 1971. *Patterns of Dominance.* New York: Oxford Univ. Press.

Massey, Douglas S., and Nancy A. Denton. 1993. *American Apartheid: Segregation and the Making of the Underclass.* Cambridge, Mass.: Harvard Univ. Press.

Mayes, Benjamin E. 1969. *Disturbed About Man.* Richmond, Va.: John Knox Press.

Mayfield, Lorraine. 1986. "Early Parenthood among Low-Income Adolescent Girls." In *The Black Family: Essays and Studies,* edited by Robert Staples. Belmont, Calif.: Wadsworth Publishing.

Mazrui, Ali. 1986. "The Africans: The Triple Heritage." London: BBC.

———. 1991. "Whole Soyinka as a Television Critic: A Parade of Deception." *Transition* 54: 165–77.

McIntyre, R. 1992. "Theories of Development and Social Change." *Rethinking Marxism* 5 (fall), no. 3.

McMurry, Linda O. 1985. *Recorder of the Black Experience—A Biography of Monroe Nathan Work.* Baton Rouge: Louisiana State Univ. Press.

Mead, George Herbert. 1934. *Mind, Self, and Society.* Chicago: Univ. of Chicago Press.

Meier, August, Elliott Rudwick, and Francis L. Broderick. 1965. *Black Protest Thought in the Twentieth Century.* Indianapolis, Ind.: Bobbs-Merrill.

———, and Elliott Rudwick. 1986. *Black History and the Historical Profession, 1915–1980.* Urbana: Univ. of Illinois Press.

Meillassoux, C. 1991. 1960. "Essai d'interpretation de phenomene economique dans les societes traditionnelles d'auto-subsistence." *Cahiers d'Etudes Africaines* 45–60.

———. *The Anthropology of Slavery.* Chicago: Univ. of Chicago Press.

Members Resolution. 1999. An e-mail sent by Dr. Bonnie Dill to American Sociological Association voting members, Nov. 5.

Merton, Robert K. 1957. *Social Theory and Social Structure.* New York: Free Press.

———. 1972. "Insiders and Outsiders: A Chapter in the Sociology of Knowledge." *American Journal of Sociology* 76: 9–47.

Messick, S. 1983. *The Effectiveness of Coaching for the SAT.* Princeton, N.J.: Educational Testing Service.

Mickelson, Roslyn A. 1984. "Race, Class and Gender Differences in Adolescent Academic Achievement Attitudes and Behaviors." Ph.D. diss., Univ. of California, Los Angeles.

Miers, S., and Kopytoff, L., eds. 1975. *Slavery in Africa: Historical and Anthropological Perspectives.* Madison: Univ. of Wisconsin Press.

Mills, C. Wright. 1977. *The Sociological Imagination.* New York: Oxford Univ. Press.

Mills, C. W., et al. 1950. *Puerto Rican Journey.* New York: Oxford Univ. Press.

Mintz, S. 1970. Foreword to *Afro-American Anthropology,* edited by N. Whitten, Jr. and J. Szwed. New York: Free Press.

Montagu, Ashley. 1964. *The Concept of Race.* New York: Free Press.

Moore, Barrington, Jr. 1998. *Moral Aspects of Economic Growth, and Other Essays.* Ithaca: Cornell Univ. Press.

Morgan, Gordon. 1973. "First Generation of Black Sociologists and Theories of Social Change." *Journal of Social and Behavioral Scientists* 19: 106–19.

Morris, Aldon. 1984. *The Origins of the Civil Rights Movement: Black Communities Organizing for Change.* New York: Free Press.

Moynihan, Daniel P. 1965. *The Negro Family: The Case for National Action.* Washington, D.C.: U.S. Department of Labor.

———, and Nathan Glazer. 1970. *Beyond the Melting Pot.* Cambridge, Mass.: MIT Press.

Mundel, David S. et al. 1976. *The Unemployment of Nonwhite Americans: The Effects of Alternative Policies.* Congress of the United States. Congress of the United States, Congressional Budget Office, Washington: U.S. Government Printing Office.

Muriuki, G. 1974. *A History of the Kikuyu 1500–1900.* New York: Oxford Univ. Press.

Murray, Charles. 1984. *Losing Ground: American Social Policy, 1950–1980.* New York: Basic Books.

Myrdal, Gunnar. 1975. *An American Dilemma—The Negro Problem and Modern Democracy.* New York: Harper and Row, 1944. Reprint, New York: Pantheon Books.

Neisser, Ulrich. 1998. "Intelligence: Knowns and Unknowns." *American Psychologist* 51: 77–101.

Newman, W. L. 1973. *The Policies of Aristotle.* Vol. 1. New York: Arno Press.

Nisbett, Richard E. 1998. "Race, Genetics, and IQ." In *The Black-White Test Score Gap,* edited by Christopher Jencks and Meredith Phillips, 86–102. Washington, D.C.: Brookings Institution Press.

Oakes, Jeannie, and Gretchen Guiton. 1995. "Matchmaking: Tracking Decisions in Comprehensive High Schools." *American Educational Research Journal* 32: 3–33.

Ocholla-Ayayo, A.B.C. 1980. *The Luo Culture.* Wiesbaden, Germany: Steiner.

O'Connor, Carla. 1995. "Ambition and Perception of Opportunity: A View from the Nexus of Race, Class, and Gender-based Inequities." Unpublished paper, Univ. of Chicago, Department of Education.

Ogbu, John U. 1990. "Overcoming Racial Barriers." In *Access to Knowledge: An Agenda for Our Nation's Schools,* edited by John I. Goodlad and Pamela Keating, 59–89. New York: College Entrance Examination Board.

———. 1994. "Racial Stratification and Education in the United States: Why Inequality Persists." *Teachers College Record* 96: 264–98.

Okigbo, Pius Nwabufo C. 1989. *National Development Planning in Nigeria, 1900–1992.* London: James Curry.

Oliver, Melvin, and Thomas E. Shapiro. 1995. *Black Wealth/White Wealth: A New Perspective on Racial Inequality.* New York: Routledge.

Omi, Michael, and Howard Winant. 1986. *Racial Formation in the United States: From the 1960s to the 1980s.* New York: Routledge.

Onimode, Bade. 1988. *A Political Economy of the African Crisis.* London: The Institute for African Alternatives; Atlantic Highlands, N.J.: Zed Books.

Osborne, Richard H., ed. 1971. *The Biological and Social Meaning of Race.* San Francisco, Calif.: H. W. Freeman and Co.

Outlaw, Lucius. 1990. "Toward a Critical Theory of 'Race'." In *Anatomy of Racism,* edited by David Theo Goldberg. Minneapolis: Univ. of Minnesota Press.

Owusu, Kwesi, et al. 2000. "Eye of the Needle." *The African Debt Report.* London: Jubilee 2000 Coalition.

Packard, R. 1981. *Chiefship and Cosmology.* Bloomington: Indiana Univ. Press.

Park, Robert. 1950. *Race and Culture.* New York: Free Press.

Park, Robert Ezra. 1924. *Introduction to the Science of Sociology.* Chicago: Univ. of Chicago Press.

Parsons, Talcott. 1951. *The Social System.* New York: The Free Press of Glencoe.

———. 1967. "The Concept of Political Power." In *Sociological Theory and Modern Society.* New York: Free Press.

———. 1981. "The Theory of Symbolism in Relation to Action." In *Working Papers in the Theory of Action.* Westport, Conn.: Greenwood Press.

———, and Robert F. Bales. 1955. *Family Socialization and Interaction Process.* Glencoe, Ill.: The Free Press.

Payne, Charles M. 1995. *I've Got the Light of Freedom: The Organizing Tradition and the Mississippi Freedom Struggle.* Berkeley: Univ. of California Press.

Peires, J. B. 1981. "Chiefs and Commoners in Precolonial Xhosa Society." In *Before and after Shaka,* edited by J. B. Peires, 125–44. Grahamstown, South Africa: Institute of Social and Economic Research, Rhodes University.

Peterson, G., and A. Harrell. 1992. "Introduction: Inner City Isolation and Opportunity." In *Drugs, Crime and Social Isolation,* edited by A. Harrell and G. Peterson. Washington, D.C.: Urban Institute Press.

Pettigrew, Thomas F. 1980. *The Sociology of Race Relations—Reflection and Reform.* New York: Free Press.

Platt, Anthony M. 1990. *E. Franklin Frazier Reconsidered.* New Brunswick, N.J.: Rutgers Univ. Press.

Polite, Vernon C., and James Earl Davis, eds. 1994. "Pedagogical and Contextual Issues Affecting African Males in School and Society." *Journal of Negro Education* 63.

Pope, C. 1979. "Race and Crime Revisited." *Crime and Delinquency* 25: 347–57.

Portes, Alejandro. 1999. "Response from Past-President Portes." *Footnotes, American Sociological Association,* November.

Powers, Donald E., and Donald A. Rock. 1998. *Effects of Coaching on SAT I: Reasoning Scores.* New York: College Entrance Examination Board.

Quarles, Benjamin. 1969. *Black Abolitionists.* New York: Oxford Univ. Press.

Rainwater, Lee. 1970. *Behind Ghetto Walls.* Chicago: Aldine.

Redding, J. Saunders. 1952. *On Being Negro in America.* 1964. Reprint. New York: Bantam Books.

Regents of the State of California vs. Bakke. 1978. 438 US 265.

Reid, Ira de Augustine. 1939. *The Negro Immigrant.* New York: Columbia Univ. Press.

———. 1940. *In a Minor Key: Negro Youth in Story and Fact.* Washington, D.C.: American Council on Education.

Rey, P. P. 1971. *Colonialisme, neocolonialisme et transition au capitalisme.* Paris: Maspero.

Rhoades, Lawrence J. 1981. *A History of the American Sociological Association, 1905–1980.* Washington, D.C.: American Sociological Association.

Rifkin, Jeremy. 1995. *The End of Work: The Decline of the Global Labor Force and the Dawn of the Post-Market Era.* New York: Putnam.

Roberts, G. 1957. *The Population of Jamaica.* Cambridge: Cambridge Univ. Press.

Roby, Pamela. 1992. "Women and the ASA: Degendering Organizational Structures and Processes, 1964–1974." *The American Sociologist* spring: 18–48.

Rodman, Hyman. 1971. *Lower Class Families.* New York: Oxford Univ. Press.

Rorty, Richard. 1967. *The Linguistic Turn.* Chicago: Univ. of Chicago Press.

Rose, H., and McClain, P. 1990. *Race, Place and Risk.* Albany: State Univ. of New York Press.

Rose, Peter I. 1990. *They and We.* New York: Random House.

Rose, T., ed. 1969. *Violence in America.* New York: Random House.

Rose, Willie Lee, ed. 1976. *A Documentary History of Slavery in North America.* New York: Oxford Univ. Press.

Rosenthal, Steven J. 1976. "Does Sociology Have Racist Assumptions?" Presented at the Massachusetts Sociological Association meeting, Boston, Massachusetts.

Rostow, Walt Whitman. 1960. *The Stages of Economic Growth, a Non-Communist Manifesto.* Cambridge: Cambridge Univ. Press.

Rumberger, Russell W. 1995. "Dropping Out of Middle School: A Multilevel Analysis of Students and Schools." *American Educational Research Journal* 32: 583–625.

Russell, John H. 1969. *The Free Negro in Virginia, 1619–1865.* 1913. Reprint. New York: Dover Publications.

Rustin, Bayard. N.d. *Report on Poland.* New York: Philip Randolph Institute.

Sampson, R. 1987. "Urban Black Violence." *American Journal of Sociology* 93: 348–82.

———, and J. Laub. 1993. *Crime in the Making.* Cambridge, Mass.: Harvard Univ. Press.

———, and W. J. Wilson. 1995. "Toward a Theory of Race, Crime and Urban Inequality." In *Crime and Inequality,* edited by J. Hagan and R. Peterson. Stanford, Calif.: Stanford Univ. Press.

Sangmpam, S. N. 1993. "Neither Soft nor Dead: The African State Is Alive and Well." *African Studies Review* 36: 73–94.

———. 1994. *Pseudocapitalism and the Overpoliticized State: Reconciling Policies and Anthropology in Zaire.* The Making of Modern Africa Series. Aldershot, England: Avebury (Ashgate Publishing).

———. 1995. "Social Theory and the Challenges of Africa's Future." *Africa Today* 42(3).

Scanzoni, John. 1971. *The Black Family in Modern Society.* Boston, Mass.: Allyn and Bacon.

Schapera, I. 1956. *Government and Politics in Tribal Societies.* London: Watts.

Schlesinger, Arthur M., Jr. 1992. *The Disuniting of America.* New York: Norton.

Schulz, David. 1969. *Coming Up Black.* Englewood Cliffs, N.J.: Prentice-Hall.

Schultz, Alfred. 1964. *Collected Papers I.* The Hague: Martinus Nijhoff.

Schumacher. 1973. *Small Is Beautiful.* New York: Harper and Row.

Schwendinger, Herman, and Julia R. Schwendinger. 1977. *The Sociologists of the Chair—A Radical Analysis of the Formative Years of North American Sociology, 1883–1922.* New York: Basic Books.

Scott, James C. 1985. *Weapons of the Weak: Everyday Forms of Peasant Resistance.* New Haven, Conn.: Yale Univ. Press.

Scott, Joseph W. 1976. *The Black Revolts: Racial Stratification in the USA.* Cambridge, Mass.: Schenkman Publishing Co.

———. 1977. "Afro-Americans as a Political Class: Towards Conceptual Clarity." *Sociological Focus* 10: 383–95.

———. 1979. "The Political Class Statuses of South African and United States Blacks." *The Black Sociologists* 8: 58–75.

———. 1985. "1984: The Public and Private Governance of Race Relations." *Sociological Focus* 17: 175–87.

———. 1986. "Models of American Race/Ethnic Relations: A Critique and an Offering." *Equity and Excellence* 22: 77–85.

Searle, John. 1995. *The Construction of Social Reality.* New York: Free Press.

Seielstad, George. 1989. *The Heart of the Web.* Boston: Harcourt Brace Jovanovich.

Sewell, William H. 1992. "Some Observations and Reflections on the Role of Women and Minorities in the Democratization of the American Sociological Association, 1905–1990." *The American Sociologist* spring: 56–62.

Shade, Barbara J. 1992. "Is There an Afro-American Cognitive Style?" In *African American Psychology: Theory, Research, and Practice,* edited by A. Kathleen Hoard Berlew et al., 256–59. Newbury Park, Calif.: Sage Publications.

Shibutani, Tamotsu. 1961. "Social Statue in Reference Groups." In *Society and Personality: An Interactionist Approach to Social Psychology.* Englewood Cliffs, N.J.: Prentice-Hall.

Shih, M., T. L. Pittinsky, and N. Ambady. 1999. "Stereotype Susceptibility: Identity Salience and Shifts in Quantitative Performance." *Psychological Science* 10 (January): 80–83.

Silberman, C. 1980. *Crime Violence, Criminal Justice.* New York: Vintage.

Simonsen, Thordis, ed. 1986. *You May Plow Here: The Narrative of Sara Brooks.* New York: Touchstone.

Skrentny, John David. 1996. *The Ironies of Affirmative Action.* Chicago: Univ. of Chicago Press.

Slaughter, Diana T. 1977. "Relation of Early Parent-Teacher Socialization Influences to Achievement Orientation and Self-esteem in Middle Childhood among Low Income Black Children." In *The Social Context of Learning and Development,* edited by John Glidewell, 101–31. New York: Gardner.

———, and Edgar G. Epps. 1987. "The Home Environment and Academic Achievement of Black American Children and Youth: An Overview." *Journal of Negro Education* 56: 3–20.

Slaughter-Defoe, Diana T. 1995. "Revisiting the Concept of Socialization: Caregiving and Teaching in the '90s—A Personal Perspective." *American Psychologist* 50: 276–86.

———, and Barbara Schneider. 1986. *Newcomers: Blacks in Private Schools.* Vols. 1–2. Report no. NIE-G-82–0040, ERIC Document Reproduction Service, nos. ED 274 768 and ED 274 769, respectively. Evanston, Ill.: Northwestern Univ. School of Education and Public Policy.

Smith, Charles U., and Lewis M. Killian. 1990. "Sociological Foundations of the Civil Rights Movement." In *Sociology in America,* edited by Herbert J. Gans. Newbury Park, Calif.: Sage Publications.

Smith, M. G. 1965. *The Plural Society in the British West Indies.* Berkeley and Los Angeles: Univ. of California Press.

Smith, R. T. 1956. *The Negro Family in British Guinea.* London: Routledge and Kegan Paul.

Southern, David W. 1987. *Gunnar Myrdal and Black-White Relations—The Use and Abuse of an American Dilemma 1944–69*. Baton Rouge: Louisiana State Univ. Press.

Spearman, 1904. "General Intelligence: Objectively Determined and Measured." *American Journal of Psychology* 15: 201–92.

Spencer, Margaret Beale, Geraldine K. Brookins, and Walter R. Allen, eds. 1985. *Beginnings: The Social and Affective Development of Black Children*. Hillsdale, N.J.: Erlbaum.

Stack, Carol. 1974. *All Our Kin*. New York: Harper and Row.

Stanfield, John H. 1985. *Philanthropy and Jim Crow in American Social Science*. Westport, Conn.: Greenwood Press.

Staples, Robert. 1971. "Towards a Sociology of the Black Family: A Decade of Theory and Research." *Journal of Marriage and the Family* 33 (February): 19–38.

Stavenhagen, R. 1973. "Classes, Colonialism, and Acculturation." *Studies in Comparative International Development* 1, no. 6: 53–77.

Steele, Claude M. 1992. "Race and the Schooling of Black Americans." *The Atlantic Monthly*, April, 68–78.

———. 1999. "Stereotyping and Its Threat Are Real." *American Psychologist* 53 (June): 690–91.

———, and Joshua Aronson. 1995. "Stereotype Threat and the Intellectual Test Performance of African Americans." *Journal of Personality and Social Psychology* 69, no. 5: 797–811.

Steele, Shelby. 1990. *The Content of Our Character: A New Vision of Race in America*. New York: St. Martin's Press.

Steffensmeier, Darrell, and Emily Allan. 1991. "Gender, Age and Crime." In *Criminology*, edited by J. Sheley. Belmont, Calif.: Wadsworth.

Steinberg, Stephen. 1989. *The Ethnic Myth*. Boston, Mass.: Beacon Press.

Stephenson, Gilbert T. 1970. *Race Distinctions in American Law*. 1910. Reprint. New York: Johnson Reprint Corporation.

Sternberg, Robert J. 1988. *The Triarchic Mind: A New Theory of Human Intelligence*. New York: Penguin.

———. 1998. "How Intelligent Is Intelligence Testing?" *Scientific American Presents* 9 (winter): 12–17.

Stevenson, Harold W., Chaunsheng Chen, and David H. Uttal. 1990. "Beliefs and Achievement: A Study of Black, White, and Hispanic Children." *Child Development* 61: 508–23.

Stone, Andre. 1997. Black World War II Heroes Finally Get Their Due." *USA Today*, January 10, 3A.

Stryker, Perrin. 1953. "How Executives Get Jobs." *Fortune*, August, 1, 17 ff.

Sumner, William Graham. 1959. *Folkways, A Study of the Sociological Importance of Usages, Manners, Customs, Mores, and Morals.* 1906. Reprint. New York: Dover Publications.

Surette, R. Media. 1992. *Crime and Criminal Justice.* Pacific Grove, Calif.: Brooks/Cole.

Taeuber, K., and A. Taeuber. 1964. "The Negro as an Immigrant Group." *American Journal of Sociology* 69.

Takaki, Ronald. 1987. *From Different Shores: Perspectives on Race and Ethnicity in America.* New York: Oxford Univ. Press.

Taylor, Howard. 1980. *The IQ Game: A Methodological Inquiry into the Heredity-Environment Controversy.* New Brunswick, N.J.: Rutgers Univ. Press.

———. 1988. "The Role of Assumptions in Heritability Estimation for IQ and Crime." Paper presented before the Departement of Sociology, UCLA, Los Angeles, October.

———. 1992. "Intelligence." In *Encyclopedia of Sociology,* edited by Edgar F. Borgatta and Marie L. Borgatta. New York: Macmillan.

———. 1995. "Review Essay: *The Bell Curve.*" *Contemporary Sociology* 24 (Mar.): 153–58.

Taylor, J. 1979. *From Modernization to Modes of Production.* London: Macmillan Press; Atlantic Highlands, N.J.: Humanities Press.

Taylor, R. T. 1988. *Hot Money and the Politics of Development.* London: Zed Press.

Taylor, R., and J. Covington. 1988. "Neighborhood Changes in Ecology and Violence." *Criminology* 26: 553–90.

Terman, Louis M. 1916. *The Measurement of Intelligence.* Boston: Houghton Mifflin.

Terray, E. 1972. *Marxism and Primitive Societies.* New York: Monthly Review Press.

———. 1975. "Classes and Class Consciousness in Abron Kingdom of Gyamen." In *Marxist Analyses and Social Anthropology,* edited by M. Block, 85–135. New York: John Wiley.

Thio, Alex. 1994. *Sociology: A Brief Introduction.* New York: Harper Collins Publishers.

Thomas, Paulette. 1999. "What Does It Take to Deem a Business 'Minority-Owned'?" *Wall Street Journal,* 1A–2A.

Thorndike, E. 1905. "Measurement of Twins." *Journal of Philosophy, Psychology, and Scientific Method* 2: 547–53.

Thornton, J. 1983. *The Kingdom of Kongo.* Madison: Univ. of Wisconsin Press.

Thrasher, F. 1927. *The Gang.* Chicago: Univ. of Chicago Press.

Tung, William. 1974. *The Chinese in America, 1820–1973.* Dobbs Ferry, N.Y.: Oceana Publications.

USA Today. 1999. "TV in Black and White." July 20, 1D–2D.

———. 1997. "Shades of Gray." June 5, 3A.

U.S. Census Bureau. 1992. *The Black Population in the United States: March 1992*. Current Population Reports, P20–471. Washington, D.C.: USCB.

U.S. Commission on Civil Rights. 1988. *The Economic Status of Americans of Asian Descent. An Exploratory Investigation*. Clearinghouse Publication 91. Washington, D.C.: U.S. Government Printing Office.

U.S. Department of Education. 1995. *Findings from the Condition of Education, 1994: No. 2: The Educational Progress of Black Students*. Washington, D.C.: National Center for Education Statistics, Office of Educational Research and Improvement.

U.S. Department of Justice. 1970, 1965, 1960. *Annual Report*. Washington, D.C.: Immigration and Naturalization Service.

———. 1971. *Our Immigration: A Brief Account of Immigration to the United States*. Washington, D.C.: Immigration and Naturalization Service.

Van den Berghe, Pierre L. 1967. *Race and Racism*. New York: John Wiley.

Vansina, J. 1978. *The Children of Woot*. Madison: Univ. of Wisconsin Press.

———. 1980. "Lignage, ideologie, et histoire en Afrique Equatoriale." *Enquetes et Documents d'Histoire Africaine* 4: 133–45.

———. 1990. *Paths in the Rainforests*. Madison: Univ. of Wisconsin Press.

Walker, S. 1985. *Sense and Nonsense about Crime*. Monterey, Calif.: Brooks/Cole.

———. 1990. "Reform Society: Provide Opportunity." In *Criminal Behavior*, edited by D. Kelly. New York: St. Martin's.

Wall Street Journal. 1997. "Federal Set-Asides: Just Another Name for Discrimination." July 9, A15.

Wallerstein, I. 1974. *The Modern World-System*. New York: Academic Press.

———. 1980. *The Modern System II*. New York: Academic Press.

———. 1984. *The Politics of the World Economy: The States, the Movements and the Civilizations*. Cambridge: Cambridge Univ. Press.

Ward, Jerry W. 1997. *Trouble Waters—250 Years of African American Poetry*. New York: Mentor Books.

Waskow, Arthur I. 1967. *From Race Riot to Sit-In*. Garden City, N.Y.: Doubleday.

Watson, Alan. 1989. *Slave Law in the Americas*. Athens: Univ. of Georgia Press.

Waters, Mary C. 1990. *Ethnic Options: Choosing Identities in America*. Berkeley: Univ. of California Press.

Weaver, J., and M. Berger. 1984. "The Marxist Critique of Dependency Theory: An Introduction." In *The Political Economy of Development and Underdevelopment*, edited by C. Wilber, 45–64. New York: Random House.

Webster, Y. 1992. *The Racialization of America*. New York: St. Martin's.

Weinberg, Meyer. 1991. "The Civil Rights Movement and Educational Change." In *The Education of African Americans*, edited by C. V. Willie, A. M. Garibaldi, and W. L. Reed, 3–6. Westport, Conn.: Auburn House.

Weinstein, Rhona W., Sybil M. Madison, and Margaret R. Kuklinski. 1995. "Raising Expectations in Schooling: Obstacles and Opportunities for Change." *American Educational Research Journal* 32: 121–59.

Wellman, David T. 1977. *Portraits of White Racism*. New York: Cambridge Univ. Press.

Were, G. 1977. *Essays on African Religion in Western Kenya*. Nairobi: East African Literature Bureau.

Wiecek, William M. 1977. "The Statutory Law of Slavery and Race in the Thirteen Mainland Colonies of British America." *William and Mary Quarterly* 34: 258–80.

Wilhelm, Sidney M. 1971. "Equality: American's Racist Ideology." In *Radical Sociology*, edited by David Colfax and Jack L. Roach. New York: Basic Books.

Williams, Robin M. 1947. *The Reduction of Intergroup Tensions*. New York Social Science Research Council.

———. 1960. *American Society*. New York: Alfred A. Knopf.

Williams, Robin M., and Margaret Ryan. 1954. *Schools in Transition*. Chapel Hill: Univ. of North Carolina Press.

Willie, Charles V. 1982. "Walter R. Chivers: An Advocate of Situation Sociology." *Phylon* 43: 242–48.

———. 1988. *A New Look at Black Families*. 3d ed. Dix Hills, N.Y.: General Hall.

———. 1989. *The Caste and Class Controversy on Race and Poverty: Round Two of the Willie/Wilson Debate*. Dix Hills, N.Y.: General Hall.

———. 1991. "Black Colleges Should Recruit and Admit More White Students." *The Chronicle of Higher Education* 37 (March 13): 48.

Willis, Madge Gill. 1992. "Learning Styles of African American Children: A Review of the Literature and Interventions." In *African American Psychology: Theory, Research, and Practice*, edited by A. Kathleen Hoard Berlew et al., 260–78. Newbury Park, Calif.: Sage Publications.

Wilson, J. Q., and R. Herrnstein. 1985. *Crime and Human Nature*. New York: Simon and Schuster.

Wilson, William Julius. 1973. *Power, Racism, and Privilege*. New York: Free Press.

———. 1980. *The Declining Significance of Race: Blacks and Changing American Institutions*. Chicago: Univ. of Chicago Press.

———. 1987. *The Truly Disadvantaged: The Inner City, the Underclass and Public Policy*. Chicago: Univ. of Chicago Press.

———. 1991a. "Public Policy Research and the Truly Disadvantaged." In *The Urban Underclass*, edited by C. Jencks and P. Peterson. Washington, D.C.: Brookings Institution.

———. 1991b. "The Poor Image of Black Men." *New Perspectives Quarterly* 8, no. 3: 26.

———. 1996. *When Work Disappears: The New World of the Urban Poor*. New York: Knopf.

Winant, Howard. 1994. *Racial Conditions: Politics, Theory, Comparisons.* Minneapolis: Univ. of Minnesota Press.

Winston, Michael R. 1971. "Through the Back Door: Academic Racism and the Negro Scholar in Historical Perspective." *Daedalus* 100: 678–719.

Wolfgang, M., and F. Ferracuti. 1967. *The Subculture of Violence.* London: Travistock.

Woodson, Carter G. 1969. *The Mis-Education of the Negro.* 2d ed. Washington, D.C.: Associated Publishers.

World Bank. 1996. *Participation Source Book.* Washington, D.C.: World Bank.

Wright, Erik Olin. 1985. *Classes.* New York: Verso.

Young, Alford A. 1993a. "The Negro Problem and the Character of the Black Community: Charles S. Johnson, E. Franklin Frazier, and the Constitution of a Black Sociological Tradition, 1920–1935." *National Journal of Sociology* 7: 95–133.

———. 1993b. "Young Black Men and Conceptions of Life Changes: An Exploratory Qualitative Inquiry." Unpublished paper. Univ. of Chicago Center for the Study of Urban Poverty.

Young, V., and A. T. Sulton. 1991. "Excluded: The Current Status of African American Scholars in the Field of Criminology and Criminal Justice." *Journal of Research in Crime and Delinquency* 28: 101–16.

Zweigenhaft, Richard L., and G. William Domhoff. 1991. *Blacks in the White Establishment: A Study of Race and Class in America.* New Haven, Conn.: Yale Univ. Press.

Index

Page number in *italics* denotes a figure.

www.ingramcontent.com/pod-product-compliance
Lightning Source LLC
Chambersburg PA
CBHW010142270326
41929CB00021B/3341